The End
of Domesticity

The End of Domesticity

Alienation from the Family in Dickens, Eliot, and James

Charles Hatten

DELAWARE

Newark: University of Delaware Press

Excerpts from TO THE LIGHTHOUSE by Virginia Woolf, copyright 1927 by Houghton Mifflin Harcourt Publishing Company and renewed 1954 by Leonard Woolf, reprinted by permission of the publisher.

Associated University Presses
2010 Eastpark Boulevard
Cranbury, NJ 08512

The paper used in this publication meets the requirements of the American National Standard for Permanence of Paper for Printed Library Materials Z39.48–1984.

Library of Congress Cataloging-in-Publication Data

Hatten, Charles, 1957–
    The end of domesticity : alienation from the family in Dickens, Eliot, and James / Charles Hatten.
        p. cm.
    Includes bibliographical references and index.
    ISBN 978-0-87413-075-1 (alk. paper)
1. Domestic fiction, English—History and criticism. 2. English fiction—19th century —History and criticism. 3. Literature and society—Great Britain—19th century. 4. Domestic fiction, American —History and criticism. 5. American fiction—19th century —History and criticism. 6. Literature and society—United States —History—19th century. 7. Dickens, Charles, 1812–1870—Criticism and interpretation. 8. Eliot, George, 1819–1880—Criticism and interpretation. 9. James, Henry, 1843–1916—Criticism and interpretation. 10. Problem families in literature. 11. Home in literature. 12. Family in literature. 13. Sex role in literature. I. Title.
    PR830.D65H38 2010
    823'.809355—dc22

2009017434

PRINTED IN THE UNITED STATES OF AMERICA

Dedicated to my parents
Louise Hatten (1920–1990),
and Barry Hatten (1917–2008)
and to my companion in life,
Tamar

Contents

Acknowledgments

IT GIVES ME GREAT SATISFACTION TO EXPRESS MY GRATITUDE TO SOME OF the many individuals and institutions who have helped me in the lengthy process of completing this book. As a child, I heard my mother, Louise Hatten, read *A Christmas Carol* to my brother and me, fostering a lifelong love of the fiction of Dickens. Perhaps those readings are the first source of this book. I am very grateful to both my parents, Louise Hatten and Barry Hatten, for encouraging in me a fascination with history, a love of reading, and a commitment to progressive politics. The earliest academic roots for this book lie in a senior essay at Brandeis University advised by Michael T. Gilmore, who patiently indulged my adolescent broodings on Henry James and Marxian literary criticism, and gave me the benefits of his shrewd insights into the James canon. The more immediate inspiration of the project was a dissertation I wrote at Yale University under the direction of Margaret Ferguson and Richard H. Brodhead on familial discourse in Milton and Dickens; Professors Ferguson and Brodhead deserve thanks for their encouragement and generous investment of time and energy in my work. During the early years of my work on this topic, a number of friends and fellow students offered assistance and inspiration, including Clem Hawes, Judy Malamut, Jaya Mehta, Susan Meyer, and Roddey Reid. Since coming to Bellarmine University, I have worked on the book for a number of years, and my colleagues in the English Department have been generous in their advice and encouragement of both my pedagogic and scholarly endeavors. The participants in the VICTORIA listserv gave me valuable bibliographic suggestions that have improved this work. I also owe thanks to Bellarmine for financial assistance and time in the form of a summer stipend and sabbatical to work on this project. Michele Thomas of Bellarmine gave me invaluable assistance in the preparation of the manuscript. I am grateful to Clive Pyne for producing the index for this volume. A portion of Chapter 1 first appeared as "Disciplining the Family in Barnaby Rudge: Dicken's Professionalization of Fiction" in *Mosaic: A journal for the interdisciplinary study of literature*, vol. 25, issue 4 (September 1992), 17–48.

Through their births during my work on this book my delightful children, Aurora and Raphael, have rendered its title in a personal sense happily ironic. They have given me much pleasure and joy as well as deepening my appreciation of the rewards and challenges of the domestic world. Finally, the contributions to this book of Tamar Heller, a skilled editor and erudite Victorian scholar as well as loving spouse, were of such magnitude and variety that they made no small contribution to the quality of the final result. It is simply a record of fact to say that without her unfailing encouragement and assistance it is doubtful the manuscript would ever have reached completion. For such generosity, encouragement, and love, and for much else as well, my gratitude is great, and this book's dedication seems a far too modest recompense.

The End
of Domesticity

Introduction:
The End of Domesticity

At the end of one of British literature's most beloved narratives, Charles Dickens's *A Christmas Carol* (1843), the hard-hearted businessman Ebenezer Scrooge, his capacity for human feeling restored by admonitory visits from three spirits, triumphantly reveals his transformation and vicariously joins in his clerk Bob Cratchit's family Christmas celebration by sending a large turkey to the Cratchit family. In his unexpected generosity to the Cratchits, Scrooge demonstrates the influence of an earlier scene in which the ghost of Christmas Present offered him a preview of the Cratchits' enthusiastic participation in the Christmas holiday. In the Cratchit family Christmas, an exuberant moment that is only marred by their memory of the baleful presence in their lives of Scrooge himself, Dickens creates a classic scene of familial warmth, depicted with verve and loving attention to details of holiday food and celebratory ritual. The scene's importance lies in how it exemplifies the idea that, away from the harsh world of the workplace, even impoverished families can form buoyant and loving communities. The Cratchit family's rich experience of Christmas demonstrates to the reader, and to Scrooge, that there are values that transcend the relentless economic calculus which has dominated his life. As the three ghosts reveal the outline of Scrooge's life, it becomes clear that the working-class family of Bob Cratchit embodies the emotional bonds and communal spirit from which the capitalist Scrooge, in the course of a life devoted to monetary gain, has detached himself. Thus, at the story's end, his generosity to the Cratchits, and his reintegration into family life through a visit to his nephew, emblematizes how the heartless ethos of the capitalist marketplace can be conquered by the loving spirit of the family.

This book centers on a seemingly straightforward question: Why, only a few decades after Dickens creates the Cratchit family Christmas, did the domestic literary mode that this scene exemplifies enter a crisis? Through what process did a contrasting literary strategy for representing the family, one in which the individual's alienation from the family is explored, become a central literary subject? The retreat of high literature in the late nineteenth century from celebrations of familial ideals represents a major change from mid-Victorian literature, when domestic fiction, replete with large claims for the spiritually and psychically restorative powers of families, was a culturally central and prestigious literary mode practiced by writers on both sides of the Atlantic. The importance of this question is suggested by the fact that in reading Victorian familial literature's decline, we can trace a genealogy for the alienation from domesticity that still reverberates in literary culture today. One of modernism's most striking differences from Victorian literature is the rejection of the celebratory and prescriptive treatment of families so common in Victorian literature. Modernism's narrative strategies, when they do not marginalize familial life altogether, relentlessly debunk the family's pretensions to embodying an idealized community. Whether in Virginia Woolf's searingly abrupt announcement in a subordinate clause of the death of Mrs. Ramsay in *To the Lighthouse*, James Joyce's tragicomically cuckolded Leopold Bloom in *Ulysses*, or the sterile couples of T. S. Eliot's *The Waste Land,* modernism is characterized by protagonists and writers alike profoundly alienated from romantic and family life. In stark contrast to the idealizing of domesticity found in Victorian literature, with its faith that even flawed families are the individual's best hope for fulfillment, modernism deploys a trenchant antifamilialism that depicts families as impediments to individual fulfillment, magnifies and emphasizes the flaws of families, and revels in alienation from the norms of family life.

Few changes in literary history entail such a dramatic reversal of conventions that were once prestigious and pervasive. As the high-water mark of Victorian familialism, Dickens's popular novels continue a long tradition of British literature that celebrated families and endorsed ideals of family life. This larger current, which derives from the increasingly familial literature of the English Renaissance, is a centrally important tradition in British literature, which finds its paradigmatic and supreme exemplar in John Milton's *Paradise Lost* (1667). In the two centuries following the appearance of this work, the familial tradition maintains a continuity that gives Victorian domestic fiction and Milton's domestic epic broadly similar preoccupations. In its nineteenth-century form, familial literature continues to celebrate the joys of familial life and to anathematize its pitfalls, to elucidate the character of an idealized familial life, and to serve as a handbook for readers to guide and admonish them in their personal lives. True to the deeply ingrained didactic impulse of this tradition, its classic topoi are often cautionary: the difficulties or failure of the marital or courtship relationship, the mistakes of parenting, and the psychic risks of childhood and early adulthood.

When we try to explain why this hoary and powerful familial tradition went into crisis so shortly after its final flowering in the Victorian novel, it is evident that it was not a case of art simply mirroring life. Major novelists did not begin writing antifamilial novels because familial life abruptly became intolerable. Though accounts of Victorian familial life can certainly be grim, family life in this era was probably less harsh than in earlier ages, and it is hard to make a case that families became increasingly unhappy as the century waned. Indeed, in the late nineteenth century, the increasing resistance, both privately and publicly, that traditional patriarchal power faced from women and social reformers probably lessened the oppressive subordination that women had long experienced in family life.[1]

Yet if literature about families did not evolve in straightforward response to an evolving reality, we must consider an alternative and influential modernist reading of the decline of Victorian familialism. This interpretation assumes that the Victorians clung to a mistakenly didactic conception of literature and that the decline of familialism was a sign of literature's maturation into a proper autonomy that allows authors to avoid the overt moralism and sentimentality of the domestic mode. The modernist disdain for domesticity's sentimental didacticism is implicit in Oscar Wilde's aphorism that "An ethical sympathy in an artist is an unpardonable mannerism of style," and it is obvious in his famous comment that "One must have a heart of stone to read the death of Little Nell without laughing."[2] Virginia Woolf, in "Professions for Women," gleefully suggests that to become a writer she had to learn to "kill" the "Angel in the House," making the demolition of the domestic legacy a necessary starting point for the modern woman writer.[3] The scornful tone of these responses to Victorian domesticity shows how violently writers of later eras react against its vigorous moralizing and intense emotionalism. If somewhat ungenerous, the modernist reaction against domesticity's moral earnestness is quite correct in noting that domestic fiction violated canons of aesthetic autonomy. Far from staying aloof from moral or social commentary or encouraging the free play of the creative sensibility, familial literature is invariably prescriptive, didactic, and moralistic. Domestic texts are the antithesis of art for art's sake; they are always a literature designed to intervene in the social world by molding the sensibilities of individuals and by influencing the families of readers. Domestic literature emphatically takes sides, not merely for families, but for specific forms and ideals of the family.[4]

But the modernist account of the decline of familialism is deeply problematic. After all, it is questionable whether overt ideological investments or
appeals to human feeling are as fatal to literary achievement as the modernist aesthetic ideology implies. Are *Crime and Punishment* or *The Divine
Comedy* vitiated as major literature because they are invested in a Christian
belief system? One can even reverse the value judgment implicit in the modernist disdain for domesticity and argue that Anglo-American modernism's
denigration of ideological commitment and sentiment is a symptom of a
weakness, its distance from widely held social values and from the communities that such values can nurture. Moreover, the disdain of sentiment typical of modernism is a historically conditioned limitation of its taste. The use
of sentimental rhetoric in Victorian fiction was an appeal to a common humanity that aspired to link reader and author in a common emotional response. It was an affirmation of a shared moral framework that supported
feelings of human solidarity across the divides of gender and social class.
Moreover, the tenuous relation to most human communities that is typical
of modernism is relevant to another weakness of its account of domesticity's
decline, its trivialization of the social context in which Victorian texts were
produced. The major Victorian writers who are the focus of this study,
Dickens, George Eliot, and Henry James, produced literature that aimed
for and frequently found a large audience (even James had a short-lived popular success); these novelists were at once serious artists and mass market
entertainers. Surely it is a paradox that critical opinion has long held against
domestic fiction the very features that made it widely popular. If a desire to
reach and hold on to a large audience encouraged Victorian authors to write
about families, the fiction's popular reach had many complex effects that are
hardly reducible to a vitiation of its literary quality. Yet the patronizing attitude of countless twentieth-century critical responses to Victorian domestic
fiction suggests that familialism's popular appeal has damaged the critical
reputation of the Victorian novelists. Even so sensitive a critic as D. A.
Miller refers grimly to the "abundance of resemblances between" the "home
and the prison-house" in *David Copperfield*, suggesting that Victorian domestic fiction was little more than a rationalization of the individual's incarceration in a stifling domesticity.[5] But to disdain a type of literature because it endorses and enjoins commitment to an institution as potent and
universal as the family may be simply symptomatic of the elitism of the
modernist sensibility.

This study will suggest that the decline of familialism in high literature
is a more complex and ambivalent process in literary history than the modernist account acknowledges. Beginning when familial writing was at the

zenith of its literary prestige with Dickens's early fiction, this study will trace a progressively less positive relation to this literary mode in the work of Dickens, Eliot, and James, writers who each evince a marked ambivalence toward familialism, both respecting and emulating earlier writers in the familial tradition while voicing a critique of domestic ideology that develops into a full-scale revolt against it. In sum, what we will trace is a change of a literary code in major literature, not so much a new reality as a new sensibility by which reality was viewed and depicted.

One of the most arresting aspects of the decline of domesticity in major literature is how rapidly major writers lose enthusiasm for the prescriptiveness and intensely normative vision of families that characterize midcentury Victorian domestic fiction. Only a few years after the midcentury apogee of domesticity's literary influence, major literary works appear that clearly challenge domestic ideology, a trend that grows exponentially in importance in later decades. In 1860 George Eliot publishes *The Mill on the Floss*, a work that powerfully undermines the orthodoxies of Victorian domestic life. In the same year, Wilkie Collins's *The Woman in White* proves an enormous success and inaugurates the fashion for "sensation novels." In narratives that often implicitly question traditional gender roles, this immensely popular genre, though less prestigious than Eliot's works, scandalized many Victorian readers with its plots centering on characters whose behavior and thoughts transgressed the norms of middle-class Victorian respectability. The rise of sensation fiction anticipates the displacement, in the last two decades of the century, of domesticity's centrality in fiction by the rise of male-dominated adventure fiction, while in their themes, sensation novels anticipate the "New Woman" fiction of the late nineteenth century, with its daring depiction of female characters living outside the bounds of convention.

Domestic fiction's rapid decline is easier to understand if we remember that the orthodoxies of middle-class domestic ideology had a less monolithic control over Victorian attitudes and behavior than we might imagine. There were always significant currents of thought and behavior in Victorian society that resisted middle-class domesticity. A long-standing tradition of radical dissent vigorously criticized the idealization of the traditional middle-class family life. In the period of the French Revolution, Mary Wollstonecraft had denounced the inequality inherent in marriage, criticized as unjust the impotence of women seduced by men, decried the economic underpinnings of women's dependent status in society, and protested that in marrying women were often "legally prostituted."[6] In their writings and their lives, major romantic figures such as Byron and Shelley disrupted and criticized the norms of conventional family life. At least in radical and socialist circles of the Victorian era, there is little doubt that these earlier critiques of the traditional moral and gender arrangements were remembered. George Eliot, for instance, wrote respectfully of Mary Wollstonecraft, linking her to the contemporary American feminist Margaret Fuller. Nineteenth-century socialists, such as the Owenites, conceptualized marriage in more egalitarian terms than did the dominant model of domesticity; they also advocated increased freedom of divorce.[7]

Moreover, Victorian society was increasingly cosmopolitan and open to influences from other cultures. French society's less puritanical sexual mores were readily available to Victorians through travel and French literature, notably in the influential works of George Sand.[8] Above all, the norms of domestic respectability were often resisted in the working-class and among social groups marginal to middle-class life, such as actors and actresses. Middle-class observers of working-class life noted that premarital intercourse was common in the working-class, that many working-class women and girls exchanged sex for money (often without considering themselves prostitutes), and working-class couples often lived in stable unions outside of legal marriage.[9] In the music halls frequented by the lower middle-class and working-class, narratives of courtship often rejected the passionless and largely asexual middle-class ideal of femininity, while on a higher class level William Makepeace Thackeray, in *Vanity Fair* (1847–48), mocks the middle-class ideal of feminine selflessness in his portrayal of the adventuress Becky Sharp, who initiates an erotic and marital history of relentlessly self-interested social climbing by symbolically throwing away Johnson's dictionary, iconic repository of moral rectitude, as her carriage departs from a genteel lady's academy.

Thus, behind the respectable center stage of Victorian middle-class life, there was a wider variety of behavior and attitudes about gender and sexuality than one might suspect from reading the censored narratives of Victorian novels. In *David Copperfield*, when Steerforth seduces David's working-class friend Little Emily, the hero, Dickens's alter ego, breaks all ties with his best friend, never seeing him again alive. If in fiction, Dickens presented a David who sternly performs a social ostracism to enforce respectable morality, in reality Dickens maintained cordial ties with individuals who violated the Victorian social code, becoming good friends and collaborating extensively with Wilkie Collins, despite the latter's sexual bohemianism. And Dickens, like many Victorian writers, was fascinated by and attracted to the world of the theater, where women worked for money, itself a violation of Victorian gender ideals, and that was known for its lax moral standards, tolerating transgressions of Victorian sexual norms by actresses. Not surprisingly, it was in theatrical circles that Dickens met his own mistress, Ellen Ternan.[10] In general, middle-class men availed themselves of a more permissive sexual ethos than they would publicly defend. Shielded by the pervasive double standard of the period, middle-class men could support and promulgate in public exactingly strict moral standards, while privately jocularly offering, as Dickens seemingly does in a letter to a male friend, to help him find the local "conveniences," that is, prostitutes, that were readily available to interested men.[11]

Such discrepancies between public professions and private behavior compels us to read domestic fiction for what it omits and elides as well as what it openly expresses. Yet what is silenced in much Victorian fiction cannot entirely explain the literary retreat from domesticity that occurs after midcentury, since what occurs is precisely the increasing acknowledgment of realities that had previously been invisible. The question that needs answering, then, is what forces allowed the speaking of aspects of domestic reality that had previously been silenced. In large measure the answer seems to be that after mid-century, several long-standing tensions implicit in familial ideology erupted into public consciousness in ways that encouraged writers to make significant shifts in the conventions by which families were represented. Foremost among the tensions causing this change in public consciousness was increasing contestation over the meaning of gender in Victorian society, particularly women's roles, but other forces in the wider culture, particularly the intractability of class conflict, the decline in religious faith, and the increasing cultural importance of imperialism, also contributed to the weakening of the consensus around domestic ideology. If the conflicts inherent in the Victorian family became more visible after mid-century, it is important to realize that domestic ideology had always both acknowledged and silenced underlying sources of domestic friction. A brief consideration of the long history of the domestic tradition in British literature shows how these underlying conflicts recur perennially, only to achieve centrality in the later years of the Victorian era.

BOURGEOIS CULTURE AND THE SELF-DIVISION OF FAMILIALISM

In its origins in the Renaissance, domestic discourse marks a break with the discursive world of the medieval era, which was largely centered on the institutions of court and church. The central innovation of early modern familial texts is to place at center stage the private family rather than the politicized feudal family of the court, to assert that domestic relationships and their moral subtext are crucially important to the human experience. Thus the roots of the English domestic literature lie in sixteenth- and seventeenth-century Britain when a discourse emerged that was aimed at the urban middle class and reflected its preoccupation with domestic affairs. Early modern familialism in a variety of genres, ranging from domestic handbooks to the increasingly domestic drama of the late Renaissance stage, initiates the long tradition in British literature that insists that the prescription of ideals for the middle-class family is both morally vital and a central business of literary texts. Such early masterpieces of domestic literature as Thomas Heywood's *A Woman Killed with Kindness* (1607) and Shakespeare's *Othello* (1603) prepare the ground for the culmination of early modern domesticity, *Paradise Lost* (1667). The great popularity and influence of that proto-novelistic domestic epic, and the rise in cultural status of that most domestic of genres, the novel, in the first half of the eighteenth century, show clearly how domestic literature grew steadily in popularity and cultural importance.[12]

In all its incarnations, familial writing has the character of a bourgeois class discourse.[13] It is not that familialism was exclusively created by the bourgeoisie or that only members of the middle-classes accepted its values, but rather that literary familialism's concerns and prescriptions were generally expressive of emerging bourgeois social norms and tended to promote bourgeois and individualist social relations. Many of the classic features of familial writing—its advocacy of individual erotic autonomy, its patriarchalism, its celebration of powerful bonds of love and loyalty between the spouses, its stress on the need to privatize affective bonds, and its intense anxiety about the importance of containing and channeling sexual desire—confirm the bourgeois character of the tradition. Moreover, the rise of familial writing to a central position in early modern Britain is a symptom of the gradual consolidation of bourgeois cultural hegemony. Undoubtedly, Samuel Richardson's great eighteenth-century novel, *Clarissa* (1747–48), a highly influential domestic novel, deploys its ferociously unflattering portrayal of the aristocrat Lovelace on behalf of a bourgeois critique of aristocratic values.[14] Though few of Richardson's immediate imitators had his literary power and intellectual rigor, his deeply sentimental and highly family-centered values, and even some of his fictive procedures, would triumph in his latter-day heirs, the creators of Victorian domestic narrative.

In its formative period of the sixteenth and seventeenth centuries, two interconnected features identify familial discourse as bourgeois class discourse. Familial texts, which often resemble religious discourse, tend to identify familial, and particularly marital, harmony with divine favor, in theological terms with election. Domestic happiness was an indication that the possessor of this attribute was one of the blessed; it served as a secular and visible counterpart to the ineffable status of being spiritually saved.[15] This identification of familial bliss and election was a key element of familialism's character as class discourse. Ever since Max Weber's pioneering insight that anxiety about election was one source of the bourgeois emphasis on individual economic achievement, we have been aware that the idea of election can function as a legitimation of the class privilege engendered by a market economy.[16] Similarly, in early familialism the idealized family was a marker of probable salvation and hence of the morally sanctified social privilege that went with being elect. Long after British society became more secular and less preoccupied with the individual's eschatological status, marital harmony was a powerful sign of middle-class status and respectability.

The other fundamental feature of early familialism is the association of ideals of family life with the maintenance of social, sexual, and moral hierarchies, specifically that of moral reason over passion, male over female, old over young, and, in general, of rulers over the ruled. In domestic handbooks and in their poetic apotheosis *Paradise Lost*, the fostering of the proper hierarchies within families is understood as the source and the model of society's necessary hierarchies generally. When Milton describes Adam and Eve, he uses language that suggests the proper hierarchy in their relationship: "Not equal, as thir sex not equal seemd; / For contemplation hee and valour formd, / For softness shee and sweet attractive Grace" (bk. 4, lines 296–98). Significantly, he adds this comment on the nature of the couple's bond: ". . . but in true filial freedom plac't; / Whence true autoritie in men;" (bk. 4, lines 294–95)[17] Politically a zealous defender of liberty, in depicting the family Milton sees freedom and hierarchy as intimately connected. The freedom within the bounds of necessarily unequal relationships that Milton posits for the Edenic pair, characterized by the benign hierarchies of God over mankind and of man over woman, is at once the prototype of domestic harmony and the model for all the proper hierarchies of a well-ordered society ("true autoritie"). All such social relations must balance respect for individual freedom with deference to the crucial hierarchies, both psychic and societal, which ensure that reason will control passion. Milton exemplifies a tendency, endlessly echoed by later domestic literature, to see the properly disciplined family as microcosm and source of the well-ordered society.

From its origins, however, familial literature harbors significant internal conflicts. For all its support for hierarchies both within and outside the family, familialism offers the individual the possibility of autonomous decisions in personal life, and such freely made decisions could undermine stable so-

cial rankings. Like all forms of bourgeois individualism, familialism enunciates a philosophy linked to the freedom available within a market economy
and hence ultimately elaborates a market-based rationality. But markets, by
virtue of their fluidity, their capacity to enable a life organized around a potentially infinite chain of freely entered engagements, have a disturbing capacity to undermine stable hierarchies and settled loyalties. Indeed, when
judged by the ethos of a traditional agrarian society, the capacity of markets
to destabilize hierarchies, undermine moral values, and disrupt communities
often generated considerable social anxiety. Milton's own effort to suggest
that the contractual basis of marriage, and its foundation on that rational
purpose, a "happy conversation" between spouses, implied the reasonable-
ness of allowing divorce for incompatibility, was a view so radical and subversive of hierarchy that two centuries after Milton proposed it, British society still resisted the degree of liberalization he had advocated. The more
general anxiety in early modern society about the amorality of markets is
visible in the moral consternation that greeted Bernard Mandeville's optimistic argument in *The Fable of the Bees: Or Private Vices, Public Benefits*
(1714) that the traditional moral vices the marketplace battened on, such as
ostentatious displays of wealth or sexual laxity, were actual goods for society
because of the economic growth they stimulated.

Because of this twin character of markets—which offer both the promise
of increased autonomy and the threat that radical individualism will engender social and moral decline—a great deal of early modern familial literature
imagines the unsettling consequences of individuals acting on the market-
based freedom to make autonomous choices in personal life. We can see the
perceived moral dangers of market-based individual choice in courtship in
the story of Charlotte Lucas in Jane Austen's *Pride and Prejudice* (1813),
who, to her friend Elizabeth Bennet's surprise and horror, coolly marries Mr.
Collins for economic reasons, despite feeling no love for him. Elizabeth's
younger sister, Lydia, makes the contrasting but equally repugnant error of
valuing passion over moral discipline, running away from her family and
cohabitating without benefit of marriage with the feckless Mr. Wickham.
Predictably, neither woman's choice results in a happy marriage. Ultimately,
however, fictions of courtship such as Austen writes typically resolve the potentially subversive tensions implicit in individual erotic choice through narratives of marital closure in which hierarchy, and social and moral stability,
is triumphantly restored. Elizabeth herself marries Darcy, a man she loves
but who also reintegrates her into upper-class society, offering her the substantial benefits of his aristocratic status. As the eighteenth and nineteenth
centuries proceed and the importance of individual freedom becomes an

ever more salient and widely accepted social value, the tension within familial literature between the valorization of individual choice and the commitment to hierarchical stability and community would only deepen. This central contradiction of familialism—its character as legitimation of social hierarchy as well as fount of bourgeois individualism—will be a recurring theme in this study because this tension contributes substantially to domesticity's collapse as a literary mode.

The conflict visible in familialist literature between supporting hierarchical bonds and celebrating individual freedom was found in human experience as much as in texts, and indeed one social function that the literary idealization of courtship and marriage served was as an imaginative solution to the tension between, on one hand, the demands of social hierarchy and economic inequality and, on the other, the desires of the individual. In such an idealization, courtship and marriage are viewed as almost spiritual spheres that transcend material pressures and constraints, an idealization that seems to have had a particular attraction for the Victorians. In fact, by the nineteenth century, courtship and marital narrative were a favorite way for British culture to imagine solutions to the anxieties engendered by an increasingly commercial society. In response to such anxieties, narratives that idealize courtship invariably define romantic love as the antithesis of market energies, even while the individualism that the ideology of romantic love posits derives its cultural energy from the increased possibilities of individual autonomy that a market society allowed.

In their elaboration of the domestic tradition, then, Dickens and other Victorian writers recast and modernize a well-established tradition. The continued vitality of familial literature in nineteenth-century Britain exemplifies the protean capacity of this narrative tradition to modernize itself continually and to articulate, generation after generation, a central theme of bourgeois culture. In the early nineteenth century, industrialization and increased commercialization brought new social prominence to the industrial bourgeoisie and encouraged new forms of social life and discipline. Familialism, in its nineteenth-century form of domestic ideology, focuses on creating in domesticity a new version of social life suitable to an age of industrial capitalism. By rewriting the existent familial narrative traditions for a new context of industrial capitalism, Victorian domestic fiction fashions itself out of energies that are at once nostalgic and innovative.

What is most distinctive about Victorian domesticity is how, in the context of the increased power of market-dominated social relations, the new degree of separation of workplace and home, the alienating character of workplaces and urban environments, and the harsh divisions of the social classes, the need for the creation of an imagined or actual domestic space resistant to the coercions and pressures of the marketplace was stronger than ever. In her classic statement of Victorian domestic ideology, *The Women of England: Their Social Duties and Domestic Habits* (1839), Sarah Stickney Ellis expresses this need to make the home a moral beacon capable of resisting the pressures of the marketplace:

> [h]ow often man returned to his home with a mind confused by the many voices, which in the mart, the exchange, or the public assembly have addressed themselves to his inborn selfishness, or his worldly pride; and while his integrity was shaken and his resolution gave way beneath the pressure of apparent necessity, or the insidious pretenses of expediency, he has stood corrected before the clear eye of woman. . . and when the snares of the world were around him, and temptations from within and without have bribed over the witness in his own bosom, he has thought of the humble monitress who sat alone, guarding the fireside comforts of his distant home[.][18]

For Ellis, as for many Victorians, the "humble monitress" of the domestic sphere was the necessary moral counterweight to the rampant egoism that industrial capitalism fostered. Building on a preexisting familial tradition in which love, in romance fashion, transcends material and social obstacles, Victorian domestic writers and ideologues gave a new cultural centrality to the ideal of the family and home as a space resistant to material pressures. More than ever, familial narrative was a culturally necessary theme, both a celebration of the individual autonomy that the bourgeoisie promised to secure for all and a dream of a world able to transcend and defeat, as the spirit of the Cratchits does the miserly Scrooge, the dark side of the market-dominated world that the bourgeoisie were creating.

One central paradox of domestic fiction's decline is that if mid-Victorian domesticity already seems to many anodyne and backward-looking by the fin de siècle, in its midcentury heyday, only a few decades before, it was an impressive weapon in the arsenal of social reform. Though it has been argued that Victorian domestic fiction was depoliticized compared to its eighteenth-century precursor (and certainly there were relatively apolitical forms of domesticity), the mode's almost sacred aura and the wide acceptance of its underlying values made it a powerful tool of middle-class self-congratulation and denunciation of social evils that reformers opposed.[19] In the early years of the century, the domestic tradition responded to the emergence of a new form of familial discipline that paralleled the new versions of social discipline disseminated by middle-class reformers and emerging in penal institutions and schools. In viewing this aspect of Victorian familialism, it is important to realize that the genuine pride Victorians took in their domestic ideals was not as irrational as it may now seem. Victorian ideals of masculinity, which reduced men's reliance on such traditional sources of masculine identity as politics and military pursuits, hunting, gambling, and drinking, and which encouraged an active involvement by men in the domestic scene and a cultivation of feelings of sentiment and compassion for women and children, have many positive elements, and may have genuinely lessened the rigors of patriarchalism at all class levels. Moreover, domestic sentimentalism was associated with humane and reforming values of the Victorian era, as seen in the growing disapproval of corporal punishment, both in the home and in the wider society; opposition to public executions (or even capital punishment itself); calls for more humane treatment of the mentally ill; and moves to discourage domestic violence and ban child labor. The deep love for and involvement with spouse and family that Victorian domestic ideals encouraged provided a standard by which excessively patriarchal or callous masculine behavior was evaluated and sharply condemned. Indeed a Victorian feminist such as John Stuart Mill, far from rejecting domesticity, would argue that the highly domestic character of the Victorian male and the closeness of the bond that ideally links marriage partners was a strong argument on behalf of reform in gender relations in the direction of greater equality.

If Victorian domesticity ameliorated relations between husband and wife and between parent and child, it was also an understandable response to harsh and divisive social conditions and was influenced by anxieties about the powers of markets, the negative social effects of industrialization, and the disquieting divisions of social class. At its most potent, domesticity in literature and society reflects ideals that transcend and critique the power of the marketplace. What Marx says of religion, that in bourgeois society it is "the sigh of the oppressed creature, the heart of a heartless world," fits familial literature also, except that domestic fictions were not only sighs at oppression, but could be shouts of protest that affirmed a set of values focused on love and loyalty to others that implicitly reject the practices typical of the marketplace.[20] As in *A Christmas Carol*, with its contrast between the isolated, antifamilial miser and the Cratchit family's exuberant warmth, domesticity can be deployed to critique market values that dominate bourgeois culture and deprive it of humanity and compassion. Indeed, at its most potent, domesticity is a mode of utopian opposition to the fallenness of the wider bourgeois society. As a vision of human community that notionally transcends material constraints, domestic fiction offered a rhetoric by which writers criticized the failings of bourgeois society, the dehumanizing effects of markets, and the brutal divisions and deprivations that separated the classes. In texts as varied as *Dombey and Son, Jane Eyre*, and *Uncle Tom's Cabin*, nineteenth-century Anglo-American familialism is typically written both *for* an emergent mode of bourgeois family life and *against* powerful institutions of repression and inhumanity within bourgeois society.

The functionality of the domestic ideal as a refuge from industrial capitalism's hurly-burly of competition makes all the more intriguing the literary retreat in the 1850s and 1860s from idealizing family life. In this period, often seen as an oasis of stability between the more tumultuous 1830s and 1840s and the more culturally anxious fin de siècle, a number of long-standing tensions in familial ideology erupt into public visibility, triggering increasingly skeptical responses and contestation over domestic life. These contentions in gender ideology occur at the very historical moment when novelists, buoyed by their unprecedented popular success and by the moral fervor of a middle-class intent on social reform, were peculiarly sensitive to responding to middle-class ideological currents and to registering changes in how such a key ideology of the middle class, domesticity, was lived.

One long-standing tension in familial ideology, as we have seen, was how it promised individual freedom while viewing the home as a hierarchically ordered glue that holds together the social fabric, two goals that are always in potential conflict. Because of the Victorians' valorization of individual freedom and the widespread desire that comes with industrialization to break with the shackles of traditionalism, this tension inherent in familial ideology gradually increases in salience. In 1857, responding to years of complaint that the ecclesiastical courts that granted legal separations were cumbersome and overly expensive, Parliament passed the Matrimonial Causes Act, which transferred jurisdiction of divorce to civil courts. By greatly reducing the expense of divorce, this act made it available for the first time to middle-class couples, though the grounds on which it could be sought were very narrow. While by our standards a modest reform, it generated conservative concern about the moral decay of British society, and its passage was a sign of the victory of an ideology of liberal concern for individual liberty over the claims of tradition and moral cohesion.

Nor was marital breakdown the only area in which Victorians became increasingly aware of the tension between the rights of the individual and the ideal of marriage as a benevolent hierarchy. In the mid-1850s, a vigorous agitation began for married women to acquire economic rights, such as the right to hold property, culminating in a large-scale petition to Parliament. Under common law they had had virtually no such rights, all property a woman brought into her marriage becoming her husband's. In 1855, as editor of *Household Words*, Dickens supports this reform by publishing an article that decried the status of women in marriage: "[the wife is] handed over to be buried in her husband's arms, or pounded into the grave with his arms . . . a wife—like a convict—cannot have or hold one iota of anything that has value."[21] And this theme of marriage as an economic imprisonment for women influences the sensation novels of the 1860s, such as Wilkie Collins's the *The Woman in White*, serialized with enormous success in 1859–60 in Dickens's *All the Year Round*. Even before these political debates brought further attention to the marital laws, radical opinion found the legal framework governing marriage obsolete and oppressive, views that influence Dickens's portrayal of marriage in *David Copperfield* and subsequent novels.

Because the separation of the middle-class woman from the marketplace was central to domestic ideology, an even more unsettling development for domestic orthodoxy was the increasingly insistent calls by middle-class women for expanded educational and occupational choices. In 1847, Charlotte Brontë makes the heroine of *Jane Eyre*, a physically and socially isolated governess, remark bitterly:

> [W]omen feel just as men feel; they need exercise for their faculties and a field for their efforts as much as their brothers do; they suffer from too rigid a restraint, too absolute a stagnation, precisely as men would suffer; and it is narrow-minded in their more privileged fellow-creatures to say that they ought to confine themselves to making puddings and knitting stockings, to playing on the piano and embroidering bags. It is thoughtless to condemn them, or laugh at them, if they seek to do more or learn more than custom has pronounced necessary for their sex.[22]

Both the sentiment and the angry tone shocked many Victorians, but Jane Eyre's comments presage a widespread debate over the lack of economic opportunities for unmarried middle-class women, a problem widely discussed in periodicals in the 1850s and 1860s. In her popular narrative poem *Aurora Leigh* (1856), Elizabeth Barrett Browning has her heroine initially refuse a marriage proposal from her cousin Romney out of a desire to pursue a poetic career. Victorian feminists quoted with approval the poem's lines:

> The honest earnest man must stand and work;
> The woman also; otherwise she drops
> At once below the dignity of man
> Accepting serfdom.[23]

A related controversy had emerged in the 1840s as advocates for improved education for women sought support for a university open to women, a debate that inspired Alfred Tennyson's famous antifeminist poem *The Princess* (1847), and that gradually led to widening higher education opportunities for women.

Such agitation for economic liberty and wider educational opportunities for women produced only incremental changes, and societal resistance to paid labor for middle-class women remained strong. *Aurora Leigh* notwithstanding, the theme of women weighing career against marriage is an unusual one before the late nineteenth century. Nevertheless, the very emergence into public consciousness of the demand of middle-class women for work outside the home powerfully influenced domestic ideology by undermining the belief that women were naturally inclined to "disinterested kindness."[24] Women had long felt the tension between the freedom of the individual that the religious and political ideologies of the Reformation and Enlightenment promised and the narrow circumscription of women within a subordinate role in domestic ideology. But the stark reality that both economic and psychic pressures were pushing middle-class women to enlarge their vocational opportunities against enormous cultural resistance fueled feminine dissatisfaction and public controversy. The paradox was that the age's dominant liberal ideology, which celebrated personal liberty in economic and political matters, made middle-class women's political and economic confinement appear, as J. S. Mill indignantly pointed out, "an isolated fact in modern social institutions; a solitary breach of what has become their fundamental law; a single relic of an old world of thought and practice exploded in everything else."[25] When Mill writes these words in 1869, his feminist stance was in a tiny minority, but the logic of his argument, that when applied to women liberal individualism made traditional gender relations unacceptable, proved prophetic, and in the following decades women sought out and found increasing opportunities for independent careers, while feminists became increasingly caustic in their critique of the powerlessness of women in marriage.[26]

So while vocational opportunities for women remained meager and unappealing, domestic fiction from midcentury begins to acknowledge that domesticity's ideal of a female life devoted to selfless domestic service might be contradicted by the desires of women themselves. We see this theme in the intensely frustrated spinsters that Dickens creates at midcentury, such as Agnes Wickfield in *David Copperfield* and Esther Summerson in *Bleak House* (the latter owing something to Jane Eyre). While these women embody familiar domestic ideals in their service to men and their relentless self-abnegation, Dickens makes it clear that they do so only at a substantial psychic cost. Caught in demanding roles as ministering angels but deprived of the status and rewards of marriage, they are tormented rather than fulfilled by their confinement within conventional feminine roles and bedeviled by repressed sexual desires, at least until long-deferred marriages finally release them to contentment. Even more clearly marked by the societal acknowledgment of the desire of middle-class women for meaningful work are Eliot's heroines, such as Maggie Tulliver in *Mill on the Floss*, who responds to her miserably circumscribed existence by oscillating with tragic consequences from religious enthusiasm, to excited intellectual questioning, to passionate and transgressive erotic dalliance. Another Eliot heroine crucified by her aspirations for a role beyond the domestic is Dorothea Brooke in *Middlemarch* (1871–72). In a poignant effort to expand the sphere of her influence and partake in the masculine world of scholarship embodied in Casaubon, she disastrously marries this coldhearted pedant. Though she is rescued from this hateful marriage by her husband's death and achieves a degree of fulfillment through her daringly unconventional second marriage, Eliot makes clear that even this more satisfying marriage to Will Ladislaw, an "ardent public man" whose reformist efforts Dorothea assists, is a compromise necessitated by social convention, one that leaves her potential achievement unrealized: "Many who knew her, thought it a pity so substantive and rare a creature should have been absorbed into the life of another, and be only known in a certain circle as a wife and mother. But no one stated exactly what else that was in her power she ought rather to have done . . ."[27] The public acknowledgment of women's desire for vocations is clearly a major influence on de-idealizing the Victorian image of the home, for it suggested that courtship, rather than being a movement toward the fulfillment of women's inner nature, was often a reluctant concession by women to limited options. On the other hand, if feminine aspirations for a public role were not abandoned with maidenhood, it was feared that continuing tensions over women's proper role would persist into the marriage. Neither alternative was easy to reconcile with the smooth and nurturant harmony believed essential to the Victorian home.

If challenges to domestic orthodoxy already have an impact on fiction in the 1850s, the 1860s bring a new departure in which the tensions that had long existed in domestic ideology become dramatically visible in public discourse and increasingly influence major literary works. This decade saw the emergence of public debate over granting women suffrage, a reform so radically disruptive of Victorian gender ideals that it was not achieved until the twentieth century. It also sees the passing of the Contagious Diseases Acts (in 1864, 1868, and 1869), statutes that attempted to control the spread of venereal disease by allowing forcible gynecological examinations of working-class women suspected of prostitution and that sparked a vociferous campaign of protests by feminists and working-class advocates who sought, eventually successfully, their repeal. The late-Victorian debate about these acts made evident the disharmony between the sexes in late Victorian England, revealing masculine fears of promiscuous feminine sexuality while inciting repeal advocates to criticize the negative social and moral effects of traditional masculine sexual license. While the increased publicity that the new Divorce Court gave failed marriages brought cultural visibility to the dangers of overbearing masculinity within the home, popular fiction began giving new exposure to the failings of men to exercise their patriarchal authority in a flexible and humane manner, as in Anthony Trollope's *He Knew He Was Right* (1869), in which the husband, Louis Trevelyan, progressively gives into his tyrannical and pathologically jealous nature.[28]

By the late decades of the nineteenth century, such publicly expressed tensions over gender roles had helped create new attitudes about domesticity itself. Especially with the return of economic difficulties in the 1870s after the boom of midcentury, economic struggles forced many middle-class men to postpone marriage or to avoid it completely. But more than economic compulsion was at work. Increasingly deriding domesticity as emotionally sterile, intellectually tedious, or simply emasculating, middle-class men came to respond to the effort to domesticate and tame their impulses, so celebrated by Sarah Ellis and other domestic writers, with a backlash that denigrated domesticity and sought a refuge from home and family. The intense popularity of sports, which enjoyed a resurgence of popularity among middle-class men, and the flourishing of men's clubs offered men retreats from the feminized world of domesticity. By the last two decades of the century, popular literature had responded to the change in mood, shifting from domestic themes to the celebrations of the male-dominated world of empire, sailing, and war, largely homosocial worlds that maintained in adult life the bracingly all-male environment of the public school. From the 1880s, this virile world began to be depicted in stirring terms by such successful writers as Robert Louis Stevenson, Rider Haggard, Bram Stoker, Arthur Conan Doyle, Joseph Conrad, and Rudyard Kipling. During a period when men often felt emasculated by the moral and social restraints of home life, or undermined in their traditional predominance by the increasingly rancorous public discourse over gender relations, the predominantly masculine world of empire, in reality or fantasy, offered them the capacity to reassert their masculine identify free from feminine influence.[29] In an age when the stability of Britain's imperial role and world preeminence was seen as potentially unstable, and when anxieties about the vitality of masculinity became pervasive, a fully masculine literature such as Kipling seemed to offer was greeted in many quarters with enthusiasm.[30] For their part, feminists and writers sympathetic to female efforts to transform gender roles in an egalitarian way contributed to the further de-idealization of domesticity by writing and hailing works that depict the high costs of masculine domination, a theme explored by writers such as Hardy, Meredith, and Ibsen. The latter's play *A Doll's House*, in which the heroine dramatically ends the play by abandoning her tyrannical husband and children, shocked Victorian audiences, but was an inspiration to many feminists.[31] It is in this context of increasingly rancorous mistrust between the sexes and constant assaults on the domestic ideal that Henry James perfects his fictions with their dispassionate dismantling of the ideal of the middle-class home as a refuge from selfishness and self-aggrandizement. For writers like Oscar Wilde and James, it is no exaggeration to say that celebrations of the intimacy of the middle-class home seemed a violation of artistic integrity, a pandering to bourgeois pieties.

Though "the flight from domesticity," as historian John Tosh has called it—the increasing masculine resistance to a domestic world seen as emasculating and constraining—is most evident in the last two decades of the century, its narrative and ideological roots can be found much earlier.[32] These strategies emerge simultaneously with the de-idealization of domesticity that begins in the 1850s and 1860s. Already in the works of writers such as Dickens and Collins in this period we see glorifications of masculine homosocial achievement in imperial, scientific, and professional activities, including professional policing and medical diagnosis of women and the home. Already such narratives of masculine identity centered on professionalism or heroic self-sacrifice, or on solidarity in an imperial enterprise, suggest that fears of class conflict and increasing awareness of the burden of empire, combined with anxieties over the continual renegotiation of masculine identity at home, encouraged male writers to develop literary modes that distance them from the domestic world.

In the later years of the century, as contention over the relations between the genders grows, and the optimism that bourgeois society could reform itself wanes, the familial mode's transformative aspirations and explosively humanistic idealism becomes less self-confident. Several important currents of change in late Victorian society undermine literary familialism. In addition to the growing contention over changing feminine roles, the rise of a wider mass culture that separated literature more emphatically into high and plebeian spheres, the crisis of religious belief, and the increased critical stress on aesthetic autonomy, itself a response to literature's more emphatic differentiation into high and low spheres, were crucial conditions that contributed to subverting the centuries-long tradition of literary familialism. Ultimately, domestic idealization recedes because major writers sense that securing their own social status can be better achieved through foregrounding communities other than families, notably communities of masculine homosociality, often linked to the project of empire, or on the other hand to the more refined communities of taste and literary connoisseurship itself, which become the basis for an emergent modernism. Given this complex development, this study suggests that the momentous change by which literary domesticity was displaced from its traditional centrality should be viewed neither as a development to be mindlessly rejected in a nostalgic longing for an age before the modernist break nor, in the manner of many devotees of modernism and postmodernism, as a rupture in literary history to be uncritically celebrated. Rather the decline of familial fiction should be understood as a complex product of a long historical development that has produced our contemporary world. The effect of the decline of domesticity on readers and society, on literature itself, remains mixed and contradictory, neither entirely a blessing nor simply a fall from grace.

Placed in the context of the broad struggle to control the representation of the family, the transformation I will be tracing can be summarized as entailing two separate captures of cultural terrain. One is the increased prominence of the theme of alienation from the family in major novels of the late Victorian period. There had long been a marginal and relatively minor strand of British cultural life that depicted an intense alienation from the family and hostility to its dominant ideological strands. Examples of this strand would include Mary Wollstonecraft's devastating critique of conventional middle- and upper-class families in *A Vindication of the Rights of Woman* (1792) and her Gothic novel *The Wrongs of Woman, or Maria* (1798) and Percy Shelley's *Epipsychidion* (1821). In this first seizure of cultural terrain, it is a significant development when the concerns of this minor strand of British cultural life, the view that traditional domestic ideology and families were often claustrophobic and confining and could engender profound alienation in individuals, seizes the terrain of the culturally prestigious, becoming thematically central to many of the most prestigious novels of the late Victorian culture. Though this consciousness of the structural failings of domestic life emerges in literary texts by both men and women—witness its visibility in Dickens—women's status within marriage and in society generally was always more problematic than men's, and domesticity's decline in large part is caused by changing conceptions of women, while the emergence to prominence of familial alienation as a literary theme is inseparable from the growing realization that the subjectivity of women put them into conflict with the hierarchical character of the patriarchal family. Familial alienation, and the inevitable recasting of the domestic literary conventions its depiction required, is explored most brilliantly by a woman writer, George Eliot. But as antifamilialism gains status as a mainstay of an emergent modernist sensibility, and the discontents of women, and often of men, in the family becomes a favored topic for literary exploration, a second and dialectical capture of cultural terrain occurs by which this literary topic is appropriated by a male-dominated high literary culture. Often, rather than being deployed in a feminist manner, the theme of individual alienation from the family or from courtship is appropriated by writers who transform it into a theme at once aestheticized and depoliticized. Moreover, the loss of the feminist energy of the theme of women's domestic discontent is accompanied by a movement by which a theme that had emerged in midcentury with particular power in women writers, such as the Brontës, Elizabeth Barrett Browning, and George Eliot, is appropriated by and most successfully deployed in the last decades of the century by male writers.[33] Here Henry James is a crucial and influential example of a writer who represents female discontent but robs it of much of its earlier feminist resonance. The result is that while many late Victorians and moderns found the questioning of domestic ideals disturbing and distasteful—Margaret Oliphant famously attacked what she called the "Anti-Marriage League" in turn-of-the-century British literature—its earlier radical character as an effort to imaginatively think through the practical problems of middle-class individuals, especially women, increasingly recedes.

Because the questioning of traditional domestic ideals is the product of a larger shift in the cultural climate, innumerable writers and texts both canonical and minor contribute to the development of the literary tradition of family alienation. For instance, such until recently noncanonical genres as sensation fiction and New Woman novels were obviously influential in raising the salience of familial conflict and alienation and changing cultural norms in the depiction of courtship and domestic life. Without denying the importance of this larger context, my concentration on the three writers that are the subject of his study has a rationale, which is that Dickens, Eliot, and James are crucial figures in the double capture of cultural terrain I describe above precisely because each aims for and indeed achieves the status of major and influential writer in the British literary tradition. In the work of such writers we can follow most clearly the shift of literary codes in canonical literature, a transformation by which the norms of traditional domestic fiction are gradually dismantled. From the ruins of the domestic tradition a new subject arises as central to serious fiction, the discontent and alienation of the individual within the family or within courtship (frequently though not always a woman) and ultimately the individual's development understood precisely as a product of that alienation.

This study begins with Dickens, the nineteenth century's greatest writer in the domestic tradition. Given the long-standing existence of conflicts within familialism, Dickens unsurprisingly finds in familial narrative an apparatus that serves contradictory functions reflected in the conflicting impulses that animate his fictions. On one hand, his familial narratives aggressively ally themselves with the emergent hegemony of bourgeois culture by promoting a novel form of the familial ideal—as well as other societal ideals—that are decidedly those of the liberal and reforming bourgeoisie, while at the same time, his fictions quickly begin to use familial ideology to criticize the incapacity of industrial capitalist society adequately to reform itself and to realize its own highest ideals. Filled with a passion to be an authoritative voice of social commentary, Dickens constantly exemplifies a general tendency in writers in the familial tradition to project onto the family the evils of the culture at large, including problems created by the power of the marketplace. Thus Dickens anatomizes the failed family and develops it as a potent apparatus with which to diagnose and castigate the failure of bourgeois society to provide individuals with satisfying communities capable of sustaining and nurturing them. For Dickens indeed, specifically familial failures are the root of the failure of bourgeois society to foster stable and coherent individual identities.

Beginning with familial literature at a high point of prestige and esteem, I show how in two important early novels, *Barnaby Rudge* (1841) and *Dombey and Son* (1848), Dickens deploys familialism in order to elevate the status of his own writing and, ultimately, of novel writing itself. In contrast to the larger trajectory I trace, in which antifamilialism becomes the mark of the most ambitious fiction, in these early novels Dickens uses familial prescriptiveness as a central part of his effort to project his own authority as a writer. At this moment of his career, the spirit of bourgeois familialism in the new form created in response to the rise of industrial capitalism was prestigious cultural capital for an ambitious fiction writer to draw on, both as a way to affiliate himself with a larger spirit of social reform and as a means to legitimate his own professional status as a man of letters.

Though a little-read work in the Dickens canon, *Barnaby Rudge* is important because it shows how intimately Dickens's early efforts at status enhancement were linked to his familialism and how, from quite early in his career, Dickens utilized specific familial ideals to make political points against what he opposed, whether classes, such as the aristocracy, or social practices, such as the draconic use of capital punishment. This polemical deployment of familialism allows Dickens to construct a coherent and sweeping condemnation of the preindustrial world of eighteenth-century England. In the remainder of chapter 1, I discuss *Dombey and Son*, the novel most fully representative of Dickens's early use of the domestic mode, and show how in it he eloquently deploys the prototypically bourgeois mode of familialism to attack the inhumanity of bourgeois society's domination by market values. At the same time, in the novel's curious absence of satisfying mothers we see proleptically the intense anxiety about femininity that will loom ever larger in Dickens's later fictions, and that indeed foreshadows his growing impatience with the domestic mode.

Even at its beginnings, Dickensian familialism is troubled and conflicted, showing signs of an ambivalence about domesticity that increases over time. By his later career, Dickens, quintessential familial writer that he is, clearly becomes eager to distance himself from too close an association with domestic ideology and the domestic site, an affiliation he now finds restrictive and inimical to the achievement of a powerful social voice. Dickens's unease with domestic sites in his later fiction, notably the exemplary novel of familial alienation *David Copperfield*, which is the focus of chapter 2, was engendered by his increasing political pessimism, his frustration over the continued difficulty of achieving status for his work, and his own doubts about the rigidities and cruelties of the domestic ideology of his day. In his late fiction, Dickens expresses his uneasiness with the domestic mode largely through his ever more tortured relationship to female characters. The deficiency of the maternal principle used to critique market-dominated society in *Dombey and Son* is developed in the late fiction into a reductive women-blaming, as female characters—above all failed mothers—are represented as the root of the failures of families to heal the psychic pain engendered by painful social divisions of class and gender.

If Dickens, Victorian familialism's most successful exponent, feels deep unease at the domestic mode, the pivotal moment in British literature's break from this mode occurs with his younger contemporary George Eliot, who thus becomes the central figure for the evolution this study traces. Chapter 3 shows how Eliot, reacting particularly against Dickens, but ultimately against the rigidities of the domestic mode generally, writes in *The Mill on the Floss* (1860) British fiction's first great novel that radically subverts orthodox domestic and gender ideology in a fully developed realist mode. This novel subtly questions the oversimplifications and caricatures of the entire domestic genre, above all its stereotypical representations of female subjectivity. Like Dickens, Eliot is deeply aware of the constraints that market forces place on her characters, and her work resembles Dickens's in its critique of a market-dominated culture. But her fiction breaks new ground in changing the relation of serious fiction to familialism. Eliot's work is profoundly influential, because by its foregrounding of the development of a female subjectivity and its exploration of a young woman's tragic discontent with her entrapment by social and familial forces, Eliot demonstrates how family life could be explored in a more nuanced and complex way than heretofore and that fiction could—indeed should—avoid the oversimplifications and evasive idealizations typical of traditional domestic narrative. At the same time, very much in keeping with predecessors in the familialist tradition, Eliot shows a deep awareness of the connections between familial dynamics and the processes of the wider society. Indeed, by realistically depicting how her protagonist's feminine subjectivity is a product of specific cultural and historical forces, Eliot subverts the static images of femininity that had heretofore dominated Victorian fiction. Thus, while working broadly within a tradition of familial narrative, she potently besieges orthodox domestic ideology by undermining its standard types and accepted silences, irrevocably undermining the prestige of the domestic mode and pointing the way to its supercession.

My fourth chapter concerns *Daniel Deronda,* which (along with *Middlemarch*) is a crucial text for the theme of familial, and particularly marital, alienation. In this impressively ambitious novel Eliot continues and develops her capacity to link the subject of a woman's confinement within a stifling domestic situation to larger issues of the failure of spiritual and political communities to inspire individuals, as well as to the problem of the power of the marketplace to coerce and dehumanize individuals and social relationships. More perhaps than any other novel in the Victorian canon, *Deronda* exemplifies how a narrative of marital alienation could resonate with the culture's largest and most basic social and political concerns. Eliot explores these connections by her juxtaposition of a plot of marital decadence with one of personal and nationalist awakening, suggesting the connections between the failures and possibilities of the most intimate communities to the stagnation and malaise of the national community and the hope for political rebirth.

If Eliot is the pivotal pioneer in the dismantling of domesticity, my last chapter looks at Henry James, the expatriate American who infiltrates and influences the British tradition, as the consolidator of the narrative tradition of early modernist antifamilialism. In this chapter I discuss James's lifelong commitment to de-idealized portrayals of women and family life, a mission clearly influenced by his self-definition as a literary artist responding to the distinction between high literary culture and degraded popular literature by bringing to novel writing an ethos of masculine professional rigor that is both ideological and aesthetic. Taking as my central example of James's late phase *The Wings of the Dove* (1902), I discuss how the thematics of fiction making in that novel are inextricably linked to a thematics of commodification, imaged as the threat of prostitution, which both demonstrates the impossibility of continued idealization of narratives of courtship and domesticity, while also figuring the ubiquitous threat of commodification faced by fiction making itself. Since with James's late fiction we arrive at the threshold of high modernism, entering a period in which antifamilial thematics have become widely and profoundly influential, his work offers a logical end point for this study. However, the afterword briefly discusses the alienation from domesticity and sexuality as a theme in high modernist literature and suggests that modernist writers develop their own myth of inevitable alienation from the domestic with which they distinguish themselves from the Victorians and from a commodified mass culture, and argue that this tradition of narratives of alienation from the domestic is still visible in contemporary literature.

To understand familial literature of the nineteenth century, both in its triumphant success and in its gradual decline, is part of a more general critical challenge of our era, the need to explore the complex relations that literature of all kinds can have to the creation and strengthening of human communities. If at times Victorian familial narratives strike us as outdated and passé, the enduring popularity of *A Christmas Carol* and many other nineteenth-century domestic and courtship narratives suggests that Victorian culture's reinvention of the domestic narrative tradition retains its enduring potency. Indeed, it can be doubted whether literature of later eras has ever imagined an alternative basis for community as successful at moving us and inspiring powerful literature as did the domestic tradition of the Victorian age. If literary art and human communities are worth conserving, it is inevitable to wonder if they cannot actively nurture one another once again in ways that respond to contemporary conditions and that move beyond both the rigid domestic orthodoxies of the Victorians and the modernist myth of inevitable domestic alienation. The story of the divorce between literature and that uniquely powerful form of human community, the family, may help us understand how such a fruitful dialectic might be again renewed.

1

Disciplining the Family in
Barnaby Rudge and *Dombey and Son*:
Dickens's Professionalization of Fiction

THE AFFINITY OF DICKENS AND THE FAMILY IS A CRITICAL TRUISM; INDEED, our image of the Victorian middle-class family is informed by scenes from Dickens's novels. Yet if we examine the shape of Dickens's career, it becomes clear that the association between Dickens and domesticity was by no means as inevitable as it now seems. Dickens's first novel, *The Pickwick Papers* (1836–37), centers largely on a celebration of the male homosocial bonds embodied in the Pickwickians and has little in common with the intense scrutiny of familial and domestic spaces that would come to characterize his later work. Early fictions such as *Oliver Twist* and *The Old Curiosity Shop* are dominated by the grotesque and often criminal world of the city and the road, not by the respectable environs of the middle-class home. Though Dickens fathered a large family, he had at best an ambivalent relation to domestic life and always keenly enjoyed all-male sociality. An examination of Dickens's career suggests that his extraordinary investment in domestic subjects was a response to a set of historical determinations as much as a personal proclivity for the domestic. One of these determinations was the potent symbolic status assigned by the Victorians to families, but equally important were the emergence of a new mode of literary production and a general impulse by middle-class men of the period toward professionalization, an impulse that Dickens fervently participated in and worked to extend to literary life. The essence of Dickens's strategy of professionalization was a strenuous effort to associate himself with two kinds of culturally powerful rhetorics that offered possibilities for elevating his status as a novelist. One was the rhetoric of the author as cultural hero, a strategy that makes Walter Scott and Thomas Carlyle important predecessors. The other was the rhetoric of social reform, in which Dickens fused the language of popular radicalism, particularly its distrust of the aristocracy, with the ideology of middle-class domesticity, an ideology that becomes a central weapon in Dickens's critique of society's failures and injustices. In two early novels, *Barnaby Rudge* and *Dombey and Son*, Dickens works to elevate his status through affiliating himself with these rhetorics, in *Barnaby Rudge* using domestic ideology to denounce the rigidities and cruelties of eighteenth-century England and its dominant class, the aristocracy; in *Dombey and Son* he uses a parallel strategy that makes domestic ideology the diagnostic tool deployed to denounce the moral failures of industrial Britain. However, even at this point in his career when his association with domesticity is most intimate, we can detect signs of Dickens's ambivalence as a male writer in associating himself with domestic narratives, and both his identification with but also his consistent distrust of the female individuality, particularly in its resistance to patriarchal authority.

Dickens began his career at a time that saw the emergence and spread of a new form of middle-class familial discourse rooted in the romantic valorization of sentiment and in the intense moral earnestness of evangelical Christianity. As social historians Leonore Davidoff and Catherine Hall have explained, such discourse articulated a middle-class identity and functioned as a response to the period's social and class conflicts.[1] In keeping with this trend, and in the interest of improving his literary status, in *Barnaby Rudge* (1841) Dickens broke with the almost picaresque openness to public sites and to diverse social strata which characterized his early fiction and focused heavily on the dissemination of this new familial ideology. In its emphasis on the family, the novel anticipates much of his later career, in which Dickens's profound investment in domesticity would intensify. From the mid-1840s, as celebrator, in hugely popular tales, of the family-centered Christmas holiday, and later as editor of the magazine *Household Words*—designed, as its title implied, to enter into and to foster the ethos of middle-class homes—Dickens continued to promote the identification of the literary and the familial.[2] But in the early move to elevate his authorial status through writing the familial narrative that is *Barnaby Rudge*, the novel's genre, the historical novel, is significant. Clearly, in Dickens's mind the elevation of the status that he desired suggested the emulation of the prestigious fiction of Walter Scott. From that writer Dickens not only borrows the confidence to comment authoritatively on the lessons of history, but as we will see, he would also learn from Scott to figure general social ills and historical processes through familial narrative.

Status Enhancement and Bourgeois Familial Forms in *Barnaby Rudge*

Dickens's initial and enormous success in *Pickwick* coincided with and formed a part of the transformation in nineteenth-century Britain of the literary mode of production from one characterized by petty-commodity capitalism to one participating in industrial capitalism, a shift of literary mode of production that involved technological, political, and institutional changes.[3] The earlier mode was characterized by the severe limitation of markets and the production of books as expensive luxury goods for a wealthy minority. In contrast, industrialization in book reading, as in other fields, encouraged and demanded a reorganization and broadening of markets and a cheapening of commodities. While the steady expansion of the reading public offered enhanced economic possibilities to the novelist, it left his or her status, both economically and socially, unstable and contested. Gaye Tuchman has pointed out the predominance of women writers among early novelists and the concomitant low status of this occupation.[4] Male writers who entered the field were anxious to elevate their status above that of female novelists. Even Walter Scott published his first novel *Waverley* anonymously, apparently dubious about the status of the genre. His works, however, were respected—critics compared him to Shakespeare—which made him an attractive model for a novelist like Dickens who intensely desired to raise his own social and literary status.

Dickens's concern with raising his status as a writer was the product of his desire to establish himself in a position higher than that of mere literary worker, one of dignity and status—in short, that of a professional man of letters. This impulse was expressed throughout his career, as in his vehement criticism of the United States for its lack of copyright protection for writers (copyright being the crucial property right that allows writers to gain economic self-sufficiency) and in his role in founding a professional association of writers, the Guild of Literature and Art. Dickens self-consciously made the promotion of the professional status of authors a goal of his own literary career, an aspiration toward professionalism that typifies the general effort in this period by middle-class men in a number of occupations to use professionalization to secure their occupations' prestige and economic position in the face of the threat of excessive competition.

In this context Dickens's agreement with the publisher John Macrone in May 1836, while he was still writing *Pickwick*, to write the historical novel that would eventually become *Barnaby Rudge* can be seen as an early effort to reimagine and elevate his own status as a writer.[5] The central strategic step that Dickens takes here is to plan to write a historical novel, thereby emulating the model of the prestigious Walter Scott. Soon after, *Pickwick* was selling by tens of thousands per part, and the formerly modest market value of writing by Dickens rose accordingly. His efforts to obtain better terms for the novel and his other writings embroiled him in disputes with Macrone and then even more embittered conflicts with his next publisher, Richard Bentley, to whom the rights to *Barnaby* were transferred. After three years of quarreling with the latter—during which Dickens both substantially raised the price of the work and, under the pressure of various other writing commitments, repeatedly postponed writing it—a lawsuit was avoided by a financial settlement that ended his relation with Bentley. The work was promised to his new publishers, Chapman and Hall, who eventually published it serially in Dickens's magazine *Master Humphrey's Clock*.

Throughout these conflicts Dickens was motivated by a desire to secure a high status as well as a high price for his writing. He wrote Bentley in 1836 demanding £500 for the novel rather than the £400 previously agreed on, arguing that he wished to write the work carefully in order to "build his fame" on it.[6] Alongside these ambitious aspirations, his letters show that his fundamental dependence on the capital of publishers, analogous to that of the proletariat who were forced to sell their labor power to the owners of the means of production to live, clearly embittered him. Thus, in January 1839 he wrote his friend and literary adviser John Forster to tell him that he was demanding another extension on *Barnaby*:

> It is no fiction to say that at present I *cannot* write this tale. The immense profits which *Oliver* has realized to its publisher and is still realizing; the paltry, wretched, miserable sum it brought to me (not equal to what is every day paid for a novel that sells fifteen hundred copies at most); the recollection of this, and the consciousness that I have still the slavery and drudgery of another work on the same journeyman-terms; the consciousness that my books are enriching everybody connected with them but myself, and that I, with such a popularity as I have acquired, am struggling in old toils, and wasting my energies in the very height and freshness of my fame, and the best part of my life, to fill the pockets of others, while for those who are nearest and dearest to me I can realize little more than a genteel subsistence: all this puts me out of heart and spirits. And I cannot—cannot and will not—under such circumstances that keep me down with an iron hand, distress myself by beginning this tale until I have had time to breathe, and until the intervention of the summer, and some cheerful days in the country, shall have restored me to a more genial and composed state of feeling. (*Letters*, 1:493–94)

Rather than suggesting mistaken business judgment in entering literary contracts before the marketability of his talents was known, Dickens's language here suggests he is engaged in a heroic struggle against tyrannical obstacles, but his rhetoric is not mere idiosyncratic bluster. Dickens is responding to the new situation of the novelist in the marketplace; he was opposing the customary copyright practice and the writer's traditional low social status, associated with a petty-commodity mode of literary production, in the awareness that the increased market for fiction afforded him the opportunity to professionalize by elevating the occupation of novelist to an unprecedented degree. The stunning popularity of his early writing allowed Dickens to secure a new social status by riding the wider economic energies of industrialization that were transforming the British economy, changes which included the explosive expansion of the demand for fiction from which he benefited.

While Dickens's rhetoric in this letter interprets his situation as an entrapment in the onerous continuance of working-class position and outmoded artisanal mode of production ("journeyman terms"), actually his demands for professional status are a new kind of response to a new economic moment. His desire to distance himself from the position of the wage laborer is rhetorically conflated with a desire to distance himself from an artisanal mode of production, an economic tyranny ("slavery"). Interestingly, when Dickens finally writes *Barnaby Rudge,* it depicts precisely a revolt against the constraints, the "iron hand," political and social, of the artisanal, petty-commodity mode of production, which suggests how for Dickens the path toward independence and status for the writer for humanity was associated with the road of progress and industrialization.

Dickens's effort to raise his social status as a literary figure involves at once a struggle for autonomy in decision making—the "independence" long prized as a moral and social virtue by the British middle class—and also a related search for social status as a moral commentator. He quarreled bitterly with Bentley over the latter's interference with his editorial control of the *Miscellany,* and after the move to Chapman and Hall he asked for complete freedom of action as editor of *Master Humphrey's Clock.* Dickens's original plans for the latter also testify to a desire to assert his status as a moral and political commentator. He proposed that it be modeled on the running social and moral commentary of canonical literary works, namely, "the *Spectator,* the *Tatler,* and Goldsmith's *Bee;* but it would be far more popular both in the subjects of which it treats and its mode of treating them" (*Letters,* 1:563–64).

Dickens's impulse toward moral and social commentary markedly influences *Barnaby Rudge* as well, since it exhibits, as John Forster noted, "strongly a special purpose, the characteristic of all but his very earliest writings."[7] Forster then identifies the two principal "vices" that the work critiques, the overuse of capital punishment and the "false religious cry" of the Gordon riots, which is both the expression of traditional religious prejudices and also the form in which class conflict appears in the novel. Closely shadowing the theme of capital punishment in the novel is the related theme of flogging and corporal violence. The significance of these themes for Dickens's project of status enhancement is that they are part of a complex of liberal middle-class disciplinary and social ideas that links the novel's preoccupation with class conflict and religious bigotry, embodied in the lower-class Gordon Riots and in elite judicial savagery, to its promulgation of new ideals of social and familial discipline.

In accordance with these enlightened disciplinary ideas, the novel powerfully indicts excessive corporal punishment in the home and by the state both for its inhumanity and for failing to control, if not for actually fostering, the class conflict that threatened Victorian society. Indeed, the obsession with modes of discipline that characterizes the Victorian period is largely occasioned by middle-class anxiety over class conflict; as critics have noted, *Barnaby Rudge* depicts a threatening lower-class violence in the historical past that would have resonated with contemporary concerns in the 1830s and 1840s about such conflict, notably the working-class political movement of Chartism.[8] By exposing corporal punishment's inadequacy to its social and familial task of maintaining order and preventing class and familial conflict, the novel implicitly promotes an alternative, historically emergent, pattern of familial and social discipline. This pattern was based not on authoritarian or physical discipline, but on emotional pressure on children and women and on the isolation of the nuclear family from larger commercial, social, and homosocial spheres. The new type of familial control is presented by the novel as the antithesis of, and presumably the solution to, the bitter class and family conflict it depicts.

It is telling that Dickens associates himself with this disciplinary mode of control at the precise moment when he was turning to the model of Scott as a way of elevating his literary status. Scott's fiction was an attractive model not only because of his prestige, but because of the moral authority that was implicit in a social commentary safely distanced from the present and couched in the authoritative terms of historical narrative. Ian Duncan has rightly stressed the importance of Scott as a model for Dickens, as for other Victorian writers: "*Barnaby Rudge* can be understood as its author's first real *novel*: for most writers of Dickens's generation, writing a historical romance was a professional rite of passage, mastering the dominant (mascu-

line) cultural model and measuring oneself against its formidable parent."[9]
By borrowing the cultural authority of such narratives, Dickens will interpret British history but also use historical fiction's authority to promote an
emergent middle-class familial ideology, which he presents as necessary to
the resolution of class conflict. Along with the adoption of Scott as model,
the growing societal importance of this emergent familial ideology and its
impeccable respectability were calculated to redound to the benefit of Dickens's literary status.

The Precedent of Scott
and the Family as History

Georg Lukács observed that Scott's Waverley novels express a deepening of
historical consciousness characteristic of the early nineteenth century, a process he ascribed to the impact of the political upheavals attending the
French Revolution and the Napoleonic Wars.[10] It is, therefore, not surprising that the process of representing the historical through the familial, a
synecdochic process that places the family's own forms within history, finds
one of its classici loci in Scott's novels. In his *Heart of Midlothian* (1819), familial rebellion figures political revolt, specifically a female-centered resistance to inadequate paternal figures. For Scott, as for John Milton before
him in *Paradise Lost*, familial rebellion is a microcosmic image of political
rebellion, as social conflict is read as familial conflict writ large. The importance of this literary tradition, which affiliates domestic with political narrative, for Dickens's development becomes clear when we note that *Heart of
Midlothian* is clearly the model for *Barnaby Rudge*; Dickens's novel, like
Scott's, has an eighteenth-century setting and is organized around parallel
societal and familial rebellions. Scott's novel centers on two sisters, Effie
Deans, who bears an illegitimate child, and her double, the virtuous Jeanie,
and puts their story in the context of the mid-eighteenth-century era when
Scottish resentment of the emergent English political domination broke out
dramatically in the Porteous riots, which are described early in the novel.
Scott's novel symbolically manages and controls the disruptive aspects of
the class and national conflict that it depicts by allying this popular rebellion with the disruptive femininity of the sexually transgressive Effie. On
the surface, Effie's sexual transgression emblematizes the comparatively
loose sexual mores of the mid-eighteenth century, and also, by middle-class
standards, of the lower class of his day. Yet in a quasi-allegorical fashion, Effie's transgression, from Scott's modernizing perspective, also suggests the

wildness and uncivilized state of the Scottish people in the eighteenth century. The narrative links political and sexual unruliness, as the rioter George Staunton fathers Effie's illegitimate child; thus the novel associates the disruptive energy of sexual transgression with the lower-class and nationalist resistance to British state authority, and more generally to the political and economic penetration of Scotland by British capital that explodes in the riots.

At the same time, Effie's sister Jeanie's autonomy from her fiancé and father, represented by her heroic journey to the heart of England in search of a pardon for her condemned sister, while also showing the weakness of the patriarchal family in its control over women, also functions as a more sympathetic symbol of the intensity of family and affective bonds in preindustrial Scotland. Jeanie's heroic journey nostalgically emblematizes the powerful loyalty to family of such a world, just as her refusal to lie to shield her sister shows her profound moral integrity. Her confidence that she can obtain a pardon for her sister (who is condemned to die for the murder of her child) suggests another aspect of this early cultural moment, the Scottish lower class's investment in the paternalism of the dominant classes. So while both Effie's transgression and Jeanie's strength of character represent the disruptive power of feminine independence and are figuratively linked to class and national conflict, such disruptions of male elite hegemony are contained by the novel's narrative, through its two parallel movements by the two sisters out of familial control; the two movements balance each other, as Effie's transgression forces Jeanie to subordinate herself to masculine authority, class authority, and English domination in her arduous journey on behalf of her sister.

Even while Scott's novel encourages a nostalgic pride in the Scottish national feeling that sparked the Porteous riots against British authority, what is lower-class and unmanageable in the resistance to central authority is located as arising in the archaic past and in women, or in dissolute men such as George Staunton. By paralleling familial and political disruption, the novel reads this irrational element of resistance to modernizing central authority as feminine, or effeminate, and lower-class, and as caused, ultimately, by failures of the archaic family. Representative here is the inadequate maternal discipline of the family of George Staunton. Effie's transgression also arises significantly from the failure by middle-class norms of her own family. Similarly, Jeanie's remarkable independence, in leaving her father to journey to England, is understood as a historically contingent and necessary revolt against the archaic and rigid patriarchalism of her father, Davie Deans, a fanatic Calvinist.

Though by the novel's end Deans has grudgingly accepted that Jeanie's spouse, Reuben Butler, is a minister for the established church that he has resisted, Deans is consistently a relic of a fanatically antiauthoritarian and narrow-minded theological position; Butler complains of his father-in-law's theology, "I cannot be persecuting old women for witches, or ferreting out matter of scandal among the young ones."[11] Moreover, Deans's rigid patriarchalism is as archaic as his theology, and Scott suggests that Deans's rigid and outmoded familial authoritarianism has been unable to manage the threat of familial and lower-class transgression that buffets both his family and the political order. In contrast, Jeanie's feminine compassion for her sister and her husband's more tolerant theology and personality suggests the flexible, sentimental, and deeply internalized bonds of family and religious life that anticipate the new ideals of family ideology in the nineteenth century. Thus, the archaic family of the elder Deans represents on the familial level the same kind of harsh and discredited repression inflicted on the lower classes on the political level by the hated Porteous, whose severity provokes popular resistance. Both Deans and Porteous embody overrigid and brutal, and hence unsuccessful, forms of social control. The disruptive conflicts of class, gender, and sexuality, the novel suggests, have their matrix in authoritarian familial and religious forms and analogous harsh modes of political control, which must be replaced by more modern and flexible forms of family and social discipline.

Scott's novel not only interprets historical tradition but is rooted in British literary tradition, specifically that of politically inflected domestic narrative. While in its depiction of Davie Deans the novel undercuts the rigid patriarchalism associated with John Milton, in another sense the novel is profoundly Miltonic, for its narrative adopts the epic poet's strategy of representing a political revolt in terms of failed family discipline. Like *Paradise Lost, Heart of Midlothian* shows how the displacement of wider ideological tensions onto a familial conflict ultimately embodies the fall into the historical truth of the limitations of revolt and the inevitable reabsorption of rebellion by a strengthened hierarchy. In both works, the emergence of a new and more adequate family and gender ideology is linked to a recurrent pattern of revolt; just as Adam and Eve, because of Satan's illegitimate revolt, must learn from their fatal rebellion against God to internalize their acceptance of his rule (and Eve her subordination to Adam), so Butler's more tolerant and sensitive masculine authority, displacing the harsh patriarchalism and archaic theology of Davie Deans, will encourage love and loyalty to the established order and to his family authority, and prevent the kind of collapse of familial and moral discipline that has led to Effie Deans's sexual fall.

THE FAILURE OF FATHERS AND
THE REJECTION OF THE GOTHIC

Scott's heroes are often considered weak, and when Dickens rewrites *Heart of Midlothian* in *Barnaby Rudge,* he imitates Scott's practice in this regard by having as titular hero an idiot who, except for a brief stint of rioting, lives with his mother. As in *Heart of Midlothian,* in *Barnaby Rudge* a weak hero, familial fragility, and effective fatherlessness provide the matrix of popular revolt. The emphasis on male, particularly paternal, inadequacy is particularly striking given that this novel represents a crucial moment in Dickens's construction of his own authority as a writer. The pen has been called a metaphorical penis, but if the authority of the writer for Dickens is invested in masculine authority, Barnaby as a central character and the novel's families generally suggest that Dickens's authority as a writer is less a function of masculine authority than an effort to compensate for its failure in the recent past.[12] This impression of inadequate masculine authority is amplified by the inadequacy of the text's paternal characters,[13] for there are no fewer than six problematic father figures (the elder Rudge, Haredale, John Willet, Chester, Varden, and on the political level, Lord Gordon) and no fully successful ones. Moreover, just as *Barnaby Rudge* imitates *Heart of Midlothian* in having a near-insurrectionary riot of the eighteenth century as a central focus, and in imaging the historical moment of this outbreak in familial terms, so Dickens also draws the reader's attention to the parallel between familial and historical situations and meditates on the historical nature of political and social authority as represented in paternal authority, using the family as his touchstone and tool for social analysis.

Dickens emphasizes the parallel between the familial and the historical by beginning with a long section that outlines the novel's familial situations, then breaks off the narrative with a five-year hiatus and, in effect, restarts the novel with an elaborate second version of the opening scene, set again in the Maypole inn on a stormy night, with a second ghostly story told to the Maypole cronies. The narrative then introduces the character of Lord Gordon and begins to describe the events leading up to the riots. If Dickens implicitly acknowledges his debt to Scott by ostentatiously shifting from the domestic to the historical, an additional function of this narrative repetition is to draw attention to the text's unease with the world that it has been depicting. The source of this unease is the novel's diagnosis, already figured in the opening chapter's image of the Maypole inn as an "old house nodding in its sleep," of a stability tending to stagnation which characterizes eighteenth-century English society.[14] This is a world where if change is difficult even to imagine, as John Willet's enormously slow mental processes comically suggest, any break with the past's inertia can occur only with the greatest of difficulty.

In the context of Dickens's career, this break in and restarting of the narrative is also a dramatization of his reorientation, with this novel, away from a popular toward a more middle-class audience. The fundamental generic change that symbolically enacts this self-conscious movement is the shift away from the Gothic narrative that begins the novel, with its characteristic elements of the mysterious stranger and the ancient murder of the master by his servant, to the historical novel that concludes it. While utilizing the formulas of the Gothic tradition, the novel also suggests, by linking the retelling of the Gothic tale of the murdered master (Reuben Haredale) and the comically static and imbecilic Maypole habitués, that Gothic narrative is no more likely to resolve the ideological issue at the root of the weakness of paternal authority in this world than are the obsessively homosocial denizens of the Maypole likely to change their accustomed rituals. The static character of the narrative and the sterility in the scenes in the Maypole of narrator and audience symbolize the inadequacy of the eighteenth-century historical moment from which the Gothic genre arises. When the novel's political plot begins, the novel's distance from the Gothic genre is restated on a political level, as the narrator labels the "mystery" associated with the anti-Catholic Protestant Associaiton with the sinister and "irresistible" power to attract and mislead "the crowd."

Dickens's generic move from Gothic to historical novel seeks to redefine his audience by asserting class status as masculine authority; for not only was the Gothic regarded as popular and frivolous, it was also associated with female writers in the tradition of Ann Radcliffe and with the evocation of feminine and domestic experience. Dickens's appeal to a middle-class audience is thus generically symbolized by a change of allegiance from the Gothic of Radcliffe to the historical novel of Scott, from the popular to the literarily prestigious and, significantly, from a maternal to a paternal literary heritage, a movement overdetermined by a desire to elevate himself above the association of novel writing with women writers. So generically, as well as narratively, the novel enacts the victory of masculine modes over feminine and domestic ones.

Abandoning the Gothic's inwardness and subjectivity, *Barnaby Rudge* turns outward toward the political and social arena. The problematic paternal characters that dominate the novel can be divided into three camps, corresponding to the figuration of three classes, a division that suggests the novel's programmatic mapping of social space, a strategy that in itself asserts moral and social authority. The most negative father, as we would expect, is the lower-class and murderous elder Rudge; his killing of his master is the transgression of domestic and familial integrity that corresponds to the sexual transgression of Effie in *Heart of Midlothian*, and that similarly symbolizes the disruptive and anarchic rebellion of the common people. Rudge's rebellion blights both the Haredale family and his own and repeats itself in the historical narrative by causing his son's eventual involvement in the irrational lower-class rebellion of the Gordon riots. With the elder Rudge gone, Barnaby lacks a controlling paternal presence to restrain him: his greed for gold, his willingness to revolt, and his general imbecility are his only inheritance from his lower-class and criminal father.

An equally destructive father is the aristocratic and cynical Sir Chester, who exercises a devious and tyrannical authority over his grown son Edward and who, for venal motives, tries to prevent his marriage. If Rudge represents the danger of lower-class rebellion, Chester represents the aristocratic irresponsibility and overrigidity that generate rebellion at every level of society, political and familial. His tyrannical authority over his son leads to the latter's deliberate rejection of his aristocratic heritage in exchange for a middle-class ethos of merit. This rejection is by far the most sympathetically portrayed rebellion in the novel because to Dickens it corresponds to the historical erosion of landed and aristocratic privilege by bourgeois social power. The irresponsibility of the landed class is embodied in Sir Chester's character, both in his role in bringing his illegitimate son Hugh to the gallows by encouraging him to take part in the riots, and in his refusal to intercede for him when he is condemned. Indeed, the procreation of such a son, coupled with the lack of concern Chester shows for his natural son's upbringing, emblematizes the absence of sexual restraint and the inadequacy of paternal authority or concern for moral education, which the novel reveals as the familial and hence the political failures of the aristocratic culture that dominates eighteenth-century society. Chester's fathering toward both his sons, the legitimate and the illegitimate, is the antitype of the good, middle-class family, and also symbolizes the callous and irresponsible stewardship of the aristocracy over the larger family of British society. The elements of irresponsibility and venality that are combined in Sir Chester are mirrored on the historical level by, respectively, Lord Gordon and Gashford. The former poses the problem of the weak father projected onto the political realm; unwittingly he misleads the people he ought to paternally guide. Literally weak of mind, and manipulated by the venal Gashford, he seems unaware of the consequences of his actions, and his moral dereliction represents, like Sir Chester, the decadence of the aristocracy.

In regard, then, to the two class extremes, the lower class (the elder Rudge) and the aristocracy (Chester), the text functions through a classic conservative ideological strategy of interpreting all threats to social authority as displacements or overflows onto the social arena from the properly self-contained operation of the family. Such a strategy discursively elides societal conflict by displacing its source from the broader social arena onto the family. The text condemns these two class poles precisely by suggesting their failure to contain the impulses of individuals within familial structures; the absence of adequate paternal authorities in Barnaby's and Hugh's familial environment is the narrative cause of their discontent, which overflows into riotous violence. Thus the riots, as Dickens presents them, have nothing to do with class resentments and everything to do with dysfunctional families. The riots are generated by such families and also by the misuse of the popular love of the feminine discursive mode of "mystery."

Not surprisingly, in this ideological schema the most interesting fathers in the novel are the middle-class ones, Haredale, Gabriel Varden, and John Willet. Their prominence suggests the text's anxiety about establishing a lineage for its own middle-class discourse, an anxiety that it never completely overcomes. In a text that implicates the bad fathers in the rise of revolt—Barnaby fights his father and joins the riots, Edward Chester rejects his father, and the people mindlessly attack symbols of authority led by Hugh, the neglected illegitimate son—Dickens's more equivocal attitude to middle-class paternal authority can be seen by noting the complex relation of these fathers to rebellion. They either incur rebellion without being unambiguous villains (John Willet and Gabriel Varden) or they act tyrannically without incurring rebellion (Haredale). In this context, the crucial point is that in contrast to eighteenth-century writers such as Richardson or writers in the female Gothic tradition, who envision families as sites of female subjectivity, in *Barnaby Rudge* families are presented preeminently as functions of masculine authority or of its lack. This preoccupation with masculine authority forms part of the novel's insistence on the literary seriousness of its enterprise, while constituting a key part of its effort to define a middle-class audience as one powerfully committed to masculine, above all to paternal, authority.

As in Scott, Dickens's families are both images of larger historical conditions and themselves examples of historically prior forms of the family, a pattern that implicitly locates Victorian familial norms as the product of a progressive correction of archaic and dysfunctional family types. Thus, the three middle-class paternal characters are each versions of Scott's Deans, the overbearing patriarch. Haredale is the most clear case; his rigid resistance to his niece's match, though excused as caused by his preoccupation with vengeance on his brother's murderer and by the deception of Sir Chester, is narratively punished by the destruction of his home and his ultimate flight into a monastery. That his daughter does not rebel is hardly surprising, given that Dickens is doubly inhibited from allowing her to do so because of her filial position and her sex. In contrast, John Willet *does* provoke his son's rebellion with his tyrannical refusal to allow him the slightest autonomy, either in his place of work, the inn, or in his erotic life. Clearly Willet, who embodies the tyrannical side of English life at this time—he heartily approves of the draconian use of hanging——is no straightforward villain such as Chester; yet the novel suggests that his son's successful rebellion is inevitable; as such, it represents the inevitable passing away of the highly patriarchal preindustrial family with its conflation of home and workplace.

In losing his arm, Willet's son eventually suffers a symbolic castration, but this is caused not by his own rebellion so much as by Dolly Varden's spurning of him, which causes him to flee into military service. This development suggests the narrative complicity in Joe's emasculation of the most positive paternal image in the novel, Dolly's father, Gabriel Varden. Like Deans and John Willet, Varden is the head of an artisanal patriarchal family. His home and his workplace are united, and the most serious rebellion he faces comes from his wife, abetted by her maid Miggs, and from his apprentice Sim, to whom he stands as both employer and in loco parentis. Varden allows his wife to rebel from his authority by her constant bad temper and, through the bad influence of her mother, Dolly has become flighty and vain, which causes her to spurn Joe. Similarly, Miggs and Sim harbor rebellious impulses that take effect during the riots, as Sim becomes one of their chief leaders, and at a crucial moment Miggs aids them in disarming Varden.

Miggs's role in the family is doubly significant; as a servant who lives with the family she serves, she represents the general threat that live-in servants presented for middle-class ideals of the family, which always stressed the importance of separating social classes within the home (and even the functions of various rooms). Such servants, who had once eaten with the family and indeed linguistically were included in the term "family," were increasingly seen as disrupting the close bonds and privacy of the nuclear family and as preventing its necessary seclusion from larger social forces and tensions, most emphatically including class divisions. Not surprisingly, given her class position, Miggs disrupts the family by representing a principle of insubordination that allies itself to Mrs. Varden's. Thanks to Miggs, the Varden household witnesses the bourgeois nightmare of class and gender ressentiments fueling one another.

Hence, the feminine insubordination of Miggs and Mrs. Varden is linked with the class violence of the riots, which are understood as arising from analogously irrational insubordination on a societal level. This connection is suggested by the women's support for the bigoted Protestant Association, a connection underlined during the captivity of Miggs with Emma Haredale and Dolly:

> And, while on serious topics, Miss Miggs considered it her duty to try her hand at the conversion of Miss Haredale; for whose improvement she launched into a polemical address of some length. She returned so often to these subjects, and so frequently called upon them to take a lesson from her,—at the same time vaunting and as it were, rioting in, her huge unworthiness, and abundant excess of sin,—she became, in that small chamber, rather a nuisance than a comfort, and rendered them, if possible, even more unhappy than they had been before. (639)

The expression of class hostility in religious language here recalls the distrust of elite society in the eighteenth and nineteenth centuries for the potentially subversive rhetoric of "enthusiasm." Mrs. Varden's aggressive use of the Protestant Manual against her husband's authority suggests the tendency for Dissenting circles to foster feminist thought, and indeed the widespread use by early nineteenth-century lower-class and feminist groups of a militantly Protestant rhetoric. In the passage above and in the novel generally, such a subversive use of religion is understood simply as a disruptive and destructive undermining of class hierarchy and paternal authority, one largely attributable to the family's inadequate isolation from the larger social arena and particularly from the influence of class discontent embodied in Miggs.

Yet the most memorable and grotesque incarnation of lower-class ressentiment in the novel is the apprentice Sim. As much as any other revolt in the novel, his rebellion is condemned and savagely punished; the loss of his legs in the riots is a hyperbolic image of castration. One reason for this punishment is obvious; his "Prentice Knights," a sort of early trade union, is represented as a moronic, indeed virtually demented, association of lower-class malcontents. In other words, Sim leads a relentlessly caricatured subversive organization of the class Other. More interestingly, perhaps, his rebellion is occasioned by sexual frustration; he is erotically obsessed with the daughter of his employer. This motivation suggests the failure of the artisanal mode of production, with its patriarchal home-workplace presided over by Varden, to control the sexuality of the worker-children it contains. This failure of an artisanal family form is analogous to how, in Scott, Effie's sexual fall is a failure caused by Deans's archaic and overauthoritarian patriarchal family. The combining of workplace with the home that was typical of the early modern family leads to a disruption of the father's authority, forced to contend with both familial and class-based subversions, and brings the destructive impulses of working-class sexuality (seen in Sim) menacingly within the middle-class familial site. Gabriel Varden, as much as he represents cheerful old England and its benign paternalism, is thus implicated in a social world characterized by an archaic and dysfunctional family structure, replete with both overrigid and overlax paternal authority, rampant female rebellion, and rebellious lower-class male sexuality turning to aggression. As a fixture of such a world, more than in any personal faults, Varden shares the problematic nature of all the novel's paternal figures.

FAMILIAL DISCIPLINE AND
THE INVENTION OF TRADITION

At first glance, the relation between Scott's *Heart of Midlothian* and Dickens's *Barnaby Rudge* seems to be one of simple continuity. Dickens quite simply learns from Scott a strategy for interpreting lower-class rebellion, one that locates it as a symptom of an archaic social order, and not as a rational behavior in the present of industrial capitalism, and that sees it as arising from dysfunctional familial forms that fail to adequately control disruptive femininity and sexuality. More importantly, Dickens appropriates Scott's overall sense of the centrality of the dysfunctional family, above all of the failure of paternal authority, as a synecdoche for the historical past; he finds in Scott a vision of history represented *through* the family, with archaic familial forms representing archaic societal structures.

As we have already seen, however, this continuity with Scott is itself not an automatic or inevitable occurrence, but rather represents a break within Dickens's career, an effort to reimagine and elevate the status of his writing, which responds to a powerful discontinuity in the structures of literary production. What appears to be mere continuity between authors is in fact a deliberate effort to create its appearance and, thereby, to create a visible literary tradition. Dickens's effort in this novel is to move into a canon of literarily prestigious novelists at a moment when such a canon was far from securely institutionalized.[15]

Indeed, the creation of the tradition of the serious novel is simultaneously a creation of the tradition of the British past, and this creation of a specific reading of the historical past inevitably entails a reading of the present which that past has produced. Both Scott and Dickens locate the "heart" of the British past in ideals of independence from tyranny and in loyalty to legal authority; Jeanie Deans and Gabriel Varden are both characterized above all by their independence, not only from the repressive political actors, but from communities infected by impulses of rebellion against authority. Rebellion, in this tradition, comes to be associated with foreignness; exteriority to the class that provides the main body of the rioters (George Staunton, Lord Gordon), to familial structures (Effie, Hugh), and finally to the religious norms that constitute the national identity: in Scott, Madge Wildfire and her mother are condemned as witches; in Dickens, Gordon becomes a Jew. Scott encourages in Dickens a tendency to stress in his writing community, as opposed to class division, continuity in British life rather than historical change, and to champion hierarchy, both formally through the constitution of a literary canon and in his fiction's content, through the promulgation of middle-class values such as the proper ordering of the family and the alien nature of class revolt.

Yet Dickens's creation of Scott as a link in tradition and as an aid to locating a British historical tradition also involves a revision or shift of emphasis from Scott's fiction, as a comparison of the structure of each novel suggests. The most obvious difference is that, while *Heart of Midlothian* begins with a public event, the Porteous riots, and then chronicles the private events that at once follow from them and explicate them, *Barnaby Rudge* begins with the narrative of private events before shifting abruptly to public ones. In *Heart of Midlothian* historical events, reasonably enough, intersect with and partially determine private narratives, but in *Barnaby Rudge* the narrative method generates the impression that the public events are caused by, or respond, to the logic of purely private events. Since this direction of causality is hardly plausible, the structure of Dickens's novel encourages a more simple reading of the historical episode it depicts than does Scott's. While Scott finds a dialectical relation between public and private spheres, Dickens suggests the historical events he depicts are merely an amplification of the same moral message that the private stories suggest. This is not to deny that there are allegorical elements in both novels, for a quasi-allegorical narrative structure linking private and public life is part of what Dickens takes from Scott. Yet clearly one ability Dickens fails to learn from his model is a profound capacity to imagine history as including autonomous forces that may determine individuals' fates irrespective of morality, an area in which Scott is indubitably his superior.

What Dickens does powerfully appropriate and recreate from Scott is the moral authority implicit in a reading of history and the understanding of the family as the crucial vantage point for an interpretation and figuring of history. He also takes from him the invocation of a sense of continuity and native values, particularly associated with a middle stratum of society (Gabriel Varden, for instance), which is embodied in a chivalrous courage and loyalty to authority, as well as in a commitment to a well-ordered household. The nature of this well-ordered household for Dickens is defined by several characteristics that embody the Victorian middle-class ideal. Most obviously, there is a preoccupation with assuring the authority of the father as a moral exemplar and source of social stability. In contrast to the text's numerous bad fathers, there is Varden who, by finally asserting his authority over his wife and her rebellious religious discourse and over his servants by firing Miggs and leaving Sim to his punishment, learns to reassert his moral authority as head of the household. A corollary to this reassertion of masculine authority in the period's emergent familial ideology is the redefinition of the maternal role, which was envisioned as being ideally nurturant and morally exemplary within a subservient position; the flaws of Mrs. Varden in this regard, who fails on all counts and as a result produces the frivolous Dolly (who is chastened and then cured by the prospect of marriage), are counterpoised to an approximation of the ideal in Mrs. Rudge, who pathetically fails morally to guide Barnaby only because deprived of the aid of a husband and father.

Most important, the proper ordering of the family was seen as fostering the internalization of values through love and moral example, not through using coercion, violence, and authoritarianism, as do all the bad fathers of the novel. To ensure such internalization, and in accordance with the individualist tendency of middle-class thought and, even more, with the economic and ideological trends that isolated middle-class women from productive labor, the family and particularly women are defined as ideally separated from the larger social sphere, including from productive activity. In this regard the triumphant scene in which Miggs, the servant and feminine confidant of Mrs. Varden, is expelled from the Varden household dramatizes the necessity of assuring this separation of the familial sphere from the economic. The scene also narratively expresses Dickens's anxiety to envision the suppression of cross-class or lower-class communities (the Prentice Knights, the habitués of the Maypole, the Protestant Association and its synecdochic image, the alliance of Mrs. Varden and Miggs, even the rioting mobs); the proper matrix of the social order, which must hold itself apart from such communities, is the individualizing and containing ambit of the isolated nuclear family. The failure, the novel implies, of moral authority in the English ancien régime is, quite simply, a failure of the family.

Standing in a certain tension with Dickens's aggressive promulgation of a familial ideology with new contours, and with the violence of his hostility to the aristocratic and authoritarian aspects of the past, epitomized in the text's polemic against capital punishment, is his appropriation of the prestige of the traditional, implicit in his picture of a past containing an idealized version of the British middle-class (i.e., Gabriel Varden). This tension emerges in the scenes of the riots, for notwithstanding its hostility to the rioters and their methods, the novel shares their animus against the repressive apparatus that the rioters attack and that symbolizes all the rigidities and authoritarianism of preindustrial England. The energy of the riots in the novel, then, is not seen as wholly negative. As unbridled and demonic as the riots become, their energies anticipate the social and economic forces that will sweep away the old order in the twin upheavals of the spread of liberal and democratic ideas after the French Revolution and the economic transformation wrought by the Industrial Revolution. If his aspirations to professionalism caused Dickens to respond with ambivalence to the democratizing potential of the new mode of literary production, his own early literary career gave him every personal reason to identify profoundly with the larger processes of industrialization of which the transformation and broadening of the literary sphere was a part. So the sweeping away of the ancien régime's Newgate prison in the riots can be said to symbolize the eventual sweeping away of the agrarian and aristocratic order and its characteristic disciplinary modes, while it also proleptically celebrates the power of industrialization to reorder the social landscape, a social restructuring most dramatically visible on the political level in the passing of the Reform Bill (1832), which substantially increased middle-class representation in Parliament.

To assert his own status as a writer for middle-class audiences in the new industrialized order, Dickens asserted as well the importance of masculine and specifically of paternal authority, and he worked to bolster that authority by promulgating a new form of familial discourse. In using the moral authority of an emergent form of familial discourse as the basis for his own professional aspirations, Dickens employed a characteristic strategy of those aspiring to professional status of linking their career aspirations with innovative discourses and practices that offer apparent solutions to pressing social problems. The sharp and bitter class tensions that accompanied industrialization, especially in the early decades of the nineteenth century, prompted a demand for such solutions, one of which was a newly flexible mode of social discipline.

The resultant shift in this period in modes of social and familial discipline was not confined to Britain; as Richard Brodhead has pointed out, a similar change in disciplinary modes and its enthusiastic promulgation by major writers occurs in America as well.[16] Viewed in a wider historical context, Dickens's strategy in *Barnaby Rudge,* of reading broad social conflicts as reducible to familial dysfunction or disciplinary failures, has a continuing appeal for apologists for capitalist societies, enabling them to explain away or to displace onto manageable local or familial problems tensions that in fact have deep social roots. Two recent instances of this ideological strategy are efforts to explain antiwar protests of the Vietnam period as proceeding from permissive parenting, and efforts to identify the allegedly pathological character of the American black family as the real root of black poverty.

In Dickens's case, by promoting a familial ideology in the form of the historical novel, he suggests the transhistorical and universal character of the theme while investigating the historical inadequacy of earlier forms of social and familial life in order to suggest optimistically the historical superiority of the social forms and familial life of the middle class of his own time. And yet as we will see, in constructing this historical myth of family life and of its complex relation to social life, he was also fashioning a strategy with which, in his later and more complex novels, he would diagnostically evaluate and powerfully criticize the contemporary social order.

DOMBEY AND SON:
THE MAN OF LETTERS AS SOCIAL CRITIC

In June 1846, Dickens writes John Forster and summarizes his activities while sojourning in Lausanne, Switzerland: "I cleared off the great part of such correspondence as I had rashly pledged myself to; and then. . . BEGAN DOMBEY!"[17] While the heavy emphasis on the annunciation of "this feat" is typical of Dickens's flair for self-dramatization, it also underlines the importance Dickens attached to the new work. As with *Barnaby Rudge,* *Dombey and Son*'s importance for Dickens lies in the opportunity he sees in it for elevating the status of his writing and, indeed, of novel writing itself. Writing *Dombey* represents a turning point in Dickens's response to the new conditions of literary production and circulation that coincided with and enabled the early phase of his career. These conditions and his own talent allowed him to earn enormous if unstable popular success, yet left him hungering for higher literary status.[18] The sales of his previous novel, *Martin Chuzzlewit,* had been disappointing, and Dickens's venture into newspaper publishing—in 1846 he briefly edited the new *Daily News*—ended disastrously with his resignation amid acrimonious disputes over the paper's finances and editorial independence.[19] Evincing a need to elevate the status of his next major fiction, Dickens took an unusually long respite between novels and relocated to Lausanne to begin the new novel. His preoccupation in this period with status is obvious when he argues in a letter to Forster shortly before beginning *Dombey* that Bradbury and Evans, his current publishers and the publishers of the *Daily News*, were not the ideal publishers for the new book, wondering "whether it is proper that a book of mine should be published at a Newspaper office" (*Letters,* 5:571). The point was, as Robert L. Patten has argued, that serial publication was still widely considered a low-status form of publication, and the association of one of his books with a newspaper would militate against the elevation of status to which Dickens aspired for his writing.[20] It is symptomatic of Dickens's difficulties in achieving such elevation that his efforts to change the address of *Dombey's* publisher failed, but he nevertheless clearly associated the novel with an effort to elevate his own status. After *Dombey's* success, Dickens, responding to a letter of Thackeray's that praised the novel, took the occasion to criticize his rival's satires of contemporary novelists in *Punch* for "depreciating and vulgarizing" the profession of novelist, trumpeting his own efforts in the opposite direction:

> I *do* sometimes please myself with thinking that my success has opened the way for good writers. And of this, I am quite sure now, and hope I shall be when I die—that in all my social doings I am mindful of this honour and dignity [of writers] and always try to do something toward the quiet assertion of their place. I am always possessed with the hope of leaving the position of literary men in England, something better and more independent than I found it. (*Letters,* 5:227–28)

If Dickens aspired to elevate the status of writing, *Dombey* was a crucial effort toward that end because it elevated his estimation of his own writing; he wrote to Forster "I have a strong belief, that, if any of my books are read years hence *Dombey* will be remembered as among the best of them[.]"[21]

In fact, of Dickens's mature writings, few achieved a contemporary critical and popular judgment so unanimously favorable.[22] But this triumphant achievement represents both domestic narrative's value for Dickens in constructing his own authority as a writer and his complex and conflicted relation to the domestic mode. If *Dombey and Son* is pivotal in Dickens's career, it has two other significant distinctions: it is Dickens's first major work to attack the entire ethos of what Carlyle called the "shabb[y] Gospel" of "laissez-faire,"[23] and it is also the most thoroughly and completely domestic of

Dickens's novels. The work's attack on laissez-faire capitalism, and by implication on the bourgeoisie in general, is the clearest sign of the new degree to which Dickens's writing in the mid-1840s attempts to redefine and enhance the novelist's cultural authority. Underpinning his immediate desires for the novel's success was Dickens's highly ambitious conception of the role of the novelist, the ultimate model for this conception being the social critic as sage or secular prophet in the style of Carlyle, a writer deeply influential for Dickens. We see the extravagance of this ambition in the famous image from *Dombey* in which Dickens aspires to reveal the evils within the domestic site, a magical image for a sweeping moral indictment of society: "Oh for a good spirit who would take the house-tops off, with a more potent and benignant hand than the lame demon in the tale, and show a Christian people what dark shapes issue from amidst their homes, to swell the retinue of the Destroying Angel as he moves forth among them!" (738). While Dickens imagines the exposure of domestic evils, his ultimate target is the competitive greed of capitalist society and its deformation of the human personality; he hopes the spirit will reveal to Victorians "their own contracted sympathies and estimates." Encouraging such moral regeneration, Dickens sees the reformed bourgeois as the potential guiding spirits of this new society. At this moment in his career, then, Dickens feels confident enough of his audience, and passionate enough in his frustrations at Victorian society, to style himself a free-ranging critic of contemporary society. In 1842 he published *American Notes*, a witheringly critical commentary on his visit to the United States, the most thoroughly liberal and bourgeois of nineteenth-century societies, and in 1843 he produced *A Christmas Carol*, with its devastating critique of the laissez-faire spirit.

Dickens deploys domestic ideals as an antidote to social ills because he sees the values inherent in the Victorian family as antithetical to those of laissez-faire capitalism. Within the family, the proper father and husband—and even more the wife and mother—were understood as founts of unselfishness and sensitive nurturance for spouse and children. Yet outside the family, men were to throw themselves with energy into "amass[ing] scalps and money" in the "war of all against all."[24] Two such diametrically opposed prescriptions for action and feeling are inevitably in a relation of potential conflict. It is one of Dickens's great themes, particularly visible in fiction of the 1840s, that the competitive bourgeois ethos inevitably crowds out and dessicates the capacity for feeling that draws people together and binds them to human communities. Bourgeois society's damage to the microcosmic community of the family, and indeed to all forms of community, was one of its most glaring flaws.[25]

Dickens can articulate this theme quite straightforwardly. For instance, in *A Christmas Carol*, when the Ghost of Christmas Past recreates a joyous Christmas celebration at Fezziwig's establishment where, as a young apprentice, Scrooge had been part of a joyous community, the Ghost makes him understand how the paternal relation between master and apprentice (the apprentices reside with the master, becoming a part of the family) transcends a merely monetary relationship. At the Ghost's prompting, Scrooge draws the Carlylean lesson of the importance of community: "He [the master] has the power to render us [employees] happy or unhappy; to make our service light or burdensome; a pleasure or a toil. Say that this power lie in words and looks; in things so slight and insignificant that it is impossible to add and count 'em up: what then? The happiness he gives, is quite as great as if it cost a fortune." [26] The good master, in other words, is a benign paternalist who leads with a fatherly mixture of inspiring values and personal behavior that promote *community*: he does not rule through economic coercion. The warm emotions Scrooge remembers here subverts the laissez-faire spirit that he has heretofore embodied, and he at once repents his coldness to his own employee, Bob Cratchit.

But if this example clearly shows laissez-faire capitalism's chilling effect on familial feelings, it does so because it represents a workplace that is also a familial space: the apprentice Scrooge lives with the Fezziwigs. By contrast, the central relationships in *Dombey* are almost entirely familial and the narrative marginalizes the workplace. In his effort at elevation of his status and formal concentration, Dickens focuses so firmly on the domestic milieu that he largely deprives himself in this novel of one of his great strengths as a writer, the satirical denunciation of failed institutions and the horrors of life lived outside the bourgeois home, as in the brilliant workhouse scenes in *Oliver Twist* or the haunting depiction of the street urchin Jo in *Bleak House*. In general, his effort to elevate his fiction by domesticating it limits the power of his critique of bourgeois values. Moreover, *Dombey* focuses on a *bourgeois* family site, which further disables his subversive project. Though Dickens often portrays unhappy families, it is within working-class or impoverished families that the ill effects of capitalism were most visible to Victorians. Such dysfunctional families are a nightmarish inversion of bourgeois norms as in the abusive brick maker in *Bleak House*, or are terrible parodies of bourgeois aspirations to upward mobility, such as Mrs. Jo and her familial victims in *Great Expectations*. Since the distorting effects of market forces are only more subtly visible in the middle-class home, *Dombey*'s tight focus on the bourgeois home tends to disable its sweeping ambitions to challenge the selfish atomization of bourgeois society.

FEMININE DEPRIVATION
AND ARTISTIC CONCENTRATION

Dickens's high estimation of *Dombey* has been vindicated by critics, who have tended to agree that it is an advance in his development in unity of theme and structural coherence.[27] And to a striking degree, this unity is achieved by the novel's concentration on the domestic scene and the family. The danger of this familial form for Dickens was that the assertion of masculine authority as writer and cultural critic to which he aspired would be subverted by the novel's emphasis on a private, feminine theme and on the degraded, feminine popular genre associated with the exploration of such themes, the Gothic. True, far from abandoning his aspirations toward achieving cultural authority through grasping historical processes, Dickens continues the method he learned in *Barnaby Rudge*. Both novels chart a familial situation and its problematic relation to and figuration of historical processes. *Dombey*, however, applies this method in a new way: to an intensely familial and domestic scene, indeed to the near-exclusion of anything except a claustrophobic concentration on the family. The two novels also share a pattern in which societal tensions between hierarchy and autonomy are figured in narratives of oppressive family situations that generate revolts against the authority of the father. Less obviously, the revolts associated with Florence and Edith, like those of the rebellious sons of *Barnaby Rudge*, are figurations of broader historical tensions. In *Barnaby Rudge*, the social correlative of the tensions manifested in familial revolts is the Gordon riots. In *Dombey and Son* the social tension figured by the novel's familial narratives is more diffuse: the emergent tyrannical power of the capitalist and the growing social and political distance between employer and employee associated with industrialization that is figured in Carker's betrayal of Dombey and in Walter Gay's disappearance and elopement with Florence. More generally, familial tensions reflect the destructive force of industrialization, understood as commercial greed run rampant, and figured in the monomaniacal commitment of Dombey to his firm. Thus Dombey's single-minded commitment to commercial values penetrates and disrupts even the home, in Victorian familial ideology the traditional sanctuary from the pressures of the marketplace.

Yet, if the novel's subtlety proceeds from its compression of the complex historical dialectic between family and history into a concentrated study of the family, the contrast with the overtly historical *Barnaby Rudge* (and its model in Scott's novels) suggests this subtlety is achieved through the loss of a coherent sense of historical narrative. In *Dombey and Son*, history itself is marginalized, for all that its effects appear everywhere in the narrative. The implicit narrative of the progress of industrialization is figured as a catastrophe, or at least an unimaginably abrupt break with the past, as in the earthquake that is the railroad's construction that transforms Staggs's garden, or in the railroad itself, a symbol of death to Dombey and the literal cause of death to Carker. But the historical narrative of industrialization in the novel does not merely mirror a process of social disruption so profound as to marginalize and dwarf the contributions of individual actors. In its focus on the domestic, the novel not only reflects the marginalization of the individual before industrialization, but also embodies Dickens's more oblique engagement in depicting and commenting on the public sphere, in contrast to the overt engagement seen in *Barnaby Rudge*'s polemic against capital punishment. Dickens's sense that domestic writing constitutes a retreat from full public engagement accounts for the novel's insistent depiction of domestic space as, above all, a site of absence. Indeed the novel imitates its heroine's renunciatory strategies by depriving itself of public dimension, except in the novel's indirect comment on child and female labor, as it elides even while responding to the explosive power of the Industrial Revolution, which, like the mysterious railroad transforming Staggs's garden, is the unseen mover behind the novel's privatized events. The novel's loss of a public dimension is dramatized early on by the death of Dombey's heir, Paul, whose poignant childhood is described in some of the novel's most powerful prose.

The senior Dombey's attitude toward his daughter Florence following the death of his son is the central and determinative instance of the theme of the domestic as absence in the novel. It is this absence, from Dombey's perspective, to which the irony of the novel's title (also the first chapter title) draws attention. From its beginning then, the novel's lack of a public dimension is linked with its focus on feminine experience. What is available for the novel, as for Dombey, is a daughter, but she is understood negatively, as above all *not* a son, as not capable of fulfilling a masculine and public position. Though Dombey's reductive reading of Florence satirizes his selfish monomaniacal desire for public status and raises the possibility that the novel will protest women's devaluation, the fact that a novel strikingly centered on feminine experience nevertheless depicts women's experience as fundamentally governed by a sense of absence suggests the ambivalence that Dickens himself, as a male writer, felt about his embrace of the domestic mode.

Dombey's failure to see Florence as a person rather than a lack is symptomatic of his larger failure to enact satisfactorily the roles of father and husband. According to Victorian domestic ideals, men should actively engage with family life and provide it with both moral rigor and emotional sustenance, a balance Dombey never succeeds in achieving. From its opening lines, the novel mocks his masculine pretensions for public status, which are embodied in his firm's title, comically juxtaposing Dombey's masculine self-assertiveness with the feebleness of the representative of maleness he has engendered: "Dombey was about eight-and-forty years of age. Son about eight-and-forty minutes. Dombey was rather bald, rather red, and though a handsome well-made man, too stern and pompous in appearance, to be prepossessing. Son was very bald, and very red, and though (of course) an undeniably fine infant, somewhat crushed and spotty in general effect, as yet" (49). The puny baby's comic disruption of the father's masculine pretensions prepares for what will become a central concern of Dombey the character and of the novel itself: the desire for a masculine heir who will embody the father's potency. And this incongruous contrast between two versions of masculinity, one rigid and overbearing, the other helpless and needy, also anticipates how the father's ambitions will blight the nurturant maternal care his infant son demands. Largely as a result of Dombey's aggressive and selfish actions, a quality of absence characterizes all the novel's female characters: Edith will be not a genuine wife, nor will Mrs. Skewton and Polly be true mothers to the children for whom they are responsible. Each female character either is viewed, like Florence, as an absence, or fails to conform successfully to a feminine role.

If Dombey's failure as a father and husband disrupts the positive potential of female figures in the novel, another dimension of his failure, as both father and employer, is his tendency to blight and feminize male characters. Thus, his son Paul, deprived of adequate nurturance by his father's coldness and Dombey's hostility to the working-class Mrs. Polly Toodles, becomes, as Nina Auerbach has pointed out, feminized to the point of death; the sinister Carker engages in the feminine mode of influence and subtlety by plotting to empower himself through marriage with Florence or by adultery with Edith; and even the hero Walter Gay is forced into a passive feminine mode of waiting, dreaming, and hoping for advancement through marriage.[28] This emasculation of male figures extends beyond characters blighted by Dombey personally to become a feature of the social landscape over which he, as preeminent capitalist, presides. The elder Carker, apparently deprived of the opportunity of marriage, lives a sexless and humble life with his sister, while the working-class male Mr. Toodles, despite Dombey's efforts to assign him masculine authority over his wife, verbally relegates authority to her ("But Polly heerd it. It's all right.").[29] Toodles's passive attitude toward his wife's autonomy links the emasculation of masculine figures in the novel to the difficulty of controlling women, which becomes an obsessive theme, not only in this novel but in a great deal of Victorian literature. Coding social ills in familial terms, *Dombey and Son* depicts a world of emasculated males and a concomitant "unnatural" power of women, which is associated with their failure to achieve their full potential as mothers and wives. All of these inadequacies of gender performance proceed from the failure of Dombey, the presiding father figure in both the family and in society, to establish a nurturant familial structure either at home or in the larger society.

Paul's death suggests that men cannot be happy unless they balance public achievement with the private familial role. In this sense, the novel reproduces the middle-class familial ideology that emphasized the centrality of nurturance and affection within the home, constructing its own textual authority by pointing out the radical failure of a masculine figure like Dombey because he has inadequately integrated himself into the domestic sphere that the novel extols. But this reproduction of domestic ideology for Dickens represents a potentially contradictory and unstable effort to appropriate a private domestic site for the public purpose of authorial self-elevation. While the new industrial order and its mass reading public generates a new kind of heroic possibility for the male writer—indeed, allows Dickens to be a literary Dombey—it confronts him with the chastening awareness that he must reside in the privatized and feminized sphere of the domestic narrative. (Significantly, the more emphatically masculine worlds of *Barnaby* and *Chuzzlewit* had not achieved great popular or critical success.) In this sense, the death of young Paul Dombey suggests the difficulties and contradictory impulses of Dickens's Pauline project of speaking in a masculine voice and converting the masses.

In this light, we can see why the novel's centering on the home is structured as a gradually growing sense of enclosure and as a failure of alternative narrative and social sites. The novel's narrative structure forces the reader to experience the same deprivation that Florence endures, the loss both of characters beloved and even of the possibility of action in their absence. Thus, in turn Polly vanishes, Paul dies, Walter and Sol Gills disappear, even Dombey leaves London; the reader is left with Florence and must share the characteristically feminine experience of isolation, tedium, and passivity while awaiting the return of important male characters.

DOMESTICITY SOURED:
THE RISE OF THE DIAGNOSTIC MODE

If Dickens's self-assertion as a writer in *Dombey* is associated here with a chastening loss of direct narrative access to the public sphere, he compensates for this loss through his vigorous espousal of ideologies of the family, which becomes the warrant for the text's moral seriousness. The novel instills the dominant familial ideology of the period, one characterized by an emphasis on the family as the site of nurturance and intense emotional life, a place where moral example and psychic influence replaces the physical coercion and rigid hierarchies of the prindustrial family, and above all, where the marketplace and the larger sociality of the community is divorced from the closed and emotionally intense domestic sphere.[30] The centrality of feminine experience in the novel suggests the centrality of women to the maintenance of the home and of the domesticity in mid-Victorian ideology.

Two different ideological accounts of the relation of family and society are at stake in the novel, both of which offer ideological solutions to the divisive forces of the marketplace and of class conflict, issues that were highly topical in the "hungry forties."[31] Victorian domestic ideology understood the larger social world as composed of mutually antagonistic and competing individuals in which men easily lost their moral bearings in a relentless striving for selfish ends; the home and the family, in particular the women of a man's family, were to embody an influence toward moral elevation and spiritual regeneration for individual men. Florence represents precisely the kind of higher moral values and suasive influence for good that domestic ideology advocated for women; she spends much of the novel as an exemplary feminine moral force, trying with little success to soften her father and waiting patiently to reap the rewards of her moral guerrilla war. Dickens himself envisioned the novel largely in these terms, calling Florence in a letter to John Forster that accompanied the first four chapters of the manuscript, Dombey's "unknown Good Genius always" (*Letters*, 4:590). Yet the crucial word for most of the novel is "unknown"; the novel revises domestic ideology pessimistically by an enormous deferral of the expected positive but subtle moral influence, a darkening and a deferral that becomes almost tragic in its dimensions.

An aspect of the novel's somber evaluation of the power of Florence's moral suasion is its awareness of the intensity of the determinations operating within the wider social world, particularly the economic world, to generate coldness and hostility even in the heart of the family, a theme that has precedent in Richardson's *Clarissa*. But a second ideological account of family and society, paternalist ideology, provides a tool with which Dickens can stress these moral and psychic failures of an urbanizing capitalist society. According to paternalist ideology, the hierarchical but benevolent relations that characterize the family should be a model for class relations, with the masters playing the role of wise and kindly fathers, and workers the role of submissive and loyal children. Hence, by entering into the workplace, the values of the family can ameliorate the social divisiveness of class conflict, as we saw in the depiction of Fezziwig and Scrooge. If *Dombey* finally affirms the validity of the ideology of domesticity, acknowledging women's transformative and redemptive potential in the home, it evaluates the emerging industrial order and its characteristic deep class divisions through the lens of paternalist thought and finds it, by this standard, utterly wanting. For in Dombey's unfeeling treatment of Walter, who, his friends optimistically point out, is potentially his son by marriage, and in his cold tolerance of the elder Carker, his role as capitalist and employer is shown to be violently at odds with a paternalistic conception of the master's role. The irony that Dombey's behavior as capitalist is the antithesis of the paternalist prescription of employing familial values in the workplace is accentuated by Walter's eventual movement into Dombey's family. The failure of paternalism in the workplace as Dombey manages it is also emphasized by the fraternal pair of the younger Carker, Dombey's agent and moral double, who becomes a malevolent agent of rebellion against Dombey's authority, and the despised elder Carker, whose theft and repentance makes him a symbolic embodiment of the sufferings of the oppressed, but morally deserving, worker.

But the central subversion of the paternalist ideology embodied in the novel is the degree to which the separation of family from society, which both domestic and paternalistic ideology presuppose, is undermined by Dombey's actions, which disrupt that separation because of the overweening ambition he derives from his powerful economic position. This necessary separation is a crucial problem for Victorian ideologies that saw the family and its influence as the source of society's moral redemption, for both ideologies—the domestic ideal of separate spheres and the paternalist ideal—imaginatively overcome societal tensions at the cost of drawing attention to the importance of policing the tension between familial values and behavior on one hand and marketplace logic on the other. How could domesticity spiritually regenerate men, or paternalism offer family ties as a model to employers for benevolent class relations, were the family itself to become part of the societal and economic struggles that it was required to cure? The influence of these two ideologies accounts for the novel's obsessive insistence on the necessity of separating family and marketplace.

In its relentless anxiety about the necessity of maintaining the separation of the familial sphere and the public or commercial sphere, the novel's diagnostic familialism emerges. By diagnostic familialism I mean a depiction of family and gender relations that deploys ideologies of class, sexuality, and gender to produce narratives of causality that explain social evils by finding their roots in familial failures. Though itself a variant of the domestic mode and rooted in similar ideological premises, the diagnostic domestic mode is more objective, negative, and satirical, more skeptical of the idealization and moral potency of the domestic than earlier domestic narrative. In contrast to sentimental domesticity's idealization of Victorian femininity (embodied in Florence), diagnostic familialism's characteristic thematics are the vitiation and failure of domestic ideals, above all of motherhood, the encroachment of greed and mercenary values, the dangers of illicit sexuality and prostitution, and the flourishing of class and gender ressentiment, the inverse of the benevolent fellow feeling promised by paternalism. This mode is diagnostic in that it offers a protosociological exposé of the normally invisible underside of public bourgeois life—of transgressive sexuality and familial malformations—as well as of the dark side of working-class life, which was often hidden from the bourgeois gaze.

The threat of these dangerous forces of transgressive sexuality and ressentiment reveal the stark limitations of traditional domesticity for the Dombeys and confirms the absence of successful paternalism—and fatherhood—in Dombey's world.[32] Throughout the novel, the failure of domesticity in the Dombey circle is the master key for diagnosing the moral bankruptcy of his bourgeois ethos. The overt and crucial sign of the pathology of this ethos is the failure of successful mothering in the milieu Dombey creates, each failure of the maternal principle generating the next in a recurring cycle of failed mothering. Beginning with the death of a mother (Mrs. Dombey), the novel repeatedly depicts forms of lost or failed mothering. Just as Florence initially loses her mother, she goes on to lose Polly (her nurse) and her stepmother Edith. Moreover, Florence precociously mothers her brother Paul, a pathetic mothering project that fails when he dies, and later she tries unsuccessfully to act as a mother to her father, who rejects her. The quasi-incestuous patterns of familial bonding in the novel are produced by the effort to restore the Dombey family's crucial missing component, which is motherhood. In its withering portrayal of Dombey's incapacity to generate an acceptably nurturant home, the novel's meditation on mothers suggests a tension between an effort to idealize the middle-class domesticity and an intense political ambivalence toward the increasing power of capitalists. Florence, a bourgeois Cinderella, suffers from the loss of the legitimate and natural mother, who can never be restored. The repeated "step" quality of parents in the novel mirrors Dombey's frantic social climbing in suggesting the difficulty of establishing various kinds of legitimacy as well as an adequately nurturant community capable of reproducing the capitalist wealth that Dombey represents. Thus, the various stepparents in the novel figure the difficulty of instilling proper moral qualities in the social world that bourgeois wealth is creating.

Through the lens of a concentration on the bourgeois home, Dickens covertly introduces anxieties over mothering in Victorian society that suggest that failed or threatened motherhood is a sign of what is generally flawed in the emerging industrial order; the images of unsuccessful motherhood figure social anxieties about the stability and health of families and of society. The novel's narrative pattern of repeatedly threatened and endangered motherhood occurs in the context of fierce debates over women's paid labor in the 1830s and 1840s, in which the presence and deplorable conditions of working-class women and children in the industrial workforce attracted much critical comment, a controversy culminating in a series of laws restricting female and child employment. Much of the rhetoric employed in opposition to female labor deployed the Victorian middle-class ideal of the family according to which the mother must be in the home and central for the children's development, and familial space must remain segregated from the world of paid labor.[33] One of the chief arguments used in opposition to female labor was that women who worked in factories or mines would be unable to live up to this middle-class ideal of family life as wives and mothers and would hence fail to socialize their children properly in moral values and social hierarchies, breeding delinquency and criminality. Another argument stressed the moral temptations and the autonomy of female industrial workers and saw such labor as leading to sexual and general immorality. In this way, too, women workers would fail to preserve the purity of the home, and would corrupt the families and class from which they came.

The character of the novel's ambivalence toward capitalism is manifested in the way the narrative twists the typical arguments critical of bourgeois workplace practices (employing women and children because they were cheap labor) and of working-class homes, into anxieties about the bourgeois home. In depicting such a home the novel obsessively depicts the vitiation of motherhood by commercial relations. Indeed, in Paul's wet nurse Polly Toodles the text imagines not so much a mother disabled by her husband's capitalist impulses (like the first Mrs. Dombey), but a working mother disabled by working *as a mother*. Polly's position is doubly problematic, for as a working mother she must work instead of mothering her own children, but her nursing of a bourgeois child transforms mothering into work; mothering can only occur in the Dombey household as part of a network of commercial relations. Dombey makes this clear when he tells Polly she must become "Richards," "an ordinary and convenient" name, insisting that there should be minimal contact between Polly and her own family, and that her relation to the Dombeys should be "a question of wages altogether" (17–18). Raymond Williams reads this passage as evidence of how the employer deprives the worker of her individuality, reducing her to an object embodying labor power.[34] But this reading misses a key point; in restricting the relationship between Polly and his son to a merely commercial one, and by his indifference to Polly's maternal feelings and responsibilities toward her own family, Dombey is not only denying Polly's humanity, he assaults her capacity to mother. Dombey's paranoid concern about Polly's moral character and degree of contact with her own family, while exaggerated for satiric effect, reflects widespread anxieties both moral and sanitary engendered by wet nurses, who were feared as sources of venereal infection.[35] These anxieties resonate with the bourgeois ideological impulse to segregate mothering from the market, an ideal that wet nurses, working-class women whose occupation combines maternal functions with commerce, inevitably disrupted. The impersonal hiring of the innocent Polly embodies the tension between motherhood as an ideal and the inhuman ethos of the commercial sphere. Yet if the novel mocks Dombey's dehumanizing suspicions of the wet nurse, it implicitly shares the anxiety he evinces about the contamination of motherhood by commerce. For this scene anticipates a central pattern in the novel, and in Dickensian familialism generally, by which the search for the good mother requires a ceaseless vigilance against the moral pollution whose ultimate source is the society's commercial character.

When Polly, too busy trying to save her own child from the degradations of the Charitable Grinders and the dangers of working-class street youths (chap. 6), fails to save Florence from falling briefly into the hands of Mrs. Brown, the demonic antitype of the good mother and procurer for her own daughter, the dangers of the mixing of motherhood and the labor market are dramatically revealed.[36] For a working mother, the novel suggests, motherhood is a disaster, one that affects both the working-class child (Rob) and the bourgeois child (Paul and Florence). Florence's loss of Polly as surrogate mother is doubly caused by Dombey's callous stress upon the commercial. He not only rigidly forbids Polly's contact with her own family, but he also cruelly punishes her for failing to keep watch over his own children and for not protecting them from contact with the working class. His commercial ethos and class snobbery preclude his understanding of the human and familial ties that bind Polly to her own children as well as to Florence and Paul. (He further contributes to the debacle by his effort to substitute for maternal care the humiliating charity of Rob's school.) Polly fails as a mother, both to her own children and to Florence and Paul, because she is a working mother for the former and a hired mother for the latter. As such, her failure dramatizes the dangers of women's paid work, even when they perform the most womanly of labors, mothering itself.

The appearance at this point in the narrative of the sinister Mrs. Brown, eventually revealed as the mother-procurer of the prostitute Alice, suggests another dimension to the opposition to women's labor, its symbolic threat to maternal purity. This character, and the thematics of sexual pollution that Mrs. Brown introduces, signals the novel's most overt investment in a diagnostic mode that implicitly draws on a quasi-medical analysis of social ills. Embodying the most lurid symptom of how the bourgeois social order disrupts its own familial ideal and vitiates motherhood, Mrs. Brown soils femininity through her complicity in her daughter's sexual intrusion into the public and commercial sphere. If Polly is a mother who is deprived of the capacity to mother by her entry into the sphere of paid labor, Mrs. Brown epitomizes the mother whose enmeshment in commerce represents a sexual degradation that prevents the inculcation in her child of proper moral values. The mother-procurer is the epitome of the mother who fails to instill in her child the correct moral principles, because she encourages horrifying moral transgression for profit. The fact that Mrs. Brown briefly captures Florence, and contemplates the symbolic defloration entailed in cutting off her hair, suggests how the confusion of motherhood with commerce that Dombey has imposed on Polly has infected the social world, ultimately threatening the bourgeois family itself, embodied in its pure essence in Florence.

Significantly, this suggestion of defloration is proleptic of the threat to the bourgeois family embodied in Mrs. Skewton and Edith, their mercenary goal replicating on another class level the degradation of Mrs. Brown and Alice. This elaborate parallel of mother-procurers on different class levels confirms what the anxiety about wet nurses suggested, that the novel's anxiety about the working mother is closely tied to an anxiety, typical of the period, about prostitution and the control of sexuality.[37] Dickens was highly concerned about the "Great Social Evil," as Victorians called prostitution, and during the period of the inception and writing of *Dombey and Son* he and the philanthropist Angela Burdett-Coutts planned the creation of an "Asylum," Urania Cottage, to reform former prostitutes (*Letters*, 4:552–56). He even developed his own system for monitoring and controlling the women's behavior, with the ultimate goal of transforming them into virtuous working-class wives.[38]

The same zeal for social reform and moral regulation that animates Dickens's proposals for Urania Cottage is deployed in *Dombey and Son*. The novel's careful categorization of characters as social types, in particular as specific types of familial dysfunction, is a mechanism of normalization that stigmatizes those characters who deviate from the norms of bourgeois domesticity. The intensely cold and ultimately physically abusive and rejecting father who is Dombey, the working mother who is Polly, and the mother-procurers embodied in Mrs. Brown and Mrs. Skewton are understood as social types who point out the necessity of normalization toward ideal forms of family life by their deviations from it. In such an ideological framework, the socially marginal prostitute takes on a disproportionate symbolic importance. Because the prostitute is the visible and overt emblem of familial and sexual incontinence, the diagnosis of the prostitute becomes a paradigm for the diagnosis of society.[39] Indeed, in a letter Dickens theorized the nature of the prostitute in a way that parallels one of the central anxieties expressed in *Dombey*, offering this reading of their typical character defect: "There seems to be something inherent in their course of life, which engenders and awakens a sudden restlessness and recklessness which may be long suppressed, but breaks out like Madness; and which all people who have had opportunities of observation in Penitentiaries and elsewhere, must have contemplated with astonishment and pity" (*Letters*, 4:555). Dickens voices the "astonishment" of the middle-class observer at working-class women's desire to escape confinement and observation and to maintain their autonomy. But this astonishment at feminine "restlessness" is obviously influenced by the middle-class obsession with the necessity of women's remaining stably within the home. This astonishment and horror at transgressive feminine autonomy suggests why the prostitute in *Dombey and Son*, whether literal or figurative (Alice or Edith), becomes a central symbol in the novel of the disturbing instability of women, their failure to remain safely in the home, outside the ambit of market relations, and under the domination of a masculine household head, and the profound cultural anxiety about the resultant threat to motherhood.

The theme of symbolic prostitution, and its meanings of commerciality and uncontrollable sexuality, dramatically reemerges in the novel with the entry into the Dombey household of Edith, Dombey's second wife. Florence's bond with her stepmother contaminates her with at first the appearance, and ultimately the reality, of rebellion against her father. True, her rebellion in leaving her home is essentially impulsive and defensive, yet the endless mitigating factors only emphasize the inevitability of the threat of "restlessness" for women, the same trait that allowed Edith to prostitute herself to one man and then flee scandalously with another. Florence's movement away from her father's house into the city is clearly understood as both traumatic and symbolically akin to becoming a woman of the streets: "Another moment, and the close darkness of the shut-up house (forgotten to be opened, though it was long since day) yielded to the unexpected glare and freedom of the morning; and Florence, with her head bent down to hide her agony of tears, was in the streets" (637). The contrast between the "glare and freedom" of the city and the claustrophic pent-upness of the middle-class home is stressed, and the chapter ends with the ominous phrase "in the streets." A Victorian reader could hardly have missed the allusion to the threat of prostitution for a woman without family or means alone in London; by ending the chapter in this way Dickens draws attention to the way that Florence's flight is a version of the same societal problem of female "restlessness" that he saw manifested in the prostitute inmates of Urania Cottage.[40] Soon after this scene, we find Florence pathetically imagining herself becoming a governess, a profession she sadly notes will debar her forever from marriage and motherhood. So even the pure Florence exhibits in her rebellious flight the "restlessness" that ideologically encodes the enmeshment of women in the marketplace and their failure to stay within the home and to remain firmly linked to marriage.[41] Moreover, by suggesting how Florence, in being expelled from her father's home, is threatened by the taint of prostitution, the novel diagnoses her family's failure as actually realizing Dombey's paranoid fantasy of his daughter's sexual impurity. Enraged at Edith's flight, Dombey has attacked Florence because he assumes her bond with her stepmother renders her as morally fallen as his apparently adulterous wife: "and as he dealt the blow, he told her what Edith was, and bade her follow her, since they had always been in league" (757). The unspoken epithet ("what Edith was") is presumably "whore," and in telling Florence to "follow" her transgressive stepmother, Dombey has given way to a tyrannical male paranoia that threatens to produce the instability of feminine virtue and the rebellion against patriarchal control that it hysterically attempts to prevent.

Thus a familial ideal is deployed as a diagnostic tool through which the social arena is read. The result is a typology of failed families that, in a scientific spirit, links characters by pathologies that transcend obvious class boundaries, Mrs. Skewton, and even Polly are failed mothers, failing to instill strong moral values through nurturance in their children; and Florence and Edith (and other women in the novel) are unstable and difficult to contain in their proper place and social role. Such a diagnostic mode, which assiduously locates hidden flaws in characters by the standards of bourgeois familial and characterological norms, foreshadows the detective narrative that Dickens will insert into *Bleak House* (1852–53) and that becomes the full-blown detective narrative produced by Dickens's friend Wilkie Collins in his influential early detective novel, *The Moonstone* (1868). This diagnostic mode evades recognizing itself as a class-based system of thought by uncovering typologies that do not overtly correspond with class boundaries, even while the ideal that structures the diagnostic method is determined by class and gender-based values.

The novel's use of processes of normalization supports D. A. Miller's reading of Victorian novels as repressive apparatuses that encourage the individual's incarceration within the domestic scene and the familial nexus.[42] But such a reading minimizes how a novel such as *Dombey* criticizes unfettered patriarchal power. It also ignores how the contrast of the ideals of love and loyalty embodied in families with the relentless competitiveness and selfishness of laissez-faire capitalism functions as a powerful rhetoric that advocates the moral reform of society and aspires to liberate the individual and enable his (or her) healthy psychic development. But for all that Dickens uses domestic narratives to castigate the ills of laissez-faire, there is a paradox inherent in his deployment of familialism, which is that, ultimately, domestic fiction was both empowering and limiting for an ambitious male writer such as Dickens. In exploring feminine experience, Dickens's domestic fictions colonize a hitherto largely female literary space associated with domesticity and with the Gothic genre, transforming this territory into a source of masculine authority. But the domestic mode also constrains the expression of a subversive vision of his culture by constricting the variety of topoi available to him, intensifying his commitment to ideological shibboleths of family and gender relations, enforcing a retreat from overt commentary on the public sphere, and above all containing Dickens's impulse toward critique of systemic structures and institutions, the capitalist marketplace and its institutional corollaries, within narratives of bourgeois personal life where the marketplace's destructive effects were least visible. Because it both constrained and empowered Dickens, the domestic mode engenders his characteristic resolution of the impasse between his aspiration for social critique and the limitations of domesticity's conventions, which is the development of the narrative apparatus of diagnostic familialism. Far from being a stable repressive apparatus, the domestic mode in *Dombey and Son* resolves only with great difficulty the tension between Dickens's impulse toward harsh critique of the marketplace's destructive impact on human relations and his commitment to classic middle-class ideological assumptions about domesticity, gender, and class that blunt that impulse. As we will see, the awkwardly willed resolution of the familial mode's inherent contradictions that Dickens achieves in *Dombey* will prove a compromise that, in the later course of his career, proves to be radically unstable.

CLASS AND GENDER RESSENTIMENT:
THE FAMILY CONTAMINATED

If the insistent thematics of vitiated motherhood and prostitution carry the novel to the point where they threaten to undermine its commitment to celebration of conventional domestic ideals, the novel's most searching subversion of familial ideology emerges through its obsession with the contaminating force of social ressentiment. This theme clearly manifests the novel's striking ambivalence toward its own social stance, which is at once celebratory of and hostile to the social changes linked to industrial capitalism. On one hand, the powerful indictment of the autocratic Dombey is a critique of the capitalist as social and familial tyrant. But that critique has been deracinated from the larger social arena in which it arises (by contrast, such an arena is much more clearly visible in *A Christmas Carol*), and is displaced to a genteel and domesticized narrative within the home.[43] If the novel displaces its antibourgeois impulses into a withering vision of a bourgeois home, it reveals an uneasiness at deploying a depiction of the middle-class family to critique bourgeois culture. This uneasiness manifests itself in its starkly divided sympathies in portraying the roots of the deep-seated malaise of such a family, for the novel is torn between its sympathetic and implicitly feminist portrayal of Florence, the neglected daughter and victim of patriarchal prejudice, and of Edith, his second wife, trapped in a mercenary marriage to Dombey, and its utterly hostile portrayal of the illegitimate class-based disgruntlement of Carker. Even the novel's feminist sympathies, which make it sensitive to the plight of the entrapped middle-class woman, prove ambivalent: with the flight of Edith from the home, the novel's sympathy for her dissipates; having left the home and become linked with the class Other (Carker), she passes the boundaries of acceptable protest.

Edith's rebellion in fleeing her marriage is damned both by its transgression of the bounds of domesticity and by its association with the figure of Carker, whose subversive energies enable Edith's antifamilial transgression. Carker's hostility to Dombey embodies the spirit of class-based ressentiment of which he, with his aesthetically polished home, his burning hatred for his master, and his self-destructive rebellion, is a classic figure.[44] The ideologeme of ressentiment, symptomatic of the pervasive anxiety about class conflict and class difference in the nineteenth century, explains the class hostility of the lower orders through invoking psychological mechanisms of destructive envy and pride. By suggesting that Carker's rebellion and Edith's have a deep affinity, the narrative that links the two of them suggests the dangerous affinities of class and gender rebellion. Indeed, Carker's hostility to his master, by providing a mechanism for Edith's rebellion, figures the tendency for the dynamics of class hostility to enter the home and to disrupt this privileged social site.

This plot enacts, therefore, a nightmarish potentiality for Victorian familial ideology. The family, instead of being a site of relief and recuperation for the individual that would free him from the brutal pressures of the marketplace could become itself a victim of the same individualistic impulses and corrosive hostilities that divided the broader society. Indeed, the family itself becomes the source of these impulses and hostilities. In a way this fictive invasion of the family by the world of class hostility is simply an anathematization of the opposite of the middle-class familial ideal. In contrast to the ideal of complete separation and withdrawal from the wider society, Dombey continually brings the world of business into the home and hence destabilizes it. But if such a rhetorical strategy of anathematization through detailing transgressions of familial insularity stresses the necessity of withdrawal of the family from the larger world, it equally tends to suggest the near impossibility of complete insulation of the family from its environment of a market- and class-dominated social world. By so doing, the novel's narrative covertly undermines domestic ideology's stress on the natural and restorative character of the bourgeois family, for the more Dickens acknowledges the inevitable determinations linking the economic and social world to the familial sphere, the less plausible become the claims of domestic ideology that an a historically static and unchanging domestic sphere is recuperative and redemptive for the individual, a universal ideal for every social circumstance.

If Dombey's central failure, which causes the drainage of emotional energy from his own family, is his inability to live up to the Victorian ideal of the father as a nurturant participant in the domestic sphere, what causes his overphallic rigidity, his refusal to be domesticated, indeed his physical and emotional absence from his family, is his arrogant desire to make his family directly serve public and class-mediated goals. In this regard his error echoes that of Clarissa Harlowe's family, who are complicit in the destruction of their daughter because of their obsessive desire for social mobility through a mercenary marriage. Dombey too reads all experience through his preoccupation with social status: his first wife is largely understood as a source of a son, the son in turn is valued largely as a source of the public prestige of the public entity "Dombey and Son";[45] Edith is criticized by Dombey precisely for not allowing herself to be used as a source of public prestige in "society." This public project is in turn the reflex of Dombey's eagerness to overcome his marginality in the public sphere (as a mere capitalist) by acquiring genteel connections, which is pathetically obvious in his susceptibility to the toadying attentions of the genteel Mrs. Skewton and Captain Bagstock. Indeed, Dombey's project of entering through marriage with Edith into an aristocratic social sphere is an effort to deploy personal relations in behalf of a project whose ultimate goal is the public prestige and power of aristocratic connections.

Obviously, Dickens uses such a plot to express his political animus toward the aristocracy. But the association between Dombey's aristocratic social ambitions and the emotionally dessicated character of his family life suggests that the novel is criticizing not merely a political and social strategy of bourgeois alliance with the landed aristocracy, but certain social values entailing subordination of familial and affective relations to public prestige. These values are stigmatized by being associated with a gentry represented as at best doddering and incompetent (Cousin Feenix), at worst dishonest and callous (Mrs. Skewton and Captain Bagstock). In this sense Dombey's flirtation with the aristocracy only literalizes his affinity with other aristocratic violators of bourgeois familial norms, such as Richardson's Lovelace. Even before his involvement with the aristocracy, he exhibits their characteristic faults in his preoccupation with public prestige and lineage, shown by his obsession with his son and neglect of his daughter. The conflation of the capitalist and the aristocrat should not surprise us. In this period, the wealth and social status that capitalists were amassing, their evident power to rewrite the physical and social world, and their impact on the political structure were relatively new and highly prominent phenomena that required new language and conceptualizations of the emergent social order. Terms like "millocrat" and "factory lord" suggest the popular associations between capitalists and the older upper class.[46] Such terminology and Dickens's use of their implicit metaphor in structuring his narrative links the novel's antibourgeois sentiments with the tradition of working-class and petit-bourgeois radicalism, which, in the face of industrialization, argued for political democracy and republicanism over what they saw as both the old and the new versions of aristocracy.[47] But if this plot expresses Dickens's conscious political impulses, he may well have less consciously sympathized with Dombey's desire for heroic public activity; indeed, given his own aspirations for a public voice, he undoubtedly felt ambivalence about being feminized and domesticated by the very literary mode that author and character alike inhabit.

Thus the antiaristocratic agenda of *Barnaby Rudge* is transformed into a critique of Dombey's bourgeois obsession with public prestige and an aristocratic alliance that causes the boundaries between the phallic energy of the competitive economic sphere to invade and vitiate the feminine sphere of familial love. Because the atomistic competition and selfishness of the marketplace invades the family, hostility and ressentiment, a mixture of envy and rage that images transgression against class and gender harmony, appear within the family as well. Because ressentiment contaminates the family, incestuous patterns emerge, centered on Dombey; Florence is his rival first for her mother, then for Paul, and then for Edith, as if his daughter's frantic efforts to secure closeness to other family members were understood as incestuously harboring sexual impulses for her mother and brother. Finally, in striking Florence on the breast, Dombey exhibits a final confusion in which Florence becomes, symbolically, a victim of his sexual frustration. Incestuous possibilities are the novel's ideologically coded expresssion of the explosive and individualist energies of capitalism redounding on the family and becoming implosive and anomic. The anatomization of such impulses is a function of the novel's general preoccupation with the maintenance of familial boundaries: it is Dombey's failure to manage and control such boundaries and the novel's refusal to affirm their inviolability in the face of the besieging energies of ressentiment spawned by assorted social frustrations, economic and political (Dombey), feminine (Edith) and lower-class (Carker), that generates the incestuous patterns that structure the novel's psychic relationships. The transgressive impulses of capitalism, figured by various characters' refusal to maintain the boundary between self-seeking and the family, emerge as confusions of roles or boundaries within the family. Beneath the placid exterior of domesticity lurks a Hobbesian psychic world in which bourgeois competition for scarce affective and sexual resources atomizes the family itself, just as the Hobbesian vision of the political economists was widely feared to threaten the atomization of social life. The climactic marker of the emergence of this relentless competition within the heart of the family itself is Dombey's assault on his daughter's breast. Not only is this a symbolic sexual violation, but it is the antithesis of the proper bourgeois family's maintenance of social norms through love and moral example. In an era when middle-class familial ideals that encouraged female passivity and decried male violence in marriage were increasingly prominent, it is a shameful return to an atavistic and discredited form of social control, corporal punishment, and spectacularly fails when Florence flees, to return only after her father's final humiliation.[48] Here the novel suggests that the dominant impulse of capitalists, their monomaniacal sacrifice of domestic and paternal feeling to commercial and public advancement, implodes upon the family and reduces it to a savage and atavistic nightmare.

SELF-CANONIZATION AND
THE IMPASSE OF CLOSURE

Even while Dickens criticizes the bourgeois values exemplified in Dombey, his aspiration as a writer toward the elevation of his social status involves him in a deep ambivalence that makes him uncomfortable with too overt a challenge to middle-class domestic ideology. The novel's relentless deployment of its diagnostic mode suggests its underlying ambivalence toward elite readers. By asserting its authority through diagnostic discourse that shows failures of familial ideals, it continually risks pursuing such a discourse to the point of undermining the middle-class familial ideology that the novel promulgates. This underlying ideological ambivalence is paralleled by the novel's generic ambivalence, which involves a self-conscious movement, designed to buttress the novel's status, into a *Clarissa*-like narrative of feminine isolation and oppression within the family, but which refuses the subversion of masculine domination that a full-blown Richardsonian narrative allows. Like his appropriation of Scott as a model in *Barnaby Rudge*, Dickens's discovery of Richardson as a model is designed to elevate his novel's status. The novel replicates many of Richardson's characteristics: the delineation of the psychology of the endlessly tormented and oppressed feminine subject, the intense moral gravity focused on the family and its reproduction through parenting and marriage, the class elevation of the central characters, and the exploitation of sentiment, particularly in an effusion of pathos. The narrative's general character strikingly resembles that of *Clarissa*. In both novels a woman of a middle-class but highly prosperous background is treated tyrannically by her family and suffers isolation and coldness at the hands of a father who is eager to move into an aristocratic social sphere. Finally, in both texts the daughter, desperate at her maltreatment, leaves her father's home and is considered to have eloped. This narrative paradigm's concentration on the constriction inherent in the position of middle-class women, while it produces a certain ascetic deprivation for the writer and reader, also empowers the writer by self-consciously emphasizing the moral seriousness of his subject. This seriousness, and the text's ambition, is further emphasized by the novel's imitation of *King Lear,* in which Florence becomes an impotent Cordelia to Dombey's King Lear.[49] So the movement into narrative deprivation after Paul's death, which deprives reader and writer of the public, the popular, and the masculine, is equally a movement to elevate the subject toward classic status and domestic purity by moving into the private and respectable confines of a bourgeois home and a lady's heart.

But the novel's movement to canonize itself by association with classic texts is a deeply ambiguous gesture. Most obviously, the mysterious and gloomy house in which Florence is left, the mystery of Solomon Gills's disappearance, and the thematics of a claustrophic and enigmatic domestic life all identify Florence as descendent of the Gothic heroine, a far less restrained and more demotic source than Richardson; moreover, as we have seen, the novel's relentless diagnostic spirit, implicating even innocents such as Polly and Florence in dysfunctional families, undermines the stark moral issues that the classic narrative paradigms suggest, and the novel veers into hyperbolic melodrama, notably in its treatment of Carker, in an effort to restore moral clarity and to limit the subversiveness of its Richardsonian exploration of female subjectivity. The novel restores moral clarity by narrative punishment, notably in the gruesome ending of Carker, who is flattened by a speeding train (horrors of industrialization indeed!), but also through reward, as Florence is rewarded through reconciliation with her father and marriage to Walter. But in endorsing domestic ideology's faith in the restorative and transformative character of feminine virtue, such an affirmative conclusion for Florence's trajectory is at odds with the tragic narrative logic that her story, following its Richardsonian and Shakespearean precedents, inevitably suggests. Hence, the novel's sense of willed resolution feels manifestly at odds with its strategies of literary self-assertion, its development of a diagnostic familialism, and its self-conscious modeling of itself on classic but tragic narrative models. The root of this tension is the clash between the logic of Dickens's literary strategies, with their tendency toward a clear-sighted denunciation of the consequences of bourgeois callousness, and his simultaneous effort to assert his status through identification with and promulgation of a comforting middle-class familial ideology.

The novel's famously problematic ending is ultimately rooted in a generic and ideological split that Dickens cannot resolve. As the novel progresses, the most subversive elements of the work, such as its satire of Dombey's failed patriarchalism and its sentimental depiction of Florence's plight, increasingly give way to diagnostic familialism, with its conservative function and its characteristic demonization of the rebellious worker and the failed mother. Ideological incoherence emerges as generic impasse as the tension between the novel's subversive impulses and its conservative commitment to domestic fiction's idealization of the redemptive potential of the bourgeois family proves insoluble, and as a result the novel ends weakly with a magical restoration of domestic harmony into which Florence and her father retreat.

Obeying the ideological need to resolve, however arbitrarily, the tension between the social and familial disorder the novel links with industrial capitalism's dynamism and the conflicting impulse to celebrate capitalism's creation of a new and prosperous social world, *Dombey and Son* abruptly and magically halts Florence's ideologically disturbing movement away from the family. Symptomatic of the aesthetic strain is the abrupt manner in which this halt is effected by the intrusion of the genre of romance, with the sudden return of Walter Gay, his engagement to Florence, and a magical reconciliation of Florence and her father, which lacks any basis in the preceding narrative. The emergence of new and improved families at the novel's end, and Dombey's well-deserved bankruptcy, signal the novel's willingness to celebrate, even as it criticizes, the triumph of an emergent industrial society. If Dombey in his familial failure is a figure for the callous capitalist in general, he is also, paradoxically, as a businessman a representative of traditional forms of economic organization based on trade and family firms. His firm's collapse, reminiscent of the railway panics of the 1840s, hints at the victory of the new economic energies of industrial capitalism over established firms and traditional businesses.[50] Dombey's fall in the familial sphere suggests the end of a preindustrial order in the economic sphere; in its transgression of boundaries between domestic and markets spheres, the Dombey family resembles the archaic patriarchal mode of family life in which productive or commercial and familial functions were united in the home. The flight of Edith from her role as part of the Dombey family and enterprise, the novel's pivotal rebellion, and the quiet return of Polly from paid work to become the unpaid but properly domestic mother and housewife of a railroad worker both figure the end of the family-based mode of production and its replacement by a new family suited to industrial capitalism, and organized more firmly than earlier family forms around the ideological imperative of women's separation from production. Torn between anxieties about the social effects of industrialization and a keen identification with this process of social transformation, which enabled the scope of his own literary success, Dickens displaces these tensions onto the newly isolated family, figuring and celebrating the process of industrialization as the development of a new and infinitely improved familial form.

At the same time, however, Dickens's championship of a triumphant domesticity is undercut by the way in which the plight of the narrative's actually or potentially transgressive women mirrors Dickens's own professional situation. In this respect, the Gothic elements in *Dombey*, given the Gothic's long history of association with subversive thought, are a locus for the articulation of the writer's subversive response to his dependent situation in the literary marketplace.[51] It is suggestive that Edith and her mother are depicted in melodramatic and sepulchral ways highly reminiscent of the female-dominated Gothic tradition. The novel's narratives of feminine entrapment and oppression, seen in Edith's miserable marriage and Florence's rejection by her father, clearly drawing on this Gothic tradition with its characteristic melodramatic images of threatened or incarcerated women, suggest how in a world permeated by bourgeois social relations, women are often commodified (Edith) or devalued (Florence). Unsurprisingly, faced with such a bleak fate within domesticity, Edith in desperation flees her marriage, if only with the repulsive Carker. It is striking evidence of the novel's ambivalence toward Dombey's genteel domesticity that the much demonized Carker, a figure from melodrama, by his quiet insight into Edith's loveless marriage, achieves the explosive rending of the mask of genteel domesticity, the ability to "take the house-tops off" to which the narrator had earlier aspired. But the more sympathetic portrayal of Edith's entrapment in this marriage, her tendency to become a mouthpiece for Dickens's critique of genteel values, suggests his sense of the limitations of his own autonomy as a literary figure. Indeed much like a writer in the marketplace, Edith complains that she must hide her true feelings, and must "sell" her "performance" to the wealthy audience she resents.[52] Like Edith, a well-paid but circumscribed performer, Dickens appears to identify with Edith's alienation from her narrow bourgeois feminine role, an identification no doubt facilitated by his feminizing confinement within a domestic fictive mode. But if Dickens sympathizes with Edith as a prisoner in a loveless marriage, when she rebels against Dombey, Dickens's evident ambivalence suggests his disquiet about feminine sexuality and about women who aggressively sought autonomy outside the home, including the women writers who were his competitors and predecessors. Indeed, Lisa Surridge, noting the novel's many destructive women, and that the heroine only placates Dombey and heals his psychic wounds through her own unmerited suffering, argues that the novel's uneasiness about the unruliness of women never allows it to completely restore women to a convincingly tranquil domesticity.[53]

The novel's identification of feminine restraint with literary restraint explains why Edith and Carker's melodramatic flight itself rebels against the text's previous decorum. Indeed, this moment of melodramatic excess, the novel's release from its claustrophic focus on feminine domestic enclosure, was sufficiently disturbing for the period that its logical corollary, Edith's sexual relation with Carker, was criticized by an aristocratic reader and critic, Lord Francis Jeffrey, who persuaded Dickens to censor himself and modify his planned narrative.[54] The need that Dickens feels to respond to genteel critical strictures and to restrain the erotic energy of his melodramatic narrative suggests that he experienced the search for literary elevation as requiring a continual domestication and suppression of erotic candor and creative energy; privately, Dickens was capable of complaining about the censorship of sexual reality that the moralism of the period imposed on his writing.

The censoring of Edith's transgressive sexuality is a symptom of the text's conflicting impulses. As we have seen, Dickens sees contemporary bourgeois familial norms as superior to those of other classes. The bourgeois familial ideology that he celebrates in *Barnaby Rudge* as superior to archaic preindustrial values, an ideology that legitimates and underwrites his own authorial moral authority, is paradoxically here deployed against the bourgeoisie itself. This strategy might work more successfully if Dickens could simply insist that bourgeois familial values are basically positive, and the elder Dombey fails in life because he reverts to an older type of familial values. But, in so doing, Dickens would sacrifice his sweeping condemnation of the cold and egotistical ethos of the bourgeoisie. Alternatively, he might follow the logic of his rejection of bourgeois values into the heart of the family and openly critique the familial norms of bourgeois culture—but at a high cost in social acceptance of his critique. Because his desire for social status made the latter alternative impossible, while he remained committed to a hostile judgment of typical bourgeois values, neither option is acceptable. Dickens's ideological impasse—one that will bedevil him for the remainder of his career—generates in *Dombey* a corresponding narrative impasse, the essence of which is that Florence is trapped within a paternally dominated space from which there is no plausible escape.

Many narratives of such imprisoning domesticities appear in earlier and contemporary domestic and familial narratives and in their cousin the Gothic, and there are a range of narrative sources of conflict to contest the protagonist's plight. One option is a cataclysmic historical outburst disrupting the repressive forces of imprisonment; another is a Byronic or seductive masculinity that sweeps the protagonist from her imprisonment, though often only to reimprison or threaten her, requiring a narrative of masculine domestication to resolve the story happily (the *Jane Eyre* plot). Another approach is that the female protagonist simply rebels against domestic confinement and by her own efforts secures her release, with positive or negative outcomes possible (the plot of George Sand's *Indiana*, and the premise of Nathaniel Hawthorne's *Scarlet Letter*); there is the frankly romance version of this narrative in which a masculine figure magically rescues the heroine, in the mode of *Sleeping Beauty;* finally, there is the possibility that female subjectivity achieves transcendence only in defeat, the tragic plot of *King Lear* and *Clarissa*.

By understanding that Dickens's project in *Dombey* is one of commitment to *domestic realism* as well as to bourgeois familial ideology, we can understand why none of these options for rescuing Florence is available to him. Quite simply, he cannot imagine a source of conflict that would sympathetically and plausibly resist the patriarchal power of Florence's father. The thoroughgoing domesticity of the novel and its contemporaneity precludes the possibility of rescue through a revolt of the lower classes. Despite the novel's harsh critique of Dombey's patriarchal rigidity, Dickens is too committed to the idealization of the pure bourgeois ideal of woman, who by definition was only threatened by the public sphere and never is imaginable as confidently entering it, to allow Florence to develop enough self-dependence to effect her own rescue. True, in the Edith-Carker plot, there are elements of the lower-class revolt narrative and the Byronic interloper narrative, but these types of plot are here trivialized and demonized, and Florence herself is carefully guarded against the taint of this melodramatic plot with its overtones of sexual passion. To make Florence's narrative denouement tragic was a conceivable option, but it would too strongly contest the optimistic terms of domestic ideology by which Florence's willingness to abide by gender norms should lead ultimately to fulfillment. More crucially, Florence never develops the powerful public presence of a Clarissa which can become a weapon she wields as Clarissa does, albeit posthumously, against the tyrannical father. If in later novels, Dickens acknowledges more doubts about the optimistic ideological and narrative outcome that resolves all irreconcilable conflicts within bourgeois domesticity, in this novel he lacks the courage of his doubts. The result is an unsatisfying closure that resembles a fairy tale and conflicts jarringly with the novel's realist vein. The awkward shift in generic register from realism to romance-influenced sentimental affirmation of filial bonds is a sign of Dickens's unsuccessful struggle to resolve his varied impulses in the novel.[55] Despite his resistance to the values of industrial bourgeois culture, Dickens was too committed to the bourgeois familial ideology, with its fetishization of the boundary between the family and the marketplace, to fully explore the entrapment of feminine subjectivity within the family, a subject that would become the specialty of his successor, George Eliot. Instead, Dickens evades exploring the threat within the bourgeois family of legitimate feminine discontent by conflating that threat with the influence of the ressentiment-filled Carker and the erotically unstable Edith. But this strategy leaves Florence, the representative of legitimate feminine frustration, isolated and besieged, requiring the miracles of Walter's love and Dombey's unexpected conversion to liberate her.

For all the undoubted brilliance with which Dickens deploys an often-sentimental domestic narrative in *Barnaby Rudge*, *A Christmas Carol*, and *Dombey and Son*, Dickens's proclivities and ambitions as a writer made this strategy ambivalent and unstable. The roots of this instability lies not just in Dickens's skepticism toward domestic pieties, but, given his aspiration to voice a social and historical vision, in the relation of such narrative strategies to their political context. Patrick Brantlinger, apropos of *Barnaby Rudge*, has called Dickens's philosophy of history "grotesque populism," suggesting that while Dickens sympathized strongly with the people, he also believed that the common people's political activism inevitably showed their vulnerability to being misled by their leaders.[56] Such an ambivalent populism helps us understand why Dickens's strategy in his early career of identifying his cultural status with domestic narratives is not sustainable. Domestic narrative as Dickens deployed it early in his career was a truly populist rhetoric; more than politics, religion, or culture, domestic sentiment appealed across class lines to both middle-class and working-class readers. While domesticity was middle-class in many of its emphases, such as in its stress on the importance of women's separation from the market and on the dangers to the home of the disgruntled workers, it also had plebeian appeal in its criticism of brutal aristocrats and callous employers who threaten to destroy family harmony. But since Dickens consistently envisions the ills of the private family as reflecting and rooted in the ills of the political family, once the collapse of Chartism in the late forties left expectations of dramatic political and social reform implausible, Dickens's vision of the political family and of the corresponding personal family necessarily becomes darker. It is in this context of increasing political pessimism that his vision of the failure of families tends to locate the root of domestic evil in the failures of political leadership on one hand and, on the other, in the unappeasable discontent of women and disgruntled working-class characters whose discontent threatens the family's stability.

Later Dickens novels, such as *Bleak House* and *Great Expectations*, with their dark sense of class division and the inadequacy of bourgeois values, will suggest the depth of Dickens's ambivalence toward the society that had emerged in his lifetime. Such novels build on and refine the diagnostic domestic mode he first fully develops in *Dombey* and use it to chart, in graver terms than are found in that work, the dangers that class divisions and market values held for family and society. The potent mask of masculine objectivity rather than feminine sentiment, comparable to the era's burgeoning discourses of professional expertise, which characterizes the diagnostic literary mode that Dickens begins to explore in *Dombey*, undoubtedly fosters his growing ambivalence toward effusive affirmations of domestic ideals. Dickens's later fiction shares with *Dombey* the sense of the failure of families to contain or heal social and economic divisions, but the later fiction tends ever more strongly to elaborate and develop the familial strand in a diagnostic rather than a sentimental mode. As Dickens's desire for high literary status comes in tension with the critical disesteem that female-centered sentimental novels fell into, and as he became aware of the limitations of domesticity as a realistic picture of families and as a tool for critiquing bourgeois society, his novels become increasingly conflicted in their affirmations of happy familial closures and ever more distanced from an idealized view of domesticity. Yet for all of Dickens's experience of the limitations of domestic narrative, he remained wedded to it as a uniquely powerful diagnostic tool with which to penetrate and castigate the deepest ills of bourgeois culture.

2

David Copperfield and After:
Dickens and the Impasse of Domesticity

Marriage, according to an old joke, is a great institution. But who wants to be locked up in an institution? This punch line, typical of the jaundiced view of the domestic in modern culture, is brought to mind by D. A. Miller's influential reading of Dickens's novels. In a thoughtful reading of *David Copperfield* (1849–50), Miller sees David as indeed falling into the conflation of marriage as prison, arguing that "the story of David's liberation runs parallel to the story of his submission," and asking "[f]aced with the abundance of resemblances between the liberal subject and his carceral double, the home and the prison-house, how can we significantly differentiate them?"[1] As my first chapter suggests, I agree that Dickens's novels participate in the development and dissemination of disciplinary discourses and argue that Dickensian familialism plays a large role in this complicity. But Miller's reading threatens to make Dickens's novels into monolithic agents of policing and conformity, while in fact *David Copperfield* and Dickens's later novels generally are clearly deeply divided and self-contradictory, never more than in their attitudes toward Victorian domesticity and gender ideology.

Moreover, a reading such as Miller's is notable for what it marginalizes as well as what it foregrounds. Most crucially, such a reading's obsession with restrictions on individual liberty minimizes the important role of pleasure in the Dickensian text. Pleasure is an underrated aspect of human experience, being both a primary glue that holds social groups together and a central component of aesthetic experience, including the reading of novels. Dickensian sociality and community, including the community of the family, may be flawed, but it is emphatically not devoid of pleasure, which is the obvious distinction between the family as Dickens imagines it and an actual prison. Miller's reading, like many in this essentially modernist debunking vein, treat the fictive embodiments of Victorian ideologies as if such fictions are purely repressive. Such readings minimize the real pleasures, even the psychic and political benefits, that such fictions offer. Against such a perspective we must bear in mind that domestic ideology and its literary offspring is more than a mass of oppressive orthodoxy against which individuals rebel and are crushed. Rather, it is a complex and diverse instrument that seduces as well as oppresses and is employed by writers for innumerable reasons, political, personal, imaginative, and psychic. Writers deploy familialism because it meets their needs and benefits their interests, both individually and as members of social classes. Not the least of its attractions is the pleaure it can bring. If we neglect the dimension of pleasure, and the larger political affiliations of Dickens's engagement with domesticity, we will fail to grasp the potency of domestic ideology, in his day and in ours.

If reducing Dickens's domestic mode to the embodiment of a repressive apparatus minimizes domesticity's pleasures and attractions, it also blinds us to Dickens's resistance to, and ambivalence about, the constraints of Victorian domestic pieties. Though, as we will see, on the surface *David Copperfield* is brilliantly organized to support the necessity of discipline of various sorts and to idealize norms of masculinity and femininity that typify the Victorian domestic ideal, a close reading of the novel reveals a subtle countertext that suggests ambivalence about and even resistance to major aspects of Victorian familial and gender ideology.[2] Dickens's own marital problems are well known, yet we must resist reading his ambivalence about domesticity merely as personal and idiosyncratic, for in his covert resistance to the rigidity of Victorian sexual and familial norms, Dickens's fiction embodies a larger cultural tension in Victorian society between, on one hand, the celebration of individual liberty and, on the other, allegiance to settled hierarchies of class and gender and the highly prescriptive domestic ideology that enforced them. Moreover, as the nineteenth century waned, this cultural tension would only intensify. Dickens's divided allegiance in regards to domesticity in *David Copperfield* is symptomatic of his growing discomfort with the ideology of domesticity which had served him so well in cementing his status as Britain's most-loved novelist. Only by noticing that the great promoter of 'household words'—the title of his popular magazine—became increasingly uncomfortable with his role as domestic writer can we understand how his novels after 1850 at once bring domestic fiction to a climax of literary achievement, but also lead literary familialism to a profound impasse out of which later major writers would extricate themselves only by abandoning the ideological shibboleths of the entire domestic tradition.

To understand familialism in late Dickens, we must bear in mind its multifaceted political character. As we have seen, in such early works as *Barnaby Rudge*, *A Christmas Carol*, and *Dombey and Son*, Dickens deploys domestic narratives as a source of his own authority as a man of letters, as a potent populist rhetoric, and as an ideal of personal community that contrasts with the heartlessness and calculation of a market-dominated world, a weapon against the corrupt and heartless values of the wealthy. The source, therefore, of Dickens's early optimistic and vigorously liberal celebrations of the middle-class home is neither merely personal belief nor native proclivity for the familial setting. Dickens's promotion of domestic values and affiliated modes of discipline that have a middle-class aura was a literary expression of the faith, pervasive and enthusiastically believed in the first half of the nineteenth century, that what the middle class was struggling for in their battles at home and abroad for greater political and individual liberty in opposition to the entrenched forces of reaction was what people everywhere wanted. In this ideological vein, the happy middle-class family (or working-class replicas of it) was the emblem of what liberty from tyrannical aristocrats and proud patriarchs that middle-class political reforms demanded was *for*. The moral superiority of the bourgeois family was what justified and would reward the middle-class fight for liberty. And, in turn, the failure by middle-class standards of families was the sign of where human liberty had been stunted or suppressed, evidence of just what was wrong with an unjust social order. Domesticity was, and still is, one of the most powerful of bourgeois ideological themes. From miserly employers and coldhearted aristocrats in Dickens to unfeeling slave owners in Harriet Beecher Stowe's fiction, in the nineteenth-century the rhetoric of domesticity was a powerful tool to castigate oppression and to recommend a remaking of the world in a mold that was at once more bourgeois and more humane.

If we understand that Dickens's familialism is tied to a specific political and historical context, we can better grasp how by midcentury, when he writes *David Copperfield*, this faith in domesticity, both as a set of ideals for practical application to life and as a mode of discourse, is already uneasy. One important context for Dickens's progressively more distanced relation to domestic idealization is that his earlier association with the feminized discourse of domesticity and human suffering, especially of women and children, was often cited by midcentury critics to trivialize his literary achievement by linking him with emotion, femininity, and the popular, rather than with literary distinction. Richard Holt Hutton would comment in 1858, "the type of Dickens' genius is, in many respects, feminine. . . . There is no intellectual background to his pictures"[3] and George Henry Lewes would similarly link Dickens's writing to women and to popular classes by reducing his achievement to the instinctual manipulation of sentiment: "With a fine felicity of instinct [Dickens] seized upon situations having an irresistible hold over the domestic affections and the ordinary sympathies. . . . Dickens sees and feels, but the logic of feeling seems the only logic he can manage."[4] Thus, in certain quarters despite his efforts to elevate himself to the level of prestigious social critic, his association with the "feminine" mode of sentimentality caused his work to be devalued. Moreover, once the collapse of Chartism took thoughts of further major political reform off the agenda, Dickens's scathing denunciations of British society's failure struck many critics as outdated emotionalism. Though more narrowly personal forces played an important role as well, ultimately the roots of Dickens's estrangement from domesticity was political, as the very literary mode that had brought him early success was used to limit his cultural status, and the liberal ideals that he espoused were chronically frustrated in the public arena. At the same time, as a restive working class caused class conflict to remain a central anxiety, Dickens, like many Victorians, grew increasingly concerned that the liberal ideas of the age would disrupt established patterns of order, leading to revolt and disorder, even while his sense of the need for social reform and passionate advocacy of individual liberty made him impatient with the traditional ruling class as well. This helps explain Dickens's great attraction to Carlyle, a writer who shared with him a disdain for the traditional landowning ruling class, but who also viewed liberal ideas with suspicion and increasingly saw such liberal ideals as individual autonomy as tending toward democracy, which he denigrated as subverting the natural hierarchies of gender, class, and race. Indeed, the profound respect for ostensibly natural hierarchies that Dickens shares with Carlyle is clearly one key source of his increasing unease with the sentimental and self-righteous moral rhetoric that characterized domestic fiction, for Dickens was clearly disturbed when such rhetoric promoted challenges to traditional hierarchies.

Dickens's general faith in the central tenet of liberal thought, however—the superiority of individual moral choices over government fiats and traditional controls—extends to his concept of marriage, and more generally is visible in his impatience with the religiously infused rigidity of sexual and moral life in his day. Liberal ideology which emphasized the importance of individual autonomy, supported by the increasing social self-confidence of the upper middle class in social life, was increasingly influential in Victorian life, and Dickens vigorously emphasized his allegiance to it in response to its repeated frustration in the political arena. Certainly the late novels, such as *Bleak House* (1852–53) and *Little Dorrit* (1855–57), are replete with signs of Dickens's frustration at Britain's political immobility.

Dickens's liberal and secularizing attitudes affect his treatment of the family by creating a sharp split in his attitudes and his fiction between, on one hand, traditional feelings and morality and, on the other, the dictates of self-seeking rationality. The chasm between these two principles of action has been a recurring problem for bourgeois ideology since at least the Enlightenment. But by tending to demystify the ritual celebrations of marital and familial harmony that were an expected part of his literary production, Dickens's belief in a liberal conception of marriage, one organized around rational self-seeking, undercuts the very basis of his capacity to emotionally appeal to his audience through the rhetoric of the domestic. Moreover, the split between traditional feeling and self-seeking rationality was particularly of concern to a writer such as Dickens, who preserved a strong respect for the traditional hierarchies that permeated the social order of Victorian England. It is easy to see that the turbulence of the first half of the nineteenth century alarmed him, because it showed signs of disrupting these hierarchies. We must not forget that both Dickens's early years and his young adulthood were politically extremely turbulent times, in which popular discontent seemed a harbinger of social tumult. In the middle of Dickens's career, revolutionary violence erupted on the Continent (1848–49), forcefully reminding the British of the threat of political instability to the new age. Under such circumstances, we can understand how a writer with strongly liberal leanings would nevertheless be concerned that liberal ideas could stimulate excessive rebelliousness or at least a widespread failure to "know one's place." Though Dickens is prone to see the cause of rebellion in excessive upper-class rigidity and punitiveness, he also evinces considerable anxiety that liberal ideals will be twisted to overcome "natural" hierarchies, which accounts for the increasing obsession his work shows with the thematics of ressentiment. This obsession with subaltern discontent takes the form of concern about gender as well as class rebellion, and is particularly notable in Dickens's long string of irresponsible women, particularly mothers. Like Milton, who in writings on divorce in the mid-seventeenth century advocated a precociously liberal doctrine of marriage long before such an individualist concept of marriage was widely accepted, but who was also intensely anxious that his vindication of marital liberty not be misused by lower-class or female readers, Dickens tends to conceptualize his liberal understanding of marriage as entailing individual male liberty from a failed marriage. In other words, the liberal conception of marriage and its consequence in the freedom to divorce was seen by both Milton and Dickens as the logical corollary and completion of, rather than as a potential disruption of, a strengthening of masculine authority in marriage. We see this in *Hard Times* (1854), a work that daringly criticizes the inaccessibility of divorce in Britain, implicitly favoring a liberal conception of marriage. But this defense of individual freedom is bolstered by a strikingly misogynistic portrayal of Stephen Blackpool's alcoholic wife, a character who blights Stephen's already dreary life as a member of the oppressed industrial proletariat. As such a plot suggests, individual liberty, as embodied in the freedom to divorce, which Stephen Blackpool as a worker is denied, is associated in Dickens's mind with the assertion of masculine dignity and independence rather than with feminine freedom.[5]

Indeed, caught between his anxieties about female and lower-class insubordination and frustration at the slow pace of liberal reform, Dickens shared his mentor Carlyle's increasing emphasis on hierarchy and a growing lack of enthusiasm for some liberal reforms. Dickens's declining confidence in progressive reform is well known; for instance, his pessimistic satire of efforts to reform prisons and rehabilitate prisoners in the late chapter of *David Copperfield*, "Two Penitents," in which the villainous Uriah Heep uses penal reform as a cover for his continuing hypocrisy and malevolence, makes clear how his political frustrations led Dickens to feel a reactionary suspicion of reforms that he felt weakened essential moral distinctions. Another liberal tendency of his day, the increasing prominence of women activists and feminist views, offended his commitment to traditional gender roles. The paradox, then, is that Dickens conceives the family and sexual life in a way that was too liberal for much of his readership, even while the sympathy for the downtrodden and for feminine experience so often at the core of domestic fiction fills him with increased ambivalence as he realizes the potential for such sympathy to subvert his sense of proper moral and social order. For all these reasons, the later fiction visibly shows increasing frustration with the domestic mode that had helped secure his status as a major writer and commentator on his society. Since domesticity was a mode he utilized for broadly political reasons, the failure of his political hopes made him increasingly conscious of domesticity's idealizations and illusions, so the picture of the family that he creates in his later fiction suggests ever more grimly the limitations of Victorian domesticity, both as a lived reality and as a set of literary conventions.

THE CRITIQUE OF MARRIAGE AND THE TEMPTATION
OF SEXUALITY IN *DAVID COPPERFIELD*

David Copperfield culminates Dickens's achievement in a domestic mode, and in its celebratory self-portrait of the rise of a novelist from humble origins to fame, it also utilizes domestic fiction to climax Dickens's project of literary status enhancement. But in its portrayal of family life it is also a transitional work that anticipates the more troubled relation to domesticity of Dickens's later fiction. Drawing on his unhappiness at his own childhood and particularly his resentment toward his mother, who had consented to his consignment to child labor, Dickens presents the Victorian family in savage colors. Though, as in *Dombey*, we see negatively depicted fathers, it is important to perceive how strikingly *Copperfield* turns much of its ire against the feminine side of domesticity. This denunciation of inadequate femininity is first visible in the withering portrayal of David's irresponsible mother, whose vanity and foolishness lead her to hand herself—and her son—over to the brutal stepfather Murdstone. The antifeminine vein of the novel continues in the scathing portrait of David's wife Dora, whose hyperfeminine inanity chastens David for his thoughtless preoccupation with the aristocratic values of gentility. Approaching but skirting the issue of divorce (though clearly alluding to it through the subplot of the extended separation between Betsey Trotwood and her husband), the novel significantly makes David's central adult crisis the breakdown of his marriage to Dora. Though the death of David's wife frees him to resume a trajectory toward marital happiness, Dickens clearly meditates here on the unattractive options that society offered individuals trapped in an unfulfilling marriage.

To grasp fully the novel's divided relation to domesticity, we must emphasize what its autobiographical character tends to make readers overlook, its strong continuity with the impulse to social reform that marks Dickens's early fiction. As in such works as *Barnaby Rudge, Oliver Twist*, and *Dombey and Son*, the characters' situations are clearly constructed to draw attention to society's evils and irrationalities, and individual failings are often exemplary of institutions or rhetorics that the text satirizes. As always in Dickens, this reforming impulse is informed by an antiaristocratic and liberal animus against social structures and traditions that restrict the individual's freedom and development. But what is unusual in *Copperfield* is how sharply the novel includes within its satiric range the Victorian family. Thus, in addition to the institutional evils of Mr. Creakle's school, run by a brutal and sycophantic master who toadies to the upper-class student, Steerforth, and the brutal callousness of Murdstone and Grinby, at once the capitalist workplace and an extension of Murdstone's domestic tyranny, we encounter wider indications of a critique of traditional domestic arrangements. Just as Mr. Creakle's school, with its archaic fawning on the aristocracy and sadistic violence, is characteristic of an outmoded disciplinary mode typical of the aristocratic past, so the gender relations we see sketched in the early part of the novel, often associated with an older generation, are clearly irrational and rigidly inegalitarian. Betsey Trotwood lives separated from a husband who "made . . . determined arrangements to throw her out of a two pair of stairs' window" (11), while Clara Copperfield is browbeaten by a Murdstonean obsession with "firmness," which David calls "another name for tyranny" (49).[6] The early part of the novel is so replete with a large number of disastrous or apparently failed marriages, including also those of Dr. and Annie Strong and the Micawbers, that Dickens clearly sees Victorian family life itself as one more of the disastrously ordered institutions that his fictions must satirize and reform. For instance, Mr. and Mrs. Micawber's marriage is repeatedly threatened by Mr. Micawber's suicidal mood swings and by Mrs. Micawber's evident disgruntlement, which she histrionically expresses by vocal reaffirmations of her marriage vows: "I never will desert Mr. Micawber. Mr. Micawber may have concealed his difficulties from me in the first instance, . . ." (151) The irony is that, though the idea of nondesertion that Mrs. Micawber voices is completely orthodox and in accordance with her marital vows, her sense of grievance at Mr. Micawber's lack of candor before marriage about his fragile economic position, and his failure to keep his family from indigence, makes her loudly reaffirmed commitment to her vows an implied protest against the frustrations and costs of such continued loyalty.

Dickens clearly identifies the roots of bad marriages, and though many of them are traditional complaints, Dickens associates almost all of them with what is obsolete, overgenteel, or rigid in his society, suggesting that they are examples of archaic and discredited social modes that should be supplanted. For instance, the novel sees an excessive emotionalism or self-indulgent romanticism as a source of much marital evil, suggested in David's father's marriage to his mother, despite her immaturity and inexperience (she is a mere "Baby," as Betsey Trotwood correctly points out and as Clara's naïveté about Murdstone will later confirm). A similarly self-indulgent romanticism, as well as a ludicrous affectation of gentility, is visible in Mr. Micawber, satirized by his continual absurd self-contradiction and self-indulgent preoccupation with his own status while his family sinks into poverty. Other salient evils are deviations from the ideal of the self-contained and nuclear marital relationship, such as in Miss Murdstone's continual interference in the marriage of her brother for the purpose of further degrading Clara, and "the general's" (Dr. Strong's mother-in-law's) bullying interference with the Strongs' marriage, as well as that old standby of domestic evil, the influence of greed or excessive egotism in marriage: both are visible in Mr. Murdstone's relation to Clara, and it is strongly suggested that Annie Strong's mother was motivated by greed in encouraging her daughter's marriage to Dr. Strong. In terms of the expected ideals of marital life, each of these marriages could be said to fail either because there is at least the appearance—often the reality—of failed masculinity and consequent female rebellion, as in the case of the Strongs and Micawbers, or the pattern is one of exaggerated gender roles that deprive the marriages of any balance and leave the women (and her child in Clara Copperfield's case) subject to masculine tyranny and hard-heartedness.

If the novel makes the point that the consequences of marital disharmony are serious and lasting, it also demonstrates that it is not merely traditions of rhetoric and behavior such as the flowery romanticism of a Micawber or the mercenary manipulativeness of a Murdstone that are flawed, but that the very institutional framework that regulates marriage is itself deficient. Dickens makes this point by having David work as clerk for a proctor, an attorney who specializes in ecclesiastical law and thus handles marital disputes. The novel's picture of Doctor's Common, in keeping with Dickens's liberal emphasis on individual liberty, rationality, and modernization, is wholly negative, the novel attributing the Common's very continued existence to British society's senseless traditionalism and to the venality of attorneys who profit at the expense of their clients.[7] In a novel that emphasizes repeatedly the disastrous character of marital choices, the episodes in Doctor's Common make the point that the institutions responsible for regulating marriage itself are in great need of reform. One episode even shows that marital law neither consistently protects marital indissolubility nor fairly operates in terminating marriages: this is the "divorce-suit" of Thomas Benjamin, which David witnesses and takes part in as clerk, which involves a suitor who had "taken out his marriage license as Thomas only; suppressing the Benjamin, in case he should not find himself as comfortable as he expected. *Not* finding himself as comfortable as he expected, or being a little fatigued with his wife, poor fellow, he now came forward by a friend, after being married a year or two, and declared that his name was Thomas Benjamin, and therefore he was not married at all. Which the court confirmed, to his great satisfaction" (405, emphasis in original). David doubts the "strict justice" of this verdict, which is a legalized version of the concubinage and abandonment that Steerforth will later commit at great cost to the affected individuals. Unsurprisingly, the case occasions a brief debate over the nature of Doctor's Commons as an institution, with David expressing to his traditionalist employer Dickens's liberal view that "we might improve the Commons" (405). In a novel filled with instances of marital failure, the point of this episode is that individual marital failures occur in the context of an irrational legal framework of obsolescent and unfair marital law administered by a corrupt institution of legal fossils "whose existence, in the natural course of things, would have terminated about two hundred years ago" (294).[8] In the context of the novel's obsession with marital breakdown, particularly David's failed marriage to Dora, what the Thomas Benjamin case demonstrates is that marriages in nineteenth-century Britain could lead to divorce (or its equivalent; the case strictly speaking involves an annulment, not divorce in the modern sense), but that such formal separations were granted on pretexts that were archaic, irrational, and open to abuse. The juxtaposition of individual marital unhappiness due to marriage for irrational motives and the exposé of the institutional failure to regulate marriage rationally suggests that marriage as it operates in Victorian society requires a more reasonable definition.[9]

Moreover, the novel hints at the nature of such a rational redefinition of marriage. Since marriages are vitiated by outside interference with the feelings of the couple, obviously the best marriage is one free from excessive control by families of origin. And clearly, too, overpreoccupation with money and status in entering a marriage are destructive; marriages must preserve their character as utterly separate from the world of commerce. Since bad marriages result from the overexaggeration of the expected masculine dominance, from an exaggeration of masculine violence, forcefulness, and feminine weakness and irrationality, reforming marriage would require a blurring of the extreme rigidity of the masculine and feminine gender role opposition as we see it suggested in the elder Copperfield's marriage and clearly visible in the Clara-Murdstone relationship, in Betsey Trotwood's marriage, and in David's marriage to Dora.

In Betsey Trotwood, in fact, we see an effort to imagine a woman who androgynously combines the forcefulness, even truculence, rational intelligence (as when she sees through Mr. Murdstone), and individualism expected of men in Victorian culture with the gentleness of heart and compassion considered appropriate for women. Betsey, often in the novel a mouthpiece for Dickens, interestingly echoes the language of Mary Wollstonecraft's rhetoric when she tells Murdstone that "you . . . beg[a]n to break [Clara], like a poor caged bird, and wear her deluded life away, in teaching her to sing *your* notes" (186). This Wollstonecraftean language clearly indicates that the danger of marriage for women is precisely in having their indi-

viduality swallowed up by marital entrapment and tyranny.[10] The implication is that women must resist losing their individuality in the marital
relationship, presumably by developing their own capacity for independent
thought, rather than merely for emotional response and the obsession with
physical beauty that characterizes Clara Copperfield and later Dora as well.
This theme echoes the radical individualism and feminism of Wollstonecraft's thought, which saw in women's development of their rational capacities and restraint of the emotional and sexual nature their only opportunity
for achieving dignity and parity in marriage. One of the central concerns of
Wollstonecraftean feminism was the utter inadequacy of feminine education
to make women rational and sophisticated partners to men, a concern that
continued to animate Victorian feminists. We in fact see David, albeit mal-
adroitly, attempting to correct the failings of Dora's education by giving her
a refresher course in sophisticated intellectual culture, a course that, had it
succeeded, would have made Dora more David's equal than she is capable of
being.

Dickens's critique of marriage here clearly suggests a subversive notion
that the rigid hierarchies of Victorian gender relations are an impediment to
happiness in marriage, and the novel's preoccupation with marital failure,
irrational marital laws, and marriage as an impediment to individual fulfillment are readable as a veiled suggestion that marriage itself ought to be more
rationally and liberally arranged by society. Such an understanding of marriage, as having the character as a vehicle for individual development and
fulfillment and ideally not obliterating the individuality of the participants
(as Clara's is), raises the issue of whether, when marriage impedes individual
development, it should not be a dissoluble contract, the position Dickens
clearly advocates in *Hard Times*. But against his own convictions, in the later
part of the novel, Dickens desperately retreats from the sweeping subversion
of the Victorian marital institution that he hints at in the novel's early part,
no doubt because he fears to disrupt his audience's acceptance of the premises of the domestic fiction that was so fundamental to his own rise to the
status of cultural icon. It is this retreat into the orthodoxy of the affirmation
of marriage at the novel's close that generates the novel's self-division over
domesticity, a division that anticipates the more radical disaffection from
domestic idealization of the later fiction.

Copperfield meditates on social class as well as marriage, and, as often in
Dickens's fiction, familial narratives in the novel encode a reading of social
class. As an important tradition of criticism has pointed out, the novel's domestic narrative has a clear class message; the two erotic objects in David's
life, Dora and Agnes, are affiliated with the aristocracy and the middle class

respectively.[11] Thus Dora's inane incapacity for housework and her emotional regression are synecdochic of frivolous aristocratic values, while Agnes's self-denial, and her moral and practical mastery of the self-abnegating feminine domestic role, are triumphantly middle-class. David, in realizing the mistake of loving Dora, and finally learning to value and to marry Agnes, is implicitly choosing to mature into a full acceptance of properly bourgeois values. Without denying the validity of this reading, I would like to more closely examine the theme of emotional discipline that Dickens uses to unify his narrative of class socialization, and to read its development as symptomatic of Dickens's increasing alienation from the idealization of domesticity and the ideologies that structured the Victorian family. Though critics and biographers have often noted how the darker elements of *David Copperfield* foreshadow the gloomier mood that characterized Dickens's fiction in his later years, there is a tendency to read this increasing gloom as simply a symptom of the increasing stresses and disappointments in Dickens's personal life. Though such stresses provide much evidence that Dickens struggled with gender and familial ideology in his life as in his art, a too narrowly biographical reading leaves opaque why Dickens's increasing alienation from a domestic mode becomes a harbinger of much serious British fiction after *Copperfield*. By reading the ambivalence Dickens shows toward domesticity as part of a politically determined crisis of the familial mode, we can better understand the proleptic role that the novel and Dickens's later dark versions of Victorian domesticity play in literary history.

To understand the role of domesticity in *Copperfield*, one must note that, as one would expect in an autobiographical narrative about a novelist, it is the work in which Dickens is most self-reflexive about the character of his own career. While modes of social and familial discipline had been a crucial Dickensian topic from very early in his career, in this novel Dickens achieves a self-consciousness about his concerns that causes him to make that subject quite explicit and to present his hero deliberately as an exemplary hero of discipline, first as a victim of its failure and then ultimately as a hero of artistic mastery and upward mobility achieved through internalized discipline. The central Copperfieldian theme is the need to instill the self with a proper psychic discipline, a process that allows and promotes familial fulfillment, while also inseparable from the achievement of a secure middle-class identity.[12] In this novel, to become a successful middle-class individual is, above all, to be disciplined. For instance, in the important subplot of Mr. Micawber and his tragicomical, chaotic family, the Micawbers' failure in middle-class domesticity shows the consequences of emotional and financial indiscipline, as Micawber falls first into destitution and debtor's prison, then later

into the demonic clutches of Uriah Heep. Meanwhile, in the central narrative of the novel, David's journey into adulthood is a continual encounter
with various forms of societal discipline, from the abusive fathering of Murdstone, to its extension in the violence and class bias of Mr. Creakle's school,
to its antithesis in the benevolent paternalism of Dr. Strong's school.

Yet Dickens is more confident in demonstrating the horrors of brutal and
archaic modes of discipline (the physically abusive schoolmaster, the debtors'
prison) than he is in celebrating the success of modern and flexible modes of
control. One sign of this lack of confidence in more flexible modes of discipline is the novel's evident anxiety about the difficulty of controlling women,
especially in marriage, seen first in the subplot of Annie Strong and her apparent disloyalty to her older husband, and then reemerging more pro-
nouncedly in David's struggle to contain both Dora's misbehavior and his
own emotions in response to it. For the bourgeois man, as he is conceived in
the novel, the control of women in marriage and in society involves a high
degree of self-mastery as well. In a crucial scene of the novel, which demonstrates how explicitly Dickens draws attention to the theme of self-discipline,
but which also shows the gaps and silences that characterize his treatment of
the theme, David awaits the news of Dora's imminent death. He rebukes
himself with the question "Would it, indeed, have been better if we had
loved each other as a boy and girl, and forgotten it?" (647) and responds,
"Undisciplined heart, reply!" (647). If we consider the implications of this
apostrophe to David's heart, we see that the novel's narrative of class mobility and internalization of proper familial discipline is deeply troubled and
contradictory, as seen in how a certain unreadability clings stubbornly to the
notion of David's undisciplined heart that is at once suggestive of the limits
of Dickens's narrative practice and his own deep ambivalence about domesticity.

David's apostrophe to his heart glosses his entire marriage; it offers a
reading of what we have so far experienced of the novel that pertains to David's courtship and marriage. It reads the failure of David's marriage by attributing it to a seemingly straightforward failure—his failure of emotional
discipline of the "heart," which some other part of David, at least in retrospect, is able to see and to rebuke and which causes his lack of fulfillment in
marriage to Dora. But this generalizing gloss on David's experience contained in this apostrophe leaves unclear exactly in what regard David's heart
has been undisciplined. The scene in which the apostrophe occurs is itself
the antithesis of undisciplined self-indulgence—David, left alone with Jip by
Agnes: "think[s] with blind remorse of all those secret feelings I have nour-
ished since my marriage" (647). True, this scene is part of the heart's being

"chastened heavily—heavily" (ibid.). Still, the scene, and the one preceding it in which David tenderly reassures the self-condemnatory Dora, eloquently contradicts the notion that David's feelings for Dora are merely shallow or self-indulgent. As if to explain in anticipation this apostrophe, shortly before it David offers a proleptic gloss of the interpretation of the marriage contained in the phrase "undisciplined heart," thinking, "of every little trifle between me and Dora, and feel the truth, that trifles make the sum of life" (647).

This line suggests clearly that the failure of David's heart to be disciplined cannot be localized to any one act or even pattern of behavior, but was manifest in the minutiae of David and Dora's domestic life, which, were it to be fully revealed to us, would presumably justify the negative gloss that the apostrophe gives on the marriage and on David's heart. Yet the sheer breadth and vagueness of the gesture of generalization ("every little trifle"), containing the entire relationship presumably, yet composed wholly of trifles, suggests the impossibility of defining or articulating precisely where the marriage's failure, and hence the failure of David's heart, has occurred. Trifles are after all by definition nearly nothing: to say that the sum total of trifles showed the tragic failure of the marriage is to perform a sort of rhetorical alchemy by which the sum of these nearly nothings becomes something quite momentous. There is a gap between the triflingly small and the tragically major that they add up to, a gap that leaves the reader with a sense that the failure of the innermost and most profound secret of happiness, as Victorian domestic ideology held loving marriage to be—and so by implication the failure of David's undisciplined heart—is a failure too multiplicitous and nearly insubstantial in specifics to be specifiable or articulable.

The invocation of and yet elision of "trifles," which rests so much weight on unmentioned and unspecifiable details, and the odd gap in the novel's narrative to which it points, is particularly telling in the genre of the domestic novel. From *Pamela* on, one of the domestic novel's features had traditionally been its openness to the quotidian and the commonplace, compared to the elevated and schematic world of romance that the novel displaces. If novels are about trifles, then the impossibility or reluctance of the novel to specify the particular trifles that have robbed David and Dora of their happiness suggests that the failed relationship with Dora represents a limit that the novel recognizes to its own narrative energies and capacities; in that sense the passage underlines a limit not so much of David, but of the kind of novel his creator can or was willing to create. The domestic itself in its essence becomes a territory beyond the narrative's confident grasp, as if David's frustration with Dora is paralleled by Dickens's unease with the minutiae of conflict-ridden domestic experience. One suspects that Dickens's fear here was that either his character's degree of hostility against a female character would become offensive to his readers, or David's (and Dickens's) preference for a liberal and individualist reading of the marital relationship and David's obvious desire to escape the marriage would become shockingly evident to his audience. Suggestively, in *Hard Times*, when Dickens does openly imply the necessity of liberating the (male) individual from domestic misery, the wife is made even more a nonentity than she is in *Copperfield*: she is simply an alcoholic monster, a millstone around Stephen Blackpool's neck. In a masculine gesture that separates author from domestic unpleasantness, *David Copperfield* says simply: all that trivial stuff, were it told, would show the emptiness of this life. This is a striking reticence given that David's and his creator's authority is constructed in part through an identification of the writer with the correct diagnosis of the ills of domestic space.

Readers tend to accept David's censure of his own failings partly because, paradoxically, he is a likable and sympathetic character and because the conventions of the confession impel assent. The logic of this convention is that, if even the character himself criticizes his conduct, surely it was indeed wrong. We are in fact given some glimpses of the trifles that make up David and Dora's life together, such as the disastrous dinner party for Traddles, but the tone of such scenes is oddly light and playful given the tragic weight such trifles are eventually expected to bear. More importantly, in parts of the narrative where we do see David struggling to realize his hopes for domestic happiness, his behavior is difficult to reconcile with heedless or overly emotional behavior as the rest of the novel exemplifies it in a Micawber or a Steerforth. David in fact shows considerable persistence, patience, and even forebearance toward Dora, despite her tendency to prove incapable of realizing either David's loftiest goals for her, as intellectual and literary companion, and his most mundane expectations, to be a competent housewife. David's gravest fault that we are shown is that, misled by his own needs, he misreads Dora's character and makes overbearing efforts to "form her mind" (585). Even in this episode, though, David's generosity in assuming a capacity for intellectual growth on Dora's part and her incapacity and childishness are far more striking than David's "undisciplined" emotion in response to her. The accusation against his undisciplined heart receives only a weak support from this episode. David's relatively restrained response to Dora's failures to perform according to his, and Victorian society's, gender expectations is especially striking given that, in every other aspect of his life, David is exemplarily disciplined and persistent. Moreover, he tells us that, having recognized his failure to adjust at first to Dora's nature, he learns to adjust and to temper his earlier demands. In short, though his heart shows some failure of emotional discipline, in the course of the marriage these wayward responses are largely corrected. And even in the early part of the marriage, on the basis of the episodes narrated, it was apparently only moderately undisciplined, if one allows for the highly trying marital circumstances that David faces.

True, in David's worst failing, his effort to "form [Dora's] mind," Dickens flirts with one of the standard plots of a Gothic variant of domestic fiction—the tyrannical husband who causes, or hastens, the fragile wife's death. Such a Gothic husband and his corresponding narrative trajectory occur in the novel in Murdstone and his sister and their browbeating of Clara (which hastens her death), and Betsey Trotwood explicitly draws our attention to the possible parallel between the two marriages (see 531 and 538). The plot appealed to Dickens as a way to encode the evils of marital entrapment, and later in *Bleak House*, in his depiction of the relation between Mr. Jarndyce and Esther Summerson, he will develop a revision of the plot in which the Gothically entrapping male is a sympathetic and well-meaning figure who inadvertently tyrannizes over a weak fiancée. This plot possibility is interesting because within the Gothic tradition it has at least a protofeminist character, especially if the entrapment of the women is acknowledged. But the plot of David and Dora's marriage is not convincing as a genuine instance of Gothic marital entrapment, largely because of how distanced we are from Dora's subjectivity, but especially because David's tyranny appears quite mild and well intentioned.

If the novel fails narratively to substantiate the notion of David as "undisciplined" in his marriage to Dora, it does offer an alternative—and indeed within domestic fiction highly traditional—proof of David's emotional incontinence by pointing to his failure in choosing wisely in marriage in the first place. In place of the elided process of marital breakdown, the novel metonymically substitutes an emblematic faulty decision that stands for, and presumably causes, the countless "trifles" that constituted David and Dora's unhappy marriage. As Dora herself says to David in her final deathbed scene, in choosing to marry her at all, David chose wrong; it would have been better, "had [we] only loved each other as a boy and girl, and forgotten it" (645).

This reading of the marriage is given authority by being offered by Dora herself on her deathbed, with the conventional preternatural wisdom of the dying. But here too, what constitutes David's "undisciplined heart" is reduced to a simple formula that resists a satisfying reading. According to this view, the only good Dora for David would have been one he had loved "as a boy and girl." This phrase clearly indicates that they should have loved each other as children, or childlike adults, too immature for the responsibilities of the adult world; as Dora explains, "I am afraid, dear, I was too young. I don't mean in years only, but in experience, and thoughts, and everything" (645). This hypothetical narrative that Dora posits, of a child-David and a child-Dora having loved one another and then foregone attempting to transfer this love into their adult lives, fits Dora quite well, because in insisting in being called "child-wife," she has shown that she failed to make the transition to full adulthood. Yet it clashes startlingly with what we know of David, who had to take on adult companionship (the Micawbers) and adult obligations at Murdstone and Grinby as a mere boy; and this has been no passing phase, but has, he asserts, helped equip him to be supremely disciplined in life: in his career he speaks of successfully learning "to turn the painful discipline of my younger days to account" (439). And David is, of course, when he meets Dora, planning to assume adult responsibilities by starting his career as a proctor and begins soon after to launch an adult career as a journalist. Given David's precociously rapid maturation, where, we might wonder, in the novel's world, is the immature boy to be the counterpart for Dora in this hypothetical "boy and girl" love that would have been the happier alternative to their married life?

But such a boy does exist in the novel, as indeed does such a boy and girl love, if we read the phrase "loved as a boy and girl" to mean loved in a way innocent of adult sexual feeling or knowledge. The phrase recalls David's childhood friendship with little Emily, of whom he says, "Of course I was in love with little Em'ly" (39). This love is explicitly separated from adult realities, including sexuality: "We made no more provision for growing older, than we did for growing younger" (ibid.). It is this love that fully fits the label of "loved as a boy and girl" and Dickens identifies this love as asexual and unknowing: "I loved that baby quite as truly, quite as tenderly, with greater purity, and more disinterestedness, than can enter in to the best love of a later time of life . . ." (ibid.). The phrase "greater purity" than loves of a more mature "time of life," emphasize the asexual purity of his love for Emily, a significant comment in view of her later sexual history.

In implicitly invoking the childish David and Emily relationship as an ideal of love that is superior to David's relationship with Dora, the novel clearly evades the very issues that it raises by its depiction of Dora, just as it does when it elides the process of the breakdown of David's marriage. If after consideration Dora and David would have preferred their relationship to be equivalent to that of David and Emily's, it is remarkable how unlike the asexual purity of this early bond *is* the actual relationship of David and

Dora. David's first experience of Dora is described in the mock-inflated language of romantic love, but that he is sexually attracted to her is clear. From his first sight of her "I was a captive and a slave" (331). Her physical charms are mentioned over and over; she is "prettily pettish" (333), "bright-eyed lovely Dora" (333); "What a form she had, what a face she had" (333), "diminutive altogether" (333); "I never saw such curls" (336). Her appearance sparks erotic reverie in David: "I was wandering in a garden of Eden all the while, with Dora" (334). David means that his mood was blissfully paradisal, but the erotic potential of the nakedness of the Edenic pair is a relevant connotation. David experiences Dora from the beginning as a sexual object and is passionately excited and in love with her as such. Thus the alternative type of relation that Dora will retrospectively recommend of "lov[ing] as a boy and girl," that is, asexually, is a profound evasion of the reality of the adult David and Dora as they always were, sexual beings. And yet this evasion is offered as the only imaginable scenario by which David could have avoided falling into the trap of vitiating his happiness through failing to discipline his heart. This evasion of sexual reality might be ascribed to Dora herself and to her general failure to mature successfully, except that David endorses Dora's view, repeating her words to him in his inward thoughts: "Would it, indeed, have been better if we had loved each other as a boy and girl, and forgotten it? Undisciplined heart, reply!" (647).

In its stubborn unreadability then, or rather its readability only as pointing toward what the narrative refuses to acknowledge in detail, the phrase "undisciplined heart," which ostensibly glosses and explains David's marital tragedy, indicates a limit or impasse that euphemistically gestures beyond itself to topics that Dickens was unable or unwilling to explore. The process by which a man and woman, once in love, become no longer in love, is a subject the novel largely elides. What is at stake here is not just a minor moment of reticence in the novel's narrative, because by its rhetorical fortissimo and the histrionic character of the scene in which this apostrophe to the heart occurs, these lines draw attention to the importance, in the context of the entire novel, of David's interpretation of his marital experience. The very forcefulness and staginess of this internal monologue are readable as an effort to leap over, by sheer rhetorical force, the chasm in the text between venial failures of David's role as husband that we see and the intense moral condemnation that his heart is judged to deserve. The fact that the novel seems to gesture in two different directions simultaneously, on one hand to David's failure *within* the marriage, through unspecifiable quotidian and psychic details ("trifles") and, alternatively, to the marriage's very existence as a result of David's sexual passion for Dora, their failure to remain "as boy and girl," offering these as alternative proofs of the general failure that David's heart has precipitated, is symptomatic of Dickens's straining to represent something that the novel's narrative mode, with its silences about sexuality and gender conflict, resists representing.

There are in fact two unrepresentable narratives here. If Dickens were to give us the "trifles" that destroyed the David and Dora relationship, he would have to confront the nature of marriage as a clashing of two individualities, which would entail a demystification of the language of duty and self-denial that cloaked the reality of Victorian marriage: though it is generally known that women were expected to be selfless and "disinterested" in marriage, husbands too were expected to be ruled by duty and self-denial. On his wedding day Betsey Trotwood specifically warns David of the role of duty in marital life: "It will be your duty, and it will be your pleasure too . . . to estimate her (as you chose her) by the qualities she has, and not by the qualities she may not have" (538). Clearly the implication is that David must learn to restrain his individuality to the extent it demands things from Dora that she cannot provide. If David has, manifestly, not been happy in this self-denying role, depicting the trifles of marital failure would raise exactly the issue of to what extent marriage should be viewed in liberal terms, as a dissoluble contract deserving of termination when it irremediably impedes the individual's self-development. When Dickens turns to this very issue in *Hard Times*, he answers in the affirmative, protesting the inaccessibility of divorce in cases of marital breakdown. That novel, of course, largely frames the issue as part of the sufferings of a working-class character, but clearly the logic of the position that marriage is a dissoluble contract between individuals would subvert Victorian society's idealization of middle-class marriage as well, a reality that Dickens carefully swerves from acknowledging in depicting David's marriage.

The alternative narrative suggested by the phrase "undisciplined heart" to explain David's marital failure, equally unrepresentable, though this narrative idea is clearly hinted at, is that David is a victim of inadequate sexual self-control, first tempted by the alluring but seemingly asexual bond with little Emily, and then decisively falling for Dora, her socially more elevated sister in sexual temptation. Because of the taboo in Victorian fiction against acknowledging the unruliness of sexual impulses in sympathetic characters, this narrative is necessarily veiled but is definitely hinted at. This narrative strand is in fact important to the novel's ideological structure since, given the novel's impasse caused by its unwillingness to express the need for a liberal redefinition of marriage to promote the individual's self-development, the only language it has available for making marital failure sympathetic is to suggest that David is betrayed into marital misery by having "abandoned [himself] to enjoyment" (307) in his sexual passion for Dora. This phrase is used to describe David's "first dissipation" of drunkenness (which is encouraged by Steerforth, later revealed as a sexual decadent), but it could equally apply to his intoxication with Dora's beauties and his surrender in loving her to sexual impulses. Dora's (and covertly Emily's) sexual temptation of David becomes the displaced locus through which the novel's ambivalence about marriage and domesticity is played out. The unruly sexuality with which these women are associated is made to take the blame for the failure of disciplined masculine heterosexuality. Hence, as the novel strives to achieve idealized disciplined sexual identity, both female characters must be banished from the novel's closure, Emily to Australia and perpetual spinsterhood, Dora to death.

These two occluded narratives are at the heart of the novel's ideological movement, because the narrative makes the failure ascribed to David's heart to be properly disciplined crucial to the meaning Dickens tries to express later in the novel—David's development from this point on is predicated on his recognition, as Dora dies, of his heart's failure. Moreover, by the novel's moral logic, the heavy chastening that David's heart receives here seems to suggest that David's heart has indeed been highly undisciplined and so requires the onerous discipline of the lengthy depression and repentance that David undergoes following Dora's death.

Though the narrative of sexual failure of discipline is largely elided, Dickens reveals through indirection why the failure of David and Dora's marriage is unnarratable, hinting that David's love for Dora was too heavily founded on her sexual attractiveness, which made David misread her, failing to notice her immaturity, silliness, and incompatibility, a product both of personality and of her overgenteel upbringing. In this regard, David has followed the romantic (but foolhardy) path of his father, who married a woman below him in class status and of weak character, but "unusually youthful in appearance" with "luxuriant and beautiful" hair (12). (Not "Rookery" but "[c]ookery would have been more to the purpose" [13] is Betsey Trotwood's apparently accurate summing up of the triumph of romanticism and erotic attraction over common sense in the elder Copperfield's marriage.) Ultimately, the lacuna in the text's narration of the dissolution of David's marriage is a product of the tension between Dickens's liberal conception of the marriage relationship, by which the individual self-seeking that has led David to Dora should be allowed to correct its error of judgment and abandon his relation to Dora, and Dickens's continuing public commitment to the ideal of Victorian domesticity, which prescribed that the husband's (as well, of course, as the wife's) love be capable of nearly infinite self-sacrifice and that partners should accept a lifetime of unhappiness rather than disrupt the sacred permanence of marriage. The discrepancy between Dickens's liberal conception of marital roles and the domestic mode that he inhabits produces an awkward gap in the novel's narrative.

To avoid exploring the interplay of maturation, sexuality, and the societal and legal bonds of marriage in middle-class domesticity, then, the novel gestures toward a superior alternative to David's vitiated domestic site: his earlier idyllic and safely asexual bond with Emily, who can be seen by the reader as the angelic substitute for the disturbingly sexually alluring and ultimately disappointing Clara and Dora Copperfield, this infantile love the preferable "love as a boy and girl" that Dora has recommended. Since conventionally the lack of mature sexual impulses is a hallmark of childhood and there is a childlike simplicity to working-class characters as Dickens represents them, Emily as a working-class child is seemingly a doubly safe love object for the young David. As a child embodying David's childlike asexual and romantic identification with working-class people, Emily as an adult continues to function as a proof of David's moral stature, as in his empathetic response to Emily's engagement to Ham. This empathetic and spectatorial response to working-class courtship, which elides the possibility of renewed erotic attraction to Emily, demonstrates David's tacit commitment to the taboo against cross-class erotic attraction. By reminding us of the innocent relationship of Emily and David, the phrase "love[d] as boy and girl," protects our image of David as successfully controlling—or seemingly lacking—unruly sexuality, and reminds us of the channeling of sexuality within proper (that is endogamous) class boundaries that we see in his avuncular relationship to the mature Emily. Through the idealization of his relation to her, Emily becomes a guarantor of David's moral status who protects him from the suggestions in his relation to Dora that sexuality is a destabilizing presence for the bourgeois individual.

If Emily is the marker of David's sexual self-control and empathy with the poor (an empathy he naively ascribes to Steerforth also), his bond with her also embodies, as we have seen, the ideal alternative to the failed David-Dora relationship. But if Emily's status as childlike icon of nonsexual love makes her the guarantor of David's sexual restraint, through her character and history the novel subverts its own careful fencing off of the middle-class male from proclivity to sexual transgression. For, given her economic vulnerability, femininity, and beauty, Emily's childlike status as working-class character causes her to be read as constantly threatened by sexuality, producing the curious effect that the character who embodies the ideal alternative to the overly sexualized David-Dora relationship ominously represents as well the pitfalls of feminine sexuality in its working-class form, both for herself and for the bourgeois male. When as a child Emily threatens to leap off a pier to her death, David admits that, given her later history, "[t]here has been a time since—I do not say it lasted long, but it has been—when I have asked myself if it would have been better for little Em'ly to have had the waters close above her head that morning in my sight; and when I have answered Yes, it would have been" (39). By anticipating Emily's later sexual fall, the scene hints that, even as a child, she is a potentially ominous love object. And by foregrounding the irresolution of the older David before the revelation of Emily's sexual transgression (ought she to have died young?), this passage suggests how Emily's fate is linked to David's irresolute character, thereby implicating him in a version of the moral weakness that will occasion Emily's fall. True, his irresolution takes the form of a hysterical desire to obliterate Emily and her sexual weakness, a position stigmatized later in the novel by being associated with the hysterical femininity of Rosa Dartle, but by its very hysteria and lack of masculine firmness, this hyperbolic moral response suggests how intimately David's own psychic development is implicated by its intimate relation to the working-class Emily's moral fragility.

One of the notable features, after all, of David as a character throughout the novel is his intense imaginative and emotional response to working-class (and lower-middle-class) people, which is suggestive of the influence of romanticism on the novel, a response first powerfully evoked in David's visit with his beloved nurse to the Peggotty family's seaside home. But given the standard association of the working class with fragile moral purity, the novel suggests that this side of David puts him at constant risk of transgressing bourgeois Victorian moral norms. Emily herself, far from being safe from erotic suggestions, accumulates them as the story progresses, and Miss Mowcher even imagines, mistakenly but understandably, that David as a young man has harbored a passion for her. Nor is Miss Mowcher completely mistaken: clearly Dickens intends us to read David's first sight of Emily as an adult woman as involving a repression, not entirely successful, of a reading of Emily as sexually attractive and morally restless, in short, as a temptation to the elite male: "a most beautiful little creature, with the cloudless blue eyes, that had looked into my childish heart, . . . with enough of willfulness in her bright face to justify what I had heard [that she was considered "wayward"]; with much of the old capricious coyness lurking in it; but with nothing in her pretty looks, I am sure, but what was meant for goodness and for happiness, and what was on a good and happy course" (262). Later events make this passage read as obviously ironic, but even on first reading the overeagerness ("I am sure") suggests David's not quite successful repression of Emily's potential "waywardness," in other words, her potentially dangerous availability for the resumption of his earlier affection for her, which would now inevitably be sexualized. Thus, Miss Mowcher's suspicious misreading of David as sexually attracted to Emily (she glances sharply at him when he first mentions Emily [285]) is in fact partly an accurate gloss of his potential for sexual incontinence and his not fully conscious attraction to his childhood friend. At the revelation of Emily's seduction by Steerforth, it is obvious that David has acted as a stalking horse for Steerforth's erotic designs and hence David feels understandably morally complicit in them. On one hand, Miss Mowcher's misreading of David is shown to be founded on a prejudice against young gentlemen, as David's suspicions of her involve prejudices against her dwarfism. The liberal point against irrational prejudice that Dickens makes here links David to Steerforth in that both are shown as capable of illiberal prejudices (Steerforth's against the working class, David's against Miss Mowcher as a dwarf). Moreover, with David's unwitting aid in lulling suspicions, Steerforth has enacted the consequences of these illiberal views by his seduction of Emily, an act with devastating consequences for her, Ham, and Mr. Peggotty. Miss Mowcher's shrewd intuition about David's sexual attraction to Emily, albeit apparently wrong, draws attention to the reality that Steerforth's seduction of Emily actualizes David's unconscious attraction to her and suggests that he might easily, given his capacity for "undisciplined" sexual passion, have been tempted to rekindle in a sexual form the love he once felt for his childhood sweetheart.

Steerforth's liaison with Emily, which results in the most dramatic rupture of a male friendship in the novel—a divorce between Steerforth and David—which is analogous to his failed marriage with Dora, is thematically linked with this marital failure by being equally an instance of sexual energy transgressing bourgeois bounds and proving destructive. Steerforth's sexual transgression, by externalizing the potential for sexual incontinence that David himself possesses, becomes a cautionary sign of how the failure of sexual control inevitably exacerbates class conflict (most evident in the angry confrontation between Mr. Peggotty and Mrs. Steerforth, the parent figures of the transgressive pair) as well as threatening to destroy individual and family happiness. No wonder David feels such intense guilt on learning of Emily's desertion and Ham's psychic devastation.

Dickens emphasizes the omnipresence of sexual temptation in bourgeois as well as working-class social space by introducing the story of Dr. and Annie Strong: this story of near-adultery and of a seemingly loveless and mercenary marriage is also presented quite evasively, since we are ultimately told—despite strong evidence to the contrary—that there is no mercenary element in the marriage nor any lasting regret of Annie Strong for the loss of her earlier favorite, the dashing and handsome Jack Maldon. Dickens underlines how Annie's "undisciplined" passion for Jack Maldon parallels David's for Dora, as both are examples of the threat that youthful sexual passion represent to rationally organized bourgeois domesticity.

Significantly, the mercenary element associated with Annie's marriage to Dr. Strong is elided in the case of David's marriage to Dora, which points to a significant difference between the representation of male and female sexual transgression. While sexual excess and transgression is threatening for both males and females, it is clearly, in accordance with the sexual double standard, more taboo for women and hence is more carefully elided from the text. In the stories of both Annie Strong and Emily, female sexual transgression is situated in an economic context, suggesting that women are particularly vulnerable to sexual transgressions when economically constrained. Social historians have noted how working-class sexuality was in fact constrained in important ways by economic deprivation, but Dickens does not explore, except in melodramatic and stereotyped ways, the subjective experience of the working-class woman. But his linking of female sexual transgression to economic contexts functions effectively to deprive transgressive female sexuality of any status as autonomous behavior, while also hinting at its "natural" inevitability, since it is linked to women's seemingly natural economic weakness. Particularly in the case of Emily, who pathetically announces that she will never "come back, unless he brings me back a lady" (383), a line that conflates the traditional seduced woman's desire for marriage with a hope for upward mobility, a sexual fall seems simply a reflex of economic discontent.

It is clear, then, that the phrase that implicitly links Dora and Emily—"loved as a boy and girl"—is founded on a real if covert affinity between these two female characters, an affinity that ultimately scapegoats femininity, and particularly sexualized femininity, for domestic malaise and masculine transgression. Both female characters essentially embody erotic temptation, in particular the temptation to let emotion overrule prudence and moral prescience, to transgress class boundaries in destructive ways, in a downward direction in the case of Emily and in an upward movement in the case of Dora. If David never falls into moral failure as deep as Steerforth's, it is because of David's superior moral and psychic sensitivities and his psychic identification with the lower classes; though working-class women may sexually tempt him, he could never be as callous toward working people as is Steerforth because he feels too great a bond of sympathy with Emily's working-class family. Nevertheless, David struggles with a parallel conflict to that which defeats Steerforth, fighting not always successfully against the lures of hedonism and sexual passion and their tendency to lead to disastrous violations of class boundaries and rational prudence. In Steerforth, this conflict leads to a complete rupture with the framework of Victorian domesticity, but in David's case, too, implicitly the lure of sexuality is untamable by, and is part of the dis-ease at the root of, Victorian marriage. David's childhood fondness for Little Emily, easily transferred to the adult realm, if only in Miss Mowcher's suspicions, marks him as particularly susceptible to the charms of working-class females, as he is clearly drawn to that class in general. David has, after all, found in the working-class Peggotty the positive version of the mother that his own mother never was, and when victimized by the callous, untrammeled bourgeois energies of Murdstone, he has shared the exploited position of the working class. Indeed the novel probably accurately reflects the social reality that there were ample psychic reasons for elite men to find working-class individuals—especially females—attractive. In Dickens, working-class people in general are consistently represented as more emotionally expressive and honest, more authentic, than elite individuals. Working-class women are associated with physicality, an emotional warmth (one thinks of Peggotty's memorable button-popping hugs) and a preoccupation with the body that would be enticing to elite men, given how physically withdrawn (Agnes) or physically fragile elite women (Dora) appear to be.[13] Suggestively, in much of Dickens, it is especially the working-class family, or at most the lower-middle-class family, that is the site par excellence of the very substantial pleasures of community (think of Bob Cratchit's family). Of course, the tendency of working-class women to stray erotically and their willingness to enter into masculine realms of economic striving or commerce make them at once more masculine in their life-strategies than bourgeois women, and also more sexually available. If the novel clearly depicts the intersection of class and gender dynamics that would have encouraged cross-class liaisons, it nevertheless refuses to explore this topic except as cautionary tale, recoding David's sexual impulses as a part of youth that he must discipline and control in order to mature fully.

THE SUBVERSION OF SEXUAL REPRESSION

Central then to understanding *David Copperfield* is Victorian culture's ideological conflation of success in terms of mastering the demands of the mar-

ket, a success that David triumphantly achieves, and success at sexual and
moral self-discipline, which he attains as well, though at a higher psychic
cost. But if there is a self-division in David's relation to sexuality that probably reflects one in his creator, there is also a counter-narrative to the novel's
epic of self-discipline that speaks to Dickens's growing discontent with the
rigid sexual moralism of the middle class. The novel links the lure of sexuality that threatens David with the working class and also with the spirit of
unfettered individualism that derives from romanticism and the ferment of
ideas that accompanied the French Revolution; the Byronic Steerforth, like
the working-class Emily, is emblematic of these forces. We see the novel's
preference for romantic over authoritarian ideals of personal and family life
in the contrast between the loving but chaotic working-class family of the
Peggottys as against the rigid and harshly disciplined familial world established by Mr. Murdstone and his sister, their insistently moralistic rhetoric
suggesting the influence of evangelical Christianity on Victorian family life.
David's return from his vacation with the Peggottys to the coldly repressive
Murdstonean family is a fall from paradise into psychic and emotional alienation. Thus, while the text tames and domesticates the transgressive sexual
impulses that threaten bourgeois stability, indeed, it has David dramatically
perform such a domestication, it also, unsurprisingly, given Dickens's passionate liberal ideals, reveals a countervailing tendency to acknowledge the
attraction of transgressive impulses and their capacity to subvert sexual and
gender norms.

From this perspective, even Dora is an ambiguous figure. Seen merely as
sexual pitfall and the epitome of failed domesticity, she seems purely negative. Yet Dora sparks not merely David's sexual energies, but also his imaginative ones. When he meets her, he feels "captive," and the scene in which
he first "falls into captivity" to her is filled with indications that she stirs
both his erotic desire and his imagination. She inspires a fairy-tale narrative
when he imagines himself as a hardy woodsman who must "take my wood-
man's axe in my hand, and clear my own way through the forest of difficulty, by cutting down the trees until I came to Dora" (439). Through his
response to her, he imaginatively creates an ideal image of her as "related to
a higher order of things," and "my refuge in disappointment and distress,"
an ideal that serves both as a psychological refuge and as a goal for his efforts to elevate his own status: "The more I pitied myself, or pitied others,
the more I sought for consolation in the image of Dora" (401).

Though Dora is only partly successful as David's muse (witness her aversion to Shakespeare), the imaginative energy that she inspires in David links
her associatively with his vocation as a writer, and he in fact first mentions

being "known as a writer" in describing his early marital life with Dora. Moreover, as a character associated with a passionate emotional response from David, Dora is inevitably linked to Steerforth; there is a sense that Dora replaces Steerforth in a metonymic set of associations. Both characters are associated with genteel activities (fencing, horseback riding): both are physically attractive upper-class figures who sweep David into their orbits. Dora functions most clearly as a substitute for Steerforth when his seduction of Emily ends David's friendship with him: "[Dora's] idea . . . made some amends to me, even for the loss of my friend" (401). Given the metonymic links between these characters, it is suggestive that, like Dora, Steerforth has stimulated David's imagination. Like Dora, Steerforth's physical appearance stirs an imaginative response in David; during his confrontation with Mr. Mell at Mr. Creakle's school, Steerforth struck David as "a noble fellow in appearance," and his speech to Mr. Creakle seems a "gallant speech" (90). Though he later regrets his partiality for Steerforth here, David's response shows how he imaginatively assimilates Steerforth to a heroic ideal; earlier, by requiring David to retell him the stories that he has read, Steerforth serves as the first spur to David's narrative gifts, a task that further stimulates his imagination.

Like Dora, Steerforth is a sexual figure as well as a muse; because of Steerforth's physical attractiveness and the wish he expresses that David would have a sister, he is, from early in the novel, a sexually charged figure. (Indeed the implied compliment to David's physical allure in his remark about his hypothetical sister has overtones of homoeroticism, or at least of highly sexualized homosociality, an early signal of the aristocratic decadence that will become Steerforth's defining trait.)[14] David's storytelling at school makes him the "Sultana Scheherazade" to Steerforth's sultan (85), imagery that situates the imaginative act of narrating in an erotic context. Even the novels that David draws on for his nightly narrations to Steerforth are linked with sexuality. In recounting the positive role that the novels have on his early childhood (suggestively, they are a legacy from his passionate and romantic father), David mentions several novels that would have been sexually scandalous for Victorian readers (*Roderick Random*, *Tom Jones*) but insists "whatever harm there was in some of them was not there for me; *I* knew nothing of it" (54, emphasis in original). The argument is less than candid. Though children are often puzzled by sexual references in books, as the child grows more sophisticated about sexuality, perhaps in part through the medium of books, he or she may glean knowledge of adult sexuality from reinterpreting narratives containing sexual elements. If David remembers the stories well enough to retell them to Steerforth, they could well aid his growing sophistication about sexual knowledge and mores. This passage's defense of eighteenth-century literature thus quietly questions the Victorian ethos that required that literature be safe for children by evading sexual topoi. Eighteenth-century literature is certainly more open about sexuality than Victorian literature was permitted to be, and Dickens implies that the effects of David's exposure to it are entirely positive. Thus, from early in the novel, and implicitly throughout in the figures of Steerforth and Dora, the power of the imagination, which the novel celebrates for allowing David both to transcend his class position through success as a novelist and to create the narrative that is the novel, is repeatedly linked to sexuality and to the passions associated with it. Steerforth in particular, the most obviously sexual character in the novel, suggests this link of sexual and imaginative energies by his association with romantic questing, as when he tells David his guiding principle in life is that he must "ride on."

Because both characters are associated with sexuality and the imagination, Dora and Steerforth express the novel's ambivalence about these affiliated energies. By implying such an affinity, the novel inevitably suggests that imaginative energies as well as erotic ones can threaten the individual who lacks sufficient discipline. True, judging from the success of David's literary career, his imaginative powers are—like Dickens's—powerfully disciplined to meet the requirements of the market, a market that policed Victorian fiction for any deviation from gender and sexual orthodoxy. Yet repeatedly Dickens suggests that transgressions against bourgeois sexual and domestic boundaries are at the heart of David's imaginative power. For instance, Dickens often celebrates the pleasures of community and friendship, and one of David's strongest early friends is Mr. Micawber, himself a devotee of extravagant and imaginative use of language. The latter's familial situation and life situation is replete with the histrionic and demonstrative, and the Micawbers, largely because they fail to conform to bourgeois social norms, become a source of both emotional and imaginative sustenance for David. For instance, in his first meeting with the family, Mrs. Micawber is breastfeeding one of the twins and comes up to show him the apartment "twin and all" (139). David says of Mrs. Micawber's incessant breast-feeding, "I hardly ever, in all my experience of the family, saw both the twins detached from Mrs. Micawber at the same time. One of them was always taking refreshment" (139). On top of the indecorousness of Mrs. Micawber's combination of maternal and commercial responsibilities and her simultaneous exposure of an intimate part of the female body to her visitor, she makes no effort to distinguish what information is appropriate to a child, immediately beginning to explain Micawber's indebtedness to David, who comments "I

never can quite understand whether my precocious self-dependence confused Mrs. Micawber in reference to my age, or whether she was so full of
the subject that she would have talked about it to the very twins if there had
been nobody else to communicate with, but this was the strain in which she
begin, and she went on accordingly all the time I knew her" (140). The Micawbers expose David to repeated violations of bourgeois ideals of the separation of domesticity from commerciality, from theatricality, and from the
indecorous, a tendency that climaxes with Micawber's move to debtor's
prison, where David witnesses Captain Hopkins cohabitating with and having fathered two children by a woman "not married to Captain Hopkins"
(147). Yet David credits this transgressive and squalid milieu, to which the
Micawbers give him access, as a source for his creative efforts, as he "fitted
my old books to my altered life, and made stories for myself, out of the
streets, and out of men and women" (149); this process is part of the "gradual forming" of David's character, which will later make him a well-known
writer. Such a narrative of the imaginative value of lower-class and transgressive milieus is analogous to how the somewhat disreputable world of the cir-
cus in *Hard Times* is linked both to a relaxation of bourgeois norms of sexual decorum (where for instance none of the women "were particular in
respect of showing their legs") but also to a realm of imagination and deep
feeling ("an untiring readiness to help and pity one another") that contrasts
with and resists puritanical utilitarianism associated with the middle class.
It should be noted that *Hard Times* will show another kind of rebellion
against bourgeois domesticity, and another argument in favor of divorce, in
Louisa Gradgrind's love for Mr. Harthouse, which is her rebellion against
her loveless marriage to Bounderby, a failed marriage caused by the coldhearted disregard of emotional life in her father's utilitarian ethos. As with
Edith in *Dombey and Son*, however, Dickens clearly censors the adulterous
potential of his plot: despite the collapse of her marriage, Louisa, rather than
acting on her feelings for Harthouse, simply abandons her husband and returns to her father. Despite the strategic censoring of narrative possibilities,
both novels suggest how Dickens saw a rigid and puritanical morality, linked
to the middle class, as hostile to the flowering of human pleasure, bonds of
affection, and creativity.

Not only does *Copperfield* celebrate the transgressive impulses of the
imagination, but it also directly criticizes the repressive spirit that responds
to sexual transgression with harsh punishment. Because of the novel's need
to emphasize David's impulse toward sexual self-control, Dickens depicts
the currents of sexuality and repression that are the subtext of David's story,
as well as their implication with the dynamics of social class, through a the-

atrical mode that in key scenes of the novel relegates him to a largely spectatorial role. This mode allows David to see the ravages of the sexual hypocrisy
and repressiveness and its poisoning effect on relations of social class, while
keeping David's bourgeois self largely immune from the forces he witnesses.
In one such melodramatic scene, while David watches in hiding, Rosa Dartle lashes out angrily at Emily, who has finally returned to London after her
sojourn with Steerforth and is on the verge of being rescued by Mr. Peggotty. In the midst of Rosa's tirade, Emily tries to defend herself by saying
that she had loved and trusted Steerforth, and Rosa fulminates, "Why don't
they whip these creatures! If I could order it to be done, I would have this
girl whipped to death" (606). She then gleefully recommends suicide to
Emily. Rosa's punitive spirit here is made hyperbolic in order to discredit the
spirit of sexual repressiveness that she represents. The reader is intended to
feel, like David, a sense of gratitude and relief when Mr. Peggoty, full of forgiveness and love, enters to rescue Emily.

   The scene epitomizes the novel's condemnation of bourgeois sexual repressiveness as inhumanity. Because Rosa presents herself as a defender of
bourgeois domestic ideals, which she defines as class-specific and as excluding the working class, her moral bankruptcy implicitly indicts the domestic
values she enunciates. Explicitly excluding a working-class girl from the
mantle of domesticity's protection, she furiously tells Emily that she has no
right to claim that her home has been violated by Steerforth, for as a working-class fallen woman she has confused the pure realm of domesticity and
the sordid sphere of commerce: "Your home! You were a part of the trade of
your home, and were bought and sold like any other vendible thing your
people dealt in" (605). Rosa expresses here what is always an unspoken but
powerful rule of bourgeois domesticity, that it defines itself as the antithesis
of commerce. By saying Emily was a "vendible thing" to her "people" she
deprives Emily, because of her social class, of the traditional sanctity of the
middle-class home. But the depiction of Emily's "people" throughout the
novel demonstrates that Rosa here is cruelly and radically misreading the
working-class home. Though Rosa correctly infers that Emily had economic
motives for her relationship with Steerforth, she ignores the reality of the
class injury that Steerforth has done to Emily's family and exhibits a bigoted refusal to see that the ethical norms of her own class that condemn
sexual transgressions can also inspire working-class families, while such
families can be the equal of their middle-class counterparts in their love for
their children. Far from callously seeing Emily as a "thing" to be commodified, Mr. Peggotty remains steadfast in his love for her despite her sexual
disgrace. The extent of Rosa's failure of sympathy is shown by her blindness

to how the economic privilege that Steerforth has used to gain access to Emily and how her economic vulnerability, rather than reducing her to a "vendible thing," makes her sympathetic and understandable even in her sexual fall.

The scene powerfully subverts the rigid punitiveness of the bourgeois sexual and familial values of Dickens's age, associating this punitive spirit with the arrogance and class prejudices of the wealthy. But Rosa's stance is further subverted by the fact that her motive is largely sexual jealousy. This fact has been implicit in Rosa's character all along, but it is shown most dramatically at the moment when Emily speaks of her love for Steerforth: "Rosa Dartle sprang up from her seat; recoiled; and in recoiling struck at her, with a face of such malignity, so darkened and disfigured by passion, that I had almost thrown myself between them" (606). She then announces her intention to hound Emily perpetually with the infamy of her fall (necessitating the eventual emigration of Emily and Mr. Peggotty). Earlier scenes have established that Rosa loved—presumably still loves—Steerforth and that he has spurned her; the scar on her face, inflicted by Steerforth, is an emblem of this lasting psychic wound. In her hysterical embodiment of sexual repression, Rosa is also hypocritically animated by her own sexual passion, mixed with discontent at her own low social status. Earlier, when David and Steerforth visit the family home, she vents her frustration at this marginal status and her erotic frustration in sarcastic remarks directed at Steerforth's class snobbery. Now, faced with a rival who has successfully won Steerforth, no matter how briefly, her animus is directed against the rival, not against Steerforth. The earlier scenes have made clear that her venomous character is the product of her own erotic and class frustration, as one who lives tantalizingly close to the upper bourgeoisie, but is permanently exiled sexually and socially from equality with them.

The scene shows the novel's profound ambivalence about the traditional sexual repressiveness that is its dominant ideology, by showing how this repressiveness can become an agent of class and gender ressentiment, and by demonstrating how domestic ideology can be wielded as a class weapon that erases sympathy for the working class and their sufferings. In this scene, such sympathy is embodied in David, who watches helplessly from his hiding place. While feeling a deep compassion for Emily during the scene, he is removed from acting in it. The narrative convention here, drawn from melodrama and Gothic fiction, allows David to witness, but not himself be affected to the point of taking action, by the powerful currents of class feeling and sexuality that so obviously affect the other characters. In this way, Dickens can point out how the workings of such currents make moralistic discourses blatantly self-serving (as in the cases of Rosa and Mrs. Steerforth). But the spectatorial conventions in such a scene also crucially function to guard David from being seen as himself vulnerable either to the powerful sexual impulses that sweep up Steerforth and Emily or to the class aspirations and frustrations that prove so insidious in the case of Rosa Dartle. In contrast to the moral weakness he exhibits earlier in the novel, here David appears to be a fully autonomous, if indecisive, bourgeois individual. Yet in this scene he inhabits a fictional world where, in contrast to the pieties of domesticity, the reader can see that both in sexual transgressions and in their policing, moral and sexual behavior is implicated in energies of sexual desire and class frustration that subvert the possibility of individual autonomy, while rigid and repressive moral discourses are revealed to be covert agents of class warfare. Such an exposure to the dark reality of repressive discourses helps us understand the roots of David's self-division.

The Threat of Ressentiment and the Neurotic Heroine

If, in a liberal spirit, the novel subverts the repressiveness of Victorian domestic ideology, it also has a profoundly conservative reading of the threat to society posed by discontented lower-class and female figures. In *David Copperfield* and much of the later fiction, Dickens perceptively shows a world as riven by seemingly insoluble class and gender conflicts. Unfortunately, this theme is generally coded through the thematics of ressentiment. An idea never absent from Dickens's work, it becomes a central theme of such late fictions as *A Tale of Two Cities* (1859) and *Great Expectations* (1860–61). Ressentiment is the product of economic differentiation, and as such it is the evil twin of David's ambitions of "cutting down the trees until I came to Dora[,]" his ambitious striving for genteel status. The ideological position of ressentiment in the novel is as demonic Other to domesticity, or more precisely, ressentiment is the infection against which domesticity, often unsuccessfully, must guard. This conflict of ressentiment and domesticity emerges in how Uriah Heep, a monstrous figure of ressentiment and Rosa Dartle's masculine counterpart, threatens Agnes, the most fully domestic figure in the novel. Yet in his portrayal of Agnes, Dickens shows the domestic women as covertly infected by her own deep discontent as much as the overtly disgruntled and vengeful Rosa, suggesting that even the seemingly ideal domestic femininity often conceals an underlying hysteria. In other words, a painful reality lurks behind the idealized image of the domestic woman.

In the early part of the novel, the polar opposition between domesticity and ressentiment adds a frisson of transgression to Uriah Heep's erotic designs on Agnes. Heep rationalizes these ressentiment-inspired designs by arguing that they are merely the idiosyncratic and personal—by which the novel understands lower-class—replication of the legitimate ambitions of the gentleman's son David. When as a youth David first encounters Uriah, the ambitious clerk of working-class origins, he mirrors David's own rise from being a child laborer "knowing" of "London life, and London streets" (199) to being a pupil at an elite school who will be socialized as a young gentleman. David himself feels the alienation of the upwardly mobile and the shame of his social origins: "I was so conscious of having passed through scenes of which [the other boys] could have no knowledge, and of having acquired experiences foreign to my age, appearance and condition, as one of them, that I half believed it was an imposture to come there as an ordinary little schoolboy" (198). Uriah, who strives for upward mobility by insinuating himself into the Wickfield business and household, experiences an analogous alienation, but for him the "imposture" is not a feeling of inauthenticity produced by chance associations with a lower-class milieu, but a genuine imposture that he deploys to resist his exclusion from privilege. No doubt because David senses both Uriah's kinship with him in social terms and the latter's sinister inauthenticity, he feels that "[Uriah] had a sort of fascination for me" (202). When, with polite condescension, David responds to Uriah's self-improvement (he is reading a law book) by suggesting that Uriah may rise to be partner in Wickfield's law firm, David is at once the child ingratiating himself with his elders and the upper-class gentleman offering polite but empty words of encouragement to a social inferior. Uriah pries from David a bland compliment of Agnes, then responds to this comment, as to David's earlier prediction of a partnership, with exaggerated gratitude. Later, when he comes to visit the adult David in London, Uriah adduces these chance remarks as David's benevolent patronage: "To think that you should be the first to kindle the sparks of ambition in my 'umble breast, and that you've not forgot it!" (323)

Uriah's covert irony here expresses his class-based anger against David; it is precisely because the middle-class David has never genuinely encouraged Uriah, or other members of his social class, that he malevolently legitimates his ambitions through David's offhand patronage. David's genteel and bloodless remark that "[e]veryone must have" admiration for Agnes (204) becomes twisted into Uriah's claim that David gave permission to desire Agnes, legitimating his class and erotic aggression in using Wickfield's alcoholism and financial mistakes in an effort to win her. Uriah's implication throughout is that what David has privileged access to—a high social status, ability to win Agnes—has not been genuinely offered to himself, but merely dangled before him as something beyond his reach. David's own aspiration to privilege becomes for Uriah an alibi for his ressentiment-filled strivings.

In this context, in which male rivalries over class position and the malevolent resentments that they engender menace domesticity's power (as embodied in Agnes), we can understand how vital is that aspect of the novel that suggests that domesticity itself is tainted by ressentiment's energies and economic self-seeking. If domesticity is besieged from without by lower-class envy and rage, it is chilling that self-seeking infects the domestic site as well. For instance, Rosa Dartle's impassioned denunciation of Emily as a "vendible thing" and hence not worthy of invoking the sacred word "home" could hardly make more clear the ideological boundary between the mercenary taint of commerce that affects the lower-class home as compared to the pure haven from economic pressures that is the bourgeois home. Yet that denunciation is itself subverted by Rosa's evident ressentiment; as a woman both socially marginal and sexually frustrated, she intrudes ressentiment into the Steerforth home, thereby ironizing the sexual morality that she enunciates. Feminine discontent arising from economic sources is not the only source of alienation that can contaminate the family. The angry disgruntlement of Micawber's son at his lack of career prospects suggests that filial discontent can do so as well, a rebellion that spurs the Micawber family's emigration to Australia.

In the larger context of the novel's depiction of domesticity and social class, Rosa is only the most lurid instance of a recurring pattern in which women in particular, and the domesticity with which they are entrusted, are contaminated by economic pressures and thus fail to rescue David, the prototypical middle-class hero, from market and class-based forces. The foundational moral failure of David's mother, Clara, is one that David is aware of even as a child: "I watch her winding her bright curls round her fingers, and straitening her waist and nobody knows better than I do that she likes to look so well, and is proud of being so pretty" (22). David's childish indulgence of Clara is calculated to provoke the reader's censoriousness, and Peggotty's moralizing gloss on Clara's behavior underscores the point that Clara cares more for her vanity and sexuality than she does her child. In death Clara receives the most damaging critique of all from David, which is the near-total psychic repression of her failure: "From the moment of my knowing of the death of my mother, the idea of her as she had been of late had vanished from me. I remembered her, from that instant, only as the young mother of my earliest impressions, who had been used to wind her bright curls round and round her finger, and to dance with me at twilight in the parlor. . . . In her death she winged her way back to her calm untroubled youth, and cancelled all the rest" (119).

As David's childish indulgence reveals its own inadequacy as a full judgment of the mother's failure, so here his repression of that failure acts in retrospect to underline it. David's childhood is so painful as to be ineffable; "all the rest" gestures at the endless horrors of life with Murdstone, a life in which Clara has suffered and from which she has failed to shield David. Indeed, as Peggotty has pointed out, it is Clara's vanity over her looks—and susceptibility to Murdstone's "admiration" of them—that has caused her to neglect her maternal duty by marrying such a man. Clara's failure allows domesticity to buckle under economic pressures, for Murdstone's motive in marrying her is clearly economic. In sending David away to labor for Murdstone and Grinby, Murdstone himself cites economic motives: "I suppose you know, David, that I am not rich" (135). Though Murdstone's language of moral rigor ("firmness") in treating Clara and David links him with evangelical Christianity's rigid version of Victorian domesticity, with its stress on breaking the childish will through stern punishment, he ultimately embodies the spirit of chilly laissez-faire capitalism and its indifference to the needs of the powerless. His rationalization for David's economic exploitation is simply that the imperatives of the economic world are more important than David's status as a child, and in fact that economic pressures will quite properly obliterate David's childish refractoriness: "a young boy of your disposition, which requires a great deal of correcting; and . . . no greater service can be done than to force it to conform to the ways of the working world, and to bend it and break it" (135).

Just as he excuses his mother's failings, in falling in love with and marrying Dora Spenlow, David again overindulges feminine weakness. Here, too, at a different stage of life, the failure of the vain and sexualized female character preeminently consists of not securing the male subject against the power of the marketplace and of inadequately aiding David in his battle with it. For what David above all lacks in Dora is a sympathetic helper in his work: "But that it would have been better for me if my wife could have helped me more, and shared the many thoughts in which I had no partner; and that this might have been; I knew" (587). Significantly, David's efforts, finally abandoned as mistaken, to "form [her] mind" are essentially efforts to make her more intellectual: "I talked to her on the subjects which occupied my thoughts; and I read Shakespeare to her—and fatigued her to the last degree" (585). The version of Dora that David tries unsuccessfully to create would at once competently and selflessly inhabit the domestic realm, outside the male-dominated world of intellectuality and commerce. Yet, paradoxically, she would have had easy and confident access to that world in order to provide an intellectually stimulating haven for David from it, a haven that would nevertheless maintain the male world's practical sense and intellectual excitement. Given the contradictory nature of these demands and the limitations of Victorian women's education, understandably Dora has difficulty fulfilling such a role, and linked as she is to gentility, especially in her obliviousness to the importance of labor, Dora herself embodies the dangers of upward mobility. The image of the hypergenteel or aristocratic person in Dickens is always of someone who by his failure to maintain proper standards for the lower orders involves them in moral destruction. And Dora's behavior, at first comically, then more insistently, partakes of this pattern: "I am persuaded we should have no right to go on in this way. We are positively corrupting people" (584), David complains to her. If the lack of a secure childhood class identity that his mother's failure has created in him generates a corresponding emphatic striving for the bourgeois ideals of discipline and moral control, Dora embodies his failure to achieve these in every stage of his life.

In this recurrent narrative pattern, there is something approaching a masculine paranoia in the repeated failure of crucial bourgeois women, the mother and the wife, to maintain the hero's class identity. As I have suggested, this failure in part reflects the novel's ambivalence toward the sexual desires and the imaginative energies with which women are associated, values that, according to the bourgeois ethos at its most uncompromising, must be firmly disciplined. As we have seen, the early part of the novel suggests a subversive reading of Victorian gender relations by showing the irrationality and unhappiness associated with failed marriages, which generally exhibit either exaggerated and predatory masculinity (Murdstone, Steerforth) or weak or undisciplined masculinity (Micawber, the elder Copperfield, Dr. Strong, David), alternatives that are linked to failed femininities, either victimized or rebellious. But in a swerve away from the advocacy of a liberal conception of marriage, in the later part of the novel Dickens strikingly rewrites these narratives to defuse their subversion of Victorian gender roles and domesticity. Thus, the seemingly powerful and masculine woman Betsey Trotwood is revealed to be still foolishly in love with her abusive husband; the apparently rebellious, straying wife Annie Strong claims to be contented and even relieved to have been saved from "the first mistaken impulse of my undisciplined heart" (558) in loving the handsome Jack Maldon, so that, rather implausibly, her seemingly asexual bond with the much older Dr. Strong is actually a blessing; Mr. Micawber redeems his family's poverty by achieving upward mobility in Australia; while in marriage to Agnes, David finds the domestic happiness that has eluded him. But the suppression of the novel's subversive energies generates a telltale incoherence (sometimes indicated by the implausibility of narratives, such as in the Annie Strong story) to the novel's ideological thrust. The affirmation of conventional domesticity as self-denial of individual passion and, indeed, as sexual repression was enough at odds with Dickens's personality and beliefs that there are traces of ambivalence toward this version of domesticity clearly visible in the novel. We see this in David's intense nostalgia for the past of his childhood and youth, as if to say that if maturation means the giving in to so much repression, how happy is it? Over and over, the novel strikes the theme of being exiled from childhood and youth: thus, when David returns from his self-exile abroad, he eats at a coffeehouse where even the waiter seems a relic of an earlier day: "which had its sanded floor sanded, no doubt, in exactly the same manner when the chief waiter was a boy—if he ever was a boy, which appeared improbable" (691). Both milieu and waiter are archaic, and David is caught in a world in which being a boy seems inconceivable, as he reflects pessimistically how Traddles will have small hopes of livelihood for "twenty years to come," and hence will be exiled in turn from the rejuvenating possibility of marriage. David is wrong about this, for Traddles has married, and clearly David is projecting his own feelings of nostalgia and exile from the promise of youth onto Traddles, while feeling exiled from Agnes in hyperbolic atonement for his "headlong passion" for Dora (698). The implication is clear that in David's depressive state he needs the solace that Traddles has found in marriage, but the nostalgia for lost youth seems ineradicable and darkens the mood of the novel's ending. The ambivalence about the success of bourgeois discipline in the novel is also suggested by the successive loss by marriage, death, or emigration of almost every character that has been associated with giving David pleasure, energy, or desire, including Steerforth, Dora, Emily, Mr. Peggotty, Traddles, and the Micawbers. The very characters who most utterly violate the norms of bourgeois discipline fill David with the most acute nostalgia—such as Steerforth, to whom David tells us he feels closer than ever after his transgression with Emily, and Mr. Micawber, whose milieu is the root of the literary achievement that defines David's later life. Even Dora continually haunts David, since Agnes's emotional claims on him is forestalled as a result of David's lingering sadness and repentance at his ill-fated first love. While David's reticence about resuming heterosexual romance in the wake of his failed first marriage seems the reverse of nostalgia for Dora herself, his emotional frozenness after her death and his inability to move the narrative forward—the degree to which his feelings for Agnes have lost all the spontaneity and energy that characterize the earlier part of the novel—enforces our sense that the abandonment of what Dora and Steerforth represent has irredeemably wounded David. While David hyperbolically performs the ritual of renunciation and atonement for his earlier failure of emotional and sexual discipline, the very excess inherent in this performance, as when he says that after his seduction of Emily his former friend is dead to him, calls into question whether Dickens fully believes in the resolution of the conflicting impulses that divide his hero and that may well have divided himself.

Nevertheless, in the last part of the novel, Agnes is envisioned as the magical resolution of the impasse created between the impulsive energies of youth and the disastrous consequences to which they led. Like David, she has been compelled to grow up too quickly and hence possesses a precocious self-discipline. Yet as a childhood friend she returns David to his original memories of quasi-familial warmth. If anywhere in the novel there is a clear celebration of domestic virtue, it is in Agnes. Yet, even in depicting Agnes, who functions symbolically to reconcile the tension in the novel between individualist desire and the nurture of others through selflessness idealized in domesticity, Dickens shows an uneasiness with the celebration of feminine self-denial which bespeaks his unease with the entire domestic mode. The prominence of Betsey Trotwood in promoting the novel's marital resolution is one clue to this unease. As a separated wife, Betsey is herself a figure of alienation from domesticity and a de-idealized view of romantic love, but unusually for Dickens, her feminine independence is treated quite positively, and earlier in the novel she mediates between the feminine extreme of sentiment and weakness of Clara and the masculine extreme of callousness and discipline of Murdstone by enforcing the discipline and practicality of the latter with the sentiment and compassion, albeit carefully veiled, associated with femininity. Once again at the novel's end she emerges to play a mediating role, this time between Agnes's feminine reticence and David's masculine self-denial. She tells David that Agnes is going to marry soon, a hint that by allowing David to realize the hidden love that Agnes has had for him all along also enables him finally to avow his own love for her.

The striking paradox of this last movement of the plot is that David has become so hypermasculine in his disciplined self-denial that he becomes feminine in his passivity; the problem of exaggerated gender roles visible in so many of the novel's marriages (Murdstone-Clara, elder Copperfield-Clara, David-Dora) has stubbornly reemerged. Agnes, on the other hand, is also hyperbolically feminine; indeed, in this part of the novel she anticipates the figure of the hysterical woman, a character type increasingly important in Dickens's late fiction, as her long years of self-denial finally culminate in an excess of pain under which even her prodigious self-control crumbles. The genealogy of Agnes's preternatural selflessness is revealed in the chapter entitled "Agnes," where David learns of how her mother suffered rejection by her father—her only surviving parent—in marrying Mr. Wickfield. The deathblow to Agnes's mother was her father's rejection of her plea to obtain forgiveness "before my Agnes came into this world" (707). Thus Agnes's mother is ideally selfless, sacrificing all for love, making a final tragic effort at restoring a relationship with her father even as she is about to give birth to Agnes, as if to create a connection not only with her own past but on behalf of the child to come. Wickfield's loss of his self-denying wife devastates him and makes him overdependent on his daughter. Thus unsurprisingly, he reads Agnes as a replica of her mother: "I have always read something of her poor mother's story, in her character" (708). David follows her father's lead, reading Agnes as perfectly suited for self-denial, particularly in love: "I felt, even [in their childhood], that you could be faithfully affectionate against all discouragement, and never cease to be so, until you ceased to live" (709).

David's reading of Agnes is valid insofar as it suggests her strong tendency to loyalty. What it fails to capture is the evident cost of her self-abnegation and sexual repression. Even the mother's story, read closely, is in part about the destructive impact of containing emotional pain. "[The mother] was always laboring, in secret, under this distress; and being delicate and downcast at the time of his last repulse . . . pined away and died" (708). Her secrecy in harboring the pain of her father's rejection—a "labor" indeed—may well have been an element of the pain itself: the mother's self-smothering concealment of her pain is part of what kills her. Certainly Agnes in turn suffers from the pain of concealing her frustrated passion for David. This pain is made clear in a passage following the one above: "For an instant, a distressful shadow crossed her face; but, even in the start it gave me, it was gone; and she was playing on, and looking at me with her own calm smile" (709). Agnes plays the piano here, an image of her general performance of her femininity; but her performance of the role of self-denying woman living only for others is finally disrupted when she has to face the reality that David's complacent reading of her character as actually thriving on self-punishment may consign her to "cease . . . to live" before he recognizes her love.

By now the reader has considerable evidence of Agnes's love for David: Betsey Trotwood has hinted to David that Agnes has feelings for someone, and in addition to her long-established loyalty to David, there are strong clues as to who that someone is. Such clues include Agnes's laying "her hand

upon her bosom" (705) upon first seeing David return from abroad following Dora's death, her keeping a shrine of his childhood possessions, her pale-
ness and flushing when David presses her for secret information she has
withheld, and her urging David not to travel again. It is David who by insisting on seeing Agnes only in angelic form as his "solace and resource . . .
always before me, pointing upward!" (709) disembodies her to the point that
he neglects to see the actual frustrated and lonely woman before him, associating her instead with her role as emblem of his childhood and surrogate
mother for her father and now for him.

Two months later, when Betsey Trotwood's heavy hints have brought
David close to understanding the truth of Agnes's eagerness to marry him,
she is pushed to the brink of hysteria by David's stubborn inability to grasp
her feelings. When he presses her for the identity of the man she loves, she
"burst into such tears as smote me to the heart" (723). David's demand that
she confide in him causes her to cry so violently that David can hardly understand her: "'Oh, spare me! I am not myself! Another time!' was all I could
distinguish" (723). Agnes, always perfectly in control of comforting and
moral utterance, can hardly speak and tries to withdraw from the conversation. She is indeed "not [her]self" even while to the end she maintains her
self-denying refusal to acknowledge her love for David until he has taken
the initiative. The scene corroborates what the earlier moment in which Agnes's expression momentarily changes suggests, which is that Agnes has two
selves, an exterior self fully compliant with, and performing superlatively,
the social role of "disinterested" woman (to use Betsey Trotwood's word for
her [704]), and another hidden self who passionately loves and desires to be
loved. Agnes's conflict only resolves itself when David finally proposes and
she gratefully accepts.

The potentially comic incongruity of the scene's sustained failure of com-
munication, which Dickens perceives but carefully suppresses, is retrospectively replayed in an overtly comic incident that follows in which David
bluntly tells Betsey Trotwood, much to her annoyance, that "Agnes is not
unhappy in any attachment" (726), whereupon he reveals the meaning of
his words by "[taking] Agnes in my arm to the back of her chair, and we
both leaned over her" (726). In both of these scenes, double meanings in
language are used to suggest the difficulty of matching one's expected gender role with one's inner feeling; David and Agnes's theatrical performing of
their bond for Aunt Betsey brings together hidden feeling with public display in a comically exaggerated form, which, of course, draws attention to
the way in which gender roles are always a performance, not merely a natural reflex of the inner nature, which is the subversive lesson that Agnes's

story suggests. Moreover, the word "hysterics," which is obviously relevant to Agnes's suppressed feelings in the earlier scene, is finally openly invoked, but this time for Betsey Trotwood's amused response to the scene of overt love rather than Agnes's intense pain of concealed love. Dickens often uses comedy for serious purposes. Here the comedy of the public acknowledgment of David and Agnes's love defuses the tension of the scene between the two of them that precedes it, while picking up some of the earlier scene's misread communicative cues. Dickens suppresses the potential comedy in the proposal scene because what is potentially comic is also, for Agnes, potentially tragic; were David to remain oblivious to the clues prompting him to avow his love for her, Agnes would suffer silently, presumably until death, rather than abandon her selfless and asexual role as spiritual guide and mother figure. She teeters on the edge of becoming perennially "not [her] self" in the role of frustrated old maid, forever pining for an offer of love that never comes.

Agnes's near-hysteria in the face of David's self-involvement is significant because it shows how David's complacent reading of her through the lens of domesticity's idealization of the self-denying woman wreaks havoc on the psyche of a real woman with passions and desires. And yet it is precisely this role of self-denying domestic spirit that David requires in order to overcome the impasse that the novel's movement has taken him toward. Having not mastered a version of the self that allows him to fulfill his sexual and imaginative energies in adult life, he psychically takes refuge in the nostalgic return to the childhood life that Agnes embodies. His actual experience of adult life and sexuality is largely elided in gesturing to his married life with Agnes, which in the novel's final lines is metonymically equated with the end of life: "O Agnes, O my soul, so may thy face be by me when I close my life indeed; so may I, when realities are melting from me like the shadows which I now dismiss, still find thee near me, pointing upward!" (737). Eloquent as this ending is, its emphasis on spiritual guidance on the path to mortality underlines how finding fulfillment through Agnes is a turn away from the vibrant imaginative and sexual energy that David and other characters in the novel show. The implication is that fulfilled domesticity is possible only through a shutting down of such unruly energies in mature life.

Mary Poovey has argued that in this novel Dickens links domesticity and the profession of writing precisely because both were ideologically constructed as transcending the class and market divisions of Victorian society.[15] Indeed, there is no question that domesticity overtly sponsors authorship in *Copperfield*, just as Dickens's celebration of domesticity endeared him to, and enhanced his status for, his Victorian readers. The penultimate paragraph of the novel makes clear how Dickens makes his writing derive its moral authority from its affiliation with blissful domesticity: "My lamp burns low, and I have written far into the night; but the dear presence, without which I am nothing, bears me company" (737). But in the earlier scenes, which show that even Agnes, the catalyst for David's inner peace, has suffered intense psychic pain while playing her assigned role, Dickens once again covertly questions his culture's domestic ideology. The sexual frustration and desire for fulfillment implicit in the pain of Agnes's tears calls into question the success of Victorian ideology in remaking bourgeois women into selfless and disinterested angels. Indeed, these final scenes suggest that the success that does occur is productive of a split between the performed role and the women's inner anguish. Agnes's "distressed look" is the incipient symptom of the discontent with her lot that Dickens diagnoses women, especially sexually frustrated women, as often covertly feeling, and that can become, in its hypertrophied form, the rancorous ressentiment of a Rosa Dartle. But if domesticity is ultimately tainted either by energies of ressentiment or frustration as in the cases of Rosa Dartle and Agnes, or subverted by feminine self-involvement or sexual desires, as in the case of Clara Copperfield, it is a fragile house indeed.

Thus, Dickens portrays domesticity as a house of cards, incapable of reliably securing the bourgeois individual's happiness; yet he accepts the bourgeois ideological norms of the centrality of family and women to individual happiness, and, like many in his age, he saw domesticity as a bastion against the class menaces outside the bourgeois home. Ultimately he shows intense skepticism about the capacity of women and domesticity to insulate men from the corrosive energies of ressentiment and economic competition, because he sees women themselves as easily seduced from their posts, either by their feminine weaknesses of vanity and sexuality, or by frustration, even brooding ressentiment, at their own limited lives.

DICKENS'S LATER FICTION AND THE RETREAT FROM DOMESTICITY

In his later depictions of families, Dickens fleshes out the skepticism about domesticity already implicit in *David Copperfield*. The hysterical repressed single woman, unable to acknowledge her inner division over sexual needs, is anatomized in much greater depth in Esther Summerson of *Bleak House*, while the profoundly ressentiment-filled woman reappears in *Great Expectations* at different class levels in Miss Havisham and Mrs. Joe; the self-involved and childish woman is anathematized again in such characters as Pet in *Little Dorritt*, Lady Dedlock in *Bleak House*, and Stephen Blackpool's alcoholic wife in *Hard Times*. In every case Dickens makes the failure of femininity to live up to its highest ideals the cause of the family's inability to bequeath the individual a secure identity and allow him to transcend the menace of class conflict. Indeed, in many cases feminine failures or malevolence substantially exacerbate class-based conflicts, as in *Great Expectations*, where Mrs. Joe precipitates the murderous ressentiment of Joe's apprentice Orlick (causing his crippling attack on her) by refusing to let him emulate Pip's holiday visit to Miss Havisham, a visit expressive of Pip's aspiration to self-improvement, and where Miss Havisham, a kind of evil stepmother, diabolically stirs Pip's disdain of his lower-class origins by holding out upper-class Estella as a prize to him and allowing him to mistakenly read his "expectations" as proceeding from her own benevolence and as intended to lift him to Estella's class status.

There is a continuity in Dickens's use of familial ideology in that he invariably uses departures from familial norms as indications of personal and social failure. In this sense, even his most negatively portrayed families can be seen as implicit endorsements of conventional ideals of gender role behavior and familial harmony. What is striking, however, are the numerous signs that beneath the surface contrast between the failure of Dickensian families and Victorian familial ideals, there is an increasingly pronounced disaffection in his novels from the orthodoxy of domestic ideology itself, and a corresponding dissatisfaction with the conventions of domestic fiction. Inasmuch as Dickens's alienation from the domestic mode derives from the tension between his strongly liberal sense of the rigidity and hyper-moralism of Victorian domesticity and the essential immobility of the culture's conservative commitment to established social and familial ideals, the root of this alienation lies in the frustration of his larger political impulses toward liberal reform. And indeed, the sense of more general political frustration has been much more obvious to readers of the late fiction than his disquiet specifically with domesticity. But Dickens's growing alienation from domesticity is also visible and important in its own right. It contributes substantially to the impasse that developed in his relation to his readers, many of whom were disappointed in his later works, and it causes major weakness in the fictive strategies of his later fiction. As he becomes increasingly cognizant of how domesticity failed to work as the dominant ideologies claimed it should, he was compelled either to offend his audience by attacking their cherished domestic ideology or to diagnose and explain domesticity's failure, primarily by blaming women, the central actors in domestic space and narrative, for not making families work as ideally as they should have. The latter literary and ideological strategy locks him into rigid and misogynistic stereotypes of women characters that, aside from their aesthetic weakness, risked offending women and feminist readers, a serious business for a writer who relied heavily on a female audience. We find as early as *Bleak House* (1852–53) his harshly negative portrayal of the female philanthropist Mrs. Jellyby and her friend the feminist Mrs. Wisk angering the women's rights advocate J. S. Mill, who comments in a letter "that creature Dickens . . . has the vulgar impudence in [*Bleak House*] to ridicule rights of women. It is done in the very vulgarest way[.]"[16] I will discuss in my next chapter the similar disdain George Eliot felt for Dickens's representation of women. Yet Dickens could not simply withdraw from familial topoi, for domesticity as a discursive mode was ineluctable for him, because it was precisely through this mode that he secured his status as a beloved novelist who deployed moral energies of middle-class feeling and sentiment against the brutality and callousness of the society that capitalism was creating around him.

Certainly in the fictions produced after *Copperfield*, signs of Dickens's lack of enthusiasm for idealizations of domestic life are everywhere. *Bleak House* is a dramatic example of this ambivalence. On one hand, it is partly narrated by the intensely domestic Esther, whose moral authority derives substantially from her exemplary performance of a domestic role, showing how self-consciously Dickens deploys the domestic mode as a voice of a simple moral authority. The triumphant tour of Britain by the American antislavery novelist Harriet Beecher Stowe as he was writing this novel no doubt reinforced Dickens's awareness of domestic fiction's moral force, though it is significant that Dickens was less than fully enthusiastic about her work, in which domestic fiction challenges a racism that Dickens shared.[17] As for Esther, despite her narrative's power, her moral authority can seem simpleminded, and Dickens subtly undermines her authority by suggesting the limits of her character, showing how she, like Agnes, is neurotically incapable of acknowledging her own feelings of repressed love and sexual desire. For example, when Esther decides to marry her guardian Jarndyce, despite her love for Allan Woodcourt, she can only comment, "I was very happy, very thankful, very hopeful; but I cried very much" (668); like Agnes, she is unable to articulate the tension between her respectable self-denial and her inner heartbreak. A split character, Esther is the voice of moral virtues whose integrity and common sense eloquently contrasts with the failed institutional life that victimizes the lives of the novel's characters. Yet at other times she is an all-too-obvious victim of domesticity's dysfunction and the feminine sexuality that domesticity cannot acknowledge—an appropriate role for the illegitimate child of a coldhearted, aristocratic woman. To the very end of the novel, Esther, as self-repressed as Agnes, is unable to admit her vanity about her pockmarked face or to acknowledge possessing the sexual passion her once-beautiful face signifies. Dickens further undercuts Esther's narrative authority by juxtaposing her with an omniscient and masculine-sounding narrator whose persona is far more cynical and histrionic and whose perspective is more wide-ranging than hers.

As we have seen, in another late novel, *Hard Times*, Dickens frontally attacks the inadequacy of divorce laws in showing the worker Stephen Blackpool indissolubly shackled to an alcoholic wife, thereby disrupting an ideological cornerstone of domesticity that saw the marital relation as permanent and sacred. It is a paradox of this novel, usually thought of as an attack upon economic liberalism and its utilitarian defenders, that it contains at its center this passionate vindication of liberal ideals in marital life. But the seeming paradox is a sign of how Dickens at once chafed at the limitations on individual liberty in his culture, including those affecting the family, while seeing the representatives of economic liberalism as lacking the proper human values to justly rule society. In the unhappy marriage of Louisa Gradgrind, Dickens repeats the failure of marital life on the middle-class level, thus reinforcing the point that failed marriages are a product of the culture's unresponsiveness to emotional life, as seen in Mr. Gradgrind, and its political immobility, as suggested by the novel's bitter refrain that life in industrial England is "[a]w a muddle" (292). In Dickens's vision, the failure of British society derives from the failure of the dominant classes to play successfully their paternalist role as generous masters of the people, and he hence depicts this failure through the disorder of individual families.

It is true that *Little Dorrit* (1855–57) has a traditional domestic finale, but its denouement, in which Arthur Clennam must be rescued by Little Dorrit from a near-coma while in prison for debt so that he in turn can rescue her from her nightmarish family, hardly constitutes a ringing endorsement of domesticity, imaging marriage simply as the last refuge of an exhausted masculinity and an exploited femininity. *Great Expectations* (1860–61), the Dickens novel most obsessively centered on narratives of class ressentiment, is also the one that most radically points to familial pathology. This dark and brilliant novel explodes the notion suggested by domestic ideology of families being capable of repressing or preventing ressentiment, by showing how the discontent of parents—especially mothers—and the helpless failures of fathers, becomes an engine that spreads the dark energies of ressentiment to the next generation. This pattern is shown through the blighting influence of Magwich and Miss Havisham on their respective pro-

tégés and symbolic "children," Pip and Estella, as well as through the destructive influence of the rebellious wife Mrs. Joe.

In the last three decades of the nineteenth century, there was a decided
backlash against domesticity among men, that culminated in the efflores-
cence of highly masculine adventure fiction, which emerged in the 1880s.[18]
This backlash against domesticity had roots in several phenomena: the contestation of masculine privilege both in the family and in society generally
that erupted in the 1850s and 1860s, the growing awareness that the optimistic vision of domesticity defusing class conflict was a chimera, and the
renewed fascination with the importance of the imperial enterprise and the
declining prestige of religious discourse, which tended to be linked with
domestic narrative. But these tendencies to displace domestic fiction's emphasis on the home with narratives in which women are either demonized
or marginalized and masculine identity thrives best in all-male environments have ideological and narrative roots as early as the later part of Dickens's career. We see this in how Dickens, both in his own work and in texts
he produces with Wilkie Collins, becomes preoccupied with producing fictions that glorify the unity across divides of class that unites men through
commitment to common imperial and scientific enterprises. In 1856 Dickens commissioned Collins to write a play (which he heavily edited), *The Frozen Deep*, designed to exonerate a lost British expedition of Arctic explorers
from allegations of cannibalism, a charge that Dickens saw as unjust and as
sullying British national honor.[19] The cannibalism charge, with its implicit
notion of a breakdown of community into a war of all against all, would
have suggested to the Victorians the nightmare of class conflict. The resulting drama presents the explorers as overcoming class differences through
exemplary self-sacrifice, with a male character who nobly sacrifices himself
for his romantic rival. Dickens responds similarly to a traumatic event for
the British, the Indian Mutiny of 1857, which dramatized the costs and
dangers of imperialism and stirred intense pro-imperialist and racist sentiments; because the reluctance of workingmen to be enlisted to fight the sep-
oys came to public notice, the mutiny also exposed the continuing class divisions of British society, horrifying Dickens. In response, he coauthors with
Collins "The Perils of Certain English Prisoners" (1857), which though ostensibly set in Central America alludes to contemporary excitement over the
mutiny and shows a community of British colonists heroically defending
themselves against attack by lower-class and racially Other pirates; once
again, British men unite across boundaries of social class, here against a bar-
baric enemy that threatens to assault feminine virtue. In such texts, imperial
enterprises allow men to assert a masculine identity far from domestic con-

fines. Indeed, by urging men to unite across boundaries of social class on behalf of a largely masculine imperial enterprise, these narratives can be read as reducing the need for domesticity's ideological role as a social glue that ameliorates class divisions.

While such works may seem a minor part of the Dickens canon, the thematic and narrative apparatus they develop has a large impact on his later work. The theme of self-sacrificing men uniting across class boundaries to defend femininity against corrosive and dangerous social divisions reemerges in the context of class violence in *A Tale of Two Cities* (1859), Dickens's novel of the French Revolution. In this novel, which reverberates with Dickens's deep anxiety about the class divisions of his own society, the ne'er-do-well Sydney Carton sacrifices himself by dying at the hands of the revolutionaries to protect the aristocratic Charles Darnay, thereby giving his life for the woman both he and Darnay love, a plot that echoes that of *The Frozen Deep*. In a parallel narrative of masculine renunciation at the end of *Great Expectations*, Pip, frustrated and humiliated at the failure of his project of class mobility and winning Estella, accepts the loss of his childhood sweetheart Biddy to his working-class stepfather Joe, apparently abandoning hopes of marriage and retreating to a self-sacrificing imperial vocation far from feminine entanglements.[20] In all of these late Dickens texts, masculine identity is secured through men's renunciation of the attractions of home and women rather than through enmeshment in them. Indeed, women (such as the demonic revolutionary Madame Defarge) are at times identified with racial or class Others that threaten society and that men must heroically resist.

Another striking early sign of retreat from celebrations of the domestic and the concomitant turn to constructions of masculine identity defined through homosociality and professional expertise is the rise of the figure of the detective. Dickens pioneers this figure in British literature in Inspector Bucket in *Bleak House*, though the role of the detective is enormously developed and the innovation of an entire novel organized around solving a crime is brilliantly introduced by Wilkie Collins's *The Moonstone*, serialized in Dickens's *All the Year Round* in 1868–69, in which the hero Franklin Blake requires the help of other males of a scientific bent to solve a domestic mystery, though one with an interestingly imperialist element.[21] This pattern of masculine homosociality and professional expertise protecting and policing a problematic and troubled domestic space, rather than entering into and forming an identity through it as in domestic fiction, becomes the model for Arthur Conan Doyle's hugely successful Sherlock Holmes stories of the 1880s and 1890s. By the end of his life, Dickens was at work on *The Mystery of Edwin Drood*, a novel in the vein of Wilkie Collins, a personal friend but also a writer with highly skeptical views of conventional Victorian morality. Dickens's attraction to the mystery genre toward the end of his career suggests how far he had moved from celebrations of masculine enmeshment in hearth and family.

It might appear that in emphasizing Dickens's ambivalent feeling about domesticity, I have cast him as the conventional figure of the Victorian hypocrite, and in his separation from his wife and affair with a young actress, Ellen Ternan, which involved him in an elaborate double life, there would seem to be evidence for the charge. But a more nuanced reading of the scandal associated with Dickens's marriage is instructive for what it tells us about the processes that characterized public image management and family conflict in the Victorian period. In 1858, after years of marital discontent, Dickens sought a separation from his wife. Frantic to minimize the damage that publicity and gossip about his marriage might wreak on his public persona, he allowed two veiled but revealing statements he had written on the separation to appear publicly. The statements blamed the separation from his wife on marital incompatibility and accused his wife of maternal incompetence, while stridently defending unnamed persons from slanders that he attributed to his wife and her family, in effect denying rumors he had committed adultery. Though the public may have been puzzled, the persons under suspicion were known by his associates to be his sister-in-law Georgina (who sided with him in the separation but whom no evidence links erotically with Dickens) and Ellen Ternan, who modern scholars believe did at some point become his mistress.[22]

Dickens's anxiety about his public reputation is understandable. Though his novels are landmarks of the modernizing process, which takes moral rhetoric out of the face-to-face setting of the parish or congregation and gives a new authority to market-mediated mass culture, in many ways Dickens himself embodied a "charismatic" form of cultural authority that had analogues with such traditional figures as the minister or the statesman and that was—and is—highly reliant upon public perception of its wielder's personal qualities. Dickens was deeply committed to enacting his public role as famed and respectable author, and by many gestures, from writing an autobiographical novel, to the words emblazoned on the cover of *Household Words*—"A Magazine Conducted by Charles Dickens"—to his highly successful reading tours, he constantly emphasized his personal identification with his own fictions and the ideals that they celebrated. If Dickens had compelling reasons to keep his public persona unblemished, its very fragility is also revealing. On a basic level, his clumsy efforts at image management shows a paradox inherent in his use of his charismatic authority at once to

promote the bourgeois ideal of personal autonomy and freedom while identifying these liberal ideals with an idealized and orthodox family form. Domestic happiness is typically envisioned as a bulwark of individual liberty
and happiness, counterposed to tyrannical opponents in the aristocracy or
bourgeoisie. But, as modern politicians and celebrities have found, the public role of model family member instigates a profoundly intrusive media examination of the private life of the individual that sharply curtails privacy
and can make a mockery of personal liberty. In this case, domesticity as discourse intersected with an emergent world of mass celebrity to leave Dickens
desperately trying to recover the privacy of his personal life and preserve his
personal autonomy.

It understates the case to say that the public statements Dickens published about his marital problems received poor reviews. Though his hysterical efforts to contain the gossip swirling around his family were maladroit,
spreading the very rumors he hoped to squelch and provoking skepticism
about his protestations of innocence, his status as exemplary Victorian family man made his public image genuinely hard to manage successfully. Significantly, many contemporary observers, even if neutral on the adultery
charges, harshly blamed him for the *publicity* he had given his domestic affairs. A writer who had fictionally expatiated at enormous length to a welcoming public on families, happy and unhappy, was widely scorned for publicly airing his own familial woes. In attempting to salvage his reputation, he
had violated a central tenet of Victorian domesticity, which was that the vi-
cissitudes of family life should remain separate from the public realm, and
he had also showed himself very publicly to be churlish to his wife. Such
criticisms must have reinforced Dickens's awareness of how familial ideals of
the period placed strict limits on individual freedom of action and further
heightened his alienation from idealizations of the family.

Critics have argued that the later fiction is influenced by the scandal of
the separation and by Dickens's relationship with Ellen Ternan. Though this
is true, one could make at least as strong an argument for tracing the path of
causality in the opposite direction from Dickens's favored gender
ideologemes to his management of his personal scandal. For Dickens's fictions, especially *Copperfield*, are eerily proleptic of the women-blaming discourses he uses to defend his own domestic behavior. Reading Dickens's letters and public statements about his separation from his wife, in which he
claims that their marriage was "as miserable a one as ever was made," that
his wife was a terrible mother, a mentally unbalanced woman who had
"fallen into the most miserable weaknesses and jealousies," one recognizes
patterns familiar from the mature novels.[23] To defend his own conduct in

real life, Dickens again produces narratives comparable to his fictive ones of a beleaguered and innocent masculinity, subverted by incompetent and malevolent women, especially mothers (he accuses his mother-in-law of falsely defaming Ellen Ternan). Though after the scandal Dickens did use fictions and subterfuge to manage his personal life, using a pseudonym when visiting Ternan, it seems likely that his obsessive, nearly paranoid narratives in life and art of male identity beset by malign or inadequate women genuinely reflected his ambivalent feelings about women. Certainly these narratives reflect preoccupations–with maternal ineptitude and feminine moral weakness—that were both culturally pervasive and personally compelling to Dickens. The subordinate position of Victorian women, the way in which their subordination was enforced by holding them to rigorous moral standards and emphasizing endlessly the importance of domestic virtues amid a culture often callously indifferent to offering assistance to nurturers of children (one that in other contexts celebrated individual self-aggrandizement), essentially made such ideological and psychic preoccupations with female deficiencies inevitable. The scapegoating of women, noticeable in Dickens's fiction from *David Copperfield* on, resonated in his life as well, as a characteristic reading of the failure of the typical marriage and as a defensive response to pervasive anxieties and incipient challenges to masculine freedom and authority. On a personal level, such scapegoating was a defense against rumors of infidelity and disloyalty to his spouse and children and was also a way of articulating his own frequent impatience with family life itself; more generally, it defended against having to acknowledge the inherent contradictoriness of Victorian domesticity, which envisioned selfless altruism and nurturance flourishing mysteriously in the midst of a culture of brutal and egotistic competition. Scapegoating women as morally deficient in domestic virtues, and consequently responsible for their own discontent, was also a defense that allowed Victorian men to gloss over and trivialize how at midcentury the inherent tension between liberal individualism and women's rigid subordination was beginning to become an overt cultural and political issue. This issue was visible in the growing evidence of feminine discontent. Agitations for changes in women's status (such as efforts to give middle-class women access to higher education and to reform property laws in their favor) begin to emerge, the plight of "superfluous women"—unmarried middle-class women with limited economic options—was widely discussed, and *Jane Eyre*, a powerful and angry novel about such a woman, appears in 1847, shortly before *Copperfield*; Jane Eyre is probably a direct influence on Esther's narrative in *Bleak House*, though Esther's discontent is far more veiled than Jane Eyre's.

The scandal of Dickens's separation and adultery also suggests the wide divergence between the emotions and opinions many Victorians felt privately about sexual and gender issues and the tenor of their public—and at times even their private—stances. In 1853, describing to his wife a trip he took with Wilkie Collins, Dickens wrote, "[Collins] occasionally expounds a code of morals taken from modern French novels, which I instantly and with gravity smash[,]" but goes on to add "these absurdities are innocent" and "[we] are all the best of friends, and have never had the least difference."[24] These complacent comments are not easily reconciled with the picture of the stern moral patriarch damning Collins's lax moral code that appears earlier in the letter. The most likely reading is that whatever Dickens's real stance toward Collins's views, a powerful bond of male camaraderie and shared masculine attitudes, much like the homosocial bonds that unite David and Steerforth, made Dickens tolerant of his friend's unorthodox moral principles, but to a female audience, he minimized the power of these bonds and depicted himself as an apostle of moral rigor. Moreover, clearly Dickens knew of Collins's common-law wife, whom he met socially. Given his private toleration of Collins's unorthodox sexual norms and his own clandestine relation with Ellen Ternan, Dickens's private opinions on sexuality were probably closer to the individualistic and transgressive code of a Wilkie Collins than he would ever publicly acknowledge. Rather than engaging in facile moral condemnation of Dickens's hypocrisy, it is probably more fruitful to see him as a man conflicted and divided over questions of gender and sexuality (as is David Copperfield), at once believing in domestic orthodoxy, the importance of feminine purity, and the separation of gender roles as the necessary moral cements of his culture, while in private yearning for, and accepting, a greater latitude toward sexual behavior than orthodoxy allowed for the pursuit of pleasure, community, and love.[25]

We find in Dickens's ambivalence toward domesticity, reflected in the subtexts of his novels, an early instance of a division, more visible in our own day than in his, of a chasm between an ideology of liberal individualism and the lingering power of a traditional rhetoric of moral restraint and conventional familialism. As British society becomes increasingly organized around principles of economic liberalism and capitalist modernization, the power of traditional moral rhetoric would wane. In our day, as in Dickens's, public figures and private individuals struggle to balance the desire to affirm community and to express the hortatory fervor that traditional domestic and moral rhetoric offers, with the reality that the lure of individualist ideologies constantly offers rewards to individual self-seeking. What is significant here about apparent hypocrisy, in the Victorians' day and ours, is both the personal anguish these divisions entail and the potentially profound difficulties that societies face in legitimating practices of domination and hierarchy, such as of men over women, given the deep tension between a society's commitment to ideals of self-seeking and competition as guiding principles and a contradictory continuing commitment to a traditional, if fraying, moral framework of familialism and general moral restraint. In truth, widespread hypocrisy, whether in the Victorian age and our own, suggests not merely individual weakness but a society in the process of changing its sexual mores and unable to confront rationally the reality of such change.

Ultimately, domesticity becomes for Dickens a highly unsatisfactory series of conventions. Yet what is striking is that without an alternative that his social position as promoter of domesticity allows him, Dickens nearly always reaffirms, at times almost mechanically, the necessity of marital resolutions. Unable to explore his impatience with his culture's sexual repressiveness openly, he largely displaces his ambivalence about domesticity into an obsessive portrayal of the failures of women to live up to its ideals. In the later fiction, even where he shows masculine selfishness and complacence as contributing to familial conflict, it is inevitably women whose roles as mothers and wives, or objects of male courtship, make their failings most disastrous and poisonous for family and society. Women, above all mothers, become scapegoats for the failure of domestic arrangements that he sensed were unsatisfactory but that his commitment to traditional gender hierarchies and his own social position made it impossible for him to openly question. The result in the late works is brilliantly vivid and powerful fiction, but fiction marred by a failure to stay consistent to the best elements of his vision, for at his most thoughtful, Dickens knew that odious personal behavior often results from malign societal arrangements, not merely from individual failings. He shows this, for instance, when Uriah Heep reveals that his duplicitous "cant of humility" (485) has been taught him by the systematically hypocritical charity schools in which he was raised and hence derives from larger structures of class domination. In contrast to such a radical insight about class domination, Dickens's keen perception and disaffection from the rigidities of Victorian family life did not prevent him from putting the heaviest blame for familial failure on women's individual moral weaknesses and psychic frailties. By diagnosing and resolving familial ills in this way, he absolves himself from complicity in the masculine privilege that Victorian gender arrangements gave him, and that his own fictions show repeatedly led to male selfishness, callousness, and cruelty.

Through his intense investment in familial narratives and his powerful celebration of familial communities, Dickens is the greatest domestic novelist of the nineteeth century. His powerful evocations of troubled families anticipate, both in their insights and their bias against women, the medicalizing and often women-blaming discourse of modern psychoanalysis, with its obsession with the figures of the female hysteric and the failed mother. But in both their achievement and their limitations, such fictions open the way to the more subversive and deeply analytical assaults on domesticity that were to come. Indeed, revising domesticity in later Victorian fiction would require both building on Dickens's achievement in domestic narrative while also resisting his all-too-evident masculine bias. So it is not surprising that such revisions would come most powerfully from a novelist more alienated from the mainstream of Victorian life than Dickens and one who was herself a woman.

3

The Crisis of Community and the Historicization of the Feminine in *The Mill on the Floss*

For George Eliot, who began her literary career when his popularity and fame were at their peak, Dickens is the inevitable predecessor. His importance as a model for her was accentuated by the fact that they shared many values and attitudes, and that she deeply admired him as a man and a writer, an admiration that was mutual.[1] Both novelists felt a strong commitment to elevating the status of novel writing and envisioned the novelist's role as a voice of social and moral criticism. Perhaps most importantly, Eliot agreed with Dickens that the world of industrial capitalism was morally repugnant, and she was as aware as he of the destructive impact of market relations and class divisions. But far more than Dickens, she was sympathetic to the difficulties that Victorian society created for middle-class women. Indeed, her fiction is in large measure a sustained effort to correct the overly simplistic and stereotyped portrayals of women and families that characterize Dickens's novels. The brilliant success of her correction of Dickens's example in the representation of the family would show later writers in the British tradition the inadequacies of conventional domestic fiction as a fictive mode and would offer an alternative model for representing the family that would emphasize, and more subtly trace, the problematic relation of the individual to the family, putting the individual's alienation from the family at the center of ambitious British fiction. Given the prestige and power of Eliot's achievement as a novelist, her influential revision of domestic fiction helps propel the representation of the family in British literature toward the focus on disaffection with family life that characterizes modernism.

As we have seen, by relying on stereotyped images of femininity as either self-sacrificing and quiescent or destructively narcissistic, Dickens pillories women as complicit in, even responsible for, the psychic and social evils of an industrializing society. Again and again, he links them to the callous treatment of children and the corrosive effects of class snobbery and ressentiment because they fail to fulfill their assigned role as bearers of values of disinterested love and fellow feeling. As horrified as Dickens was by the inhumanity of industrial society and despite his genuine sympathy for women trapped in oppressive circumstances, he opposed any major change in conventional gender roles, rather implying that women needed to emulate models of domestic perfection. In contrast, Eliot understands more deeply and commits herself more strongly to showing how the subordination of women was a nightmare for individual women, and what is more, she reads the frustration of women in a confining family life as a symptom of the nation's political and social malaise. Though she shares with Dickens a willingness to subvert domestic ideology's rigid conventions, she is more willing than Dickens to exculpate women from blame for failures of social harmony and compassion. Eliot was cautious in her expression of feminist impulses, but *The Mill on the Floss* (1860), arguably her most subversive novel, takes as a central theme the barriers to women's development and delineates how the tensions arising from economic conflicts caused by an emergent industrial capitalism are displaced into a tragic scapegoating of the heroine. Because these themes so precisely mirror and rewrite the disproportionate blame for social ills that women had been assigned in Dickens's novels, they suggest that Eliot was deliberately correcting the misogynistic bias of her masculine predecessor. Indeed, by infusing the representation of feminine subjectivity with the sense of women as a product of particular historical moments, she showed the importance of feminine subjectivity as a topic while irrevocably disrupting the tradition of static and stereotypical images of women in the home.

The radicalism of Eliot's project in revising conventions of domestic narrative has been underappreciated because inadequate consideration has been given to two crucial contexts for Eliot's work. One such context is the insidiously rigid and women-blaming conventions of domestic fiction to which she responds, and which we have noted in Dickens's late fiction. Another crucial context for Eliot's representations of women is her profound concern, which she shared with many Victorians, with the coming of industrialism and her awareness of its often deleterious effects on human communities. The basis of Eliot's powerful revision of domestic narrative is her insight into the societal impact of industrial capitalism. No British novelist more astutely connects this social transformation to its effects on women's lives. Eliot's dark vision of nineteenth-century femininity sees it as impeded and trapped by the problematic societal matrix that industrialism creates. She shows a shrewd understanding of how in the nineteenth century women were constrained by both long-standing traditional barriers to their development and by the profound and novel impact on communities of the transformative forces of commercialization and industrialization, an intersection of social forces that caused women's aspirations to rise but left them with few opportunities for fulfilling them.

ELIOT AND THE CRITIQUE OF DICKENS

Eliot's differences from Dickens are of a piece with the larger trend in nineteenth-century fiction toward increasing realism. Eliot defined her fiction as programmatically realist in intention, and this is a significant way in which she distances herself from Dickens. But this aesthetic credo glosses over how her dissatisfaction with Dickens's precedent also derives from specific moral and political values. Though she shares with Dickens a commitment to the reform of a British society transformed and polarized by industrial capitalism, there is a political agenda undergirding her moral legitimation of her own fictive practice. For Eliot sees her inward-turning and psychological fiction as more capable than earlier fiction was in promoting sympathy and understanding across boundaries of class and circumstance—a stress on the power of feeling and compassion for others that links Eliot to the spirit of romanticism. She believes that to bridge the gap between the social classes—and the genders—will ultimately promote social reform. Eliot's project of writing a new kind of realist fiction to heal social chasms is inextricably bound up with her revision of the Dickensian approach to character, particularly to women characters. While her fiction's ostensible goal was the fostering of cross-class understanding, she inevitably found her fullest fictive vocation in exploring female subjectivity. Though her fiction turns only gradually toward the discovery of this subject, her reaction against the Dickensian mode is, from the beginning, complexly overdetermined by aesthetic, moral, and political values, values informed by her middle-class radicalism as much as by her gender.

In her 1856 essay "The Natural History of German Life," written shortly before her turn to fiction, she praises the concreteness of the German social scientist Wilhelm von Riehl's depiction of German social classes, and contrastingly condemns Dickens (not named but the clear referent) for failing to depict his characters from within and his inability to understand how social conditions actually affect human sensibilities: "We have one great novelist who is gifted with the utmost power of rendering the external traits of our town population; and if he could give us their psychological character—their conceptions of life, and their emotions—with the same truth as their idiom and manners, his books would be the greatest contribution Art has ever made to the awakening of social sympathies. But . . . he scarcely ever passes from the humorous and external to the emotional and tragic, without becoming as transcendent in his unreality as he was a moment before in his artistic truthfulness."[2] This passage clearly shows Eliot's eagerness to understand, from a notionally "objective" middle-class standpoint, the position of the lower orders ("our town population"); this impulse is part of her articulation of a middle-class reforming impulse at a time when pressure from below is viewed with intense suspicion by British elites. The mere representation of the lower orders as Dickens practices it, she argues, is not enough. Their inner feelings and conceptions must be carefully read by the middle-class writer.

Eliot's stress on the importance of a mediated and skillfully interpreted perception of the lower classes' inner selves—for how could such a mystery be plumbed without enormous skill and knowledge—is suggestive of her elite-dominated conception of the nature of social reform. It also reminds us of the political basis of her ideal of fiction. Though sharing with Dickens an aspiration toward social and political reform, her work is largely devoid of the ambivalent sympathy for populist outbursts that Dickens's work can evince or his often affectionate acknowledgment of the virtues of popular sociality; for the older writer, revolution still has the prestige attached to it of the progenitor of bourgeois democratic ideals. It is clear that for Dickens combustible pressure from below, though potentially terrifying and often distrusted, offers hope for the achievement of democratic, antiaristocratic goals: the broadening of democracy and the reform of an industrial society. For this reason, in Dickens's fiction, sheer anger against the established order (as in the tragicomic fulminations of the "man from Shropshire" in *Bleak House*) is given a certain respect. In contrast, Eliot, responding to an era in which pressure from below seemed to generate only the success of reaction, as in the failed Continental revolutions of 1848–49, or the frustrated Chartist movement in Britain, and mistrustful of the growing clamor for a more widely based democracy, places her hopes for reform in morally sensitive elite reformers who will carefully manage aspirations for social change.[3] Indeed, by her programmatic effort to enlist her reader's sympathies for the humble, she casts the novelist herself—one with sufficient skill to understand the lower classes' inner selves—as a crucial agent of political reform. The combination of profound appeals to sentiment and serious intellectual argument that typifies Eliot's best fiction, and that encourages the reader to contextualize and sympathize with her characters' situations, is motivated ultimately by Eliot's commitment to an elite-led social reform. She devises this new fictive strategy by drawing on the increasing prestige of scholarship and scientific knowledge, forms of knowledge that hold themselves aloof from traditional and popular biases and assumptions. Her clear-eyed distance from domestic pieties and ideals is part of this emulation of sociological objectivity, a key inspiration for her rigorously de-idealizing form of realism. The stately, essayistic, and elaborately nuanced prose and intellectual manner of her fiction, so strikingly different from the theatrical, emotive, and demotic prose of Dickens, embodies her elitist and intellectualized agenda. Both in how she writes and in what she says about the lower classes, and in her very obsession with the nuances of elite personal behavior, she reassures her middle- and upper-class readers that in her fiction *they* are in control and that *their* values will predominate.

If the class aspect of Eliot's project is to rearticulate the dominant fictional mode in a more elitist and intellectualized way than had Dickens, her subversiveness and originality as a novelist derives largely from how she also rearticulates fictional priorities away from the masculine-centered values and preoccupations of Dickens to focus on subjects and concerns that express feminine values and preoccupations. Her critique of Dickens quoted above is coded in a suggestively gendered manner. The very areas that were traditionally considered feminine fortes, of creating sympathy and understanding inner feelings, are seen as the sites of Dickens's complete inadequacy. He is stigmatized as merely an observer of "external" manners; since Victorian women were associated with internal space, both domestic and psychic, this attack suggests his work is vitiated by an overly masculine mode. Even the damning insistence that he is "transcendent[ly] unreal" in his "tragic" and "emotional" mode suggests that his failings are gendered. Although traditional tragedy had been a male-dominated genre, the Victorians tended to associate deep and tragic emotion with the feminine. The tragic operas of the period usually have feminine protagonists; Cordelia loomed large in the Victorian conception of *King Lear*, and even Hamlet was, in the Victorian conception, a feminized figure. Dickens himself, from Little Nell and Florence Dombey to Little Dorrit (the latter two visibly derived from Cordelia), consistently uses women as centers of pathos. To call this tragic vein in Dickens "transcendent[ly] unreal" is hyperbolically to minimize Dickens's achievement in the depiction of femininity and to trivialize him as a writer of moral seriousness and tragic weight.

At its root Eliot's critique of Dickens has a moral basis in that, for her, Dickens's fiction fails adequately to teach the reader the moral virtues of sympathy and understanding. But this critique is rooted in both her gender and in her class stance as a middle-class reformer. By stressing the need for an understanding of the inner emotional life of characters, she privileges the educated elite's strongest suit, their capacity to analyze and interpret. She distances herself from merely external depictions, which she suggests are by their shallowness and lack of intellectual depth akin to the common people that they depict. In contrast, her critique claims that inward-focused representations possess superior efficacy for promoting social reform and stirring human sympathy. While the goal of promoting reform is implicitly universal, the inward-focused and cerebral representations are those most likely to interest well-educated elite readers. In advocating a universal goal, she implies criteria that are exclusive and class-biased. But her class politics are inextricable from the gendered nature of her discourse. By emphasizing the value of feminine specialties of understanding and sympathy, and Dickens's failure in such feminine spheres, she suggests that a feminized fictive mode could achieve more than Dickens's novels could "to . . . awaken . . . social sympathies," and hence spur reform.

In short, it could be claimed that Eliot's hidden agenda in critiquing Dickens is essentially feminist and designed to undermine the masculine bias of her predecessors. Though Eliot's feminism was a very cautious one, it is certainly true that in her acerbic essay "Silly Novels by Women Novelists" she argues that the elevation of the status of the novel—one of the few intellectual or literary genres readily accessible to women—was a vital prerequisite to a vindication of women from masculine prejudice. She caustically criticizes the failures of many "women novelists" because they do not take the genre of the novel with sufficient seriousness to elevate both the genre and, implicitly, the status and esteem granted women writers. Whatever her degree of feminism, Eliot is indubitably a pioneer in developing the novel as an agent of the exploration of feminine consciousness and feminine self-assertion. Her fiction takes up the opening that Samuel Richardson (one of Eliot's favorite writers) had offered middle-class women. By framing the novel as having as its preeminent subject a minute attention to inner and domestic experience, Richardson had elevated the status of the novel and made it thoroughly bourgeois, but he does so in a way that left it ripe for feminine exploitation as a genre both prestigious and yet peculiarly suited to the training and proclivities of women writers.

Yet if there is a feminist impulse to Eliot's redefinition of fiction, there is also a clear class politics to her strategy, one with ultimately conservative consequences. Eliot, like Richardson before her, elevates the social status of the novel by feminizing its content and thereby stresses the psychological richness of its potential subjects. The turn from the male-centered fictive procedures of Dickens to the female-centered one of Eliot's is a movement toward the reassertion of middle-class identity within literature, both in its emphasis on the novel's social status, its impeccably high tone and bourgeois seriousness, and by linking the entire middle-class habitus with the literary. This repositioning of the novel builds on the preexistent social identity of the middle class, an identity already feminized by being organized around the sacred influence of the privatized bourgeois home, the site par excellence of female influence. So, while conquering a valuable territory for feminine subjectivity, Eliot's project also inevitably narrows the implied audience of serious literature. By her sheer sustained inward focus, painstaking development of character and intellectual substance, and subordination of the external details and melodramatic narrative elements of earlier writers, Eliot advances significantly the process, which reaches its pinnacle in our age, by which high literature is set off from the popular in a radical way, so that it goes without saying that serious literature is not a popular concern. Her intellectual bent and detachment from the idealization of family life makes it not surprising that she will trigger an epoch of literary innovation, in large degree because she begins the search for a new moral center of gravity for serious fiction, a search advanced innovatively by Eliot herself, especially in her late novel *Daniel Deronda,* one that could substitute for the stability that had once been provided by domesticity itself.

It may seem curious that Eliot's procedures prove so unstable and prone to provoke further innovation when in fact she is traditional enough to replicate the literary strategy of the eighteenth-century Richardson. After all, like him, she takes a literary culture with a rather rambunctious masculine cast and feminizes its dominant genre, redirecting it toward a profound inwardness, a fixation on domestic sites and on intense evaluations of the fine moral questions of personal life in which women specialized. But Richardson's strategic move occurs in a vastly different moment, when the reassertion of the familial still has an implicitly popular overtone in contrast to the gentry-dominated literary culture against which this innovation occurs (as witness the wide success of *Pamela*, the story of the virtuous serving-maid): Richardson is still enacting an intrusion of demotic and quotidian concerns into an elitist literary tradition. Writing when so few in the population could read, his sentimentalization of literature was an innovation in content that was part of a larger movement in which matters of plebeian concern shoulder their way into the forefront of the elite sphere of literature, thereby making its concerns more relevant to a wider readership. By Eliot's day, this movement has long since succeeded, and what is at stake is not a broadening of the literary audience but its internal differentiation into "serious" elite readers and a critically disdained popular audience. Eliot's intellectual tone, subordination of sensationalist plot elements, and preoccupation with the upper orders, with rural venues and with the past (*Middlemarch* is set in the 1830s, *Romola* in the Renaissance), all function to narrow her audience, not to widen it; her turn toward feminine subject has little of Richardson's plebeian appeal.

Walter Scott and the Nostalgia for the Past

While the Richardsonian example, with its massive development of the subject of individual, and particularly of feminine, subjectivity, is a powerful precedent for Eliot, her early fiction shows little evidence that she consciously planned to make discontented femininity her central subject. At first, when she dilates on women, it is often on their failure to live up to societal ideals, a topos deeply rooted in a conservative and moralistic tradition of representing women. Rather than Richardson, the masculine novelistic precedent (along with Dickens) most visibly present in her early work is that ubiquitous influence on nineteenth-century novelists, Walter Scott. He gives her access to a prestigious topic, well suited to enhance fiction's stature, which was of little interest to Richardson: history itself. While for Richardson, religious meanings provide the ultimate rhetoric of moral suasion, Eliot, writing in an age when scientific and scholarly projects had undermined the cultural authority of religion, sees a key source of her moral authority as a writer in the careful understanding of the historical past. In particular, the subject that fascinates Eliot in her first two novels is the passing away of preindustrial English country life, and in depicting, as she does in these novels, the contrast between the modernizing and the archaic features of the early nineteenth-century rural life, Scott's juxtaposition of the emergent and the disappearing features of historical eras is a powerful model. We see the impact of Scott clearly in Eliot's first novel, *Adam Bede* (1858), which takes its title from its hero, an artisanal craftsman, and describes his various tribulations, most importantly the seduction of his intended bride, Hetty Sorrel, by the local squire's son, Arthur Donnithorne. In this deceptively simple story, Eliot suggests the historical process of the decline of the entire rural, preindustrial way of life, its utter and irremediable obsolescence for industrial England. Though set only six decades before its composition, the novel begins with a reference to the immemorial past, as if to emphasize the hoariness of its setting, the profound pastness of the past it will depict: "With a single drop of ink for a mirror, the Egyptian sorcerer undertakes to reveal to any chance comer far-reaching visions of the past. This is what I undertake to do for you, reader."[4]

All historical novels gain their effect by the contrast, implicit or explicit, between the historical era depicted in the work and the present in which the work is written and read. But in *Adam Bede*, to an exceptional degree, the pressure of the seldom acknowledged, but always understood, present is peculiarly strong and pervasive. The novel's deep nostalgia for the remembered past of preindustrial England, a nostalgia intensified by a crosscurrent of sardonic criticism, gains its full power only when read as implicit comment on the contemporary world of industrial England. In a mid-Victorian England, where workers were notoriously bound to their positions in the economy only by the impersonal cash nexus, Adam Bede attaches profound moral meaning to his work. While Victorian workers were degraded in crowded and violent urban slums, Adam works with simple dignity in a peaceful rural setting. While industrial workers, as Elizabeth Gaskell had recently dramatized in her novels, often harbored deep distrust, if not outright hatred, toward their employers, Adam is bonded to his social superiors by mutual ties of respect and even affection, bonds solidified through rituals of community sociality exemplified by the elaborately described Birthday Feast.

In its central irony, however, what the novel shows is the failure of this seemingly stable preindustrial world to reproduce itself, its self-destruction through psychic and moral torpor. These weaknesses, embodied in the morally feeble squire's son Arthur Donnithorne and in the well-meaning but feckless pastor Mr. Irwine, doom this idyllic world in the face of the new economic and psychic landscape represented by the itinerant preacher Dinah Morris's stern methodism and the industrial center from which she comes. Arthur's seduction of Hetty Sorrel, a callous destruction of Adam's hopes and dreams, typifies the failure of rural paternalism and of the communal bonds that sustain it. Though Eliot never completes the historical narrative she implies, her readers would have understood that the grim industrial landscape of "Stonyshire," from which Dinah emerges to preach her fervent brand of Christianity as if from a landscape of the damned, represents an image of the future that will increasingly replace the Adam Bedes of England and the communal bonds of rural England that sustain him.

For Eliot's development as a writer of feminine subjectivity, it is significant that the central example of failed community in this narrative is precipitated by the failure of female subjectivity to withstand the social and psychic forces impinging upon it. Hetty is inextricably both in love with desirable commodities and with the sexuality that Arthur offers her: "[Arthur] would like to see her in nice clothes, and thin shoes and white stockings, perhaps with silk clocks to them; for he must love her very much—no one else had ever put his arm around her and kissed her in that way" (147). Pathetically narcissistic, she worships her reflected image in a battered mirror obtained "at a sale of genteel household furniture" (145). Much like Dickens's Little Emily, but presented with far more detail and psychological astuteness and with an unsparing and unsentimental realism that fully elaborates her self-delusion and infantile narcissism, Hetty is shown to lack the capacity to resist the lure of commodities and hence the attraction of the higher class status that Arthur seems to offer, lures metonymically linked to her beloved earrings and to her battered hand-me-down mirror. Hetty's temptation by specious but genteel commodities suggests how the power of the marketplace, which looms on the historical horizon to threaten this rural backwater, is as subversive of this world's moral values as it is disruptive of its social and economic structure.

It is striking how fully Eliot replicates in *Adam Bede* the typical narrative displacement of larger societal dynamics onto failed femininity that we typically find in Dickens. The failure of values rooted in a particular class structure, in this case the solidarity of the rural preindustrial manor-based community is, as with Little Emily, rooted in feminine inadequacy. Superficially, in that her discontent with her lower-class position disrupts the solidarity of the working-class world and brings painful sexual and class realities to male characters, Hetty closely resembles a Little Emily or a Mrs. Joe. But the tone and implicit moral stance is utterly different than we find when Dickens tells a similar story. Arthur and Hetty are depicted analytically and even ironically, shown as inevitable products of the social determinants that produce them, rather than being treated with the sentimental and romantic emotion that characterizes the narrative of Emily and Steerforth. Moreover, Eliot revises Dickens's narrative procedure in two significant ways. By emphasizing the potent social determinants of failed femininity (the moral laxity of the gentry, the rigid subordination of women among the lower classes, the rural poverty and limited sophistication of Hetty), Eliot deliberately distances her narrative from a conventional misogyny. (To underline the absurdity of dogmatic woman-bashing and acknowledge the intellectual limits of this provincial world, Eliot introduces a superfluous friend of Adam's, Bartle Massey, who monomaniacally explains life's mysteries through the simple theory that women are the root of all evil.) And by placing the determinants of this failed femininity in the context of a larger historical movement in which the agrarian community is inexorably supplanted, she implicitly raises the possibility that the novel historical context of the present might allow for a more successful realization of femininity. In the context of a somewhat derivative novel, Eliot has already begun to subtly subvert the notion that female moral failure is a static and historically unchanging phenomenon.

At the novel's end, the Methodist preacher Dinah Morris agrees to marry Adam and to accede to the change in Methodist policy, which silences women as preachers, while the highly voluble Mrs. Poyser, stern matriarch of the yeoman farm, is chastened by her farm's threatened destruction after she rashly offends the landlord. These episodes hint that preindustrial society possessed social roles allowing female self-activity and authority that disappear as society industrializes and becomes increasingly commercial, confining women to a circumscribed private sphere. The novel does not unduly emphasize these chastenings, but stresses the collapse of the bonds that once held the preindustrial community together. Nevertheless, they are suggestive of Eliot's decided ambivalence about the role of women under industrial capitalism. These circumscriptions of female autonomy amid an emergent industrial world that will widen individual horizons and raise feminine aspirations are reminders of the paucity of opportunities for female self-development and authority that industrial capitalism brings, the subject that Eliot's next novel explores in far greater depth.

MAGGIE TULLIVER AND THE IMPRISONMENT OF FEMALE SUBJECTIVITY

The problematic status of women in an industrializing and increasingly commercial society hinted at in *Adam Bede* is central to Eliot's second novel, *The Mill on the Floss*. One of the first major works of fiction in the British tradition that radically subverts the assumptions of domestic ideology, this novel deserves careful consideration both for this reason and because it sets the mold for Eliot's later highly influential fiction. Thematically similar to *Adam Bede*, the novel centers on the contest between the stubbornly traditional preindustrial way of life and thought embodied in Mr. Tulliver and his son Tom and the modernizing impulse represented by the intellectual Phillip Wakem and the industrialist Stephen Guest, each of whom tugs in different directions at the heroine, Maggie Tulliver. This plot shows again the strong influence of Scott; Mr. Tulliver, and later his son, a sort of surrogate father for Maggie, are stern patriarchs trying at once to control his daughter and to resist the forces of historical change; they are versions of Scott's patriarchal

Mr. Deans from *Heart of Midlothian* transplanted into the nineteenth century.[5] As in *Adam Bede*, the decline of an archaic way of life and its supercession by modernizing agents is the central subject; indeed, in this novel the forces of commercialization and industrialization are far more overtly visible.

Though I emphasized how Eliot built on major masculine precursors, how she continues Dickens's preoccupation with the power of economic processes on familial and personal life and Scott's interest in large historical expanses and gradual processes of social change, in doing so my goal is not to minimize the radicalism of Eliot's innovation in the British novelistic tradition. Rather, it is precisely her willingness to carefully emulate models as prestigious as Scott and Dickens that allows her to insert herself successfully into the canonical tradition they embody and makes uniquely powerful her original and influential revision of the conventions of representation affecting women and the family. Eliot's emphasis on female subjectivity and feminist subversion of conventional domestic ideology is of course not without some precedent in British fiction, and indeed she was clearly influenced by some significant precursors, such as Charlotte Brontë and Elizabeth Gaskell, as well as the French George Sand. Margaret Doody argues persuasively that Eliot's focus on idealistic feminine characters struggling with the limitations imposed on them by society has precedents in Richardson and in the tradition of eighteenth-century women writers who follow him, and are often influenced by him;[6] certainly the Gothic tradition is filled with dark readings of the threats domestic sites hold for feminine subjectivity. As early as Mary Wollstonecraft's Gothic novel *Maria, or the Wrongs of Woman* (1798) we find an overtly feminist novel that locates the entrapment of women in Gothic spaces (the heroine is placed in a lunatic asylum) as a fitting image of how domestic ideology imprisoned women in a legal and cultural oppression. Closer to Eliot's time, Dickens had explored the oppressive father in *Dombey and Son*, the Brontës in their novels had shown women rebelling radically in thought and deed against conventional feminine subordination, and Elizabeth Gaskell had attacked masculine sexual privilege in *The Moorland Cottage* (1850) and positively portrayed a fallen woman in *Ruth* (1853). But none of these predecessors alter the momentous originality of what Eliot achieved, which was by the originality and power of her example to irrevocably alter the conventions by which women and their place in the family were represented in the British tradition of serious fiction. It is not for nothing that Henry James looked back on her achievement with awe (though also with ambivalence) and elevated the ambition of his own fiction by self-consciously revising her work in *The Portrait of a*

Lady, while other major writers who develop subversive readings of gender roles, such as Thomas Hardy and D. H. Lawrence, were influenced by her example.

Much of the *Mill on the Floss*'s startling originality is attributable to the fact that, if Scott's fiction provides the basic framework, the development of the subject shows that Eliot had assimilated a quite different influence, the notorious and highly popular French novelist George Sand. What Eliot derives most crucially from Sand is suggested in the following passage, in which Sand describes Marcelle, the heroine of *The Miller of Angibault* (1845): "She was one of those simultaneously tender and strong souls who need to devote themselves to something, and who can conceive of no greater happiness than that which they themselves confer. Unhappy in her household, bored by the world, she had abandoned herself with the romantic trust of a young girl to this sentiment, which soon became her religion."[7] We recognize here the source of the essential situation of Eliot's heroines, such as Maggie Tulliver and Dorothea Brooke, who chafe at the restrictions of the patriarchal family and seek to transcend its limitations through a spiritual commitment to an altruism that yearns to serve a cause larger than the self. Such an ideal cause can be circumscribed and Christian in character as it is in Maggie, or it can open into an enthusiasm for social reform as in Dorothea or Sand's Marcelle, but in each case the commitment to a larger cause allows the woman to transcend at least inwardly the constraints of the patriarchal family while remaining true to what Sand and Eliot conceive as women's nature in their unselfishness and lively concern for human feelings. (For Sand, and to a degree for Eliot also, the Christian impulse and the socialist, or at least reformist, passion are closely akin, as Sand justifies her socialism on the basis of Christian principles and Eliot, too, admires Christian ethical principles.) Such heroines, who move from the confinement of patriarchal family life to religious enthusiasm and ultimately to the secularized altruism of social reform, inevitably remind Eliot's readers of her own life, its dramatic movement from her provincial and deeply religious upbringing to the break with family's religious orthodoxy and her eventual decision to pursue an intellectual life and the socially unsanctioned union with George Lewes. Significant though the influence of her own experience was, the relation between Eliot's life and her art was not simple, and there is every reason to think that she discovers the power of such narratives of women struggling with societal constraints and moving through a spiritual phase by means of the mediation of similar narratives in George Sand, a writer she greatly admired. Both in her own autobiography and in her novels, Sand repeatedly writes narratives of women who are swept up by altruistic passions. As Sand recounted in her memoirs, as an adolescent, she had gone through a phase of deep religious passion, which ran its course and led her ultimately to secularize her spiritual and altruistic impulses into enthusiasm for the radical reform of a society disfigured by industrial capitalism. Whether Eliot patterned her life on Sand or simply had similar experiences because she was another highly intelligent woman living in the same historical epoch, Eliot clearly used Sand's work as a model for her characteristic narratives of women rebelling from patriarchy into idealism.

Both writers adhere to the pervasive nineteenth-century notion of women's character as qualitatively distinct from men's, as less selfish and more drawn to feelings and ideals. But the traditionalism of this conception of feminine nature should not blind us to the way Sand conceives feminine personality and aspirations in a radically original way by seeing it as fulfilled through engagement with a rapidly changing social order. In the passage that follows the paragraph quoted above, Sand comments of her heroine's socialist ideals:

> she had glimpsed . . . the social crisis that shakes this century. The women of our time are no longer strangers to these higher realms of thoughts. According to the bent of their minds, and without affectation or mockery, all of them can now read daily in the great, sad, amorphous, contradictory, but profound and significant book of real life: in all forms—journal or novel; philosophy, political discourse, or poetry; official statement or private conversation. So she was well aware, as are we all, that this bloated, diseased present time is at odds with the past which holds it back, and the future which calls it forward. She had seen lightning-flashes hurtling over her head, she could foresee a monstrous battle, more or less distant. (18)

For Eliot, as for Sand, the crucial change in women's position is that women can now read the book of "real life"; that they are beginning to acquire the intellectual reach to develop their minds and to question society's most basic structures. The importance of Sand as a model for Eliot is that she gave a fictive form to what was a central issue for Victorian women who aspired to move beyond their traditional limitations, the question of the relation women should take to the rapid social change that industrialism had brought. As society becomes wealthier and educational expectations rise, the limited education of even the most elite women begin to attract comment as arbitrary and a waste of human talent; the intense controversy that erupts about whether women should have access to university education is a symptom of the topicality of this question for Victorian women in the 1850s. The novel responds to this larger context by making the subject of education and

Maggie's relation to it central to its theme of the power of the repressive and parochial environment to thwart human development.

What is radically new in fiction was not new in political speculation. Mary Wollstonecraft, in *A Vindication of the Rights of Woman*, had powerfully formulated a radical solution to the problem of the relation of middle-class women's self-development to historical progress. In the ferment of ideas sparked by the French Revolution, Wollstonecraft argues that women's apparent moral and intellectual weakness was the result of society's refusal to acknowledge their human potential; humanity could only advance if there was a "revolution in female manners" which would awaken women's reason and make them an influence for rational benevolence,[8] rather than as they all too frequently had been, mere embodiments of vice and triviality, pernicious failings that they passed on to their children. Though her thought anticipated and influenced that of Victorian feminists, an anticipation that Eliot appreciatively noted in her essay comparing Wollstonecraft to Margaret Fuller, Wollstonecraft's radical conception of the necessity of women participating in the progressive movement of history through expanded education had little immediate impact. But as the passage I have quoted shows, in Sand's writing, women's conceptions of themselves and their relation to their families and to society in general are directly and powerfully influenced by the stormy movements of human history. Rather than assuming, as had previous writers, that women were outside of history or inevitably lagged hopelessly behind it, Sand conceives women to be, as Wollstonecraft had suggested, capable of standing at the forefront of social change through their self-development toward rationality. By giving Eliot narrative material and character-types through which realistically to embody and work through this radical political idea, Sand has a strong influence on Eliot. With the possibility that self-definition and psychic liberation could help make women agents of history, Sand creates a conception of the feminine personality that irrevocably changes the character of women's relation to society and to domesticity, and it is this change that Eliot brilliantly imports into British literature.

Eliot's indebtedness to Sand is suggested by *Mill*'s numerous parallels with her novels. *The Miller of Angibault* shares more with *The Mill on the Floss* than a title that refers to rural mills. Sand's novel tells the story of a young aristocratic widow who moves to the countryside to live out idealistic and democratic ideals, only to find her estate and the rural landscape of which it is a part inextricably caught in the web of a grasping rural capitalist. The novel's basic tension between a feminine idealism and the masculine forces of capitalist rapacity, found in a pastoral landscape where they are least expected, anticipates *The Mill on the Floss*'s relentless focus on the help-lessness of Maggie's spiritual idealism before the economic forces that en-mesh her and, indeed, her entire rural world. Maggie is clearly descended as well from another kind of Sand heroine, the passionate and transgressive heroines first seen in Sand's *Indiana* (1831).[9] Like *Indiana*, *Mill* focuses on pastoral innocence and suppressed feminine subjectivity, and figuratively they both make use of images of drowning and water and associations be-tween an oppressed woman and a dark-haired, Other femininity. In Sand's novel, her heroine Indiana has a Creole servant, Noun, who, seduced by the aristocratic man she loves, drowns herself in her despair. Later Indiana her-self, frustrated in her love for the same man, attempts suicide by drowning. Indiana's tortured and stifled female bourgeois experience thus is shown to strikingly parallel the lower-class and racially Other experiences of her maid, creating a narrative that links oppressions of class, race, and gender. Maggie Tulliver is similarly linked by plot and imagery to racial Others, drifts into sexual passion while on a boat with Stephen Guest, and finally is drowned in a flood. The most arresting parallel with Sand's work, though, is the rep-etition of the general pattern of character relationships. *Indiana* is structured around an adulterous triangle consisting of a patriarchal, quasi-paternal hus-band whose property contains a mill, an upper-class rake, and the heroine, a passionate woman linked to Otherness who turns to the rake more out of frustration with her own life than out of genuine love; Sand gives Indiana another man in her life, Ralph Brown, a fraternal admirer who suppresses his own love for her while loyally sympathizing with her oppression in her loveless marriage. This quartet of characters is carefully reproduced in *Mill*, with the significant deviation that the adulterous passion of the heroine is suppressed, though Eliot comes very close to it in her depiction of the trans-gressive love between Maggie and Stephen, who is at least tacitly betrothed to Lucy Deane. All of Sand's central characters reappear; the stern patriarch, who in accordance with the suppression of the adultery plot is not the hus-band but Maggie's father (and a similarly patriarchal brother), the upper-class rake (updated to industrialist scion), Stephen, and finally the sympa-thetic friend, Philip Wakem. Moreover, Eliot follows Sand in making her novel a political and intellectual allegory in which characters are associated with intellectual positions: the patriarch with stubbornly conservative nos-talgia for the past, the male friend with rational benevolence and belief in progress, the upper-class rake with moral laxity and subjectivism. And very much as Indiana voluntarily seeks death with Ralph, her ideal alter ego, so Maggie seeks death with her brother, her own embodiment of conscience and higher morality.

What is ultimately more significant than these numerous character and narrative parallels is Eliot's interest in Sand's treatment of her character's psychology, particularly the sympathetic portrayal of the passionate protagonist's unhappiness with the restrictions on her freedom, and the link between this unhappiness and her erotic attraction to the rake. Beyond the numerous narrative parallels, what Eliot clearly found an inspiration for in Sand was her willingness to write a narrative that challenges rather than supports the gender assumptions of Victorian culture, and Sand's ability to link the unconventional behavior of her heroines with a radical questioning of feminine social roles. When Eliot writes in an early letter to a friend that what she valued in Sand was her ability to "delineate human passion and its results," what she suggests is that she admired Sand's realism for its willingness to represent sympathetically characters who are at odds with the dominant social forces and codes of her day, which inevitably includes Sand's avoidance of the conventional moral hostility to feminine sexuality and her strong sympathy with feminine discontent. (Characteristically, in this letter Eliot carefully evades endorsing Sand's unconventional moral views.)[10] Eliot borrows from Sand the very plot devices, such as the link between the heroine and racial Otherness and the presence of a masculine friend who embodies a rational critique of patriarchy, that Sand uses to figure feminine alienation, especially of passionate and sensual women. She uses them for purposes similar to Sand's, to underline the painfulness of women's self-suppression and their passionate, if often self-defeating, response to their oppression by masculine domination. True, in accordance with British sensibilities and her own Protestant values, Eliot tames the amoral passions of Sand's heroines. Sand's heroines typically rebel against patriarchal restrictions through love for a man other than their husband. Given her awareness of the harshness of patriarchal domination that women experience, and with the relatively relaxed attitude toward sexual impulses of French culture, Sand often portrays such adulterous feelings sympathetically. Such moral latitude is a logical corollary of Sand's belief that women must inevitably free themselves from a stultifying domestic situation to realize their natures, which as we have seen she identifies with the progress of human history.

Sand's readers were often dismayed by her candor in discussing sexual feelings, and frequently disapproved of how her novels seemed to rationalize sexual immorality. Certainly, in suggesting that women's capacity to read and respond to the "real life" of their times could put them reasonably at odds with the authority of fathers and husbands, Sand's work does break in a startling way with the moral rigidity of previous domestic fiction and raises the possibility that adulterous loves were understandable, if not virtuous. Adulterous love in the context of a Sand novel can seem a moral failing but an inevitable one, at least a natural reaction to an oppressive social situation. Henry James, reflecting the English-speaking world's intense sexual moralism, would caustically remark of this aspect of her work: "if her heroines abandon their lovers and lie to their husbands, you may be sure it is from motives of highest morality."[11] If Sand most significantly influences Eliot in encouraging her to represent women's self-development as an inevitable aspect of historical progress, Eliot was clearly reluctant to defy her contemporary's moral sensibilities with Sand's audacity, and Eliot also faced in the British context a more moralistic reading public. Yet, within the limits of her more cautious strategies, Eliot is clearly influenced by Sand's representation of sexuality. Traditionally, women had been endlessly condemned by association with their sexuality, a fact of which Eliot is intensely aware of and which she thematizes in all three of her early books of fiction. Thus, it is a significant element of Eliot's imitation of Sand's advocacy of sympathy for women's situation that to a degree she adapts her analytical and dispassionate stance toward sexuality, a stance that defuses the traditional hysterical condemnation of sexual transgression and the inevitable concomitant denigration of women as morally frail or dangerously tempting. Given the greater latitude allowed to men in sexual matters, Eliot's clinical attitude toward sexual transgression is often most clearly visible in her representation of male sexuality. As early as *Adam Bede*, her dispassionate representation of Arthur Donnithorne's lust for Hetty had been detailed and objective enough to shock Victorian readers, and the representation of Stephen and Maggie's mutual attraction in *Mill* (much more openly explored on Stephen's side) provoked harsh condemnation from some reviewers.[12]

As if anticipating such responses, the novel stigmatizes the self-righteous condemnation of Maggie's alleged sexual fall as reflecting irrational prejudice on the part of the "world's wife," adding one final telling blow of prejudice to the long string that dogs Maggie's career.[13] As Eliot cynically points out, society ("the world's wife") typically "judge[s] others according to results" (490). If Maggie had secured a desirable marriage to Stephen Guest, moral condemnation would have faded ("What a wonderful marriage for a girl like Miss Tulliver—quite romantic! Why, young Guest will put up for the borough at the next election. Nothing like commerce nowadays!" [491]). Since her flirtation has not so ended, moral condemnation descends upon her in full force. Here we see the bringing together of the two thematic strands that dominate the novel: the growing power of the market in the novel's social world and the development of the heroine's character and her rebellion against society's constraints upon her, above all her struggle against the intense sexism that she faces at every step.

❦   ❦   ❦

The theme of the development of Maggie's personality has tended to dominate critical discussion of the novel, and the unification of the novel around Maggie is indeed an impressive achievement. This carefully controlled unity is another symptom of Eliot's efforts to elevate the status of fiction by respecting both tradition and contemporary critical ideals. Contemporary critics sought novels that were clearly unified, not split into various parts by extraneous characters and plots; Eliot responds to this demand by creating an unusual degree of unity around a single character's situation and personality. Indeed *Mill* is one of the first British novels to achieve this degree of unity. While Jane Eyre and David Copperfield are the center of their respective novels, they coexist with characters in striking contrast to them who distract to some degree from the central focus on the character of the protagonist. In *Mill*, on the other hand, though there are long sections that appear to neglect Maggie and focus on her father or her brother, both narratively and thematically everything in the novel is tightly linked to tracing the influences on Maggie's development. Mr. Tulliver's every action and trait, his stubbornness and practical independence, his love of the mill, his capacity for deep love, are expressions of a version of Maggie's own character. She shares her father's intense independence and passionate nature, his bond to the land, his great capacity to love, not least of the parent whose favorite child she is. She replicates her father's strengths and weaknesses even while suffering from his faulty decisions. Similarly, Tom, exactly in being revealed as "a stolid British type," is shown to be the striking contrast with Maggie, with her rebellious and darkly passionate nature. This contrast between siblings is not at all extraneous to the novel's themes, both because the conventionality of the father and brother are the embodiments of the parochial world that confine Maggie and because, paradoxically, Maggie finds in her father and Tom her refuge and her purpose, a loyalty and a passionate attachment that links Maggie first to the father and then to the son in an intense love that may well be intensified by her inevitable rebellion against their authority. Thus Maggie's love for her family bursts with a tremendous and self-lacerating loyalty to men who repeatedly deny her sufficient love in return. In this way, the more we see the obstinate mule-headedness and insensitivity of Tom's character (and also of his father), the more fully we understand the difficulty of the situation that Maggie faces in her commitment to such a man and to the male-dominant yeoman world he embodies.

Even the painful scenes of Tom's education, which show him struggling vainly to learn Latin and geometry, only to have his brighter sister, despite her educational deprivation, help him to understand the most basic fact about Latin—that it was once a spoken language—makes a point that is essential to our understanding of Maggie, that she is constantly and systematically deprived, by irrational social prejudice, of educational and cultural opportunities that she is far better suited to than her obtuse brother, a deprivation synecdochic of the pervasive foreclosure of economic and intellectual opportunities that middle-class women face.[14] When Tom's education is shown to be outdated and worthless for the career of businessman, the deprivation of education Maggie has suffered is further ironized; what had effectively excluded Maggie from male privilege does not even enable Tom to meet the requirements of a changing marketplace. And after her father's decline, Tom, a caricature of the worst features of the father, will dominate Maggie's situation. When the children are forced by their father's ruin to focus on practicalities, it is the stern and unbending brother as much as the unfeeling family clan that are the restrictive environment against which Maggie inevitably rebels.

The situation in which familial closeness is interrupted by the harsh dictates of the wider world has fictive precedents; for instance, David Copperfield's intense intimacy with his mother and the servant Peggotty is disrupted by the advent of Murdstone, the mercenary second husband. But Eliot tightens the screw of criticism of Victorian families by making the harsh bringer of the bad news of market-dominated and class-structured selfishness and competitiveness, not the forbidding stepfather but the apparent equal and playmate Tom. Dickens allows us to imagine that the problems of the family are external ones that descend cruelly from the outside to infect the family, or are the result of individual moral failure, such as Clara Copperfield's failure to protect her son or Mrs. Steerforth's overindulgence of Steerforth. But Eliot, more clear-sighted and analytical, portrays family life more realistically, showing that Tom's stubbornness and lack of feeling, his tendency to domineer over his sister, is neither a product of forces external to the family nor simply an individual moral failure, but is behavior rooted in the masculine privilege that has always characterized traditional families. The harsh economic world to which Tom must subject himself, and which he in turn embodies for his sister (in his unforgiving hostility to his father's economic opponent Wakem and his son Philip), simply reinforces his original tendency to dominate and oppress her with his masculine privilege. Where Dickens reads failed families as signs of individual moral failure, Eliot understands the power of the structural imbalance of power between the genders of the typical Victorian family and the devastating results of this imbalance. It is true that in depicting her heroine as alienated by her family's gender inequality, particularly a favored and tyrannical brother, Eliot builds on a theme that earlier women writers had addressed; Elizabeth Gaskell's *The Moorland Cottage* has a heroine, Maggie Browne, who faces a similarly arrogant and sexist brother, and like Maggie Tulliver, that character struggles to balance her own desires with loyalty to her brother. Eliot's originality, however, is that while clearly showing the typical gender inequality of the Victorian home, she creates out of that context a genuinely complex female heroine who is not a pattern of moral perfection but a complex woman whose development is warped by her oppressive family situation.[15]

Important as Maggie's psychological progress is in unifying the novel, the larger significance of her progress is only comprehensible in the context of the second major thematic strand in the novel, the increasing power of market relations in her world. Her father's commitment to his mill and to his traditional wisdom by which "water is water" faces a losing battle against the forces of commercialization and, ultimately, industrialization, that the Wakems embody. Mr. Tulliver's ambivalence toward education, desiring it for his son as a practical necessity but fearing the larger impersonal world of law to which education gives access, is characteristic of his conflicted and ultimately bewildered relation to the processes of economic and cultural modernization: "I want to give Tom a good eddication; an eddication as'll be a bread to him. . . . It 'ud be a help to me wi' these lawsuits, and arbitrations, and things. I wouldn't make a downright lawyor o' the lad—I should be sorry for him to be a raskill—" (9).

Mr. Tulliver, a small farmer and miller enmeshed in legal conflicts over water rights with a prosperous lawyer and his wealthy client, epitomizes the declining yeoman class. Though Eliot undoubtedly knew that in this period the yeomanry struggled against difficult odds, she presents Tulliver as complicit in his own defeat because of his fierce pride and passionate attachment to the land. This attachment is never more touchingly presented than when, after his financial collapse, Tulliver is offered employment on his former land under his enemy Mr. Wakem: "But the strongest influence of all was the love of the old premises where he had run about when he was a boy, just as Tom had done after him. The Tullivers had lived on this spot for generations, and he had sat listening on a low stool on winter evenings while his father talked of the old half-timbered mill that had been there before the last great floods which damaged it so that his grandfather pulled it down and built the new one." Eliot contrasts Tulliver's love of place to how "Our instructed vagrancy, which . . . runs away early to the tropics, and is at home with palms and banyans, . . . can hardly get a dim notion of what an old-fashioned man like Tulliver feels for this spot, where all his memories centred, and where life seemed like a familiar smooth-handled tool that the fingers clutch with loving ease" (263). As this scene progresses, Tulliver connects the mill to memories of his family, which associatively is linked to his love for Maggie: "my mother—she was a fine dark-eyed woman, my mother was—the little wench 'ull be as like her as two peas" (264). Even as Tulliver in memory tries to hold on to the continuity that memories of the past and a preserved relationship to a place can provide, his interlocutor suggests the forces that are altering the world and threatening a stable connection to place: "'Ay, sir,' said Luke, with soothing sympathy, 'what wi' the rust on the wheat, an' the firin' o' the ricks an' that, as I've seen i' my time—things often looks comical'" (263–64). Luke's reference to the violent protests against the introduction of threshing machines suggests the market and technological forces that will devastate the yeomanry and their sentimental bonds to the land; modernization will favor landowners with access to capital, encourage commercial speculation in land, and militate against small landowners like Mr. Tulliver.

Even while cognizant of the harsh social context such a yeoman faces, Eliot does not present Tulliver as a sentimental figure of declining rural virtue; indeed, to a striking degree, she shows the irrationality and prejudice with which he interprets his situation, thereby hastening his own defeat. From the novel's opening pages, Eliot stresses how he irrationally reads his opponent Wakem as an agent of the devil, foolishly takes the auctioneer Mr. Riley's advice to educate Tom as a gentleman under a parson (despite the irrelevance of such genteel education for Tom and his son's unfitness for it), and proudly quarrels with his wealthy in-laws, a quarrel that compels him to mortgage his property. His hubristic and disastrous decision to "go to law" with Mr. Wakem is spurred by an impulse to defy the demands of his wife, seen as "representative" of his in-laws, the proud and genteel "Dodson family" (157), that he not do so. His naive eagerness to defeat those above him in class status, by genteelly educating his son, adds to his expenses and contributes to his defeat. Moreover, this vindictive plan is further vitiated by his overreliance on his male child; his traditionalist male prejudice causes him to ignore systematically the potential contributions of the female members of the family. Though he admits of Maggie that "It's a pity but what she'd been the lad—she'd ha' been a match for the lawyers *she* would" (19), Maggie is of course denied the education to which her precocity might have entitled her. Her father admits that he "picked the mother because she wasn't o'er 'cute," but this characteristic distrust of female intellect contributes to his failure to reproduce his own values, as his son represents the father's character frozen into mindless traditionalism, continuing his father's resentments and rigidity, while lacking his saving capacity for love.

For in Tulliver's conflict with his wealthy relatives the Dodsons, we see the country farmer Tulliver's capacity for love contrasted with the unfeeling pride and mercenary spirit of the urban middle class. The most striking instance of this tension and of Tulliver's loving nature occurs when, in desperation to pay back a loan he owes his brother-in-law, Tulliver goes to his sister and her husband, poor farmers, to demand repayment of money owed him. At the last minute he relents and abandons hope of repayment, moved by the association of his sister, Mrs. Moss, with Maggie: "he was not long in seeing his relation to his own sister side by side with Tom's relation to Maggie. Would the little wench ever be poorly off, and Tom rather hard upon her?" (81). Because of the power of Tulliver's love for his daughter, feeling trumps financial calculation: "his love and anxiety for 'the little wench' had given him a new sensibility toward his sister" (84).

This scene is proleptic of how, throughout the novel, Maggie represents the passionate and loving side of the Tulliver nature. After the financial and physical collapse of her father, it is she who angrily rebukes the Dodsons for their money-obsessed hard-heartedness in presiding over the auction of her mother's household goods. But it would be a mistake to see Maggie simply as a representative of a wild and untamed preindustrial spirit in feminine form rebelling consistently against the commercial logic of a modernizing world. Eliot is perfectly aware of this as a potential narrative possibility; that Maggie shares a name with Scott's Madge Wildfire, just such a passionate relic of the past, may not be coincidental. In an early episode in which young Maggie, angry at her family's mistreatment of her, runs away to join the gypsies, we see Eliot playfully toying with, even while rejecting, such a narrative development. Young Maggie, with her grandiose and painfully naive ideas about becoming the gypsy "queen" and civilizing these wild characters, becomes a figure of fun, though also of pathos, as she is menaced by the somewhat bewildered gypsies. Clearly a return to a preindustrial wildness is not a realistic possibility.

Yet if Maggie is not a preindustrial woman tout court, her development is incomprehensible without considering that her conflicts are largely a product of her archaic and traditional preindustrial milieu. Thematically, it is central to the novel that she suffers from the extreme traditionalism of her father's and brother's attitudes. As in her flight to the gypsies, Maggie consistently rebels against this rigid prejudice. The very violence and helpless impotence of her rebellions, both as child and as grown woman, are products of her social world's rigidity and narrowness, on which Eliot constantly harps. In a famous passage Eliot calls the Tullivers and Dodsons, and the limitations of their mental outlook, irksome even to the reader: "you are irritated with these dull men and women, as a kind of population out of keeping with the earth on which they live—with this rich plain where the great river flows for ever onward, and links the small pulse of the old English town with the beatings of the world's mighty heart." Even "a vigorous superstition" "seems more congruous with the mystery of the human lot, than the mental condition of these emmet-like Dodsons and Tullivers" (272). The enormous condescension to which the central characters are subjected here is crucial to the novel's meaning. The narrative is centrally concerned, Eliot suggests, with the struggle of her characters against the limited thinking of these middle-class people of preindustrial England. The "oppressive narrowness" of this milieu must be depicted, "if we care to understand how it acted on the lives of Tom and Maggie—how it has acted on young natures in many generations, that in the onward tendency of human things have risen above the mental level of the generation before them, to which they have been nevertheless tied by the strongest fibres of their hearts" (272–73). This passage summarizes some of the novel's key themes. On one hand, her central character, Maggie, is representative of and beneficiary of the Enlightenment's classic narrative of progress ("the onward tendency of human beings"); but, on the other hand, this progress occurs at a great cost, given her environment and sex. She is "acted on" by the "oppressive narrowness" of the mental worlds of her community. Nor is the conflict merely between her and others; it is above all within herself; for Maggie is bound to the "generation before [her]" by the "strongest fibres of [her] heart[.]"

Eliot's use of the romantic topos of ties to native place and family is complex and somewhat self-subverting. On one hand, Maggie's deep feelings for her family are repeatedly linked to the power of the natural world over her. Like her father, she loves the landscape in which she has grown up and this love helps connect her to the people with whom she shares it. Yet the natural world's very transcendent immensity ("the great river flows for ever") embodies an ideal compared to which her two families of origin ("the emmet-like Dodsons and Tullivers") seem petty and parochial. While the romantic celebration of feeling rooted in particular natural space explains what binds Maggie to her specific geographical locale, the novel's current of romantic imagery and emotion also, by suggesting the human capacity for development and for awe before the transcendent, engenders a revulsion against the inadequacies of the historical and cultural milieu of that place, one that relentlessly restricts and limits Maggie's development.[16]

The lofty abstractions of this passage leave unclear in what way precisely this world is "oppressive[ly]" constricted, but in Maggie's case the answer is clearly largely through the prejudice against her gender rooted in the preindustrial traditions of her community and family. By the values of the mid-Victorian age, in which the idea of sophisticated education for middle-class women was becoming increasingly accepted, the Tullivers are aggressively and excessively denigratory toward feminine intelligence. Mr. Tulliver complains of Maggie. "[A] woman's no business wi' being so clever; it'll turn to trouble, I doubt" (17). Tom is even more convinced of the uselessness of female intelligence. When Maggie boasts, understandably, given her intellectual superiority to her brother, "I shall be a *clever* woman[,]" Tom is certain that such a trait in a woman will be despised: "O, I daresay, and a nasty conceited thing. Everybody'll hate you" (146). Later, when Mr. Stelling confirms Tom's prejudiced view, he exults to Maggie: "You'll never go far into anything, you know" (145). And Eliot tellingly comments, "And Maggie was so oppressed by this dreadful destiny that she had no spirit for a retort" (146).

Not only are Maggie's intellectual efforts discouraged and scorned, but she is continually attacked by one of Western culture's most traditional and archaic misogynistic beliefs, women's superior susceptibility to moral temptation. In this period, the cult of domesticity often elevated women precisely for their superior capacity to resist temptation and indeed to rescue men (or erring women) from moral falls. In this context, the gloomy sense of the Tullivers that Maggie is to be blamed for any desires at all is an archaic and distasteful reliance on traditional misogyny and women-blaming, one that almost comically compels Maggie to achieve domestic moral perfection. In a striking illustration of the theme from Maggie's childhood, she is offered a half of a pastry puff by her brother. As always, she desires to please him and would like to give him the superior half, the one with more jam. But he compels her to choose with eyes closed, which gives her the more jam-filled half. Maggie then offers the superior half to Tom, but he declines. Nevertheless, when she becomes preoccupied with eating her share of puff, he accuses her of being "greedy." Despite Tom's blatant unfairness, Maggie feels guilty: "She would have given the world not to have eaten all her puff, and to have saved some of it for Tom . . . she would have gone without it many times over, sooner than Tom should call her greedy and be cross with her" (47).

This odd childish scene is undoubtedly created by Eliot because it perfectly exemplifies the irrational rigidity and tyrannical tendencies that Tom has inherited from his family, and shows how a misogynistic feminine socialization inevitably stigmatizes female appetite and desire. The charge of being considered "greedy" traumatizes Maggie, despite the obvious reality that her impulses were merely those of ordinary appetite (combined with generosity toward her brother), not greed. Eliot is deeply aware of how the traditional scapegoating of women makes them experience their own appetites and desires as a central source of alienation. It is this very problem of feminine desire that becomes precisely Maggie's central problem in life.

Thus the pastry puff scene is proleptic of how a very similar irrational hostility is directed toward her natural appetite for companionship, affection, and intellectual development as expressed in her relationship with Philip Wakem. Not surprisingly, given her family's hostility to her mind, Philip functions primarily as a catalyst for Maggie's intellectual development. She says of their friendship, using the language of oral pleasure: "It has been very sweet, I know—all the talking together, and the books, and the feeling that I had the walk to look forward to, when I could tell you the thoughts that had come into my head while I was away from you" (335). And once again, as in the childish dispute over the puffs, her brother reads her behavior as simply feminine willfulness and weakness before temptation and thus as a sign of Maggie's incorrigible feminine rebelliousness leading to willful opposition to the family's goals. Having discovered her bond with Wakem, Tom tells her, "while I have been contriving and working that my father may have some peace of mind before he dies—working for the respectability of our family—you have done all you can to destroy both" (343).

Maggie thus faces, even as an adult, the crushing sense that her family—and the provincial society of which they are representative—is because of her sex unalterably hostile to the development of her individuality. The only way for her to be acceptably feminine is to abandon her deepest sense of self, which desires to develop into a "clever woman." Maggie confronts as a grown woman the kind of devilish double bind that, as a precocious child, she had noticed that suspected witches were once placed in: "That old woman in the water's a witch—they've put her in to find out whether she's a witch or no, and if she swims she's a witch, and if she's drowned—and killed, you know—she's innocent, and not a witch, but only a poor silly old woman. But what good would it do her then, you know, when she was drowned? Only, I suppose, she'd go to heaven, and God would make it up to her" (18). In this scene young Maggie (whose father quickly decides her reading material is unsuitable), sees and questions the prejudice against women of traditional culture and its threat to female survival—what good indeed is innocence to the victimized? The condemned witch was typically a victim not merely of prejudice but of scapegoating. The anxieties and superstitious fears of her culture were displaced onto her unfortunate head. Maggie's empathy for the victimized witches is proleptic of how she will become her brother's scapegoat for his rivalry with the Wakem family, and ultimately for the economic failure of the Tullivers to successfully adjust to the forces of commercialization and modernization that the Wakems embody. Like the accused witches, she will struggle, unsuccessfully, to avoid transcendence through innocent victimhood.

Just as the accused witch must look for a compensatory reward in heaven, so the only solution Maggie can find in young adulthood to being cast in the role of scapegoat and victim of displaced masculine anger is in a spiritual consolation. For if Maggie confronts prejudice against her aspirations, her confrontation with Tom over Philip dramatizes how she confronts conflicts that are not merely external but also internal. Tyrannical relatives are not uncommon in Victorian literature, and were Tom and her father's disapproval the only obstacle to her happiness, the novel would be far more conventional than it is. But Maggie, while resenting the injustice of her brother's prejudice against Philip and herself, feels an ambivalence about the wider social and intellectual world to which Philip introduces her. We can see this by completing the passage that I quoted above, in which Maggie tells Philip about what their relationship has meant to her: "But it has made me restless: it has made me think a great deal about the world: and I have impatient thoughts again—I get weary of my home—and then it cuts me to the heart afterwards, that I should ever have felt weary of my father and mother" (335).

THE HISTORICAL FORMATION OF WOMANHOOD

The full depth of Maggie's ambivalence flows from her deeply ingrained passion for self-abnegation. In one of the novel's most original and subversive episodes, Eliot makes Maggie's development a microcosm of the development of the Western mind from medieval otherworldliness to awakened rational self-interest. It is probable that Eliot was influenced in this novelistic strategy by the Hegelian philosophy that she had studied, which was fond of discovering such parallels of microcosmic and macrocosmic development and which stressed the historical influences on intellectual development. Consequently, this novel about the development of a nineteenth-century woman shows its protagonist going through a rapturous identification with medieval asceticism: "It flashed through her like the suddenly apprehended solution of a problem, that all the miseries of her young life had come from fixing her heart on her own pleasure, as if that were the central necessity of the universe; and for the first time she saw the possibility of shifting the position from which she looked at the gratification of her own desires—of taking her stand out of herself, and looking at her own life as an insignificant part of a divinely-guided whole" (290). One might cynically wonder if Maggie's ascetic phase is not a perfect preparation for the self-abnegation expected of women in conventional Victorian domesticity.[17] But the novel presents this phase quite otherwise, as a homeopathic and compensatory response to the intense self-denial and deprivation that her family's failing financial situation has forced upon her and her resultant intense alienation. (Certainly when we encounter Maggie's cousin the prosperous Lucy Deane, we see little sign of self-denial defining bourgeois femininity.) Facing the tightly drawn restrictions caused by her father's archaic economic position, Maggie's embrace of Christian asceticism replicates and exaggerates on a psychic and spiritual level the archaism of her economic situation. Far from being part of a smooth acculturation into Victorian womanhood, this development is rather an embrace of what is in any case Maggie's painful and inevitable economic fate as a member of a declining social class. Yet it is also a subtle response to her profound dissatisfaction with the limited psychic and intellectual rewards of that existence and, unconsciously, a rebellion against it. Eliot makes it clear that Maggie turns to religion precisely out of a lack of a meaningful narrative by which to incorporate and understand her suffering, and hence her religiosity expresses her alienation from her unfulfilling lot. If such asceticism is not likely to make her life any easier, it at least gives a meaning and a purpose to her life, and allows her the opportunity to make a strong sense of self out of what otherwise would seem meaningless deprivations. True to her commitment to exploring the inner life of characters of humble class status, Eliot stresses the class element of Maggie's situation and her urgent need for a sense of purpose in her deprived circumstances:

> In writing the history of unfashionable families, one is apt to fall into a tone of emphasis which is very far from being the tone of good society, where principles and beliefs are not only of an extremely moderate kind, but are always presupposed, no subjects being eligible but such as can be touched with a light and graceful irony. But then, good society has its claret and its velvet-carpets, its dinner-engagements six weeks deep, its opera and its faery ball-

rooms; rides off its ennui on thoroughbred horses, lounges at the club, has to keep clear of crinoline vortices, gets its science done by Faraday, and its religion by the superior clergy who are to be met in the best houses: how should it have time or need for belief and emphasis? But good society, floated on gossamer wings of light irony, is of very expensive production; requiring nothing less than a wide and arduous national life condensed in unfragrant deafening factories, cramping itself in mines, sweating at furnaces, grinding, hammering, weaving under more or less oppression of carbonic acid—or else, spread over sheepwalks, and scattered in lonely houses and huts on the clayey or chalky corn-lands, where the rainy days look dreary. This wide national life is based entirely on emphasis—the emphasis of want, which urges it into all the activities necessary for the maintenance of good society and light irony: it spends its heavy years often in a chill, uncarpeted fashion, amidst family discord unsoftened by long corridors. Under such circumstances, there are many among its myriads of souls who have absolutely needed an emphatic belief: life in this unpleasuarable shape demanding some solution even to unspeculative minds; . . . require something good society calls "enthusiasm," something that will present motives in an entire absence of high prizes, something that will give patience and feed human love when the limbs ache with weariness, and human looks are hard upon us—something, clearly, that lies outside personal desires, that includes resignation for ourselves and active love for what is not ourselves. (291–92)

Rarely is Eliot so openly caustic in commenting on the class division that separates her characters from her readers, who she anticipates will find the account of Maggie's religious phase "very far from the tone of good society." Linking class structure to individual psychology, Eliot sees religious passion as an effort to respond to alienation and the failure of human community ("human looks are hard upon us" "family discord unsoftened by long corridors"), a failure that she places in the context of a class-divided society in which the privileged have little understanding of the religious sentiments of the poor because they "float" obliviously above the hardships of their lives. Without endorsing Maggie's religious devotions, Eliot sneers angrily at "good society['s]" probable scorn for her heroine's "enthusiasm," placing such disdain in the context of the privileged classes' blindness to the anonymous labors that sustain them.

It is typical of Eliot's strategies of complex indirection that another obvious reason for Maggie's need for religious meaning in her life—her victimization by gender prejudice and her exclusion from the masculine project of actively restoring the family's fortunes—is not explicitly stated here, though it is obviously relevant. Maggie's fervent Christian forbearance and self-abnegation represent both a homeopathic embrace of her gendered role of quiet sufferer under the family calamity and a sublimated protest against the insistent masculine selfishness of her father and brother. In stubborn contrast to the relentlessly mercenary and egotistic behavior of the masculine part of the family, Maggie's deep spirituality and altruism constitute a quiet rebellion against their materialism and selfishness; as the chapter that discusses Maggie's conversion ends by pointing out, "Mr Tulliver did not want spiritual consolation—he wanted to shake off the degradation of debt, and to have his revenge" (294).

The most subversive element of this turn in Maggie's story is that Eliot clearly demonstrates how Maggie's profoundly feminine self-abnegation is not, as Victorian domestic ideology insisted, a natural outgrowth of woman's nature. Rather it is a twisting of her strong-willed nature in response to contingent and social forces rooted in class deprivation and gender prejudice. And, just as human history as read from the vantage point of the nineteenth century by a secular intellectual such as Eliot appeared as a movement from unreasoning faith and irrational self-denial to a rational pursuit of self-interest, so Maggie's development evolves in parallel fashion.

Bearing in mind that Maggie's ascetic religiosity is a gendered response to deprivation allows us to understand the novel's and Maggie's ambivalence toward Philip's blunt message to her, which amounts to: this is the nineteenth century, not the thirteenth; in this age, obsessive self-denial is unnatural and absurd. While deeply appreciative of his encouragement of her intellectual development, Maggie resists his dismissal of the impulse behind what he calls her "wilful, senseless privation." Having suffered considerably from individualist masculine self-assertion, she clings—even while implicitly accepting Philip's critique of her self-denial—to the sense of the importance of bonds of community: "it cuts me to the heart afterwards, that I should ever have felt weary of my father and mother" (335). While not rejecting Philip's rationalism, Maggie clings to a sense of obligation to human relationships and the communities they form. This sense of obligation—for Eliot a transcendent value—leaves Maggie unhappy with both her alternatives, the aspiring cosmopolitan Philip and the provincial yeoman Tom. For each are merely variants of egotistic masculine self-assertion, the former lacking respect for her loyalties to community, the former selfishly and pettily manipulating such loyalties. Unsurprisingly, given her intense ambivalence toward what he represents and her lack of passionate love for him, when her brother compels a separation between her and Philip, she even feels a "dim background of relief in the forced separation" (348).

THE SEDUCTIONS OF SELF-COMMODIFICATION

At this moment of blockage in Maggie's life, Eliot embodies Maggie's conflicts in a new form as the novel turns, with the appearance of the industrialist scion Stephen Guest, toward a Richardsonian—but also Sandean--narrative of seduction. It was this portion of the novel that generated the most adverse contemporary comment and that remains critically disputed today. What shocked Victorians was the candid admission of the physical basis for Stephen's attraction to Maggie—memorably embodied in a passage that minutely describes his fervent response to the beauty of her bare arm—and the novel's clear hints that Maggie has a similar physical attraction to Stephen. Victorian prudery aside, modern readers simply find Maggie's lapse from idealism into passion disappointing. But Eliot is logically developing Maggie's character: always willful and passionate, she has experienced a long period of stultifying deprivation as a schoolteacher against which she understandably rebels when faced with the gratifying pleasures of Lucy's bourgeois world and Stephen's seductive attentions; she has, as she says, "[gotten] the bad habit of being unhappy" (373). Philip's rationalist prophecy about her ascetic phase has proven accurate, that she "will be thrown into the world some day, and then every rational satisfaction of your nature that you now deny, will assault you like a savage appetite" (329). But the rational pleasures of which Philip speaks—music, fine clothes, masculine attentions—are inextricably bound up with her temptation to passion for the wealthy Stephen.

Eliot sees Maggie as faced with two tensions caused by the social change transforming British society. As we have seen, one tension is between her loyalty as a feeling and caring woman to her family and their local ties and connections to the rural world as against her attraction toward a more cosmopolitan and more enlightened world that, by breaking with the parochialism and patriarchal prejudices of the rural milieu, would offer her as a woman greater freedom to develop her individual talents. Eliot shows Maggie in her reading self-consciously resisting the sexist prejudices encoded in literary conventions, as when she notes playfully but correctly that such conventions show bias against women (such as herself) with dark hair. Such women had long been associatively linked both with unruly sexuality and with racial Others. She objects to Philip, "I'm determined to read no more books where the blond-haired women carry away all the happiness . . . If you could give me some story, now, where the dark woman triumphs, it would restore the balance. . . . Since you are my tutor, you ought to preserve my mind from prejudices" (332). In suggesting that dark-haired women and the qualities associated with them, such as sexual passion, are typically punished in novels, Maggie self-reflexively suggests how her own situation entails a struggle against both oppressive realities and also the prejudices and traditions of representation that support these realities. (Maggie's comment shows that Eliot is self-consciously combating sexist prejudices and traditions of depicting women, though it is sadly symptomatic of the novel's judgment of the stubbornness of social prejudices that Maggie's comment on the inevitable fate of dark-haired female characters anticipates her own.)

In a larger sense, Maggie's objection to the prejudice against dark-haired women suggests her growing consciousness and her creator's realization of the toll taken by the prejudices against women's self-development—which was often literarily coded as the necessarily tragic destiny of unruly, and often sexually transgressive women who were indeed generally dark-haired. The association of dark-haired women with tragic ends also suggests the way women were often associated—as Maggie is with historically defeated races of dark-skinned people—with those traditionally thought of as lagging behind or outside history. Traditionally, in both literary and philosophical texts, women had been put in a similar category, as necessarily embodying an earlier phase of historical progress; Hegel, for instance, reads women this way. But as we have seen, Sand offered Eliot a radically different reading of women's relation to history, in which their self-development could be seen as part of humanity's historic progress, indeed as furthering it, and in depicting Maggie's objection to the traditions she finds in literature, she is clearly reflecting Sand's influence and her own appreciation for the potentially liberating character of modernization for women.

But if Maggie's indecision between loyalty to family and tradition as against the embrace of modernization and self-development dramatizes the historically contingent nature of femininity, and sharply raises the possibilty that, as Wollstonecraft had argued, the advancement of women could ameliorate the human condition generally, by depicting in the last part of the novel a second tension in Maggie's position, Eliot also shows herself profoundly aware of the dangers for women deriving from the processes of industrialization, commodification, and the erosion of cultural traditions. This danger consists in that deprived of the moral and emotional mooring of traditions, Eliot sees women as potentially becoming mere commodities, indeed sexually degraded commodities, compelled by their lack of genuine autonomy and by the loosening of restrictions on sexuality, to purchase social position at the cost of marketing their integrity and, she covertly implies, their sexuality.

In Maggie's near-seduction by Stephen Guest, Eliot also reexplores Richardson's great theme, the feminine tension between love and the duty to family and honor. The eighteenth-century writer discovers the power of this theme when the new spirit of reason and the emergent bourgeois celebration of rational self-seeking began to make the situation of women, their individuality rigidly subordinated to family dictates, peculiarly fraught and potentially tragic. Clarissa Harlowe must choose between an understandable desire to express an individual self—a desire in a woman that premodern cultures would have laughed at or anathematized, but that the eighteenth century world begins to find deeply sympathetic—and the strict moral norms that require duty to a tyrannical family. For Eliot, too, Clarissa's dilemma remains the quintessential problem for women. Having suppressed herself to the point that she has been deprived of "rational" pleasures, Maggie now is prey to the return of these suppressed desires as "savage appetite," an appetite that threatens to burst through the bonds of familial and moral duty.

The crucial difference between how Richardson and Eliot conceive the problem of women is that for Richardson, Clarissa's self-suppression is inadequately successful (though she may not fully know it, she loves Lovelace), while in contrast Eliot conceives the fundamental problem as the very existence of limitations on the individual's development imposed by social and psychic forces. Compared to Clarissa, Maggie has *too* successfully starved her passionate self of its development, and she is as a result vulnerable to the surge of passion that Stephen incites. If Eliot reads rebellious individuality more generously than does Richardson, the two writers are equally diametrically opposed in their reading of the context of human community for their respective heroines. Richardson has a qualified confidence in the moral ethos of the human community embodied in Clarissa's friends and acquaintances. He shows how this community's moral values are potent enough that Clarissa is able, albeit only in death, to invoke them successfully and through her very public death and the agency of her posthumous letters to punish devastatingly her oppressors. But though Maggie as much as Clarissa is an innocent fallen woman, such a recourse to communal moral judgments is not available to her. In her fall she is utterly alone and estranged from her community, which responds to her situation only with hypocritical rejection and condemnation.

And while Eliot returns to the highly traditional Richardsonian topos of the conflict between passion and duty, she places her updating of this topos in a context highly subversive of Victorian domesticity. Conventional domestic narratives saw women's nature as static and unchanging. But Maggie's entire psychic development, from the novel's beginning to its end, is linked to the larger social context that molds her, and thus her individual development parallels and recapitulates mankind's historical development. In her early days her passions both for love and for anger are untamed; she resembles a wild animal or uncivilized human, an early phase of human existence, and as Susan Meyer has shown, she is in fact frequently associated with people that nineteenth-century British society considered primitive.[18] It is the business of civilization to tame this wildness. But Eliot suggests that British society goes too far in domesticating Maggie's independence, driving her into the extreme of a revived medieval asceticism. Just as human history has progressed beyond this phase, the novel suggests, so must nineteenth-century femininity. Through Philip's influence, Maggie allows herself to awaken to a new sense of her own individuality. In the novel's book 6, the arrested development of her selfhood reaches its culmination as she reacts against her self-abnegating existence as schoolteacher by savoring a number of the conventional delights of bourgeois Victorian womanhood: music, a charitable fair, and flirtation with men.

Eliot is as critical, if not more, of this self-commodifying phase of Maggie's career as of her ascetic moment, of which it is the logical corollary. Clearly the later phase, with its languorous and leisurely erotic rivalries and playful delight in sensual experiences—above all, the erotically charged world of music—is an emphatic reversal of the values of the first. By depicting Maggie's psychic development, from her spiritual awakening into self-denial to her fall into luxurious and then erotic temptation, as a series of understandable responses to precisely specified historical circumstances, Eliot suggests that each version of femininity that Maggie embodies is a product of the social and historical environment in which she is placed. By demonstrating that women are products of their time, the novel disrupts the conventional view of women as always identical to the static stereotypes of femininity promulgated by domestic narrative. And most startlingly, by encouraging us to sympathize with Maggie's temptation to erotic transgression—albeit one to which she never fully succumbs—Eliot daringly suggests that the respectable middle-class woman concealed some of the untamed passion that her stereotypical lower-class cousin, the fallen woman, so shockingly exhibited. Nor, crucially, does this hidden passion dehumanize Maggie by making her merely "fallen." It shows her fallibility, but as part of a sympathetic and complex view of her personality that understands her passion as an inevitable rebellion against the deprivations and barriers to her development that she faces, which are caused by her family's class position and its persistence in a stifling and archaic traditionalism.

Like Clarissa, Maggie ultimately comes to consciousness of the magnitude of her fall, not in conventional social terms, but in terms of her commitment to the moral values of loyalty to honor, unselfishness, and family. Above all, Maggie feels a commitment to those for whom she feels a sympathetic identification. As in her ascetic phase, in refusing to accede to Stephen's efforts at seduction, Maggie represents a feminine commitment to relationships and connections with originary loyalties, and a repudiation of the masculine values of selfishness and the commodification of the self that the novel suggests a commercializing society increasingly tends to demand of women. Thus, when Stephen points out to her that by leaving her home with him she has already lost her public reputation and has no recourse from scandal except in marrying him, she responds, emphasizing her moral obligations to others:

> "I do care for Philip—in a different way: I remember all we said to each other; I know how he thought of me as the one promise of his life. He was given to me that I might make his lot less hard; and I have forsaken him. And Lucy— she has been deceived—she who trusted me more than any one. I cannot marry you: I cannot take a good for myself that has been wrung out of their misery. It is not the force that ought to rule us—this that we feel for each other; it would rend me away from all that my past life has made dear and holy to me. I can't set out on a fresh life, and forget that: I must go back to it, and cling to it, else I shall feel as if there were nothing firm beneath my feet." (478)

In a profoundly feminine way—even amid her violation of traditional feminine norms of decorum—she finds her moral center in living for those whose feelings she empathizes with and to whom she has long-standing connections derived from her native place and family, just as she has always lived her life primarily not for herself, but for her family, above all for her father and brother. Indeed, though ostensibly the issue here is her compassion for Philip and Lucy, her words "that my past life has made dear and holy to me" suggests the crucial issue is the continuing power of Maggie's loyalty to her brother and father and the stern patriarchal values they embody.

When Stephen offers her marriage, he gives her a chance to join the winning side of history, the commercializing and modernizing world that the Tullivers have been victimized by and have resisted. All Maggie must do is accede to a willingness to commodify the self and to give up her values of loyalty to her family and friends, above all her commitment to selflessness. The earlier scene at the charity fair, where Maggie's public attractiveness causes her goods, despite their inferior quality, to garner disproportionate masculine attention, shows Maggie successfully rehearsing such a commodi-fication and anticipates her capacity to "win" Stephen. This scene demon-strates that her sexual attractiveness and passionate nature gives her a self that is easily commodifiable. But for Maggie, disrupting local and familial loyalties to rise socially and economically in the world would be to betray all that her family have been fighting against and to accede to the increasing power of commercialization and wealth. In her eyes, having the "firm[ness] beneath my feet" of loyalty to her rural place and its personal ties means re-turning to her highest moral duty. Maggie's strong sense of loyalty here stands as a transcendent call to selflessness and represents a scathing critique of the sexual and social opportunism embodied in Stephen Guest.

However, Eliot unsentimentally makes clear that Maggie is sacrificing herself for an ideal of community even while the actual community around her is irredeemably corrupted by the tide of modernization and rural small-mindedness. The very impulses of loyalty to community and empathy for the feelings of others that caused her to resist Stephen's seduction are gener-ally enfeebled, leaving her self-sacrifice in refusing Stephen construable as mere fallen virtue. As Dr. Kenn, the irresolute pastor of her parish, coldly explains, "At present everything seems tending toward the relaxation of ties—toward the substitution of wayward choice for the adherence to obli-gation, which has its roots in the past" (495). Ultimately he advises her to submit to a hypocritical social prudery: "I ask you to consider whether it will not perhaps be better for you to take a situation at a distance, . . ." (496). Though he shields her from ostracism briefly by employing her, he ultimately gives in to social disapproval and fires her. Thus, Eliot bitterly reveals the distance between the lofty ideals of Christian compassion and the sordid reality of the church's imbrication in the chilly social fabric of St. Oggs. Thus, like her precursor Antigone, Maggie defies social norms by sacrificing her individual self-interest to moral scruples and loyalty to family.

At first blush the novel's famously strange and tragic ending, in which Maggie and her brother die in a flood that destroys their ancestral property, is readable as simply a histrionic resolution of Maggie's—and Eliot's—nar-rative impasse. Having staked her entire social being on loyalty to ideals of connection with others and community, Maggie could only be saved by the emergence of a rational and compassionate community, which, the novel makes clear, is highly unlikely. Instead, she finds in death the fraternity and love with her sibling, the idealized community of equality and selflessness transcending barriers of gender that had eluded her in life. Moreover, her death, a desperate sacrifice of self in a futile effort to save her brother, eloquently epitomizes and climaxes the values that have guided her life. It is important to note, though, that the sweeping away of the mill also symbolically culminates the novel's sense of the losing struggle that the small proprietor faces against the overwhelming force of industrialization. At the novel's close, the business concerns that have defeated Tom's father are on the verge of converting his mill to steam power, a sign of the victory of the new forms of economic and social power that emerge with the rise of industrial capital. Above all, in the context of Maggie's entire life, the death of Tom and Maggie embodies a nostalgic return to the deep bond that they shared as children, allowing Maggie a tragic return to the moment of closeness with the brother that adulthood has taken from her: "brother and sister had gone down in an embrace never to be parted: living through again in one supreme moment the days when they had clasped their little hands in love, and roamed the daisied fields together" (521).

Indeed, the strangeness of the novel's ending draws attention to the powerful originality of the novel's relentless realism up to the ending and the ideological and formal impasse this realism reveals. Following a narrative and ideological precedent found in Sand's novels of rural life, Eliot finds in the backwardness of a rural milieu the perfect image and exemplar of the constraints and mental and emotional confinement that women experienced in Victorian culture. While women had long been associated with the natural, either as untamed antithesis to the cultural or as a romanticized yet ahistorical maternal principle, Eliot radically revises the association of women with the rural by showing its tragic dimension for female subjectivity and its historical contingency. That tragic dimension emerges through narratives that explore the vast chasm between the growing desire of women to develop themselves and the actual underdevelopment of their own capacities (which are imaged in their backward rural setting) and by the harsh and unforgiving patriarchalism and growing commercialism of the pastoral milieu that impedes at every turn feminine efforts at self-development. Eliot elaborates further on this powerful strategy of exploring women's tragic position through the thematics of rural backwardness in *Middlemarch*, and the theme will later be taken up by such major novelists such as Hardy and Lawrence. Invariably, however, what is powerful as an image of the feminine self confined becomes as narrative a confining framework for the author, since there is always a significant distance (which is often openly acknowledged through ironies of narrative tone) between the inevitably limited perspective of the characters, including the protagonist, who is, by realistic conventions, locked within the confines of narrow limitations of rural worlds and the narrator's sense of the tremendous intellectual and moral poverty of this environment. The tendency toward a certain narrative violence toward the rural setting, as instanced in the destruction of the mill in *The Mill on the Floss* or the melodramatic plot developments at the end of *Middlemarch*, is a product of the unbridgeability of the chasm between the author's judgment of the world and the judgments and actions that are realistically available to the characters.

Unsurprisingly, given the criticism the novel attracted because of its daring candor, Eliot would in her later fiction shy away from even *The Mill on the Floss*'s subtle openness about female sexual passion. Unable to marry her companion, George Lewes, and keenly aware that her personal life put her outside the margins of Victorian respectability, Eliot was clearly eager not to push her analytical and subversive dissent from Victorian domesticity to the point of scandal. But in later novels she would return to the difficulty of finding a firm foundation of community in which to build a subjectivity, particularly for those, such as independent-minded women, seeking to transgress social conventions. Modern readers, imbued with individualist sensibilities, tend to be impatient with Eliot's self-sacrificing heroines, feeling that their impulse to live for others is too much of a concession to Victorian ideals of feminine altruism and disinterestedness. Certainly Eliot does not completely transcend these nineteenth-century ideals of femininity. But such impatience with Eliot's narratives neglects how the values of her heroines represent a powerful critique of the obsessive self-interestness of an industrial society and of how nineteenth-century society was "rationalized" through the ubiquitous pursuit of a possessive individualism utterly at odds with a respect for societal or community well-being.

Equally unfortunate is that such dismissive readings fail to perceive how, given the static and ahistorical models of femininity that pervaded her cultural moment, Eliot's stress on the interaction between a familial and historical moment and psychic embodiments of femininity, her unwavering demolition of gender prejudice, and her willingness to make sexual desire part of a sympathetically portrayed female character were explosively unsettling for her Victorian readers. While she did not single-handedly explode unreflective domesticity as a fictive mode, Eliot's demonstration of the contingent social forces molding Maggie's personality, her innovative openness in addressing female sexual passion, and her sympathetic portrayal of the tragic cost of Victorian culture's gender prejudices and scapegoating of women, undoubtedly offered her readers a devastating critique of domestic pieties and the standard idealization of women's family roles. At a cultural moment when the less-prestigious but wildly popular "sensation fiction" of the 1860s and 1870s was also subversively exploring transgressions of female roles, Eliot offered her readers—and the most ambitious writers of the next generation—a profoundly sophisticated and, paradoxically, deeply traditional, in some senses conservative, model for how elite fiction could explore this topical but ticklish topic. Eliot's radically unconventional treatment of domestic themes is part of the complex movement through which she rarefies fiction by elevating it toward the intellectual and the refined and makes it more fully bourgeois by at once feminizing it and intellectualizing its character. And yet, exactly because a feminine subjectivity that was not at rest in the conventions of Victorian culture was the implicit source of the fictive experience she creates, as well as often its subject, Eliot's fiction powerfully corrodes domestic truisms and gives center stage to the consciousness of individuals who felt separated from familial life as much as from a wider communal life.

ELIOT AND THE CENSORING
OF FEMININE SUBJECTIVITY

We can best read the cultural significance of the consternation with which some Victorian readers responded to *Mill on the Floss* by putting such negative reactions in the context of the furor of critical alarm that it anticipates, which soon after greeted the emergence to popularity of sensation fiction. With the success of Wilkie Collins's *The Woman in White* (published serially in 1859–60), Ellen Wood's *East Lynne* (1861), and Mary Braddon's *Lady Audley's Secret* (1862), this subgenre of popular fiction, with its riveting Gothic and melodramatic plots, quickly becomes the dominant form of popular fiction. Sensation fiction may have displaced the more staid domestic fiction in part because readers simply found sensation writing more exciting: "the well-known old stories of readers sitting up all night over a novel had begun to grow faint in the public recollection. Domestic histories, however virtuous and charming, do not often attain that result . . ."[19] But the contrast between the subject matter of domestic and sensation fiction is not a clear-cut one, since the typical sensation novel was highly familial in its subject matter. What chiefly distinguished sensation fiction, and alarmed many Victorian critics, was exactly the genre's emphasis on the potential for the sinister or transgressive within quotidian family and domestic life. In a highly censorious essay on the genre published in 1867, novelist and critic Margaret Oliphant, one of the most noted opponents of sensation fiction, argued emphatically that its most objectionable feature was its failure to respect the conventions of Victorian gender ideology. Oliphant particularly

considered vital that ideology's insistence on feminine passionless and innocence of sexual subjects: "[w]hat is held up [in sensation fiction] to us as the
story of the feminine soul as it really exists underneath its conventional cov-
erings, is a very fleshly and unlovely record."[20] For women writers to articulate such "fleshly" themes and women readers to be enthralled by them was
particularly disgraceful: "the fact that this new and disgusting picture of
what professes to be the female heart, comes from the hands of women, and
is tacitly accepted by them as real, is not to be laughed at" (176). Echoing
the concerns of many Victorian critics of sensation novels, Oliphant declares
that because they violated the norms of what middle-class women were
taught to feel, the emphasis in such works on the power of erotic impulses in
women was inherently unrealistic, that such fictions were inevitably immoral
and vulgarizing in their influence, and that the distasteful topics typical of
the genre were in any case the mark of an inferior brand of fiction. Though
Oliphant's strictures present themselves as descriptive, they clearly express a
widely shared prescriptive impulse anxious to police fiction for deviations
from traditional class and gender norms.

In its emphatic insistence on the need to maintain clear boundaries between what was acceptable in fiction and what was not, Oliphant's polemic
exhibits obvious inconsistencies. Sensation fiction's violations of taboos
against respectable women exhibiting transgressive desire allegedly did violence to what was characteristically British ("That sublime respect for sentimental morality and poetic justice which distinguishes the British public")
and even failed the test of fidelity to actual life because such transgressions,
or transgressive thoughts, were inherently alien to proper middle-class femininity. Yet Oliphant ruefully acknowledges that this allegedly external pollution of the British female mind was produced by British women writers
and avidly read by British women readers! "These ladies [sensation writers]
might not know, it is quite possible, any better. They might not be aware
how young women of good blood and good training feel. The perplexing
fact is, that the subjects of this slander make no objection to it . . ." (175).
No wonder that such anxious policing of moral and social boundaries in
literature would be ridiculed by Oscar Wilde in *The Importance of Being Ear-
nest*, when the modern young lady Gwendolyn announces, "I never travel
without my diary. One should always have something sensational to read in
the train."[21]

But the furor over sensation fiction is more important than its air of
moral panic might suggest, for in defining what was properly British literature in opposition to a moral radicalism and openness about sexuality seen
as alien and threatening to the social order, such strictures operated to re-

duce the possibilities for writers, especially women writers, to deploy familial narratives to explore controversial subjects. Given such a hostile response to the exploration of sexual transgressions, especially by women writers, it is little wonder that in her later work Eliot (and other writers, especially women) censored their openness in addressing such topics. Indeed, given that such subjects as the bigamous marriage or the adulterous or near-adulterous female were inevitably at the margins of literary respectability, it is intriguing to wonder why Eliot and the sensation writers were so attracted to them. The answer is probably that a major factor in engendering the allure of these themes was the growing consciousness of middle-class women of the arbitrary and oppressive nature of their legal and social position. Though sensation novelists were rarely overt feminists, some sensation writers, such as Wilkie Collins, would use the genre to expose the legal and social disabilities that women faced. Moreover, the 1850s and 1860s saw controversies erupt over the legal and economic disabilities that women faced, while the 1857 reform of the divorce laws and the subsequent public reporting of divorce cases greatly increased the visibility of the destructive effects of unrestrained patriarchalism in marriage. In the midst of the rising social awareness of feminine alienation, narratives of sexual transgressions were also a traditional language for addressing feminine discontent. The plot that Eliot uses to dramatize Maggie's tragic situation, of a woman tempted by a transgressive love because of her profound discontent with her oppressive circumstances and family situation, was a well-established narrative device in European fiction, having recent precedents in Charlotte Brontë and George Sand and a more distant but highly prestigious one in Samuel Richardson. Narratives of sexual transgression offered Victorian writers a well-established fictive language for exploring the dilemmas of women's unfree social position.

Critics of sensation fiction and its characteristic plots of sexual transgression were not unaware of the genre's intimate relation to expressions of feminine discontent. Oliphant writes that "[t]he change [in British fiction toward sensation fiction] perhaps began at the time when Jane Eyre made what advanced critics call her 'protest' against the conventionalities in which the world clothes itself. We have had many 'protests' since that time, . . ." (173). *Jane Eyre* (1847) was indeed in a mid-Victorian context startling in its open expression of feminine discontent. Oliphant is uneasily aware that the subversions of conventions of literary representations of women visible in *The Mill on the Floss* and the sensation writers (some of whom were directly influenced by Brontë and Eliot) were symptoms of a society increasingly willing to question the habits of thought that held women in subjection.[22]

For all her moral outrage, Oliphant was surely correct to see a connection between protests against women's inferior social position such as Jane Eyre's and the new directions in fiction written for, and often by, women that she denounced. Modern critics have noted that from the 1860s, fiction read by Victorian women, by foregrounding transgressive behavior in elite women, would begin to lessen the class distance between the traditional lower-class fallen women of earlier fiction and the experience of middle-class women readers. An identification with or sympathy for transgressive women could become a way in which readers and writers developed an awareness of and a critical response to women's oppression. Josephine Butler, later a prominent social purity and feminist campaigner, was inspired to enter rescue work with "ruined" women after reading Elizabeth Gaskell's *Ruth* (1853), a precursor of sensation fiction that sympathetically portrays a working-class fallen woman, and such rescue work reinforced her indignation at the masculine sexual exploitation of women.[23]

But if Victorian sensation fiction, much of it written by women, fostered the beginnings of a feminist sensibility in Victorian readers, there is a poignant irony in the literary history of the decades that follow. While women's subjectivity, particularly their struggles with the confinements of gender roles, becomes a major literary preoccupation in late nineteenth-century British and European literature, and figured prominently in the New Women fiction of the 1890s, much of it by women writers, most of the canonical explorations of this theme were written by men. When male writers such as Henry James, Henrik Ibsen, and Thomas Hardy explore the turmoil of female subjectivity in their works, even if they are sympathetic to women's situation, they often read female experience through the lens of the period's increasing obsession with a scientific language of sexuality and race, products of the cultural salience of imperialist and Darwinian ideas, and hence see women as victims of the impersonal force of sexual drives as much as of society's restrictions on their gender. Indeed, the emergence of a scientific approach to sexuality, in contrast to an earlier language of passion and moral fervor, undermined women's ability to speak authoritatively about their situation, since such scientific rhetorics were dominated by male professionals and left even "advanced" women feeling defensive and marginalized.[24] It is for this reason that paradoxically the decline of domestic fiction, for all that genre's tendency to stereotype women, was almost immediately followed by a weakening of women's rhetorical power in literature.

Given the hostility that *The Mill on the Floss* and its sensational cousins generated, one can understand why Eliot never again creates a treatment of female subjectivity, particularly of sexual passion, as daring as her portrayal of Maggie Tulliver. In her most acclaimed novel, *Middlemarch*, Eliot carefully separates the two kinds of female rebellion that are fused in *The Mill on the Floss*. In the later novel, the feminist impulses of Dorothea Brooke, whose effort to use marriage to as a way of expanding her horizons leads to a disastrously unhappy marriage to a domestic tyrant and whose subtle rebellion is treated sympathetically, is sharply distinguished from the materialism and sexuality of Rosamund, who is condemned with harsh moralism for the unrestrained appetites that destroy her idealistic husband. The taming of Eliot's subversive impulses in the portrayal of feminine rebellion and the limiting of her capacity to depict a complex feminine subjectivity suggests how effectively woman writers were restrained by social disapproval from following in the literary path that *The Mill on the Floss* opened. In later decades, British fiction would increasingly explore the subjects that Eliot and the sensation writers had brought to prominence, women's discontent with the restrictions on their roles and transgressions by members of the middle class of the Victorian sexual code. But the vehement opposition of critical opinion to such exploration, especially by women writers, explains why such explorations were most successfully carried out by male writers. Unlike women, they were free from the consciousness of being already in a marginal relation to high literary culture and of needing to defend the very legitimacy of their literary careers. Men also had easier access to the scientific language and sensibility that became increasingly favored for the treatment of sexuality, which was often seen as the determining factor underlying heterosexual romance. Indeed, the rising masculine obsession in late-nineteenth century culture with exposing sexual pathologies through journalistic or scientific investigations was an uncongenial terrain for women writers, because their very existence as professional women or as feminists could be and sometimes was read as symptomatic of such pathology. Thus, as domestic fiction declines and becomes increasingly the fictional exploration of familial pathology, the literary field is remasculinized in part because men have privileged access to intellectual and scientific frameworks with which to address marital and sexual issues and deploy a quasi-scientific rhetoric to do so, which is utterly different from the sentimental and moralistic rhetorical authority that writers, male and female, had deployed in the middle years of the century.

In the case of Eliot, it is something of a paradox that a writer so obsessed with the threat to community represented by industrialism should have helped foster an antifamilial tradition of writing that subverts one of Victorian culture's most durable and potent rituals of community, the domestic narrative. This paradox is an aspect partly of her feminism but also derives from a self-contradictory aspect to Eliot's literary project in that, while her goals were progressive, her literary methods were elitist. Aesthetically, Eliot sees herself as refining and elevating fiction, interestingly by aggressively foregrounding mundane and undramatic material, emulating what she called the "precious quality of truthfulness" of "Dutch paintings, which lofty-minded people despise" [*Adam Bede,* 173]. The quality of the *treatment* of this material, she implies, is what elevates it to moral and hence to literary significance. The result of such a program is a fiction that asserts its sympathy with the oppressed while, by its inwardness and self-consciousness about its literary style and the pervasive reflectiveness of its tone, distancing the reader from the demotic, the popular, and the immediate. Despite her reformist sympathies, Eliot's style lays claim to a refined and privileged readership. The source of this paradox lies in how Eliot's work responds to larger social forces that sharply differentiate types of fiction by their social and aesthetic status. Such distinctions function increasingly to make one of the defining features of elite communities a shared capacity to appreciate the culture and sophistication that Eliot's fiction so clearly embodies and that, to much Victorian taste, was absent in even such a major writer as Dickens. The elitist distance from communal social life that Eliot's fiction encourages was a high price to pay for her achievement. Her work helps inaugurate a sharp split between literature as a distanced and dispassionate reflection on society and literature as a celebration of human community. Since a connection to a strong sense of communal life can sustain and enrich literature, one of the central problems of fiction after Eliot becomes the difficulty that writers have in imagining and representing a community that their work can, however ambivalently, celebrate and nurture.

In our era, historical trends have reinforced our awareness of the pervasiveness of beleaguered community even while rendering more fragile the bonds of communal and family life. Moreover, in an age of heightened awareness of the destructive environmental effects of economic development, Maggie's stubborn love for the beauty of her native place does not seem irrational. And while Eliot was right to understand that there could be no simple turning back to a preindustrial past, her disquiet before the decline of traditional communities still resonates today. Market forces have continued to show an infinite capacity to disrupt and destroy communities. While individuals and groups who fear they may, like Maggie, suffer the consequences of violating societal norms often see communities as prisons that must be ruptured, Maggie's contrasting belief, that without the support of strong values and the communal ties in which they are embedded, without goals beyond the endless marketing and promotion of the self, there is ultimately "nothing firm beneath [one's] feet" still resonates. Our feelings for familiar places and the communities that they nurture is an irreplaceable source of our humanity. As market forces more pervasively and globally overwhelm and subordinate all other values, Maggie's story remains eloquent testimony of the power of the commercializing juggernaut to crush the human spirit beneath its onward rush.

4

Marital Alienation, National Destiny, and the Novel of Spiritual Malaise in *Daniel Deronda*

IN A CONTRIBUTION TO A SPIRITED DEBATE CONDUCTED IN NEWSPAPERS and magazines in the 1890s about whether marriage was a hindrance to women's development, Miss H. E. Harvey wrote an essay proclaiming "[i]t is only during the last twenty years or so that the voice of women has really been heard in literature." Later in this feminist critique of societal attitudes toward women, Harvey comments that "[t]he unmarried woman who is deserted by her lover has, of course, always been a scapegoat in the eyes of society, and it is only since George Eliot took up her cause that it has become the fashion to interest ourselves in her."[1] Harvey's implication that Eliot single-handedly transformed society's response to the fallen women is dubious literary history. In the 1850s and 1860s a larger context of increased compassion for such women occurs, and writers besides Eliot play a significant role in this change.[2] But Harvey's juxtaposition of the newly audible literary "voice of women" and praise of Eliot for challenging social prejudice toward one type of women suggests how, as a woman writer whose fiction questioned women's subordinate status, she was seen as an iconic pioneer. Strikingly, while subversively rewriting the representation of women, she also became a uniquely prestigious female author in nineteenth-century British fiction; indeed, after the death of Dickens, she became Britain's most respected novelist of either sex.

As we have seen, in her early novels, such as *Adam Bede* and especially *The Mill on the Floss*, Eliot had explored the historical contingency of femininity in ways that subverted the ideological underpinnings of the domestic novel and had placed alienation from family life at the center of feminine experience. In so doing she offered an alternative and more profoundly imagined understanding of feminine subjectivity than had hitherto appeared in British fiction, thereby showing the inadequacy of earlier fictional treatments of women. But it is particularly in her later fiction that she establishes herself as a central model for later serious fiction in the British tradition, developing a model of fiction in which intense familial alienation is a central subject. What distinguishes her later fiction from the triumphs of her earlier work is less her increasing formal control or her interest in revising conventional narratives of domesticity, which is a constant in her work, but her capacity to assert her work's authority by linking her characteristic subject of feminine subjectivity to the most prestigious of novelistic themes, the historical and political development of society itself. In this regard the political turmoil in Renaissance Italy, which is the subject of *Romola* (1863), a work much admired by Victorians though now less read, is a turning point in her fiction,[3] while in later novels she brings her heightened fascination with the interpenetration of political and personal contexts closer to her own age. Thus, we see in *Middlemarch* (1871) that Dorothea Brooke's entrapment in a stultifying marriage to a backward-looking pedant is not merely her idiosyncratic misfortune, but is linked by innumerable strands of plot and imagery to the larger immobility of British society as it resists the forces of reform, including political reform, just as Dorothea's eventual liberation through marriage with the culturally suspect outsider Will Ladislaw is part of the novel's celebration of the possibilities of breaking with insular British tradition. However, in no Eliot novel is the link between marital alienation and ideas of political and national destiny made so emphatically, or is marital alienation as central to a work's high literary ambition, as it is in her final novel, *Daniel Deronda* (1876).

SENSATIONALISM AND THE
PROBLEM OF THE RAKE

Even at her most innovative—and *Deronda* is a highly innovative work—Eliot is a writer steeped in, and reverent toward, tradition. It is therefore typical of her strategies that the novel begins with a narrative organized around a moral question traditional enough to serve as the framework around which Richardson had organized his masterpiece of domestic fiction *Clarissa*, whether a *"reformed rake makes the best husband."*[4] For in the narrative that dominates the early part of *Deronda*, Gwendolen Harleth, a genteel woman in straitened economic circumstances, faces exactly this moral quandary of how to deal with the rakishness of a prospective suitor. While being courted by a wealthy aristocrat, Henleigh Grandcourt, she is abruptly confronted by her suitor's mistress, Lydia Glasher, who informs her that

Grandcourt has fathered four children by her. Lydia argues that Grandcourt is morally obligated to marry her and legitimate their children, and suggests that for Gwendolen to marry Grandcourt would make her complicit in his betrayal of his obligations to herself and her children. Glasher's appearance raises the Richardsonian question of how an elite woman should respond to the libertine sexual behavior and masculine privilege embodied in Grandcourt's relationship with his mistress. Initially, Gwendolen responds by fleeing Grandcourt, and as the novel begins, we see her in the aftermath of this flight desperately trying to bolster her economic position by gambling at a Leubronn casino. She loses, and her gambling losses are echoed by the news that her family's investments have failed, leaving her facing the threat of poverty. Her economic plight threatens to compel her to take the degrading position of a governess, the typical destiny of the poor but educated Victorian single woman.

Desperate for economic security, Gwendolen changes her mind about her rakish suitor and marries Grandcourt, making the Richardsonian error of deciding that a confirmed rake will make at least an acceptable husband. The choice is disastrous. Grandcourt is a moral monster and domestic tyrant. Indeed, one must go back to Richardson's Lovelace to find an equally memorable portrait in British literature of an erotic sadist. Lest the reader not notice the parallel, at a crucial point of the novel, immediately after Gwendolen's marriage, Eliot provides a sly allusion to *Clarissa* when the hero Daniel Deronda, a man notable for his sympathy for and kindness to women, is playfully called by his adoptive father Sir Hugo "a kind of Lovelace who will make the Clarissas run after you."[5] Though Deronda has the personality and good looks that will draw Gwendolen to him, Sir Hugo's playful reading of Daniel as a brutal rake is spectacularly wrong and typical of this good-natured but intellectually limited character. Eliot intends the reader to correct the allusion by seeing that the Lovelace figure in the novel is not Deronda, but Grandcourt, whose villainy is more dangerous for being invisible to the world's imperceptive Sir Hugos.

If Gwendolen's essential moral dilemma—how respectable women should deal with male sexual license—is a hoaried subject in domestic fiction, the novel's treatment of this subject also responds to a cultural theme of topical interest in the 1860s and 1870s. Andrew Dowling has pointed out how *Deronda* responds to a growing cultural appetite for details of marital breakdown stimulated by the Matrimonial Causes Act (1857), which, by liberalizing requirements for divorce, generated an enormous increase in its frequency and public visibility; moreover this interest was fed and encouraged in this period by sensation fiction's wildly popular narratives of marital breakdown.[6] In this cultural context, other major novelists, such as George Meredith, Anthony Trollope, and Thomas Hardy, explored the terrain of marital disharmony, but none would do so more powerfully and influentially than Eliot. In *Deronda* the impact of the sensation genre reverberates in the Lydia Glasher plot, a variant on the bigamy plot so popular in sensation novels that it was ridiculed in parodies of the genre.[7] Such plots in part reflected the increased interest in the tension between marriage understood as a contract and potential site of individual freedom and the more traditional notion of it as an indissoluble sacrament. The reform of the divorce laws made the collapse of marriages and the possibility of their legal dissolution a far more readily conceivable alternative than it had been in the past when divorce was inaccessible to the middle class. But the overwhelming social disapproval of divorce and the limited grounds allowed for it (adultery needed to be proved, and for women even this was insufficient grounds without aggravating causes) left it a practical impossibility for many trapped in miserable marriages.

Bigamy plots were a way of imaginatively working out this tension between the heightened salience of the idea of marital dissolution and the continuing harsh barriers that prevented the realization of an individualist and contractual definition of marriage.[8] Such plots could also be used, as they are in *Deronda*, to criticize masculine misbehavior at a time when legal and cultural expectations for masculine behavior were increasingly requiring men to moderate their use of patriarchal authority and cultural awareness was growing that abuse of the marital relationship could extend beyond the traditional concern with physical violence. In 1870, British courts first recognized that marital cruelty, one of the aggravating causes required in addition to adultery for women to seek divorce under the 1857 act, did not require the presence or threat of physical violence.[9] In this cultural context, by making masculine psychic cruelty central to the novel's depiction of Grandcourt and Gwendolen's marriage, Eliot demonstrates that the overt violation of gender norms seen in male violence was not necessary for men's traditional authority in marriage to be misused. She also reflects a new societal awareness of the moral seriousness of masculine sexual license by demonstrating that to tolerate such license, or rakishness in the earlier language, can lead to an acceptance of a pernicious masculine privilege and gender inequality that inevitably bled into married life. The novel's representation of Gwendolen trapped in marriage with the sadistic Grandcourt links the theme of male sexual license to the increasingly prominent feminist concern with how women's socially and legally weak position subordinated them within marriage.

If the plot reflects concerns about the position of middle-class women, it also reflects changing views of the largely working-class fallen woman. Because she feels complicit in the injustice to her husband's mistress committed by Grandcourt, Gwendolen's obsessive guilt after her marriage was also highly topical in the 1870s. Gwendolen's guilt about the male exploitation of fallen women reflects a new kind of sympathy toward such women, who in liberal circles were no longer seen only as errant sinners in need of reform or stern punishment but, increasingly, as human beings victimized by social prejudice and masculine misbehavior who had moral claims on society. Eliot's implication that elite women should consider such moral claims raised by fallen women like Glasher, rather than relegating them to the subhuman status of wicked women from whom respectable women must disentangle their men, reflects the rising feminist concern with society's complacent acceptance of masculine sexual predation and the increasingly vocal critique of the culture's sexual hypocrisy and double standards. The feminist concern over society's condoning male sexual transgressions was reflected in the public furor of the 1870s that rose over passage of the Contagious Diseases Acts, laws that, by requiring legal supervision and compulsory medical examinations of suspected prostitutes, but not of their customers, gave legal support to the double standard (as did the Matrimonial Causes Act, in that it made adultery sufficient grounds for a man to seek divorce, but not for a woman, except with aggravating circumstances). The Contagious Diseases Acts, which were openly defended as allowing men to sow their sexual oats, shocked feminists and radicals who saw in them evidence of the arrogance of both gender and class privilege. Though critics sometimes express surprise at Gwendolen's growing revulsion at her complicity in Grandcourt's injustice to Glasher, it is a sign of how Eliot's heroine slowly gains the capacity, as did many elite women of the period, to transcend class and gender-based prejudices against fallen women and acknowledge their claims to fair treatment as human beings. Gwendolen's guilt reflects as well her profound revulsion at the egotism and irresponsibility of masculine sexuality, a revulsion that, far from being idiosyncratic, would become a major theme of late Victorian feminism as activists urged women to "banish the beast" of untrammeled masculine sexuality.[10]

Essentially, in drawing on these contemporary concerns about the nature of gender division and sexuality and reframing them within her own refined and self-consciously literary style, Eliot is deliberately elevating into the realm of high literary art concerns that had already been popularized by the enormously successful genre of sensation fiction, a genre that plays a significant role in modernizing Victorian conceptions of the reality of familial life and gender relations. Interestingly, the subject of the Lydia Glasher plot, the objection of the mistress of an upper-class man to his marriage, is anticipated by a passage in one of the most famous of sensation novels, *The Moonstone* (1868). Near the end of the novel a suitor of the heroine, Rachel Verinder, has been exposed as having stolen the fabulously valuable Indian diamond, the moonstone (originally taken violently by a British soldier from its Hindu protectors), and pawned it to obtain funds to cover up embezzlements he had committed. The suitor, Godfrey Ablewhite, desperately needs to raise adequate funds to redeem the diamond in order to convert it into twenty thousand pounds, which he has embezzled, and proposes marriage to the heroine in hope of obtaining access to her wealth. He is frustrated in this attempt by finding out that Rachel has only a life interest in her mother's substantial estate, but he is also frustrated, as the novel's detective explains to the hero, Franklin Blake, by the presence of a previous commitment to a mistress:

> The lady at the Villa had heard of his contemplated marriage. A superb woman, Mr Blake, of the sort that are not to be trifled with—the sort with the light complexion and the Roman nose. She felt the utmost contempt for Mr Godfrey Ablewhite. It would be silent contempt, if he made a handsome provision for her. Otherwise, it would be contempt with a tongue to it. Miss Verinder's life interest allowed him no more hope of raising the "provision" than of raising the twenty thousand pounds. He couldn't marry—he really couldn't marry, under all the circumstances.[11]

Lydia Glasher is a full-blown character, not just a plot device as is Ablewhite's mistress, but the situation described here is parallel to that of Lydia Glasher and Grandcourt: an upper-class man's mistress is "not to be trifled with" and stands as an obstacle to his planned marriage. Lydia Glasher's discontent emphatically has "a tongue to it." In general, *The Moonstone* is a probable influence on *Daniel Deronda*, not only because of the parallel use of the plot of the mistress as impediment to marriage but in that both novels are centrally organized around the juxtaposition of a narrative alluding to imperialism, specifically the hero's encounter with racial Others who remind him of his implication in Britain's international role, and a domestic plot revealing the troubled relations between the sexes. Both novels, moreover, implicitly suggest parallels between the masculine behavior abroad in imperial ventures and at home in the treatment of women. The likelihood that *The Moonstone* is an influence on *Deronda* is increased by Eliot's prominent deployment of jewelry as a multivalent symbol, which parallels the moonstone's function as a central and complex symbol in Collins's novel.

For Collins, the moonstone is simultaneously an image of the corrupting power of greed and commerce, but also a metaphor for women's "jewel," their chastity, which men lust for and seek to possess. In *The Moonstone*, the shadowy repeated thefts of the jewel figure not only masculine greed and lust, but also hypocrisy, most obviously in the case of Godfrey Ablewhite. Even the more likable Franklin Blake's rakish side is hinted at by his night-time theft of Rachel's jewel from her boudoir while under the influence of opium, an act that also figures men's desire to control female sexuality. *Deronda* uses jewelry in a strikingly similar way as a complex image of the corruptions of commerce as well as of the potential violence, associatively linked in both novels to imperialism, of male sexual lust. In the beginning of the novel, Gwendolen loses a necklace she has pawned to cover gambling debts, only to have the necklace redeemed by Deronda in an implicit criticism of Gwendolen's impulsive immersion in the materialistic world of gambling. Later Lydia Glasher's necklace, given to her by Grandcourt and compulsorily returned to Gwendolen, becomes an image of the corrupting power of Grandcourt's tyranny and sexual license: the necklace moves from Lydia to Gwendolen just as his control of his mistress is displaced by his domination of his wife. In both novels, not only does jewelry figure masculine sexual acquisitiveness, but the contested circulation of jewels is linked to female ambivalence about male sexual power. It is suggestive as well that in both novels central male figures are tested by the degree of humanity with which they treat fallen women of various kinds, though Eliot highlights the feminist potential of this theme by having her heroine also have to confront her relation to a fallen woman.[12]

Indeed, the figure of the fallen woman who refuses to accept society's marginalization, and the heroine's complicity in that marginalization, is central to the Gwendolen Harleth plot. Later in the novel, the development of Gwendolen's conscience will be fostered by Deronda himself, but the role of an external conscience is played first by Lydia Glasher. Having failed to prevent Gwendolen's marriage, Glasher, in a gesture both vindictive and moralistic, sends Gwendolen the family necklace she has received from Grandcourt, accompanied by a letter ominously predicting that Gwendolen's marriage to him will make her "miserable." "The willing wrong you had done me will be your curse" (359), the letter prophetically intones. Gwendolen, her guilt at displacing Glasher reawakened and mingled with foreboding, shrieks hysterically: "[Grandcourt] saw her pallid, shrieking as it seemed with terror, the jewels scattered around her on the floor. Was it a fit of madness? In some form or another the Furies had crossed his threshold" (359). The reference to the Furies, who in Aeschylus's *Oresteia* haunt Orestes after his murder of his adulterous mother, Clytemnestra, is appropriate in that Glasher, like Clytemnestra, is both mother and sexually fallen woman. But this classical allusion distracts the reader from Eliot's borrowing from a less prestigious source, *The Moonstone*, with its similar use of jewelry to figure overweening masculine power, sexual lust, and the hypocrisy behind conventional domestic surfaces.

Drawing on her sensational predecessors, Eliot makes Glasher's refusal to be forgotten disrupt conventional moralistic narratives, which conventionally marginalized fallen women just as they were deprived of access to respectable society. The fury (or Furies) of Glasher's vengeance rebels against the symbolic violence done her by Gwendolen and Grandcourt's marriage, a violence that relegates her to ostracism and her children to illegitimacy. Glasher's letter diagnosing Grandcourt's "withered heart" (359) and prophesying marital unhappiness proves all too accurate. What is fascinating is that Gwendolen's guilt-stricken response to her letter shows that the fallen woman has succeeded in establishing herself as a woman, especially a mother, worthy of legitimate rights, a psychic response that echoes the increasing willingness of elite women of the 1860s and 1870s to empathize with their primarily lower-class fallen sisters.[13] Gwendolen's guilt and foreboding, though it may seem excessive, responds to the identification that women were beginning to make across boundaries of social class with victims of masculine sexual predation and license, as well as their growing awareness of the cost of such masculine types of power.

Women in the Marketplace

Despite her debt to sensation fiction, however, Eliot's creative task was not to introduce lurid themes of the consequences of masculine sexual license or feminine transgression and the hypocrisy behind the repressive framework that governed Victorian marital and sexual life, a task already performed in the 1860s and 1870s by sensation writers and their journalistic brethren. Though often conservative in their moral trajectory, sensation novels, with their obsession with sexual transgression, their willingness to emphasize feminine passion, and their tendency to draw attention to the structural weakness of Victorian family life, disrupted the conventions of Victorian domestic fiction and prepared the ground for Eliot's more refined novel of marital alienation. Eliot's fictional project is essentially to take the explosive themes of the sensation writers and refashion them into prestigious cultural capital by transmuting these themes into novels that were indisputably literarily high in manner and thought. She does so in *Deronda* largely by creating a meditation on the nature of modernization, defined as the unleashing of market forces, the increasing domination of life by markets, and the increasing tendency of people to seek liberty, both as individuals and collectively.[14] Even as Eliot echoes a traditional moral framework of domestic fiction derived from Richardson, she also radically modernizes this framework with her emphasis on the ubiquitous power of the market. The novel's most obvious modernization of the Richardsonian narrative of the naive heroine pursued by the predatory rake is the heroine's new relation to the marketplace. Clarissa Harlowe falls tragically into degraded economic space (she is confined by Lovelace in a brothel) but this fall occurs only when the mercenary brutality of her family causes her to flee her family home. In contrast, Gwendolen Harleth—the surname's similarity to Harlowe as well as "harlot" is probably deliberate—actively seeks enmeshment in the marketplace. The famous opening scene of the novel shows Gwendolen desperately engaged in "the new excitement of gambling" (156), an image that the reader sees through the eyes of the morally fastidious Deronda, who looks on with disgust at her greed and self-preoccupation. For Gwendolen, a genteel woman, to gamble publicly was itself a shocking sign of her modernity, and also emblematizes how by the 1860s (for unlike other Eliot works, the novel is set in contemporary England), the traditional gender distinctions between male involvement in the marketplace and female avoidance of it, though still significant, were under powerful pressure from the economic need that drove thousands of middle-class women into the paid labor force. Indeed, responding to the evident need for many women of all social classes to support themselves by work, from the 1850s campaigns to widen employment and educational opportunities for women became a basis of feminist activism, which Eliot was well aware of, as her friend Barbara Bodichon was an important feminist activist. Our initial image of Gwendolen as gambler reflects the modern reality of educated women drawn to and threatened by their potential enmeshment in the marketplace.

As Gwendolen struggles with her newfound poverty, the dangers of the market's lure quickly become evident. In one of her most powerful comments on the inadequacy of feminine education, which is also a major theme of *Middlemarch*, Eliot creates a scene in which Gwendolen, fearing poverty and desperate to find a career, appeals for advice about a professional career in theater to the continental musician Herr Klesmer. In a brilliant and painful scene, he tells her that should she attempt a career on the stage she would merely make herself a sexual object: "[O]n the stage, beauty is taken where there is nothing more commanding to be had." He implies that Gwendolen would be reduced to marketing her sexuality, engaging in a kind of prostitution: "[such a woman's] career will not be luxurious to begin with: . . . and the indignities she will be liable to are such as I will not speak of" (260). But on the other hand, he crushingly tells her, a more dignified career as a genuine artist is beyond her reach, given her "inexperience—lack of discipline— lack of instruction" (257). Thus, Gwendolen's situation is that of a woman who both faces the traditional moral dangers of women's entry into the marketplace—the danger of sexual transgression and victimization—but also confronts the more modern problem that a woman must consider: whether she has amassed sufficient education, training, and cultural capital to be marketable on terms more dignified than those of self-prostitution. The novel's striking modernity is visible here in its blunt acknowledgment that women must struggle against self-degradation and sexual victimization in the marketplace not merely by retreating from it into domesticity but by taking on the burden of acquiring the human and cultural capital to market themselves successfully.

In fact, Gwendolen's naive relation to the historical forces that are modernizing feminine gender roles is her central weakness. Her enmeshment in, and inability to withstand, market forces, so visible in her chastening audition for Herr Klesmer (whose name suggests his Jewish origins), will prove thematically pivotal for the novel since it is the key to the relation between Gwendolen's narrative and the novel's other main plot, Daniel Deronda's growing commitment to Jewish culture. From Eliot's perspective, both women and the Jews must confront the power of the marketplace as a central obstacle to their self-liberation. Though the ethical dilemma that Gwendolen faces concerning Grandcourt's preexisting family might seem a moral issue that transcends history, because of the thematic centrality of market relations in the novel, Eliot carefully identifies Gwendolen as a woman whose behavior and attitudes, including her eagerness to go riding, her gambling, her willingness to pursue a performing career, and her confidence that she will have great freedom in her marriage to Grandcourt, are products of recent history, which is modernizing women's roles and their relation to the marketplace. Indeed, in her materialism and lack of moral seriousness, Gwendolen resembles the late Victorian "Girl of the Period" "whose sole idea of life is plenty of fun and luxury," famously denounced by antifeminist novelist Eliza Lynn Linton, who accused her of imitating the dress and perhaps the moral character of the prostitute.[15] As we will see, in her mercenary marriage, Gwendolen similarly approaches the moral status of the prostitute. But Gwendolen's central error is that she egotistically imagines society's structures to be less hostile to her independence and freedom than they are precisely because she does not understand her place in history. Eliot's implicit ideal of femininity is similar to George Sand's, that of a woman who, without abandoning her essential femininity, is aware, in Sand's phrase, of the "crisis of our times," who is able to understand the deep thoughts of the time and who recognizes "diseased present time is at odds with the past which holds it back."[16] But if Gwendolen is a product of her times, she is not a heroine out of Sand's novels who can grasp the intellectual, social, and political changes of her time and respond to them. Though Eliot does not define her ideal of a woman self-conscious of her position in history as bluntly as does Sand, that Eliot shares this ideal is implicit in her quietly damning characterization of her heroine: "Gwendolen was as inwardly rebellious against the restraint of family conditions, and as ready to look through obligations into her own fundamental want of feeling for them, as if she had been sustained by the boldest speculations; but she really had no such speculations, and would at once have marked herself off from any sort of theoretical or practically reforming women by satirising them" (53). If Gwendolen has the satiric attitude of superiority to "theoretical or practically reforming women," there is no rational basis for her assumption of superiority to them. The satiric target of this and many other passages in the novel is Gwendolen herself, whose insouciant and genteel feelings of superiority and unawareness of practical or theoretical criticisms of the feminine position leave her doomed to be a victim of history's progress. Rather than being an autonomous subject acting within history, she is as unaware of history's movement as she is of how to adequately prepare herself for the stage or the concert hall.

Thus Eliot implies that Gwendolen, a woman whose desire for freedom outruns her capacity to earn it, fails because she lags behind the progressive movement of history that women must join. If the historical character of femininity potentially liberates women from the stereotyped images and ideological norms of domesticity, it also stands as a condemnation of a woman such as Gwendolen who has inadequately readied herself to join the march of progress defined as individuals and groups who strive for freedom. As the narrator summarizes Gwendolen's delusive state before marriage: "What she was clear upon was, that she did not wish to lead the same sort of life as ordinary young ladies did; but what she was not clear upon was, how she should set about leading any other, and what were the particular acts which she would assert her freedom by doing" (52). Gwendolen's relation to historical change is contradictory, for she is both a product of the era's widening horizons and increased material wealth for middle-class women but unaware of how the "past," which "holds back" the present, will also hold her back. Eliot emphasizes this flaw by making Gwendolen oblivious to the political movements of her time, including momentous struggles for human freedom:

> Could there be a slenderer, more insignificant thread in human history than this consciousness of a girl, busy with her small inferences of the way in which she could make her life pleasant? —in a time, too, when ideas were with fresh vigour making armies of themselves, and the universal kinship was declaring itself fiercely: when women on the other side of the world would not mourn for the husbands and sons who died bravely in a common cause, and men stinted of bread on our side of the world heard of that willing loss and were patient: a time when the soul of man was waking to pulses which had for centuries been beating in him unfelt, until their full sum made a new life of terror or of joy. (124)

The immediate reference is to the American Civil War and the sympathy of British workers for the Union cause, despite the economic cost to workers of the interruption of cotton supplies, but the larger theme is the spread of human liberty and "the universal kinship" of humanity. These themes will reverberate powerfully through the novel, forming a crucial context for Deronda's growing fascination with and commitment to the Jewish people, another community deprived of liberty and also suffering, because of anti-Semitism, from the lack of feelings of "universal kinship." In the cosmic context of this struggle for human liberty, Gwendolen is so oblivious to the march of ideas freeing slaves everywhere as to enslave herself through her loveless marriage. Her deepest weakness is her failure to recognize her relation to history's progressive movement.

Paradoxically, Gwendolen's marriage to Grandcourt confirms her blindness to the forces of historical progress while being very much the product of contemporary women's problems; indeed, in her desire for freedom in the married state, she exemplifies the general march of ideas ("ideas were with fresh vigour making armies of themselves") that is causing humanity to fight for freedom. Yet she lacks the awareness of how to seek freedom effectively, and expecting freedom in marriage finds only imprisonment. Moreover, the couple's descent into a hellish state of mutual animosity and poisonous idleness figures a culture's larger malaise, the nation's lack of vigorous spiritual energy and its stultification by a decadent elite. As a landed aristocrat heedless of the society changing around him, Grandcourt parallels in masculine aristocratic terms Gwendolen's solipsistic version of femininity. The novel is set shortly before the 1867 Reform Bill, which dramatically increased the size of the electorate by enfranchising much of the male urban working class; in this context, Grandcourt embodies an aristocracy woefully unprepared to face the changing reality of a democratizing society. This sense of a traditional aristocratic order ill-prepared to face an emergent mass political society extends to the hero as well. Daniel Deronda's indecision about his vocation—Sir Hugh urges him to pursue a political career, but he feels that politics is corrupting—typifies a cultural elite unable or unwilling to respond adequately to a modernizing and democratizing world, torn between the need for modernization and a stubborn commitment to a traditional past that is ebbing away.

Cultural malaise is also suggested by Gwendolen's fateful decision to marry Grandcourt, which becomes an emblem of a culture without strong moral direction, for her choice is repeatedly associated with her propensity for gambling and thus figures the breakdown of the mental division between the world of commerce and of womanly behavior as well as the weakening of traditional moral restraints. Hesitating before her marriage, Gwendolen reads it as an ominous sign of her breaking free from moral and religious bonds:

> She seemed on the edge of adopting deliberately, as a notion for all the rest of her life, what she had rashly said in her bitterness, when her discovery had driven her away to Leubronn; that it did not signify what she did; she had only to amuse herself as best she could. . . . [A]ll the infiltrated influences of disregarded religious teaching, as well as the deeper impressions of something awful and inexorable enveloping her, seemed to concentrate themselves in the vague conceptions of avenging power. (311–12)

Gwendolen's spiritual vertigo captures the experience of many educated Victorians that the period's doubts about religious faith left them without a clear moral compass. Her fondness for gambling suggests how that pursuit becomes an image for accepting the world as determined by random forces without moral purpose or meaning, a profoundly morally disturbing image of the world that late Victorians were forced to contemplate in the wake of Darwin's evolutionary theory, with its emphasis on the role of chance in nature, and the decline of belief in God's intervention in history. Moreover, as Deronda points out to her, gambling places the individuals in an amoral relationship to society, since it implies complicity in profiting parasitically and without deserving from the losses and suffering of others. In her spiritual crisis, as in the naive aspiration for "the imagined freedom she would create for herself in marriage," Gwendolen is a product of her time, while her tragically mistaken choice of Henleigh Grandcourt is a symptom of her inability to respond adequately to the realities of her historical moment, above all as these realities affect women. As we have seen, the Lydia Glasher narrative is designed to remind readers that the sexual norms followed by elite Victorian men and women were often strikingly different. Yet, at a time when male sexual license was becoming increasingly controversial, Gwendolen complacently assumes that Grandcourt is no worse in this regard than other men. Similarly, though Victorian women were angrily protesting their legal disabilities in marriage, Gwendolen, who imagines she will "manage" her husband, is as ignorant of the realities of marriage as "of magnetic currents and the law of storms" (298). The limits of Gwendolen's feminine education figure how she is above all a heroine who fails to respond to the promise and challenge of her historical moment in her failure to understand the confining realities of Victorian marriage.

Gwendolen's premonition of an "avenging power" awaiting her suggests how profoundly moralistic is the narrative sensibility that judges her. Eliot is famous for redirecting the fictive universe away from conventional religious doctrines: having lost her own evangelical Christian faith, she nevertheless still believed in largely Christian moral categories and urged a morally guided life, but now not directed toward God but rather toward human progress. But just as Christian thought typically envisions damnation and hell as the "avenging power" awaiting the sinner, Gwendolen intuits that such a power awaits her. Indeed, she is right, but it is not the Christian afterlife that awaits her, but the hell of marital alienation and self-recrimination.

WOMEN AND JEWS

As Gwendolen suffers from the tragically unhappy marriage that results from her marital choice, she turns in desperation to Deronda for spiritual and psychic support. In this part of the novel, Gwendolen's narrative is interwoven with the increasingly prominent narrative of Deronda's fascination with a group of Jews, particularly the beautiful singer Mirah whom he rescues from attempted suicide. Deronda is also drawn to a sickly boarder of the Cohen family, eventually revealed to be Mirah's brother, the mystical and charismatic Mordecai. The issue that has puzzled readers of the novel since its original reception is by what logic these seemingly disparate narrative strands are linked.[17] The obvious connection between women and Jews is that both are preeminently victims of prejudice in the dominant culture. Though antifeminine bias is not as obvious a theme in *Deronda* as in earlier Eliot novels, it is clearly not absent from a novel in which Grandcourt says, "[i]nfernal idiots that women are!" (350), and Lady Mallinger is viewed by popular opinion as "the infelicitous wife who had produced nothing but daughters, little better than no children" (442). As the Lydia Glasher plot and Grandcourt's treatment of Gwendolen shows, women suffer in concrete and demonstrable ways from male sexism and tyranny. Indeed, Grandcourt's brutal tyranny over the heroine, combined with his contemptuous treatment of his mistress, are the novel's central examples of how sexism often renders women's lives miserable. The novel links these two kinds of victimization by prejudice and unjust power by making Deronda, a male character raised as a Gentile who initially believes himself illegitimate, show an unusual degree of sympathy for the situation of both women and Jews, most obviously in his rescue of the female Jew Mirah.

Daniel's unusual sensitivity is shown to be the result of both temperament and early environment, specifically his fear of his own illegitimacy combined with a definite moral fastidiousness. This trait is emphasized immediately before Deronda rescues Mirah as she is about to commit suicide, when the narrator remarks that Deronda's indecision about his career arises from his intense moral earnestness and sympathy for others: "the strong array of reasons why he should shrink from getting into that routine of the world which makes men apologise for all its wrong-doing" (188). Shortly after, acting out of spontaneous empathy for Mirah in her despair, he rescues her from attempted drowning. He sees in her plight an image of the sorrows of women, especially fallen women, a socially despised group for which his own probable illegitimacy makes him feel empathy: "The agitating impression this forsaken girl was making on him stirred a fibre that lay close to his deepest interest in the fates of women—'perhaps my mother was like this one'" (190–91). His interest in her destiny is not lessened by learning of her Jewishness, and indeed his search for her relations leads him to meet and become friends with a family of Jews, the Cohens, and ultimately to concern himself with the fate of the Jewish people.

Beyond the obvious link of victimization by prejudice, the novel suggests a deeper and more subtle connection between the situation of Jews and women. Equally important is that the social process menacing both groups is the encroaching or, to use a favorite metaphor of the novel, imperial power of the market. Women are particularly threatened by the market because they can be reduced to being sexual commodities, metaphorically mere slaves. It is this danger of commodification that Klesmer sneeringly warns Gwendolen she would face by becoming a public performer without adequate training. Mirah's emergence in the novel further develops this theme, as her history embodies this danger for women. Compelled by her greedy and gambling father into public performances, a career she finds distasteful and degrading, she finally flees from home when threatened by the prostitution of being compelled to marry for money. Though she is a talented singer, her repeatedly expressed dislike for public concerts suggests her lasting resistance to the pressures of self-commodification, which have dominated the early part of her life. Mirah's function in the novel is thus to embody in stark form the dangers of degradation to the status of sexual commodity that women face when forced to market themselves openly for money. Superficially, Gwendolen has averted this fate after the warning from Klesmer. Yet her marriage to Grandcourt is repeatedly referred to as a disastrous gamble, while its chief benefits are economic (the wealth and status available to her as an aristocrat's wife and the income given her impoverished mother). Such imagery links the desperate and disastrous entry into commercial life seen in the novel's opening scene, in which Gwendolen gambles away money, and the similarly costly surrender to economic coercion she makes with her marriage. As her marriage to Grandcourt deteriorates, Gwendolen becomes little better than a slave, as the narrator compares her husband's control of her to the policy of a brutal colonist: "If this white-handed man with the perpendicular profile had been sent to govern a difficult colony, he might have won reputation among his contemporaries. He had certainly ability, would have understood that it was safer to exterminate than to cajole superseded proprietors, and would not have flinched from making things safe in that way" (594). The reference is to Governor Eyre, whose harsh suppression in 1865 of a Jamaican rebellion caused a furor; Eyre's actions were directed against former slaves inhabiting the British colony. The parallel between Mirah and Gwendolen's being reduced to becoming human commodities, the impoverished Jewish woman and the wealthy Gentile, suggests that women at every class level are equally threatened by the imperial power of the market. Born into a more privileged class status than Mirah, Gwendolen is nevertheless like her in being threatened by economic coercion. But unlike her, she has willingly given in to economic pressure and prostitutes herself in marrying a man she does not love.

If women are victims of the power of the market, in her representation of Victorian Jews Eliot clearly implies that the Jews as a people face potential dehumanization by their enmeshment in the marketplace. While a Jew such as Mirah is an unwilling victim of the marketplace, Eliot's development of the theme also suggests that many Jews (such as Mirah's father) use the market to victimize others, or at least have become imbued with an excessively commercial sensibility, a pattern in the novel that echoes a traditional theme of anti-Semitism, which associated Jews with materialism and economic predation. Unquestionably in her treatment of Mirah's father and of the Cohen family, the paterfamilias of which Ezra Cohen is a cheerful pawnbroker (a kind of jovial Shylock), Eliot draws on such traditional images of the Jews as archetypal capitalists, a use of anti-Semitic imagery that understandably disturbs modern readers.[18] It is important to note, however, that even in deploying this anti-Semitic theme, Eliot takes pains to place it in the context of Deronda's increasing respect for the Jews he meets. Moreover, through Deronda's growing understanding of the cultural and social situation of the Jews, the novel distinguishes his sense of the dehumanizing character of market relations from reflexive hostility to a people long linked with commerce or a belief in their inherent moral deficiency. By learning to distinguish the revulsion he feels at the materialism of the Cohens from reflexive prejudice against Jews, he comes to reject traditional anti-Semitism. Even in his initial distaste for Ezra Cohen, Deronda's response is dominated by an aristocratic disdain of the commercial spirit of the archetypal small businessman, and the narrator acknowledges that what most strikes Deronda is the man's mundane bourgeois characteristics, which subvert Gentile fantasies of the Jews as an inherently romantic and poetic race: "no shadow of Suffering Race distinguished his [Cohen's] vulgarity of soul from that of a prosperous pink-and-white huckster of the purest English lineage" (391).[19] Essentially what Deronda dislikes about the Cohens is not their Jewishness but their immersion in commerce; he shares his creator's sense that excessive materialism deadens humanity's higher capacities. By teaching Deronda this distinction between a materialism that characterizes some Jews and derogatory Christian stereotypes of the Jews generally and by representing Jews such as Mirah and Mordecai, who themselves vigorously reject the preoccupation with commerce that characterizes many Jews, the novel clearly attempts to disrupt the reader's anti-Semitic assumptions. The novel's subversion of traditional anti-Semitism (combined with satiric depiction of the ignorance and reflexive anti-Semitism of even good-hearted Christians such as the Meyrick family) includes showing how Gentiles such as Gwendolen fall into materialism and greed as much as do some of the novel's Jewish characters. At the same time, the novel carefully contextualizes the materialism of Jewish characters by suggesting that, to the extent modern Jews do have materialistic tendencies, these are the product of their oppressed and deracinated social situation rather than of their essential nature.

It is typical of much social thought of the Victorian era to evince anxiety about the increased commercialization that industrialization brought with it and to decry the negative effects of markets on men as well as women, Christians as much as Jews. Not only for socialists, but for such conservative thinkers as Carlyle and Ruskin, the destructive impact of markets and market-based thinking is one of the central themes of their critique of an industrial society. Eliot shares this anxiety, writing as a young woman in a letter to friends to praise those who have "a presentiment, a yearning, or a clear vision of the time when this miserable reign of Mammon shall end."[20] She never lost her dislike of the power of money, which she eloquently expresses in *Deronda* as in her other novels. But she puts Jews and women in a special category as groups particularly threatened and adversely affected by the power of the market. Women risk being degraded as virtual slaves of men, or if not slaves, female performers such as Mirah, their self-marketing associated with the degradation of actual prostitution. For Eliot, such self-marketing is not just degrading in the sense that all human involvement with the market risks degradation, but it particularly violates a basic nature of women in their capacity for altruism and purity. Thus, a relation to the market requires them to constantly be on guard against the degradation that the self-marketing of the female body entails.

Similarly, Eliot suggests the market has particular dangers for Jews. In their case, as with women, there is both a particularly historic talent for doing good, but also a peculiar vulnerability. Their gift for good lies in their historical capacity for moral seriousness and respect for moral law; their vulnerability derives from how, as she saw it, the Jews' spiritual character had been exhausted and stunted by two forces, their historic religious traditionalism and their condition as a persecuted and despised people. Deronda's Jewish mentor Mordecai forcefully expresses this idea of contemporary Jews as spiritually exhausted and giving in to materialism when he tells Ezra Cohen's young son Jacob, "A curse is on your generation, child. They will open the mountains and drag forth the golden wings and coin them into money" (478). Later, in discussing the destiny of the Jews with a group of self-taught, working-class intellectuals, Mordecai elaborates his diagnosis of the spiritual failings of modern Jews, ascribing it to their segregation and persecution in Gentile culture: "the dispersion was wide, the yoke of oppression was a spiked torture as well as a load; . . . What wonder that multitudes of our people are ignorant, narrow, superstitious? What wonder?" (532) Jews can only rise above the materialism of the wider culture, above a "selfish ambitious and rivalry in low greed" that assimilation into an industrializing Gentile society offers them (528), Mordecai argues, by committing themselves to a higher ideal than personal enrichment. In accordance with Eliot's ideals of secular human liberation, the ideal Mordecai proposes for the Jews is the settling of a new homeland and the creation of a "new Jewish polity" where there will be "equality of protection" for the long-persecuted Jews, which will end their status as outcast people in Christian culture.

The problematic relation that both Jews and women have to the marketplace, then, is for Eliot a symptom of arguably the deepest and most profound link between the two groups, that neither have fully reaped the benefits of human progress. For each group, moreover, Eliot suggests that to envision its progress one must understand carefully the nature of historical progress itself. Traditionally, women were seen as outside of history or as lagging behind it in their concerns. Eliot explores such a type of femininity in Maggie Tulliver, whose primarily familial and atavistic loyalties leave her helpless before the forces of a commercializing world. Despite, by some measures, her modernity, Gwendolen Harleth emblematizes feminine backwardness, as when Klesmer sneers at the amateurism of her musical training. Similarly, Deronda summarizes a key point of Victorian feminism, traceable to Mary Wollstonecraft, when he tells her that women must accept what Carlyle had called the "gospel of work." Women, Eliot implies, must remold their femininity so that it aspires to a more elevated social status than it has heretofore achieved and allows a greater self-realization through commitment to disciplined labor, a radical departure from what had been the expected role of elite women. At the same time, Eliot is also deeply concerned with the violence she sees women doing to their dignity and nature as women when they surrender to the pressures of the marketplace; in this regard Mirah's experience of the dangers of commodification are a cautionary tale. In her infatuation with wealth and horseback riding, her eagerness to gamble, and even her willingness to consider becoming a public performer, Gwendolen has shown herself to be superficially a modern woman. But Eliot's point about her is that while she unthinkingly embraced the worst side of modernization in the form of heightened materialism, by so doing she has been unaware of the potential of her historical moment for feminine self-liberation through disciplined labor and sympathy for a wider community beyond herself and family.

The novel's plot harshly chastens Gwendolen for this blindness to her moment's historical promise. The passages in the novel describing her marriage to Grandcourt summarize and refine a tradition of Gothic and sensation fiction in which women's oppressive position in patriarchal families is linked with the threat of madness and imprisonment.[21] Gwendolen is not literally imprisoned, but she is consistently silenced and subjected by her husband's "empire of fear" (425) and is bereft of the capacity for individual choices. If not literally insane, she feels intense psychic torments because of her disappointment in failing to achieve any autonomy in her marriage and even more because of her remorse and guilt over the wrong she now understands she has done Lydia Glasher, a sin for which her miserable marriage seems a retribution. But these emotions are inseparable from the tyranny of her husband, who becomes a figure reminiscent of the worst villains of

Gothic fiction. Revealing his underlying sadism, he brutally forces Gwendolen to wear the necklace that Lydia had sent Gwendolen with her premonitory letter, thus subjecting his wife to the same complete control to which his mistress submitted, while fully enjoying her crushed resistance: "[s]he fancied that his eyes showed a delight in torturing her" (427). The necklace becomes an image of his utter possession of her, a status that she bitterly reflects she has earned by "robb[ing] another woman" (427). Her sense of deserving "some retributive calamity" aids Grandcourt's sadistic project: "her fear of him . . . had reached a superstitious point" (427), while his total control of his wife is a source of satisfaction to him. Having put the necklace on her "Grandcourt inwardly observed that she answered to the rein" (428).

Gwendolen's only relief from her status as possession and damned soul is to seek both spiritual and psychic redemption through an increasingly strong relationship with Deronda. In an emblematic scene, she wears the necklace that he had redeemed for her in Leubronn to a party that he attends, thus signaling to Deronda her mood of repentance. Having heard the story of Grandcourt's preexisting family, he shares Gwendolen's sense that she has been complicit in wronging Grandcourt's mistress. Indeed, to a striking degree, he sympathizes with the fallen woman and her offspring and judges Gwendolen accordingly: "His own acute experience made him alive to the form of injury which might affect the unavowed children and their mother. . . . Gwendolen's view of her position might easily have been no other than that her husband's marriage with her was his entrance on the path of virtue, while Mrs. Glasher represented his forsaken sin. And Deronda had naturally some resentment on behalf of the Hagars and Ishmaels" (43–35). Accordingly, when Gwendolen appeals to him for means to show her repentance, he sternly advises her, in a summary of Eliot's own ethos, to educate herself and broaden her field of sympathies: "Look on other lives besides your own [he tells her]. See what their troubles are, and how they are borne. Try to care about something in this vast world besides the gratification of small selfish desires. Try to care for what is best in thought and action—something that is good apart from the accidents of your own lot" (446). Naturally Gwendolen will have difficulty following this advice, since the novel's image of the world she lives in is of an upper class obsessed with the fulfillment of their "small selfish desires." The Arnoldian ring of "what is best in thought and action" suggests an ambiguity in this ethos between a recommendation to pursue what is aesthetically best and elevated, a project that could coexist with a lack of sympathy for actual human suffering, and the main thrust of Deronda's recommendation, encouraging sympathy for other humans and their communities. This ambiguity derives from the difficulty of realizing in concrete and practical terms the romantic faith in the idea that the awakening of the emotional life through nature or art, that is through aesthetic experience, will have meaningful effect in the world of human sympathy and action for others. As we will see later, this ambiguity between aesthetic and moral sympathy will loom large in the Jamesian revision of Eliot's ethos and fictional practice.

Modern readers of Eliot have been dismayed by the failure of her heroines to assert their independence against the restraints of a patriarchal culture. But it is a mistake to see her heroines as passive. Eliot's convention for representing female resistance is largely through the plot of women drawn emotionally to men who society forbids them, but whose personalities offer a contrast to stultifying masculine authority figures. We see this in Maggie Tulliver's attraction to Stephen Guest, in Dorothea Casaubon's attraction, while her husband Casaubon is still alive, to Will Ladislaw, and in Gwendolen's attraction to Daniel Deronda. There is reason to believe that this plot had a personal resonance for Eliot, as biographers believe she twice fell in love with married men (her employer John Chapman and George Lewes), and she seems to have feared that the passionate side of her nature was a threat to her sense of morality, as when, on the eve of her conservative father's death she wrote her friends the Brays, "I had a horrid vision of myself last night becoming earthly sensual and devilish for want of that purifying restraining influence [of her father]" (*EL*, 1:284). But this theme of transgressive passion is not only autobiographical, as it draws on a literary tradition, most powerfully represented by George Sand, that represents women's rebellion against a patriarchal lot through their sexual passion. Interestingly, when she encountered a version of this plot in Charlotte's Brontë's *Jane Eyre* (1847), Eliot complained of the conservatism of Brontë's handling of it. Writing of Jane's refusal to stay with Rochester, the man she loves, because his insane wife is still alive, Eliot writes: "All self-sacrifice is good—but one would like it to be in a somewhat nobler cause than that of a diabolical law which chains a man soul and body to a putrefying carcase" (*EL* 1:51). This abrupt dismissal of the laws limiting access to divorce as "diabolical" suggests a paradox of Eliot's stance toward marriage and the family, which is that while considering the traditional legal and moral structures that governed marital life excessively rigid, she also had a profound fear of allowing erotic behavior to be guided by individual self-interest. Thus Eliot uses plots of women who struggle between passion and social conformity to suggest the intolerable nature of women's confinement within patriarchal familial structures while also warning against a selfish individualism which she saw as allied with materialism in subverting the possibility of human community.

Ultimately, through Grandcourt's abrupt death in a boating accident off the Italian coast, the narrative magically liberates Gwendolen from the Dantean hell of her marriage. Yet her husband's death also further chastens Gwendolen's rebellious nature. Gwendolen has failed to aid her husband with sufficient speed to save him, and the moral ambiguity of this failure underscores how the accident answers Gwendolen's largely, but by no means completely, unconscious desire to liberate herself from her purgatorial marriage by murdering the patriarchal tyrant. Aware of how fate has brought to life her not-quite-buried transgressive and homicidal wishes, Gwendolen is overwhelmed with remorse and again turns to Deronda, who is providentially in Italy, to comfort her and help her expiate her sinful desires.

Deronda has meanwhile been pursuing an immersion in Jewish culture and history and deriving from it the lesson that Jews must hew a middle course between a rigid adherence to religious and ethnic tradition on one hand while, on the other, avoiding a complete surrender to the forces of modernization and assimilation into a bourgeois and Gentile culture that would cause the Jews to disappear as a distinct cultural group. In her representation of how Mordecai teaches Deronda to be inspired by his vision of Jewish nationalism—a vision to which Deronda, on learning of his own Jewish parentage, resolves to wholeheartedly devote himself—Eliot offers a salvation for the Jews that both gives them a future as a people while breaking decisively with what she considers their rigid religious traditionalism. Though this plot has generated some unease in modern readers, [22] in sending Deronda off to seek avenues of Jewish liberation abroad she emulates in an idealistic form the narrative pattern deployed by Dickens when he sends Pip off at the end of *Great Expectations* to expiate his complicity in class snobbery and class conflict through the self-sacrifice of working in the "East." Both writers are participating in a larger cultural movement by which British society subordinated the centrality of internal and especially class reform in national life to a new fervor in dedication to imperialist projects, interpreted as Britain's civilizing and governing duty. Though external colonization had long beckoned as a safety valve for the discontented and economically deprived, in the last four decades of the nineteenth century, British society committed itself to its imperial mission with increased vigor.[23] If Eliot's thinking is influenced by a broad acceptance of Britain's imperial role, she clearly also found herself disturbed by national chauvinism and the arrogance and brutality of some of Britain's imperial behavior, as is suggested by her consistent linking of Grandcourt with the darkest side of imperialism (as when he is implicitly compared to the brutal colonialist Governor Eyre).

As Amanda Anderson has pointed out, Eliot's narrative of Jewish nationalism involves a complex compromise between allegiance to an ethnic-based identity that is prereflective and a relation to tradition open to revision by self-conscious reflection.[24] The novel's suggestion that the Jews can liberate themselves through a secular nationalist political project leaves radically uncertain the status of religious traditionalism, and Deronda suggests that he will respect such traditionalism only to a degree. Despite these limitations, the general thrust of Eliot's plot, which is to both encourage respect for identity rooted in traditionalism while modernizing such tradition by affiliating it with modernizing goals, specifically nationalist ones, expresses Eliot's consistent distrust of parochialism combined with her belief in organic communities as counterweight to the atomizing force of the marketplace. Though the celebration of an ethnically homogenous nationalism has troubled some readers, in its treatment of the Deronda-Mordecai relationship, the novel revises one of the most liberal elements of *The Moonstone*. In both novels there is a crucial alliance between the hero and a mysterious and racially Other man who is a source of knowledge. In *The Moonstone*, it is Ezra Jennings, the enigmatic mixed-race doctor's assistant, who provides Blake with the key to the mystery of the moonstone's fate. In *Deronda*, Mordecai gives Deronda not only a profoundly sympathetic and insightful understanding of the Jews and their situation, but offers him nothing less than his ultimate destiny. Both Jennings and Mordecai are mortally ill, perform their salvific function for the hero, and then expire nobly. Moreover, both characters are named Ezra (Mordecai's true name) a name that means "helper" in Hebrew and thus corresponds to the role each character plays for the respective heroes.[25] But Eliot's novel dramatically shifts the weight given to the hero's confrontation with prejudice and his rejection of racism. In *The Moonstone*, Franklin Blake must overcome prejudice against racial Otherness to find an ally in achieving a successful manhood, yet the hero's victory over social prejudice, while highly significant, is a secondary theme to the solution of the mystery. In contrast in *Deronda,* the hero's personal victory over social prejudice and his enlarged field of sympathy is central to his development.

Unsurprisingly, given the novel's parallel between the two groups, women and Jews, Eliot's implied solution to feminine discontents is analogous to that which she imagines for the Jews. For women, as for the Jews, the solution to the problem of historical progress lies in a balance between modernizing and traditional impulses, in avoiding both modernity's drift toward amoral self-commodification and self-marginalizing confinement in a privatized realm cut off from self-development and progress. The confluence of these two compromises between tradition and modernization is embodied in Deronda, a modernizing Jew, and his friendship with Gwendolen. As we have seen, he becomes an apostle to the intellectually and spiritually backward Gwendolen, indeed a messianic figure (implicitly modeled on Christ), who offers Gwendolen a modernized gospel of moral rectitude to heal her moral anguish and drift. Moreover, this development reinstates the Jews' traditional role, since in Eliot's mind the great Jewish contribution to world culture was their focus on moral law. If Eliot turns her back on unreflective moral traditionalism, in an aspect of her sensibility that has been disconcerting for modern readers she equally rejects a full-blown project of modernization of feminine roles, which she identifies with a complete surrender of feminine identity to the dictates of the marketplace. She sees women as ideally and naturally embodying noncompetitive and nurturant values that the culture needs; she feels that women must learn to become more altruistic, not less, rather than sacrifice their womanliness to conform to a market-dominated world. While sharing the Wollstonecraftean skepticism about women's allegedly innate nature being inferior, or superior, to men's, Eliot follows George Sand in valuing women's tendency to find their highest goal in an altruism that transcends their individual desires. It is due to her commitment to women's altruistic role that Eliot disappointed some of her women friends by declining to support the demand for women's suffrage.

Eliot's middle-ground position between modernity and tradition is not simply the smooth mediation of unsatisfactory extremes, but is clearly the product of her intense ambivalence about Victorian women's growing determination to find fulfillment and autonomy through education and labor. Creative labor was particularly inviting and fulfilling for women, for in certain fields, such as music and drama, by the nineteenth century women already had a strong tradition of achievement on which to build. Essentially Eliot's project as a woman determined to become one of Britain's major novelists was to extend that tradition of culturally acknowledged creative achievement by women into literature. Her predecessors in other arts were significant to her: in a letter to a friend she in fact announces, "I have turned out to be an artist . . . with words."[26] But in this project of feminine conquest of the literary sphere, she had to confront the powerful cultural anxieties in her society about feminine creative achievement, in particular the fear that such achievement was a sign of rebelliousness, neurosis, and unwomanliness that could lead women to become sexually compromised. All of these issues are at stake in Eliot's portrayal of Princess Lenora Halm-Eberstein (the Alcharisi), the woman who, in acknowledging herself as Deronda's long-absent mother, reveals both his Jewish identity and also her hostile relation to that cultural tradition.

The dominant note of Lenora's character is her intense rebelliousness against the male-dominated religious tradition of her ancestors. Defying the authority of her father and his Jewish religious tradition, she has become a well-known singer who abandons her child in order to focus on her musical career. Eliot, who similarly broke with the evangelical Christianity of her family and sought an independent life through rupture with religion, almost certainly identifies with her character's defiance of masculine religious tradition. Indeed, a crucial advantage of the Jewish plot for Eliot is that it allows her to depict sympathetically a woman violently breaking with patriarchal religious traditions. To Eliot's primarily Christian readers, such a rebellion against Jewish tradition would easily awake compassion, because Christian readers would tend to agree that Jewish traditions were an overly rigid obstacle to human fulfillment. Yet Lenora states her refusal to remain simply a vehicle for the transmission of masculine culture in terms that could apply to any oppressive tradition: "I tell you, [my father] never thought of his daughter except as an instrument. Because I had wants outside his purpose, I was to be put in a frame and tortured. If that is the right law for the world, I will not say that I love it" (662). The complexity of Deronda's response to his mother's defiance of patriarchal authority suggests Eliot's own ambivalence about women's rebellion against tradition. Thanks to his friendship with Mordecai, Daniel is by now imbued with a deep respect for the Jewish heritage, which he will now accept as his own. He feels angry and disappointed that Lenora's rejection of Judaism has had the effect of concealing from him his ethnic heritage, and he is also understandably disappointed at his mother's abdication of a maternal role in his life. Yet he listens sympathetically to her insistence that she had a right to assert her own creative individuality. Showing him a picture of her young self, she asks, "Had I not a rightful claim to be something more than a mere daughter and mother? The voice and the genius matched the face. Whatever else was wrong, acknowledge that I had a right to be an artist, though my father's will was against it" (664). Deronda can only agree.

But Lenora is a tragic figure, her violent rebellion against her father's religion chastised, most notably in her son's refusal to follow her in rejecting Judaism—a chastisement parallel to the punishment of Gwendolen's violent impulse to rebel against patriarchal authority. In creating Lenora, Eliot at once defends her own transgression against patriarchal, especially religious, tradition and defends her right to "be an artist," while also warning against the dangers of the violent break with the past that Lenora represents. A key sign of the novel's ambivalence toward Lenora is that, in striking contrast to the anxiety about the marketplace the novel expresses generally, she transgressively glories in the freedoms that the marketplace afford women: "[My father] hated that Jewish women should be thought of by the Christian world as a sort of ware to make public singers and actresses of. As if we were not the more enviable for that! That is a chance of escaping from bondage" (631). Further evidence of Eliot's ambivalence about Lenora are the Gothic associations that hover around her; called a Melusina, a half-serpent fairy, she imparts the secret of Deronda's origins in the Gothic context of responding to a curse that dooms her to a fatal illness in apparent punishment for her defiance of her father's wishes. As a character she is visibly derived from the driven and tortured female artist figures that Sand and de Staël create, and thus she represents a tribute to an emergent tradition of feminine literary creativity.[27] But this tradition was molded by the culture's conflicting feeling about female artists, which admired their creativity while fearing that their achievements would vitiate their femininity. In her hate-filled and violent break with tradition and in her thoroughgoing unwomanliness, the Alcharisi recalls not only artist figures but the demonic unsexed revolutionary woman depicted in the conservative tradition of whom Dickens's Madame Defarge from *Tale of Two Cities* (1859) would have been a recent example. This literary type derives from Carlyle and ultimately from Edmund Burke's images of "the vilest of women" who join the revolutionary crowds demanding the arrest of the French royalty during the Revolution.[28] While Deronda's generous feelings toward his long-absent mother encourage the reader to extend some compassion to Lenora and to empathize with her burning desire for freedom from a stifling traditionalism, she is finally not a sympathetic character, because in refusing to accept the role of mother, she rejects women's nurturant role. In this refusal we see epitomized the cost of a radical and destructive break with tradition, which the novel reads with a conservative horror as an inhuman assault on feminine nature.

In contrast, Deronda will offer Gwendolen liberation from traditional femininity, which preserves, rather than does violence to, women's essential nature. Though some critics have seen Deronda as embodying merely a more subtle form of masculine authority than Grandcourt, a more fruitful way of reading Deronda would place him in the tradition of the masculine confidants Sand gives her heroines, such as Brown in *Indiana*, who sympathize with the heroine while providing an external rational commentary on her situation. As a confidant of Gwendolen, Deronda's role builds on the foundations of the conscience awoken by Lydia Glasher to confirm the justice of Gwendolen's sense of complicity in evil, and then begins to suggest ways in which she may expiate her guilt. The central point he makes to her is that she must move beyond the limits of her gender and social class by learning about the wider social world, what Sand called the "crisis of our age." As we have seen, though Deronda recommends that Gwendolen develop her individuality through education, which is a potentially self-liberating activity ("care for what is best in thought and action"), he clearly frames this education as not merely striving for individual fulfillment, but as directed toward the goal of broadening one's sympathies and increasing one's capacity to help others. The implication is that broadened knowledge and sympathy will lead Gwendolen to reject a life of idleness and luxury and work for the good of others through philanthropic or reform activities. If education is central, as we have seen, "the gospel of work" is also a key part of Deronda's message to Gwendolen. "What sort of earth or heaven," he sternly asks her, "would hold any spiritual wealth in it for souls pauperised by inaction?" (451). The stigmatization of idleness here reverberates not only with the Carlylean criticism of the aristocracy for their life of leisure but also with Wollstonecraft's insistence that women would become rational and dignified beings by abandoning the idleness traditional to their gender.

In essence, Deronda gives Gwendolen a more ambitious version of the lesson that Philip Wakem offered Maggie Tulliver: respond to your age and move with its progressive currents. After Grandcourt's death, when Gwendolen again seeks his advice, he returns even more insistently to similar themes. Having learned, he tells her, the dangers of a selfish and amoral life from her marriage, she must now learn to live through serving others, which given her class position, suggests living through philanthropy. It is a life devoted to such projects that he seems to envision when he prophesies that she will make herself "among the best of women, such as make others glad that they were born" (769). His final conversation with her in England makes clear that his advocacy of a modernized version of femininity is linked to his larger progressive vision of history; in this scene he also tells her of his commitment to Jewish nationalism and the travel abroad that that commitment will entail. But Eliot emphasizes how Gwendolen's newfound knowledge of the extent of Deronda's commitment to a larger historical project, while offering her a model for the life of wider sympathies and engagement with history that Deronda urges on her, is initially experienced largely as a shattering blow to her own sense of self-importance:

> There comes a terrible moment to many souls when the great movements of the world, the larger destinies of mankind, which have lain aloof in newspapers and other neglected reading, enter like an earthquake into their own lives. . . .

> That was the sort of crisis which was at this moment beginning in Gwendolen's small life: she was for the first time feeling the pressure of a vast mysterious movement, for the first time being dislodged from her supremacy in her own world, and getting a sense that her horizon was but a dipping onward of an existence with which her own was revolving . . . (803–4)

If the scene is a painful experience, Eliot clearly feels it is a salutary one for Gwendolen, not only chastening her for her self-involvement but indicating how completely her insulation from the "great movements of the world" has left her vulnerable to bewilderment and disappointment. Most obviously, Gwendolen loses Deronda as a potential husband as well as an available source of emotional support. At the same time, the scene reinforces the idea that Gwendolen must understand and participate in the historical change that will inevitably affect her. Though she ends this chapter in nearly hysterical grief, by the last pages of the novel she is writing Deronda that she remembers his words *"that I may live to be one of the best of women, who make others glad that they were born"* (810; italics in original). This line suggests that Gwendolen intends to commit herself to the altruistic and philanthropic ideals that Deronda had recommended to her and that she will in future avoid being a "soul pauperised by inaction." Deronda has agreed to continue counseling her through letters, and, given the grandiose philanthropic and political project he is about to embark on, it would be surprising if he did not continue to urge her to participate in such pursuits. Modern critics have tended to see the endings of Eliot's novels merely as reinforcing an ethos of feminine self-abnegation, but this reading ignores how a life devoted to a larger cause can be deeply fulfilling. Such a reading also fails to acknowledge that in the Victorian era such philanthropic and reform projects were a promising field in which elite women were able to more fully develop their capacities and through which they launched novel and significant public roles.[29] A philanthropic career was an avenue by which a woman could both fulfill her individuality and influence the larger world, while remaining an upholder of the values of an essential femininity by resisting egotism and the aggressiveness of the dominant culture.

REALISM AT THE BREAKING POINT

If Eliot's ideological positions in *Deronda* have alienated not a few modern readers, the novel also disconcerts by the sheer originality of its generic character, in particular its movement in its later half from the domestic realism of the Gwendolen narrative to the mythic narrative that dominates the Jewish plot. One influential response (represented by Leavis among others) has been simply to read the novel as a formal failure. A more useful response may be to acknowledge the aesthetic challenge the novel offers us but to try to read that aesthetic difficulty as a response to a particular historical situation, and to Eliot's goals in responding to that context. Most basically, the novel's generic shift suggests Eliot's sense that the ideas she desired to express exceeded what could be said within the conventions of domestic realism. As a mode realism creates an implied agreement with the reader founded on shared assumptions about the plausible and the acceptable; the realist writer agrees tacitly to limit or minimize narrative developments that would be judged wildly implausible, as well as those that could be seen as morally and socially unacceptable. It is of course crucial to the ideological and aesthetic effectiveness of the realist mode that there is a large area of overlap between what is judged plausible and what is morally and socially acceptable. The hostile reception of much sensation fiction, and in some quarters of *The Mill on the Floss*, shows that the violation of the perceived norms of the socially acceptable could easily be translated into the language of indignation against both a fiction's inappropriateness and its narrative implausibility. In this context, it is suggestive that the reception of the later half of the novel, with its plot of Deronda's increasingly powerful friendship with Mordecai, was sharply more negative than that accorded the first half, a response that Eliot seems to have anticipated. In *Daniel Deronda* Eliot expresses ideas so radically divergent from what the majority of her culture would find readily acceptable that she could only imagine these ideas being narratively expressed through romance or epic narrative conventions, not through realistic ones. The ideas and narrative material that interest her were subversive enough of prevailing ideas in the Victorian age that they would inevitably be read as unrealistic by readers.

So it is not surprising that Eliot felt that her concerns could hardly be conveyed through a realistic narrative. The ideas central to the novel—that upper-class women could feel they shared a common plight of victimization by prejudice and the power of the market with Jews, who Eliot understood typically as workers and small businessmen; that a Gentile aristocrat could identify with oppression of lower-class Jews, indeed with Jews as a people; that a hero should be able to empathize with a woman's sense of entrapment in the constraints of patriarchal culture's limitations on her subjectivity— were all quite radical ideas in Victorian culture, at odds with traditional thinking and prejudices. Even more subversive is the idea that women and elite men ought to act on these insights, as we see Deronda doing. In *Deronda* the domestic realism of the Gwendolen Harleth plot founders under the pressure of reading marital breakdown as an opportunity for feminine self-development, but also as a sign of national, at least upper-class, moral exhaustion, and as a moment of feminine recognition that one's human identity is most properly realized through identification with a collective and historical project. Thus the novel's reliance on romance or sacred epic mode in its later half is an effort to express ideas of radical human liberation in a context in which social expectation and the closely related realist conventions would inevitably limit it. Eliot, knowing that her readers would probably reject the direction in which her narrative is going, makes a virtue of the narrative's defiance of readerly expectation by making the narrative deliberately wondrous and, indeed, miraculous, the numinous air that results being appropriate to the high seriousness of her religious and national theme. Eliot in a sense uses the mythic mode that she adopts in the Mordecai-Deronda parts of the plot to emphasize the sense of wonder about the sheer strangeness and power of these moral truths. Despite society's rejection of such ideas, Eliot suggests, they are wonderful because they are true.

Eliot links the alienation she finds in the microcommunity of the family to the macrocommunity of the nation-state through the plot of Jewish nationalism because she reads both as resulting from the ideological crisis caused by political modernization, which required that society find a moral basis to unify itself. This problem of weakening moral consensus was intensified by the abandonment of religious faith by intellectuals such as Eliot. In response to this problem of declining faith, the novel, as Jonathan Loesberg points out, has a paradoxical double-sided attitude toward nonrational beliefs. Such beliefs, such as Gwendolen's superstitious feeling of guilt and fear of retribution in her marriage or Deronda's investment in Mordecai's prophetic utterances, are at once subjected to rational scrutiny in the novel, inviting the reader's skepticism, even while the novel endorses the moral value of the underlying emotional and ethical impulses that these belief systems embody. The model for this combination of rational distancing and emotional investment in ethical belief systems is the Feurbachean critique of Christianity, a lifelong influence on Eliot, which rationally doubted the objective truth of Christian doctrine even while endorsing its ethical thrust.[30] But clearly this resolution of the dialectic between rational subversion of beliefs and emotional recuperation of them is vulnerable in that such a voluntaristic and cerebral response to moral crisis, of affirming values embodied in a theology one cannot rationally defend, is a dubious solution for society generally, which needs a belief system that successfully integrates the claims of rationally understood reality with the pull of emotion toward ethical norms. In creating a nationalist commitment as the counterpoint to her narrative of marital alienation, Eliot suggests that she senses the problem created by the critique of traditional religious faith and offers investment in a revived national community, whether Jewish or British, as her desired solution to the problem. There is, moreover, a logic linking these two kinds of community, for the microcosmic community of the family is governed by laws determined by the political community of the entire nation, and thus the failure of the microcommunity of the family can serve as evidence for the need to reassert a morally purified national community. The nationalist narrative that Eliot envisions, the details of which are left scrupulously vague, is above all a marker of a renewed idealism that would link individual and nation and find embodiment in a collective sense of purpose, a renewal of idealism that for Eliot was what her market-obsessed culture desperately needed.

Ultimately Eliot may link familial alienation and the revival of a national idealism because she reads her era as a period of cultural transition caught, as Arnold said, "between two worlds, one dead, / The other powerless to be born."[31] As we have seen, Gwendolen's central problem is that her egotistic and modern desire for greater personal independence must confront the reality of which she is supremely oblivious, the social and historical barriers limiting women's self-development. Daniel Deronda's parallel problem as a character is defined as having no clear goals in life, as a result of being both in a privileged position as the foster child of an aristocratic family and, because of his assumed illegitimacy, lacking a confident relation to that privilege. His anxieties about his own social position, both within privilege and outside it, are extended to cosmic heights by his conflicting loyalties to established tradition combined with sympathy for historical progress. Both central characters' ambivalence about personal identity mirrors the Victorian age's ambivalence about whether to embrace a break with tradition or to resist such a rupture. Eliot chooses to resolve these problems by a shift from a realist narrative mode to a mythic one because of a genuine insight, namely, that conflicts over the very nature of society's goals and purpose and the position of individuals in relation to them are not resolvable on an individual level, just as the problem of the relations of genders, social classes, or nations is not resolvable through individual action or personal transformation alone. Eliot's insight in this regard remains valid. She is also a shrewd critic of a bourgeois society in her implied solution to the problem, an effort to clarify and strengthen collective purposes so as to strengthen community and detach individuals from relentless and often self-destructive pursuit of individual self-interest. Like Carlyle, Ruskin, and Arnold, Eliot decries her culture's tendency to promote narrow-minded striving for individual interest, particularly through seeing commerce as the highest good. Like other writers of the period, she felt the attraction of the ideal of collective rebirth, which would subsume the fate of the individual but would also liberate society and individual alike from the constraints of oppressive traditionalism. In essence, her cultural aspiration and the plot that expresses it are designed to promote a modernizing project that avoids both the extremes of cultural traditionalism and of a violent, radical break with the past, a middle-ground position suitably embodied in the idea of the Jewish homeland, which would serve as a bridge between the East, generally understood as a place of static traditionalism (as were the Jews), and the West, site of a potentially atomistic and deracinating process of modernization; as Mordecai describes it "a community in the van of the East which carries the culture and the sympathies of every great nation in its bosom." (535)

If there is a complex movement of compromise between individual and collective aspirations in the Jewish plot, or rather an effort to imagine how an individual aspiration for a middle way between innovation and traditionalism could work on a collective level, there is a corresponding revision of tradition and search for compromise in the novel's meditations on gender. One of the signs of the ambivalence and complexity of Eliot's meditations on gender is how radically the narrative revises earlier stereotypes of courtship and marriage plots, even while ultimately vindicating the notion of an essential femininity. For instance, a plot that had a strong association with women, of an individual who finds fulfillment in the abandonment of an original cultural role to unite with an alien culture—such as the Jewish Rebecca in Scott's *Ivanhoe* who falls in love with a Christian—is assigned to a man, Deronda, while a classically masculine plot of a hero who sacrifices ties to family and community to pursue a vocation is given to a woman, Daniel's mother. Similarly, the self-sacrificing role of the individual who desires above all to live through others is assigned to a man (Mordecai, who dies passively of consumption in another traditionally feminine narrative act). All of these reversals of gender expectations, and above all Deronda's own feminine sensitivity to nuances of sympathy and moral virtue, are clearly also designed to express that just as women must abandon their seclusion from the wider world, they must enter history not in a degraded way through the marketplace but rather in a spiritual way, while their traditional self-sacrificing nature should be ideally extended to men on behalf of a noble national or imperial goal.

The novel's vision of a compromise between tradition and modernization, and between male and female roles, undoubtedly was attractive to Eliot because of her own painful life experience of moving from a highly traditional childhood to a radically individualist adulthood. Her life consisted of a series of rebellions against convention, such as breaking with the religious faith of her family, transgressing the customary bounds of her gender by becoming a well-known intellectual, and, in her relationship with George Lewes, openly violating Victorian society's codes of sexual conduct. But Eliot's unconventionality took a toll, as she was forced to pay the price for her individuality by enduring the rejection of her family and, because of the unsanctioned partnershop with Lewes, ostracism from much of a respectable society. Because Lewes's marriage had collapsed, but he had no access to divorce (which forced him and Eliot to live outside of marriage), Eliot, like Dickens and George Meredith, was a major Victorian writer who had personal experience of the limitations and frustrations engendered by Victorian marital law. However, she was able to transmute her personal exasperation with the conventions of family life into statements of broad significance because her experiences and intellectual development gave her a commitment to the advancement of progressive ideals. She read her own experience of social disapproval and alienation as linked to society's general failure in marital life as in other areas to realize ideals of progress. The result is that we find in her fiction a profound ambivalence toward the individual's response to community norms, which some readers have read as inconsistency. Her contemporary Eliza Lynn Linton snidely complained of the contrast between her unconventional life and her highly moral art: "all her teaching went to the side of self-sacrifice for the general good, of conformity with established moral standards, while her life was in direct opposition to her words" (233). Unfair as this comment is, it nonetheless draws attention with polemical sharpness to a genuine tension in Eliot's work. In *Deronda*, Eliot clearly shows Gwendolen's situation in her marriage to her husband is intolerable, but as for how to deal with her natural rebellious feelings toward her husband, Eliot sees no remedy for Gwendolen but repentance for her own sins. This impasse epitomizes how for Eliot, women must both liberate themselves and yet must also avoid striving so strenuously for independence as to surrender to the wider culture's growing materialism and individualism. Rather than the tension between conformity to social norms and the desire for individual freedom manifesting itself, as Linton claimed, as an inconsistency between life and art, the tension between these two impulses is visible in the novels as much as it was in Eliot's life. We see it in Eliot's depiction of the tragic dignity of Lenora, the artist who abandons all tradition and family ties to achieve creative self-realization, and in her sympathy for a Dorothea or a Gwendolen in their passion for men who offer sympathy and relief from their subjected roles as wives. The mirror image of Eliot's understanding of the dangers of excessive focus on self-realization is her ambivalence toward community. For while she is intensely aware of the capacity of existing communities to oppress and seclude the outsider or the underling, and while she proselytizes for a more tolerant world in which communities would less invidiously discriminate against minorities, she also desires strong communities enriched by a continuing respect for tradition.

Eliot's experience of alienation from her culture and her longing for a more vital sense of community was not so idiosyncratic as to make her fiction outside of the mainstream of British literature. On the contrary, so significant is her achievement and so high her cultural prestige that the narratives of domestic breakdown and familial alienation that she creates in novels such as *The Mill on the Floss, Middlemarch,* and *Daniel Deronda,* while expressing her own alienation from her culture because of its oppression of women, its materialism, and its commitment to stultifying traditions, transcend the autobiographical experience in which they are grounded and succeed in substantially recasting the domestic narrative tradition. In so doing, she creates a model for writers in the late nineteenth and twentieth century, for whom marital and familial alienation becomes a central way of expressing alienation from bourgeois culture. Because, as we have seen, the alienation of gender that Gwendolen experiences is complexly linked to the very different alienations emphasized in the portion of the novel focused on Jewish characters, *Deronda* is a striking example of how familial alienation can figuratively be linked to a wide spectrum of alienations. However, the abstractness of the connections between these various kinds of alienation is a clear sign of the novel's immense ambitions and the limitations of its achievement. For the very abstractness of the connections linking the various themes and narrative strands of the story elevates the cultural capital that the novel embodies above that of all but a tiny number of previous novels, and in so doing helped make it a new model for the novel as art object. The truth is that very few novels written in the nineteenth century—or since—attempt to answer as weighty a question as to whether an individual's capacity to find the correct relationship to historical progress can resolve individual alienation and collective oppression. Yet this issue is ultimately the thematic idea linking the novel's two major narrative strands. While such a formulation may seem abstract and cerebral, this abstractness is a property inherent in the novel. In passages where, as we have seen, Deronda and Gwendolen confront their relation to history, or in a passage such as the one in which Mordecai and Deronda attend a meeting of self-taught worker-intellectuals who discuss the roots of historical progress and debate how to apply their progressive principles to the situation of the Jews, the novel requires that the reader consider such demanding and abstract intellectual issues.

In reading the concrete problems of an oppressed ethnic group and women in highly abstract terms, Eliot both represents the concerns of such groups while speaking for them in a way that largely excludes the voice of the groups whose oppressions she depicts; for most members of these groups the requisite cultural capital to understand her formulation of the issue would be inaccessible to them. And unsurprisingly, given the intellectuality of the novel's construction of its concerns, the central representatives of the novel's ideas, Gwendolen and Daniel, are characters who from a conventional and surface appearance are highly privileged. It is only by abstracting their dilemmas from any pressing material or economic pressure that Eliot can give herself room to explore the nuances of the intellectual and emotional issues that interest her. If these innovations are a gain for the intellectual subtlety and range of the novel as a genre, *Deronda*'s combination of cerebral concerns and a focus on economically privileged characters is clearly a loss for the genre's appeal as an agent of either mass entertainment or political reform.

Thus, if we see in *Daniel Deronda* the novel of familial alienation emerging in something like its modern form, there is loss as well as gain inherent in that transformation. On one hand, in a novel of this kind, familial alienation, particularly marital alienation, at least for individuals of a privileged class, has enormous importance as the sign of a failed relationship of the individual to society and to history. On the other hand, the abstractness of the mediations linking familial alienation and national and historical decadence are sufficiently complex and abstractly imagined as to leave solutions to both marital and historical alienation verging on the phantasmic. Of course, Eliot does imply specific directions that she believes both women and Jews should move in working toward their liberation. But the connections Eliot suggests between the two realms operate at such a high level of abstraction that it is only with great difficulty that a set of either ethical standards or a political praxis could be derived from such a narrative. In the narrative of Lydia Glasher and Gwendolen, as we have seen, Eliot uses as the germ of her narrative a difficult ethical dilemma in the tradition of Richardson's novelistic explorations of moral issues. But as the novel progresses, the ethical realm increasingly gives way to both the mysterious depths of psychology, as in Gwendolen's never fully acknowledged homicidal rage at Grandcourt, and her similarly repressed but evident passion for Deronda, and also to the abstract issues of the individual's relation to history. It is in this transformation of what novels do, the shift from the mobilization of powerful moral responses, which dominated earlier domestic fiction, to the pondering of the individual psyche's confrontation with the inscrutable realities of history, that Eliot's creation of the modern novel of familial alienation is so original and seminal, looking forward to modernist fiction. Unlike traditional domestic narrative, such a novel by the very abstractness of its concerns radically complicates the uses to which it puts familial narrative, a subject matter which no longer functions primarily to offer moral guidance in personal life or to mobilize moral fervor in reforming society. By creating her original but intensely intellectual version of domestic narrative, she put alienation from the family at the center of serious fiction's purview, but she also prepared the way for the more depoliticized version of this theme that would appear in the modernist works to come.

5

The Smashed Window:
Henry James, the Fin de Siècle,
and the Prostitution of Love and
Art in *The Wings of the Dove*

A CHILD IS ABANDONED BY HER DIVORCED PARENTS, EACH PREOCCUPIED with new liaisons; two young orphans are raised by a hysterical governess obsessed with sexual evil; a guest at a country house endlessly theorizes about and investigates the illicit relationships of other guests; a man pursues an affair with his father-in-law's wife. One need only recall some plots of major texts Henry James wrote after 1895 to see that in his late career any idealization of romantic and family life has been left far behind. Indeed, one can argue that in the later part of his career James's central preoccupation is how sordid and corrupt such central areas of life have become in the fin de siècle world. In this sense, James's late fiction participates in the moral panics of the last two decades of the nineteenth century, and the public discourse expressing anxiety about gender roles, sexuality, and family life, which were seen as symptoms of larger cultural decline at a time when anxieties about the stability of the British Empire and Britain's global dominance were becoming increasingly salient.[1] But while James's late work surely reflects this cultural environment, there is something deeper at work in James's resistance to traditional domestic narrative, a pattern visible already in his early career, when he tries to position himself as the successor of George Eliot and Nathaniel Hawthorne as the English-speaking world's preeminent novelist. What is distinctive about James's relation to domesticity is that he makes skepticism, even antipathy, to the idealization of romantic and familial life a more central part of the definition of what serious writers do than any comparably influential novelist in the English language before him. For earlier writers in the Victorian novelistic tradition failures of family life or courtship were symptoms of individual moral failure and sometimes also signs of the discrete and practical failures of specific institutions or the negative effects of specious beliefs. Even in depicting the failure of Gwendolen Harleth's marriage, which epitomizes a broad-ranging cultural stagnation and philosophical impasse, Eliot never implies that family life itself is irremediably flawed; rather, she suggests that the family has been corrupted by moral and cultural failures that require further moral growth and social change. It is in part to enforce this point that Gwendolen's failed marriage and moral isolation is juxtaposed with the more hopeful marital and political prospects of Daniel and Mirah, a marriage seen as likely to thrive because of its inclusion in an idealistic effort at cultural renovation.

In contrast, James's commitment to the de-idealization of courtship and marriage is of a quite different kind: we do not find the career pattern notable in earlier writers such as Dickens, in which there is an evolution from novels with conventional treatments of love and marital closure to those of greater ambiguity in depicting courtship and increased emphasis on familial alienation. Instead for James the resistance to idealizations of romance and family life, the prominence of alienation from courtship and marriage, and the avoidance of the traditional closural device of marriage for central characters are there from the beginning of the career and are, indeed, always central to his self-definition as a writer. This is not to suggest that James, the expatriate American who infiltrated himself into the British literary tradition, is able to single-handedly supplant Victorian domestic narrative traditions. Clearly, had James never written a word, the idealizations and stereotypes characteristic of domestic tradition current in midcentury would have been challenged as the century progressed. Indeed, these challenges were everywhere by the 1890s, from feminists questioning the value of marriage for women, "New Woman" and decadent novelists, many of them women, who developed innovative fictive trajectories for unconventional heroines, to numerous major writers such as Ibsen, Meredith, and Hardy, who took seriously the changing situation and aspirations of women as a literary subject and who began to undermine Victorian reticence about sexual matters. Ultimately, the source of all of these disruptions of the traditional gender figurations were late Victorian women themselves, who by pursuing education, moving into newly expanding fields of work, and demanding a growing political role rendered implausible the traditional image of women presiding over a domestic space consecrated by its remoteness from economic exchange and political competition. James's uniqueness in this sphere does not lie in his challenge to Victorian domestic narrative traditions, but rather in that throughout this career he consistently resisted conventional narratives of gender, courtship, and family and the moral certitudes that they were designed to inculcate. Most important, James is unique in the degree to which he makes resistance to traditional domestic narrative the basis for his innovative and brilliant late style; it is preeminently through this late style and anxieties and themes it expresses, aesthetic and moral, that he bequeaths a powerful model for literary distinction to his modernist successors. To trace the connection between his response to domestic narrative and his late style, in this chapter I will sketch James's evolving relation to courtship and domestic narratives, situate the development of his late style in the fin de siècle period, and read James's tragic late novel *The Wings of the Dove* as exemplary of James's characteristic alienation from, and subtle revision of, Victorian family and courtship narratives.

JAMES AND THE MASCULINE CORRECTION OF DOMESTIC FICTION

If by the 1890s James's de-idealizing of gender roles and sexual relations had become highly topical, the curious truth is that one can hardly find in James's long career a moment when an impulse to debunk idealizations of gender relations and family life is not present. As Alfred Habegger has demonstrated, James's early critical work, undertaken in his twenties, was often directed at denouncing the sentimental or overly didactic writing of popular female novelists of his day.[2] If sentimental idealization of love or family life were anathema in James's critical practice, he was similarly hostile to any impulse to use fiction to further feminist ideals or to imply that traditional family life might imprison women. And James practiced similar aesthetic values in his fictions to those he preached in his criticism. Thus, a very early story, "The Story of a Masterpiece" (1868), shows how James could appropriate predecessors' work yet scrub it clean of any feminist impulse. In this story, a wealthy man decides to have a portrait painter create a picture of his fiancée as a nuptial present. The painter, who we learn from a narrative flashback has experienced the fiancée's shallowness and duplicity, creates a work of art that captures her "levity" of soul, a moral blot that becomes immediately evident to the wealthy prospective bridegroom when he sees the picture. He resignedly carries through with the marriage, though not before angrily slashing the portrait with a dagger. In addition to showing the influence of Hawthorne, the story draws on Browning's "My Last Duchess," in which the brilliant painting of the young bride of a Renaissance nobleman captures her emotional receptivity, a trait interpreted by the nobleman as symptomatic of a fatal independence of character or perhaps infidelity; he arranges, as it seems, for the wife's murder. James draws the idea of a painting that hints at sexual wantonness from the Browning poem, to which his story openly alludes. In his rewriting of the poem it is fascinating how many typical Jamesian themes the young writer discovers in Browning's concise masterpiece and carefully reproduces in his much longer story, including the morally ambivalent relation between wealth and creativity, the distrustful relations of the sexes, and the power of art to tell truths and inform perceptions of life; these are topics that James will return to throughout his career. But the most striking feature of James's use of his source is that the feminist impulse so evident in "My Last Duchess" is in James's imitation sternly erased. In "My Last Duchess," the Duke is a horrifying domestic tyrant who has seemingly misread the painting and the woman it portrays to find sexual immorality and occasion for murderous retribution where, in reality, there was only youthfulness and romantic impulsiveness. But in James's version of the story, the painter's imitations of the woman's moral wantonness are accurate, male violence is directed against the painting rather than the woman, and male artist and patron are painfully united in recognition of the unpalatable truth revealed by art, namely the flawed moral character of the painter's, and James's, female subject; in contrast to Browning's feminist poem, James's story suggests that the best art helps men to resist romantic illusions about women.[3]

This impulse to make women the subject of masculine art but to correct any impulse toward idealization of them or, even less, any sympathy with feminine waywardness or rebellion against feminine roles, is not merely a youthful crotchet, but becomes a distinctive aspect of James's entire career. Far from idealizing relations between the sexes, he regularly raises his readers' expectations for the possibility of marriage for his characters, only to follow his de-idealized vision of his characters and frustrate his readers' expectations. His early novel *The American* was lambasted by reviewers and even some of James's correspondents for not bring together the wealthy American hero and the Frenchwoman he planned to marry. In response to criticism on this point from Elizabeth Boott, James loftily responds, "I am a realist," suggesting that his self-definition as a serious artist precluded a crowd-pleasing, if artificial, happy ending.[4] Even when James's intention involved concluding a novel with an imminent marriage, he was careful to remove sentimental idealization; thus, at the end of *The Bostonians* (1886), when Basil Ransom, the masculine Southerner, rescues Verena Tarrant from domination by the powerful feminist Olive Chancellor, who has drawn her into a life of political activism, the narrator cynically remarks that Verena's tears "were not the last she was destined to shed."[5] It is thus simply the statement of years of practical resistance to the powerful convention of the closural affirmation of marital happiness when he writes caustically in *The Art of Fiction* (1884), his major contribution to the debate about British fiction of the 1880s, listing the various philistine ways of evaluating a novel:

> One would say that [a novel] being good means representing virtuous and aspiring characters, placed in prominent positions; another would say that it depends on a "happy ending," on a distribution at the last of prizes, pensions, husbands, wives, babies, millions, appended paragraphs and cheerful remarks. . . . The "ending" of a novel is, for many persons, like that of a good dinner, a course of dessert and ices, and the artist in fiction is regarded as a sort of meddlesome doctor who forbids agreeable aftertastes.[6]

There is more at stake here than James's unwillingness to affirm the marital state as the psychic and moral end point of the story, which it so often was in Victorian fiction. The sentimentality and idealization about marriage and family in conventional fiction had been disrupted by earlier writers; but even when he imitates a precursor who was at pains to de-idealize marriage herself, James was at pains to correct what he considered insufficiently disciplined and, as he thought, characteristically feminine fiction making, which gave away too much in realistic rigor on behalf of feminine aspirations. I am referring to James's rewriting in one his most brilliant novels, *The Portrait of a Lady* (1881), of two of Eliot's late novels. The magnitude in this novel of James's debt to Eliot has long been noted, and Richard Brodhead has usefully contextualized the unusual intensity of James's investment in rewriting his recent precursors and contemporaries, arguing that such investments were a measure of James's strenuous effort to define a new identity for the novelist as practitioner of a fully serious art form, one clearly distinguished from mere popular entertainment.[7] The broader cultural situation of this Jamesian ambition is a professionalizing impulse that was characteristic of many skilled and educated workers in the nineteenth century, a widespread effort to secure or consolidate their own social status and economic privilege. James's impulse within fiction writing responded as well to the emerging tendency in literary criticism to distinguish with greater rigor between the highest level of literary work and the merely pedestrian, to carefully locate, in the Arnoldian phrase, "the best that is known and thought in the world."[8] Moreover, for a writer such as James, who despite his best efforts was consistently disappointed by his lack of popular success, the effort to define the self as literarily distinguished quickly becomes an effort to compensate for lack of financial success by redefining a limited audience as a sign that his creative efforts were a more elevated project from that undertaken in the degraded and philistine arena of an emergent mass culture.

For James's larger project, remaking himself from American provincial to member of the British literary tradition while modernizing and refining that tradition, George Eliot was an appealing model. By the 1870s Britain's most prestigious living novelist, especially in such ambitious works as *Middlemarch, Romola,* and *Daniel Deronda,* Eliot had built on an earlier tradition of British novels and exemplified the strength of that tradition herself in a particularly ambitious, modern, and refined mode. James's at once admiring and competitive impulse toward Eliot is captured in a letter of 1873 to a friend: "To produce some little exemplary works of art is my narrow and lowly dream. They are to have less 'brain' than *Middlemarch*; but (I boldly proclaim it) more *form.*"⁹ Undoubtedly, *Portrait*'s debt to *Deronda*'s plot and figurative strategy is obvious; again, we have a woman seeking freedom in marriage who finds herself married to a rakish and hypocritical man who is revealed to have a preexisting family, including a malevolent mistress who has given him a child (or children). But if *Portrait*'s plot is modeled on *Deronda*'s, Isabel Archer's character is in many ways at least as indebted to Dorothea from *Middlemarch,* and Isabel resembles Dorothea more than Gwendolen in being associated with books and ideas and in trying to live a life of unworldly idealism.

Though lack of space precludes a detailed reading of the novel, we can see how James's rewriting of these Eliotic models eliminates traces of romance or Gothic conventions, such as the romantic appearance of Will Ladislaw to replace Casaubon in *Middlemarch* or the Gothic intrusion of Lydia Glasher in *Daniel Deronda.* But these generic cleansings have an ideological agenda as well. They eliminate those parts of each novel that draw attention to how Eliot's heroines are victims of their society's restrictive opportunities for educated women, how their anguish is thus representative of conflict between the need for radical change and the society's resistance to it. While like Gwendolen, Isabel marries a rake, she is deprived of the powerful motivation of poverty that causes Gwendolen to err, nor does she, like Gwendolen, consider a career as a professional performer, making Isabel's error less representative of women's economic vulnerability than Gwendolen's. And if, like Dorothea, Isabel tries to use her economic privilege to move beyond the limited horizons available to her sex, one of James's most profound changes from Eliot as a model is to excise the political context of her narratives, the interpenetration of social and philosophical issues with her character's dilemmas and personalities. While Dorothea's efforts toward greater self-realization as an educated woman are largely thwarted, they are given dignity by how her aspirations resonate with the larger theme, developed at great length in *Middlemarch*'s complex narrative, of various attempted reforms that characterize early nineteenth-century Britain.

In contrast, Isabel has no context for her effort at self-realization but the relentlessly satirized Henrietta Stackpole, the gauche feminine reporter, who tramples on the boundaries between public and private life and is clearly the model of what Isabel should not be. Equally, James excises from his revision of *Deronda* any figure as ambiguous as Lydia Glasher, the mistress Gwendolen displaces, who raises the issue of how women should respond to masculine sexual license and to the moral claims of fallen women (the corresponding figure, Madame Merle, in *Portrait* is a conventional villainess), nor is there any counterpart in *Portrait,* for the Deronda-Mordecai narrative with its aspiration toward cultural and political renewal, nor any suggestion, as there is with Gwendolen, that Isabel's failure to find happiness is due to her failure of sympathy with the social currents liberating humankind. Eliot makes her characters' situations part of the limitations of their historical moments and balances Gwendolen and Dorothea's failure with a compensatory if modest move toward feminine liberation, as in the case of Dorothea through the development of her more egalitarian and passionate relationship with her second husband, Will Ladislaw, and their joint commitment to philanthropy. In Gwendolen's case this compensatory movement is suggested through her learning to extend her field of sympathies beyond herself and to the newfound commitment to altruism she learns from Deronda's example. In contrast, Isabel's development is largely toward increased aesthetic understanding and resigned acceptance of social boundaries; nor is there in *Portrait* any sense of a compensation for marital failure other than deeper psychic and aesthetic insight. Moreover, in contrast to his models, James takes away any sympathetic context for Isabel's blunder into marital catastrophe. While Gwendolen's choice of Grandcourt is a desparate response to economic coercion, and Dorothea's choice of Casaubon is part of a sympathetically portrayed quest for purpose in life, by making Isabel's choice of Osmond a sign of sheer naïve idealism, *Portrait* virtually reverses the feminist impulses of Eliot's novels and suggests that women should confine their efforts at freedom within the psychological and aesthetic realms to which Isabel ultimately consigns herself.

In one regard, however, *Portrait* exceeds its models in radicalism, and that is in the formal radicalism of its notoriously ambiguous ending, in which Isabel rebuffs the continuing love of Caspar Goodwood and returns to her unhappy married life with Gilbert Osmond in Rome. Eliot had anticipated James with her refusal (much to many readers' disappointment) to bring Deronda and Gwendolen together, a refusal of readerly expectations of the "fairy-tale" ending that often concluded traditional domestic fiction. James, however, goes a step beyond Eliot's defiance of readerly expectations by emphasizing the irresolution of Isabel's situation and by leaving this uncertainty the dominant note of *Portrait*'s ending. The effect is created largely by the absence of any other major plotlines than Isabel's failed marriage: by contrast, *Deronda* ends with the more traditional closural devices of marriage (Deronda and Mirah), the death of a major character (Mordecai), and the suggested beginning of new directions created by the resolves that both Deronda and Gwendolen have made to live altruistically for others. Isabel's fate is unsoftened by such a context of personal renewal or other marital commitment, and is made particularly startling by the grimness of the marital destiny she embraces. Isabel returns to Rome, a place associated with tradition and tragic history, as if bowing and surrendering to the weight of both historical and marital tradition.[10] While Isabel's return to Rome and to Osmond is studiedly ambiguous, leaving the reader to wonder how long Isabel will have to endure her nightmarish marital situation, it emphatically reaffirms traditional marriage as the governing framework of women's lives, suggesting a firm refusal of any feminist subversion of women's traditional position within domestic space.[11]

In closing the novel with such ambiguity, refusing to resolve Isabel's struggle for freedom and her conflict with her husband either in the direction of tragedy or in that of romantic fulfillment, and leaving the tension between these options as a spur to the readers'—and Isabel's—aesthetic development, James makes a move of momentous portent for the history of the novel, for such an indeterminate ending anticipates the sustained ambiguities of modernist fiction. James was well acquainted with various alternative endings for such a plot, such as Isabel's rebellion into adultery or her escape from Osmond through his death or conversion. Plots of magical escapes from intolerable marriages had often been used in earlier narratives where the fiancé or husband is a bigamous rake or tyrant, as in the dramatic moral conversion of Rochester in *Jane Eyre* or the fortuitous deaths that eliminate *Deronda*'s Grandcourt and *Middlemarch*'s Casaubon, which clears the way for a more satisfactory pairing with Will Ladislaw. Such potential closures would either cast Isabel as a stubborn rebel against her sex's position or imagine love and feminine autonomy as compatible, if only in the aspiration of writer and reader suggested by a romantic ending. If by avoiding such possibilities James's ambiguous ending reaffirms the necessity of women making peace with their traditional role in marriage, even more important is the message of the ending on a formal level, which is that the aesthetic logic of the work must take precedence over his readers' desires for the conventional romance ending, a stance that sharply rejects the commitments to feminine liberty that plots of romantic escape from failed marriages had often expressed. Instead, the ending's ambiguity suggests the superior truth to history of James's masculine narrative over the formally defective works of his feminine predecessor. This formal innovation both imitates and resists Eliot's example, pointedly declining to affirm her support for the progressive development of the feminine role, but also withdrawing the novel from the ritual affirmation of the family as a source of consensus and community that had bound reader and writer on behalf of the higher value of the novelist's artistic freedom. The novel as a genre becomes aestheticized.

THE CRISIS OF REALISM AND THE
ORIGINS OF THE LATE STYLE

Though *Portrait*'s ambiguous ending anticipates literary modernism, James, in the thick of his midcareer effort to write popular novels that were also distinguished realist fictions, shows little immediate sign of having recognized the possibilities for further innovation that he had opened. The focus on inward emotional growth and pervasive moral ambiguity that this ending anticipates would only achieve its full flowering in works written in the mid-1890s and after. But in the later novels of the middle period, James continues to warn his readers against the dangers of women defying their nature and pursuing power too aggressively in other figures that repeat the warning against power-hungry women embodied in Henrietta Stackpole: characters such as Olive Chancellor, the power-hungry feminist, or Christina Light, the society lady who dabbles in radical politics and whose indifference sends the hero of *The Princess Casamassima* into suicidal despair. One important context then for the development of James's late style, and in particular his increasingly critical relation to earlier courtship and domestic narrative, is his sense that his worst fears about the deterioration of the female character were being confirmed. In a passage in his notebook, which is adjacent to his first note for what would become *The Awkward Age* (1899), a novel in which many of the themes that dominate his late fiction are already visible, James writes an approving comment on a French commentator on English society, Brada: "the 2 most striking notes to him, are *Primo*, The masculinization of women; and *Secondo*, The demoralization of the aristocracy—the cessation, on their part to take themselves seriously; their traffic in vulgar things . . ." Later he transcribes a long passage from Brada, prefacing it with the comment "the idea . . . is the Revolution in English society by the *avènement* [advance] of the women. . . . I saw it long ago."[12] Such a passage shows James complacently casting himself as a prophet of female degeneration and of the negative effects of this "masculinization" on society.

In the last decades of the nineteenth century, as British society became preoccupied with the threat of the New Woman and sexual scandals repeatedly rocked the culture, one might imagine that James would have felt that the wider society was waking up to evils of which he had long warned. But no one who has read James's stories of literary life from the mideighties and the nineties could confuse James with a writer complacent in his relation to the society in which he lived. Instead, the dominant note both in the letters and the fiction is of the indifference or hostility of the mass audience to his literary labors. In 1888, after the limited sales of *The Bostonians* and *The Princess Casamassima,* he writes to his longtime friend and supporter William Howells that these books "have reduced the desire, & the demand, for my productions to zero" (*LL* 196). His next major novel, *The Tragic Muse,* did little better, and by the nineties James's sense of estrangement from literary modishness has become almost biblical: "I *have* felt, for a long time past, that I have fallen upon evil days—every sign or symbol of one's being the least *wanted*, anywhere or by anyone, having so utterly failed. A new generation, that I know not, & mainly prize not, had taken universal possession" (*LL* 277) The final collapse of James's hope for a lucrative rapprochement with popular taste came with the humiliating failure of his play *Guy Domville,* jeered off the stage, along with its author, in 1895. It is in the context of his sense of waning popular appreciation and literary isolation that James writes tale after tale, which implies the limitations of the literary marketplace and of the audience, of the tension between material success and aesthetic refinement. Such stories include "The Author of Beltraffio" (1884), in which an author has a wife whose moralistic hostility to his writing leads to tragic consequences, and the enigmatic "The Lesson of the Master" (1888), in which a writer immersed in public popularity and family life warns a young aspiring writer that he will inevitably compromise his art if he marries. While the young writer hesitates, the opportunistic older writer, whose wife has since died, appropriates the young writer's beloved and marries her, leaving ambiguous whether the older writer's advice was sincere or cynical. Other stories that suggest the opposition between literary ambition and popular success include "The Next Time" (1895), in which a naturally refined but impecunious writer tries desperately but unsuccessfully to write crassly enough to achieve popular success (a theme James saw as autobiographical), and "John Delavoy" (1898), in which a writer tries in vain to publish a discussion of the works of a well-known author whose life is of interest to the public but whose work is considered too immoral to be acceptable for public discussion, another story based on James's own experience. James's vision of literary culture in these stories is of a marketplace ruthlessly dominated by concern with circulation and by journalistic prying into personal lives and with hypocritical moral puritanism leaving scant interest in genuine literary distinction.[13]

This vitiation of literary culture by popular writers and journalists' and its link to evolving gender roles which also alarmed James, is expressed with particular clarity in his late story "The Death of the Lion" (1894), in which a young reporter discovers a great but nearly forgotten novelist as a potential subject for journalistic exploitation. The young man's editor insists he write a sensationalized account of the novelist's life, an agenda that reflects the marketplace's indifference to the quality of the writer's work. But having been converted to a belief in the hermetic nature of the novelist's art, the young man abandons his job as reporter. Meanwhile, the long-neglected novelist is increasingly overshadowed by two gender-ambiguous popular writers, a male novelist with a female pseudonym and female writer who impersonates a man. At long last, in the former journalist and his betrothed, who is a devoted fan of the novelist, the great writer finds a faithful and adoring audience. But rediscovery comes too late, and even as he dies, the manuscript of his final masterpiece, which he has entrusted to the ex-journalist, is lost as the androgynous popular novelists are lionized. Such a narrative makes very clear that James saw his own version of literary art as superseded by fictions that pandered to a literary marketplace dominated by journalism and sensationalism, and links this pessimism about the rising tide of market-dominated popular culture to his obsession with the theme of gender role transgressions.[14] In contrast to the truly masculine devotion and dedication of the serious writer ("the lion"), we find the self-involved yet crowd-pleasing gender confusion of the popular writers. Gender transgression and literary feminization become marks of the literarily crass, of modern life's vitiation and neglect of quality through a blurring of necessary boundaries, including those between art and life, male and female, commerce and private life.

It is only in the context of James's profound alienation from a wider audience that he understood as feminized and corrupted by mass culture that we can fully understand his elaboration of the late style that emerges in the late 1890s and the decade that follows, a style characterized by a continued, indeed, heightened resistance to idealizing courtship or domestic narratives, and that breaks with the stark moral polarities such conventional writing traded in, replacing them with an increasing focus on psychological and moral ambiguity and formal difficulty. In addition to his failure to achieve the wide audience and financial rewards he had hoped for and his disquiet at gender role trends in the culture, several other contexts are useful to understanding James's late style. One is the rise of literary aestheticism, with its slogan of "art for art's sake" and its fetishization of intense aesthetic, often visual, experience as a central purpose in life. Though the aesthetic movement had undoubted affinities with James's own project of promoting literary refinement, James clearly felt there was something morally dubious, and subversive of proper gender roles, in aestheticism and its representative artists. Yet notwithstanding his disapproval, aestheticism and its even more disreputable cousin decadence, embodied for many Victorians in the notorious magazine *The Yellow Book* (published briefly in the 1890s), offered a welcoming hand to James in his late career. Despite feeling real ambivalence about the publication, James, lacking strong demand for his work elsewhere, published some of his late fiction in this avant-garde setting, and at least one of his late novels, *The Sacred Fount* (1901), has a decided decadent aura to it. Despite his misgivings at the association of his writing with aesthetes and decadence, some contemporaries detected an affinity. Margaret Oliphant shrewdly noted of James that "[t]he art of the American cosmopolitan is at all times conspicuous as art. It is impossible to lose sight of the skill with which he whips up the very light materials at his command."[15] Such a criticism, that James's work was all manner and little matter, which registers James's obsession with formal perfection and stylistic elevation, was much the same criticism Oliphant and others would level at aesthetic writers.

In addition to being relegated to an uncomfortable avant-garde position in the literary marketplace, James also witnessed how the tradition of literary realism to which he had devoted his life was becoming controversial, even while it was losing its preeminence in the marketplace. To many late Victorian critics, the "new realism" that had begun to invade British letters in the 1880s was morally suspect, both foreign in origin— French, American, or Scandinavian—and less morally uplifting than the native strain of realism embodied in George Eliot.[16] According to this argument British writers, James included, were dragging literature into a tedious and morally suspect focus on mere actuality rather than higher things. Such a position became a weapon of moral traditionalism, and in 1888 Henry Vizetelly, a publisher of writers such as Flaubert, Daudet, Maupassant, and Tolstoy, was prosecuted for publishing a translation of Zola's *La Terre,* a novel that authorities labeled a work of "bestial obscenity"; the subject was taken gravely enough that members of Parliament denounced the demoralizing effects of Zola's fiction in the House of Commons. British writers said to be influenced by the nat-

uralist tradition were stigmatized by critics as contributing to the moral decline of the British Empire. Novelists on their part in this period were increasingly inclined to attempt greater openness in addressing sexuality,
gender conflicts, and the evils of class divisions, and found themselves drawn
into open conflict with the gatekeepers of moral propriety and political conservatism, such as circulating libraries, magazine editors, and reviewers. Writers such as George Moore, Arthur Morrison, George Gissing, and Thomas
Hardy appalled many late Victorian readers by their bold and often grim
presentations of sexual life or social problems, and took a defiant joy in disturbing the reader's complacencies or in transgressing the norms of literary
propriety.[17] As realism as a movement insisted on transgressing bounds of
propriety or dredging up unpleasant aspects of social reality, critics saw such
writing as morally threatening and politically questionable. Ibsen, whose
writings first became known in the mideighties, and whose *A Doll House* was
first produced in England in 1889, added to the cultural distaste at texts in a
realist vein. Ibsen's plays, with their complex portrayal of middle-class
women discontented with their limited roles, generated fervent enthusiasm
among some theatergoers, including many feminists, but provoked violent
disapproval from conservatives. Equally abhorrent to many readers and critics were the New Women fictions by writers such as Sarah Grand, Mona
Caird, Grant Allen, and Thomas Hardy, with their exploration of changing
gender roles and their female characters who question traditional marriage,
which burst into prominence in the early 1890s. New Women novels were
inevitably denounced, as had been "naturalist" fiction of the 1880s, as the
morally noisome product of "Zolaism" and feminism. Enraged critics such as
Hugh E. M. Stutfield saw New Women novels as preaching decadence and
immorality: "[t]he sacredness of the marriage-tie is apparently mere old-fashioned Tory twaddle in the eyes of our *révoltés*."[18] Hysterically replaying the
anxiety over sensation fiction, critics denounced such novels because their
narratives featured women transgressing traditional sexual roles, allegedly a
sign of cultural and moral decline and an incitement to such violation of
gender and sexual norms. Ironically, many New Women writers were in fact
puritanical in their attitudes about sexuality and raised sexual issues to promote masculine sexual purity; nevertheless, their novels did challenge conventional gender roles.

Even as new trends in realism struck many critics and politicians as a sign
of unsound morals, feminine revolt, and political subversion, a more pragmatic threat to realism in the fin de siècle was that its market position was
challenged by the roaring success of adventure, fantasy, and mystery fiction,
genres that writers such as Robert Louis Stevenson, Rider Haggard, and

Rudyard Kipling turned into lucrative literary mines. Romance and adventure fiction was lauded exactly for avoiding realism, for providing a welcome escape, in Haggard's words, to "minds jaded with the toil and emptiness of our competitive existence."[19] It need hardly be said that the rise of such escapist fare was an unwelcome development to a writer such as James. Responding to these contexts of moral controversy and of censorship regulating the status of realism along with the rise of adventure fiction, which menaced realism's marketplace position, James writes sourly in his critical essay "The Future of the Novel" (1899):

> Nothing is so striking in a survey of this field, and nothing to be so much borne in mind, as that the larger part of the great multitude that sustains the teller and the publisher of tales is constituted by boys and girls; by girls in especial, if we apply the term to the later stages of the life of the innumerable women who, under modern arrangements, increasingly fail to marry—fail, apparently, even, largely, to desire to. . . . The sort of taste that used to be called "good" has nothing to do with the matter: we are so demonstrably in the presence of millions for whom taste is but an obscure, confused immediate instinct. (*AC,* 243)

By literature for boys ("great fortunes, if not great reputations, are made, we learn, by writing for schoolboys"), James clearly meant the fantasy and adventure fiction so popular in this era, while his designation of all unmarried females as "girls" suggests both his discomfort with changing gender roles and his sense of the constraints that writers suffered under in having to avoid shocking virginal readers. Whether boys or "girls" were the audience, James defines the problem of novelists as facing a huge and largely philistine audience devoid of sophistication about life, and certainly about sexuality, as about cultural distinction.

In response to this situation, James recommends that the novel engage in "experiments," including, significantly, ones in which the novelists "untie" the "long and most respectable tradition of making it defer supremely, . . . to the inexperience of the young" (*AC,* 248). James is referring here to the powerful belief in Victorian culture that novelists must avoid representing sexuality, what he calls the "great relation between men and women, the constant world-renewal" (*AC,* 248) lest their tales corrupt young readers. Such suppression, "too many sources of interest neglected" (*AC,* 249) James argued, was morally useless and retarded the development of fiction as an art. He goes on to note that if the goal of such reticence was traditionally to protect women's sensibilities, this group was visibly transforming its own social role and defying the conventions ostensibly designed to protect them: "nothing is more salient in English life to-day, to fresh eyes, than the revolution taking place in the position and outlook of women . . . we may very well yet see the female elbow itself, kept in increasing activity by the play of the pen, smash with final resonance the window all this time most superstitiously closed" (*AC*, 250). In such a passage James has in mind the New Woman, and New Woman writers in particular. In effect he argues that the sexual reticence of the Victorian age is inevitably giving way to the new frankness that women themselves are demanding. James was quite correct in noting the increasing frankness of writers, including women writers, in this period: for instance, in 1893 Sarah Grand published the best-selling novel, *The Heavenly Twins*, in which a woman refuses to consummate her marriage because her husband's sexual history causes her to fear infection with a venereal disease—a subject that shows both how fin de siècle fiction prominently aired feminist themes and reflected a new openness about sexuality.

It is important to remember, too, that in addition to literary trends, sexual transgressions were topical in this period because of a series of scandals that punctuated the fin de siècle years, beginning with journalist W. T. Stead's sensational 1885 exposé of the prostitution of girls and young women, a scandal that led directly to increased state regulation of sexuality, including homosexuality, in an atmosphere of moral panic and heightened press attention to the dangers of illicit sexuality. Since Stead identified the villains of his exposé as upper-class men purchasing the virginities of working-class girls, his work had significant class implications as well as exciting the concern of feminists. Moreover, the tightening of legal prohibitions on homosexuality that occurred in the wake of Stead's exposé set the stage for later scandals such as the 1889–90 Cleveland Street scandals about male prostitution and the 1895 trials of Oscar Wilde. Thus, in his increasing focus on transgressive sexuality, James responds both to the topicality of the subject and his sense of the obsolescence of much Victorian restraint about sexual matters in the novel. His treatment of this topic, however, is filled with an ambivalence that helps stimulate the formal inventiveness of his late fiction. The fact that he was addressing subjects of gender roles and sexuality that clearly provoked cultural conflict rather than consensus encouraged James to experiment with efforts that minimize and make unobtrusive the authorial narrative voice, which had in earlier Victorian fiction been the formal device implying a community of values between author and reader. In the 1890s James becomes quite inventive and sophisticated in this regard, by developing to a new degree of sophistication the strategy of focalization, the use of narration to focus on one character's thoughts and point of view; he also experiments with first-person narration (which of course eliminates impersonal narrators), and, building on his dramatic experience, makes heavy use of dialogue, a tendency that was brought to an extreme in *The Awkward Age* (1899), which consists, except for minimal scene-setting descriptions, almost entirely of dialogue.[20]

In content as well as form, James's late fiction is haunted by the preoccupation of the period with illicit sexuality and gender role changes. Fictions of this period are frequently structured around characters who become aware of or are affected by sexual immorality, but who by virtue of youth (*What Maisie Knew, The Awkward Age*), low social class and temperament (*The Spoils of Poynton, In the Cage, The Turn of the Screw*), or sheer personal eccentricity (*The Sacred Fount*) are able to gain their knowledge, or perhaps their fantasies, of sexual immorality only indirectly through fragmentary evidence, inference, and imagination. By exploring the possible moral and psychological effects of this indirect contact with usually upper-class sexual moral transgressions, James addresses the topic of the "vulgarization" of the upper class and that of sexual transgressions while adhering to the letter, though hardly the spirit, of the tradition that fictions should not impart knowledge unsuitable to young persons. Indeed, in some cases these fictions expose the hypocrisy of such restrictions on the discussion of sexuality in fiction by showing young persons exposed directly to the sexual immoralities of their elders about which they are not allowed to read literary accounts. In an anticipation of the late fiction, such situations also allow James to scrutinize the moral ambiguity of transgressive sexuality itself and of the intense puritanical restriction of it, since characters that obsessively and punitively regulate sexual behavior are at times as disturbing as those who transgress. This is notably the case in *The Turn of the Screw*, in which the hysterical concern of a young governess for protecting her two young charges from the ostensibly corrupting moral influence of two ghosts, remnants of morally dubious former servants of her master, lead to the death of one of her charges. This narrative is also striking because of its cruel parody of the female-centered and often domestic world of Gothic fiction, another case of James drawing on but correcting his feminine precursors. The governess-narrator, clearly a latter-day Jane Eyre, tells her story with the overinsistent narrative intimacy and emotional excitability, and the obsessive and irrational dread of sexuality, that James associated with women writers and readers; though the story is famously ambiguous, clearly James judges the governess's hysterical effort to shield the children from sexual corruption pathetic in its failure of emotional distance and at least as destructive as the evil she resists.[21] A similar moral ambiguity is found at the end of James's gloomy novel of divorce, *What Maisie Knew* (1897), in which the young protagonist, abandoned by her biological parents, while in France has an opportunity to be raised by her beloved stepfather Sir Claude, who offers to keep her on the Continent. But the implacable moral condemnation by her morally strict governess, Mrs. Wix, of Sir Claude's relationship with his mistress deprives the girl of her last chance at some semblance of family life, and she returns, utterly bereft, with her governess to England.[22]

PROSTITUTION AND AESTHETIC COMMODIFICATION
IN *THE WINGS OF THE DOVE*

In James's last great period his work builds on the formal innovations of the 1890s, while remaining preoccupied with the transgressive sexuality central to all three of the major final novels, *The Ambassadors* (1903), *The Wings of the Dove* (1902), and *The Golden Bowl* (1904). But in the late novels, the narrative material to a striking degree also circles back to quite conventional, even hackneyed, domestic and courtship narrative models of the mid-Victorian era. Yet building on his ability to create moral ambiguity and psychological subtlety, which he had developed in the previous decades, James writes these novels as if to demonstrate the impossibility in the modern era of telling the courtship and domestic narratives of the Victorian period with the old moral clarity. Thus, a fundamental impulse of these novels is to rewrite such traditional narratives to show the crudity of their moral assumptions and the inadequacy of the depiction of social and psychic complexity, to replace such crude moral assumptions with the drama of refined aesthetic, psychological, and moral discriminations.

In each of these final major novels, a morally problematic situation is created by the power of money, in response to which some characters, deploying language corrupted by the taint of literary conventionality or journalistic cliché, try to justify and explain, both to themselves and to others, their complicity in a morally sordid situation. However, a central character, in some sense James's surrogate, resists this debasement of language and the accompanying blurring of moral distinctions. The tension over the misuse of language and the intricacy of moral distinctions, while it surrounds the protagonists, is not external to them. Rather, compelled by their own economic and psychic constraint and moral indecisions, the protagonists carefully weigh and evaluate their situations, and generate a creative response to the morally problematic situations that confront them. It is through the dialectic of such competing deployments of language and moral sensibility that the late Jamesian text makes its own style a significant subject, one that is fraught with moral as well as aesthetic import.

Underscoring the centrality of gender role transition to these fictions, each is haunted by the figure of the New Woman, a female character who seizes masculine power for herself through enmeshment in the marketplace, and this enmeshment is often figured as the danger of prostitution. It should be remembered that though many actual late-Victorian feminists were stridently puritanical in accordance with the Social Purity movement, popular constructions of the New Woman figured women's increased resistance to marriage and desire to enter into masculine realms of privilege with sexual looseness or even prostitution. In a play sending up the New Woman, the following exchange occurs between two advanced women:

Enid: And *I* say that man reeking with infamy, ought not to be allowed to marry a pure girl.
Victoria: Certainly not! *She* ought to reek with infamy as well![23]

The link between the New Woman and the prostitute in James's mind suggests his visceral discomfort with women who seized masculine prerogatives, but also figures his gloomy reading of the degrading power of the marketplace, a subject that, given his view of the negative effects of mass culture and journalism on literature was of enormous personal importance to him. Moreover, the twinned themes of prostitution and the New Woman represent the antithesis of traditional domesticity's rigid separation of male and female characters into separate forms and channeling of sexuality within the family. Both also demonstrate the obsolescence of the ideological insistence on rigid boundaries between commerce and love or family life; all three of the major late novels thematize the power of wealth to distort and corrupt sexuality and feature transgressions of traditional gender roles.

Though prostitution, the paradigmatic example of sexuality corrupted by economics, has a major symbolic significance in earlier Victorian fiction, what is new in James's late works is not only the centrality of this theme but the way the situation of the prostitute is linked to that of the creative individual or writer.[24] While the upwardly mobile David Copperfield witnesses the danger of prostitution for those of a lower social class, such as Little Emily, James's characters in the late novels, like Fleda Vetch in *The Spoils of Poynton* and Kate Croy in *The Wings of the Dove*, are threatened by the possibility of prostitution in a much more intimate way. This intimate threat of prostitution suggests how the dark side of human existence, including the intractable pressure of sexual and economic impulses, are seen as more fully constitutive of human, including middle-class, life than they were in mid-Victorian fiction. Indeed, in James's late fiction, the typically self-enclosed, separate, fictive world and the consciousness that it creates in the reader, and also represents in the consciousness of characters, tends to figure itself repeatedly as a response to the threat to the artistic consciousness of the danger of self-prostitution, or a response to a symbolic prostitution already suffered.

Prostitution is an important ideological theme in this period because it epitomizes in a stark form anxieties about ideals that were notionally distinct from market valuation, of the feminine, of the child, of whatever was ennobling, being reduced to the status of mere commodity. In such a context in which social and political anxieties were aroused by prostitution, the subject becomes a privileged marker for anxiety about reifications in general, of detachments of behavior from their accepted systems of meaning, especially detachments involving personal and sexual life. In the subject of prostitution, the widespread suspicions, partly caused by changing gender and sexual norms, that the naked power of money was having shocking effects in corrupting public morals and that social morality could no longer be trusted to channel sexual impulses into acceptable forms found its perfect image. As manifest victims of forces beyond her control, the prostitute could be a sympathetic figure. But her refusal to conform to the culture's asexual ideal for single women could also confirm sexist preconceptions of women as essentially carnal and sexually voracious. The image of the prostitute was thus available in the culture to express increasing fin de siècle anxieties about the reifications that were salient in a modern industrial society and the profound tensions everywhere visible over class and gender inequalities. For instance, by melodramatically exposing the exploitative practices and sexual deviance of wealthy males who purchased young girls for sex in "The Maiden Tribute of Modern Babylon," W. T. Stead stirred passionate outrage, especially among workers and women.[25] But the image of the prostitute also allowed the containment of such explosive social anxieties within moralistic narratives that ultimately reassured society about the nature of the subversions and instabilities that made reified social relations disquieting. By displacing anxieties about the general processes of the reification, modernization, and commodification onto the scapegoated figure of the sexualized women or prostitute, or her evil twin the procurer, narratives about such women could at once register general anxieties and yet reassure society that the problem was rooted in the class or ethnic Other (sexually threatening women of foreign extraction are everywhere in fin de siècle literature), or that it lay ultimately in the traditional threat of the demonic woman.[26]

What is most original about James's use of the prostitution theme is that he elaborately explores the parallel between the position of the creative or sensitive individual writer and that of the prostitute.[27] Particularly overt in depiction of these themes is *The Wings of the Dove*, perhaps James's most moving late novel. Its protagonist, Merton Densher, is James's most sympathetic and successful portrait of the literary aesthete caught in a world in which literary production is fully commodified. (Strether in *The Ambassadors* is another brilliantly imagined example, though he is more an aspiring aesthete than the real thing.) Painfully aware that his poverty makes him helpless to rescue his fiancée Kate Croy from her impoverished and sordid family, Densher finds "funny . . . the innermost fact, so often vivid to him, of his own consciousness—his private inability to believe that he should ever be rich" (54). Densher's alienation from wealth is a direct result of his position as a talented aesthete who is incapable, or constitutionally unwilling, to conform to a market-dominated social world by marketing his literary talents aggressively:

> It was a line on which his fancy could be admirably active; the innumerable ways of making money were beautifully present to him; he could have handled them for his newspaper as easily as he could have handled everything. He was quite aware how he handled everything; it was another mark on his forehead: the pair of smudges from the thumb of fortune, the brand on the passive fleece, dated from the primal hour and kept each other company. He wrote, as for print, with deplorable ease; since there had been nothing to stop him even at the age of ten, so there was as little at twenty; it was part of his fate in the first place and part of the wretched public's in the second. The innumerable ways of making money were, no doubt, at all events, what his imagination often was busy with after he had tilted his chair and thrown back his head with his hands clasped behind it. What would most have prolonged that attitude, moreover, was the reflexion that the ways were ways only for others. (55)

The paradox here is important; Densher's inborn native talent, which allows his fancy to be "admirably active" on the subject of making money, is precisely that innate superiority that prevents him from being willing to market himself successfully.[28] In a market-driven literary world, Densher's characteristic literary superiority becomes a mark of Cain "brand[ing]" him as exiled from market success. Through the romantic convention of Densher's innate artistic nobility, the tension, rooted in the organization of cultural production of James's period, between the market dictates of commercialized production and the writer's desire for aesthetic autonomy, which James forcefully defended in his critical prose, is here represented as an internal tension between Densher's desire for wealth and his innate unwillingness to prostitute his literary talents for money. The novel will dramatize Densher's internal conflict as precisely embodied by the danger of such a genteel form of prostitution.

If Densher is the novel's central creative figure, it is a striking feature of the novel that all three major characters (and even some minor ones) use creative abilities to make fictions, so that the novel enacts the fate of various kinds of fiction makers and their fictions in competition with one another.[29] A particularly influential fiction maker is Kate Croy. If Densher, as journalist, must pander to the market's demands, his willingness to acquiesce in the successful marketing of himself that he fears he can never successfully achieve occupationally is externalized in his lover Kate Croy. One of James's most fully imagined female characters, she combines the rebellion against feminine impotence of Isabel Archer with the deviousness and mercenary motives of her precursor in the James canon, Madame Merle. Like Densher, Kate has internalized a position within a society structured by commodification; as a woman valued for display purposes, she sees herself as having already suffered the commodification with which Densher is threatened. In the first chapter of the novel, she appeals to her disgraced and ruined father, Lionel Croy, to take her in and prevent her from becoming the tool of her wealthy aunt Maud Lowder, an influential personage in the family who has demanded that she break all ties with her father. Her willingness to sacrifice mercenary advantage for family loyalty shows Kate's basic character, its tension between idealism and materialism. But her father cynically tells her that her only reasonable hope to escape poverty is to make a mercenary marriage under the direction of Mrs. Lowder. A less-idealized portrayal of family relations than the one found in this scene would be difficult to envision, as each character manipulates and voices scorn for the other. The grim naturalism of this opening scene sets the tone for the depiction of the world that has created Kate Croy and will determine her later actions.

Despite having an idealistic side, Kate is forced throughout the novel to bow to the commodification of the self to which her father abandons her. Her idealism and aspiration toward intellectual and aesthetic life is embodied in her love for the impoverished but intellectual Densher, but entrapped by the domination of her mercenary aunt ("Britannia of the Marketplace" as Kate calls her), she must play a theatrical role in her aunt's household, since her position with her wealthy relative is a "great value" "the only one they have" (59), as she caustically says of her family. Kate's dilemma throughout the novel is that her mercenary situation cripples her ability to live for higher values, despite her desperate aspiration toward them. As she points out in an image of commodification to the more economically privileged Milly Theale: "I *am*— . . . on the counter, when I'm not in the shop-window; in and out of which I'm thus conveniently commercially whisked: the essence, all of it, of my position, and the price, as properly, of my aunt's protection" (169; emphasis in original). Anxious to avoid the poverty of her own family and to rebel against her socially defined feminine role as passive object, Kate seizes a masculine role by controlling her relation with Densher. (Tellingly, she begins the novel by *waiting*: "She waited, Kate Croy, for her father to come in, but he kept her unconscionably . . ." [21], an action synecdochic of the enforced passivity against which she will rebel.) At the novel's beginning, her aspiration for masculine power in response to the family disgrace is a key note of her character: "she quite visibly lost herself in the thought of the way she might still pull things around had she only been a man" (22), and her rebellion against feminine passivity aligns her with the fin de siècle figure of the New Woman. Appropriately, given Kate's surrender to the dictates of the market and her desire for masculine power, she will eventually complete the gender reversal that her domination of Densher has begun by placing him in a prototypically feminine position, that of prostitute, when she plans, like Madame Merle with Gilbert Osmond, to have Densher marry Milly and gain her wealth. Symbolically her willingness to be a procurer, to market Densher to Milly, threatens to place him in a position that embodies his threatened commodification in the literary marketplace. Densher in turn, resisting his feminized role in her plot and eager to restore his sense of masculine control over his domineering fiancée, demands that she prostitute herself in turn, requiring her to "come to him" in his room for intercourse in return for his participation in their mercenary scheme. This sexual act in turn figures how both characters are fully enmeshed in a reifying world that requires that the most intimate relations be objectified.

If Kate's role in the novel, then, is to be the figure for the market pressures that bear on the creative Densher, she is also a fiction maker in her own right. With her brilliant improvisations, theatrical sense, and callous Darwinian logic of might over compassion, she figures the maker of fictions who is fully complicit with a surrender to the market—the writer as prostitute to the market. Though not literally a writer, she uses her imagination for gain, like the popular writers of the day. In her masculine plotting for power, her greed, her fetishistic investment in health, reminiscent of the association of New Woman writing with eugenicism, Kate resembles the writers in that tradition. "I'm a brute about illness," she tells Densher: "It's well for you, my dear, . . . that you're sound as a bell" (215); Kate's pride in the couple's physical health, and her dismissal of the scruples of conscience Densher eventually develops, suggests her materialist worldview and a nearly Social Darwinist contempt for the physically weak.[30] At the same time, with her dark beauty (she is a brunette who in key scenes wears a black dress), aesthetic aspirations, and sexual looseness, she is also something of a female decadent, a type James associated with women enmeshed in the market-place.[31] Kate is the culmination of a number of late James female characters doomed by their affinity with the New Woman type who face a symbolic prostitution in the marketplace; Fleda Vetch, in *The Spoils of Poynton*, is a female aesthete and former art student drawn into an upper-class woman's feminist rebellion against her son's appropriation of valuable art objects. The older woman, in her desperation to defeat her son, urges Fleda to "let herself go" by seducing the son away from his fiancée, a symbolic exchange of sexuality for wealth. Nanda, in *The Awkward Age*, though not as economically vulnerable as Fleda, must "work" other characters for economic benefit, calls herself a "modern, slangy hack," and loses the man she loves and hopes to marry because he comes to associate her with women from the immoral French novels she reads. Her name, one letter from Nana, hints that one such woman is the courtesan heroine about whom Zola wrote a notorious novel.[32]

Given how Kate epitomizes commodified modern femininity, it is no surprise that she is perfectly practical and businesslike in understanding the necessity of the commodification her lover faces as a journalist. When Densher, in a sign that he is at last learning to market his aesthetic talents, is chosen by his company for the mission of writing on America (often seen in this era as the heartland of commercialization), Kate fully approves the scheme:

> He was struck at the same time with her happy grasp of what had really occurred in Fleet Street—all the more that it was his own final reading. He was to pull the subject up—that was just what they wanted; . . . It was just because he didn't nose about and babble, because he wasn't the usual gossip-monger, that they had picked him out. It was a branch of their correspondence with which they evidently wished a new tone associated, such a tone as, from now on, it would have always to take from his example. (67–68)

Kate approves and applauds Densher's complicity in the paradox of aestheticism; the aesthete's elevated "tone," ostensibly a defense against surrendering to the degradation of the literary market, against becoming the "usual gossip-monger," becomes by virtue of its apparent elevation above the market a peculiarly valuable commodity in the market. As a master of commodification, Kate understands this strategem; later, she will have Densher play a similar role toward Milly, another paying audience, a role that mirrors the paradoxical situation in which Densher's professional role places him. His cultured tone and *appearance* of disinterestedness will become his most marketable asset, the perfect cloak for an all-too-interested grasp at Milly's money.

In the ensuing dialogue about Densher's career, James telegraphs to the reader how, in contrast to Densher's intuition that the imagination must remain inviolate, Kate unsentimentally categorizes the imagination as an economic resource:

> "How you ought indeed, when you understand so well, to be a journalist's wife!" Densher exclaimed in admiration even while she struck him as fairly hurrying him off.
>
> But she was almost impatient of the praise. "What do you expect one *not* to understand when one cares for you?"
>
> "Ah then I'll put it otherwise and say "How much you care for me!"
>
> "Yes," she assented; "it fairly redeems my stupidity. I *shall*, with a chance to show it," she added, "have some imagination for you." (68; emphasis in original)

While Densher is rather ruefully "hurri[ed] off" to market his imagination, Kate is all too eager to put her imagination to the work of securing the couple wealth, to use it to "redeem" herself from her feckless love for the impoverished Densher. It is characteristic of the novel's linking of economic pressures with gender role disruptions that Densher and Kate reverse Victorian gender expectations; he is sentimental and feeling, expecting her to show emotion at his impending departure, while she is briskly practical, "hurrying him off." This moment is typical of how for James, Victorian conventions of gender become a potent, nostalgic residue, powerful by their absence. Moreover, Kate's language here ("redeems") suggests the commercial nature of her impulses as well as how for her, as James envisioned the typical woman writer, the deployment of the imagination is firmly part of an economic calculus. Ultimately, the "imagination for you" that she delivers to Densher will be her skillful reading of Milly and her stage-managing of Densher's relation to her in the plot to ensnare her wealth.

We see this stage-managing particularly clearly and its link to Kate's role as a figure for public and commercial uses of the imagination in the crucial scene in which Densher demands that Kate sleep with him. This scene shows that a central feature of this relationship, and indeed a fundamental feature of the novel, is that the courtship narrative of Densher and Kate will be the quintessence of romantic love corrupted; their story will show how the romance of traditional courtship becomes indistinguishable from that of commodification and comes to resemble its antithesis, commercialized sexuality. In essence, the romance of courtship is ironized and revealed as inapplicable to modern conditions. Kate and Densher's entire relationship has been conducted amid publicity, which has required duplicity and stage-managing to conceal itself from a watchful society ("the beginning of everything" [50] occurs on a crowded underground train). Given the association in the novel between public spaces and publicity, including journalism (Densher's profession), it is fitting that this crucial scene of Kate's self-prostitution occurs in the square of St. Mark's in Venice while Densher and Kate await their traveling companions. When Kate urges Densher to enter into her scheme more fully by deceiving her aunt about his feelings for Milly, he responds by demanding her sexual acquiescence. Her response reveals how her very nature is at one with clarity, openness, and lucidity, characteristics the novel links with commercial uses of the imagination and with a surrender to the "highly modern" (50) world that Kate embodies:

> She listened as for the good information, and there was support for him—since it was a question of his going step by step—in the way she took no refuge in showing herself shocked. He had in truth not expected of her that particular vulgarity, but the absence of it only added the thrill of a deeper reason to his sense of possibilities. For the knowledge of what she was he had absolutely to see her now, incapable of refuge, stand there for him in all the light of the day and of his admirable merciless meaning. (294)

Kate's only immediate response is to tell him to restrain his physical gesture of holding her arm—as always, she manages appearances. As they approach the others, he confidently exults in the success of his request: "Yet what he was possessed of was real—the fact that she hadn't thrown over his lucidity the horrid shadow of cheap reprobation" (295). James thus links the very qualities that makes Kate symbolically a master of fiction making on the commercial model—her lucidity, clarity, acceptance of publicity, in short, her modernity and unsentimental valuation of moral norms—to the pressures that here sexually degrade her. The lucidity with which she is consistently associated here "in the light of day" makes clear "what she was"—a whore—a word the novel suggests but tactfully does not employ. In the next chapter, in which Kate exacts Densher's agreement to court and propose to Milly in return for which she will sleep with him, it becomes clear that each character is acceding to acts of self-prostitution, agreeing to acts of love for mercenary motives.

James suffuses these scenes with bitter irony. Given Densher's violation of norms against nonmarital sexuality, readers might well have doubted that his meaning was "admirable," and his proposal, not her potential refusal, could be considered "vulgarity." An even harsher irony arises when she agrees to his request—in conventional terms, the sacrifice of her honor—with the words "On my honour" (312). But these ironies only draw attention to the thorough reversal and subversion that James reveals in his characters of the values typically embedded in traditional domestic and courtship narratives. Far from courtship and the family being sites dictated by honor and free from market considerations, the sexual impulses that underlie such narratives are revealed to be deeply implicated in market-determined power relations. Just as the imagination of a writer such as Densher cannot transcend its enmeshment in the literary marketplace, neither can human sexuality and its embodiment in romantic love remain free of economic taint. As if to suggest that there is no morally secure position in a fully market-saturated world from which to condemn Kate and Densher, James allows their own language to condemn them implicitly. Rather than overtly condemning them in the manner of an earlier more didactic style of fiction, he extends the subversion of the "normal" metonymically from their illicit behavior to their perverse language, as both the language they speak and that of the narration itself become twisted into perverse meanings to capture their perverse actions, which are grotesque in their cool calculations and thoroughgoing reversal of conventional morality. James's strategy of having language porously absorb the moral ambiguity of his character's behavior is highly germane to the parallel the novel suggests between literary and sexual prostitution. In James's vision, the debasement of moral and sexual life, and of a commodified language that expresses that debasement, are not merely linked but become nearly identical.

The phrase "what she was[,]" elliptically suggesting the word whore, is also important to the meaning of the scene and to the novel's larger structure. This silent but palpably present word becomes the first of several tangible silences in the novel, notably the famously absent scene in which a chastened Densher says good-bye to Milly shortly before her death. We never see this scene, and indeed Densher is acutely embarrassed at the idea of having to describe it to Kate ("He had fairly fancied her even wanting to know and trying to find out how far, as the odious phrase was, he and Milly had gone" [359]), but whatever Densher has done in this scene, whether silent sympathy or physical expression of affection, this is clearly Densher's moment, corresponding to Kate's coming to his room, to offer love which will be financially rewarded. Though clearly enough implying the act Kate performs sexually for wealth, to what degree Densher has acted the role of lover to Milly the novel declines to specify, a crucial example of how the novel's reticence favors Densher's dignity and resists Kate's degrading "lucidity," which is linked with the acceptance of commodification.

It is because the resistance to the commodification of language and experience is so central to the novel's themes that of all the late fictions, *Wings* most fully suggests the deeper thematic meaning of the endless narrative obliquity of James's late style. It does this by making the novel's increasing linguistic difficulty a sign of the moral subversion his characters are performing on traditional moral values, but also makes this narrative complexity and retardation become the formal correlative of Densher's growing resistance to the moral perversity of the role that Kate's fiction making has created for him. For if Kate's pragmatic complicity in mercenary and commercial fiction making requires a "lucidity," a "light of day" that is ultimately oppressive and specious in its "merciless meaning," the necessary resistance to this market-tainted fictive practice, tainting like the thumbprint on Densher's head, lies in the resistance that both he and the narrative develop to lucidity itself.

The novel stages on many levels Densher's increasing resistance to Kate's insistent reification of language, of morality, and of sexuality, which figures James's resistance to the commodification of literature as mass-produced domestic, courtship or adventure narratives. The novel does so formally by its withdrawal into a dreamy and ambiguous prose; generically by its insistent refusal of the reader's narrative expectations, which derive from conventional courtship narrative, and literally through Densher's retreat from the present of his relationship with Kate into a nostalgic obsession with the past and Milly's memory. The immense retardation of the narrative movement from what begins as a simple story of courtship and marriage, a strategy that defeats the reader's expectation of a narrative organized around courtship, is pervasively motivated by first Milly's and then Densher's complicity with, but finally resistance to, processes of commodification that are epitomized in Kate Croy. Early in the novel, Densher generates a narrative retardation by his morally confused incomprehension of Kate's plan for Milly and himself and his reluctance to act on it; finally, the novel comes to a different kind of retardation as it centers on his inner consciousness as he experiences remorse, which further slows the narrative's pace in the novel's final books.

Milly is an appropriate magnet for Densher's aesthetic and moral resistance to Kate's greed, because Milly's tale is largely that of the talented pupil educated to see the necessity of aesthetic perception of her own life by those around her, who encourage her to aestheticize her experience, though they do so for their own self-interested reasons.[33] Milly herself is something of a fiction maker, though largely her fictions amount to the creation of the image and style of herself as the American patron of culture, ensconced in a Venetian palace no less, who by sheer willpower and optimistic fiction making will hold death at bay. It is around this poignant image of a largely defensive fiction making, in which Milly craves to create "life"—and specifically a romance with Densher—as an embodiment of her will to live that James develops most fully the symbol-laden, fairy-tale world characteristic of the late fiction, as suggested by Milly's resonant titles of "princess" and "dove." The image of Milly as dove, a word with biblical resonances that also recalls Hawthorne's saintly American virgin Hilda from *The Marble Faun*, is the most straightforward example of the aestheticization and sentimentalization that Milly undergoes. In the novel's nearly allegorical structure, Milly's dovelike status symbolizes the idealism associated with the bourgeoisie of an earlier moment (to Densher she is "the American girl as he had originally found her" [302]). Her girlhood and Americanness, her love of freedom, and her innocence of European corruption are the markers of this status. Appropriate though the image may be for her, in its emphasis on her fragility and sexual innocence, the metaphor also serves the purpose of her pursuers, and it is typical of the novel's ironic relation to sentimental language that the character who actually assigns her this name is the manipulative Kate Croy. As the novel progresses, Milly's dovelike "wings" are a euphemism for her great wealth, further ironizing the image's spiritual connotations. Deployed in such a context, this biblical image is degraded and robbed of its spiritual and sentimental significance.

The reader of this novel, used to the tradition of narratives of courtship and domestic drama, might well have wondered why James felt it necessary to slow so dramatically and, indeed, even in certain places to truncate the novel's narrative, as in the missing scene where Densher says good-bye to Milly, while enormously expanding the degree to which we enter the consciousness of the characters, above all, of Merton Densher. From a certain point of view, the narrative material in *Wings*, as in all the late novels, is strikingly and banally conventional; Kate and Densher, the impoverished couple waiting anxiously to have the resources to marry, seem merely stock figures in Victorian domestic narrative. Moreover, Kate and Densher's plot and the resultant courtship of Milly by Densher generates a variant of the bigamy plot in which an innocent woman (or more rarely a man) becomes aware of the sexual looseness of a lover, fiancée, or spouse and of the reality of their preexisting sexual bonds; it is the plot of *Jane Eyre*, of many sensation texts, and reappears in *Daniel Deronda* and in *The Portrait of a Lady*. What is original about James's use of this hackneyed domestic plot is precisely his complete transformation of its moral coordinates; he transmutes the banal narrative into something of great complexity by the nuance with which both victim and villains are treated, which disables the expected simple moral response to such a plot. Essentially James rewrites melodrama so that neither villain is in any simple sense villainous, and indeed, the later part of the novel becomes a narrative of moral and aesthetic discrimination, as Densher gradually comes to reject Kate's modern lucidity, and to prefer Milly's ambiguous and imaginatively colored traditional femininity. In short, Densher reflexively reinterprets the narrative of which he has been a part, and comes to understand Kate as aesthetically and morally vitiated by her enmeshment in the marketplace and spiritually inferior to Milly. Moreover, this process of discrimination and moral reevaluation on Densher's part is affiliated with a general cultural critique that is not merely that of the character but resonates with that of his creator.

There is a crucial moment in the novel where we can see James's method with particular clarity. Densher, paying court to Milly in Venice, has for the first time been refused admission to Milly's palace and feels a confusion of emotions as he leaves, including embarrassment at her servant Eugenio's evident low opinion of him. A storm has broken out, and the gloomy weather reflects Densher's storm of conflicting emotions. In indirect discourse James tells us that this moment was also one of epiphany for Densher:

> It was a Venice all of evil that had broken out. . . . a Venice of cold lashing rain from a low black sky, of wicked wind raging through the narrow passes, of general arrest and interruption, with the people engaged in all the water-life huddled, stranded and wageless, bored and cynical, under archways and bridges. . . . The wet and the cold were now to reckon with, and it was to Densher precisely as if he had seen the obliteration at a stroke, of the margin on a faith in which they were all living. The margin had been his name for it—for the thing that, though it had held out, could bear no shock. The shock, in some form, had come, and he wondered about it while, threading his way among loungers as vague as himself, he dropped his eyes sightlessly on the rubbish in shops. There were stretches of the gallery paved with squares of red marble, greasy now with the salt spray; and the whole place, in its huge elegance, the grace of its conception and the beauty of its detail, was more than ever like a great drawing-room, the drawing-room of Europe, profaned and bewildered by some reverse of fortune. (325–27)

A reader might well wonder how one gets from Densher's social embarrassment before a servant ("One had come to a queer pass when a servant's opinion so mattered" [326]) to "the drawing-room of Europe, profaned and bewildered" and to the sense of a lost idealism "in which they were all living." The economic metaphor of a failing "margin" suggests a pervasive moral bankruptcy now suddenly visible to Densher, but what is striking here is the breadth and the depth of the implicit moral jeremiad against a "profaned" Europe. The precipitating events—a check in his relationship with Milly, a rainy day, a disrespectful servant—seem disproportionate to the epochal import this passage assigns it. But the connection between Densher's personal frustration and his sense of cultural crisis becomes readable if we understand that James is operating, for all of his ironizing of courtship narrative traditions, within the conventions of domestic fiction, in which historical and cultural conflicts are figured through narratives of courtship and domesticity.

Thus James invites us to read through the lens of these conventions so that the ultimately permanent disruption of Densher's courtship of Milly becomes the beginning of a turning point in his consciousness that will end his relationship with Kate, a moral reevaluation to which the novel assigns a large moral and cultural resonance. For in the narrative of Milly and Densher's relationship, both in its apparent character and in its reality, James creates images that reflect larger cultural concerns. As a young and idealistic American, Milly figures the promise of American idealism, which for James always combines moral high-mindedness and commitment to individual freedom with moral rigidity and cultural impoverishment. Such a representative figure could benefit from what Densher, as a representative educated Briton, could offer her, a cultural and historical knowledge that would broaden her. At the same time, Milly's idealism and belief in freedom could inspire a European sensibility understood as increasingly cynical and decadent, as imaged by the "bored and cynical" gondoliers and the "rubbish in shops" in Venice. If America could learn from European cultural richness, Europe, a world "profaned" by the domination of commerce over moral ideals, could benefit from American idealism. Densher, who writes for a living and struggles against the corruption of a rigid and mercenary social order, embodies a Europe requiring an infusion of the moral idealism Milly symbolizes.

But at this point in the narrative, as Densher becomes painfully and guiltily aware, the reality of his courtship of Milly lies not in an idealistic fusion of American idealism and European sophistication but rather enacts Milly's other significance in the novel, as a bearer of vast wealth. Densher and Kate Croy's plot to gain that wealth figures Europeans as motivated indeed by a failing "margin," not only literal need of money, but an economic collapse that figures a moral bankruptcy. Britain had in fact suffered serious economic reverses in the years before this novel was written, the 1880s and 1890s having been decades of economic recession and rising working-class militance, facts that add to the resonance of the metaphor. But James clearly wants us to envision economic need ("the margin on a faith in which they were all living") as merely symptomatic, as figuring a deeper moral failure of society, which Densher's epiphanically intuits. It is this moral failure that Densher feels complicit in, a feeling that immeasurably deepens and fills him with guilt in the next chapter, in which Mrs. Stringham reports to him that Milly, informed of Densher's engagement to Kate by the callous aristocrat Lord Mark, has "turned her face to the wall" (331), surrendering to her fatal ailment.

Mrs. Stringham urges him "to save [Milly's] life" (344) by denying the truth of what Lord Mark has told her, in effect to continue fiction making on behalf of Milly's health rather than greed. As we have noted, James never gives us the crucial scene where Densher returns apparently ready to admit the truth to Milly, and in the novel's only indirect account of the scene, Densher tells Kate that Milly has never asked him for the truth; but his epiphany, in which he sees the failure "of the margin, on the faith of which they were all living," suggests his real motive for resistance to further lying. Urged though he is to such an act by Mrs. Stringham, with her sentimental and melodramatic notion that such a lie at the last hour could save Milly's life, and also presumably by loyalty to Kate, who will later understandably demand why Densher did not lie, he is unwilling to falsify reality and corrupt further his relation to Milly in an act of fiction making that would be the final surrender to his fiancée's mercenary plot. In personal terms, Densher values an honest relationship with Milly above all else; but as the passage quoted above suggests, Densher's choice of integrity has a wider cultural import, suggesting a refusal of complicity in a general moral corruption and dishonesty, in a profanation of European culture, which Kate, the lucid and modern, all-too-masculine woman embodies and encourages. If the narrative's implication that the gender role reversals and dishonesty of Kate and Densher's relation is symptomatic of a general cultural decline seems overblown, this figurative link must be put into the context of how the fin de siècle New Woman and decadent writing were seen as symptoms of a nearly apocalyptic cultural degeneration that threatened Britain's social health and imperial position.[34]

Though by betraying her trust Kate and Densher could be said to hasten Milly's death, James is too partial to the idealism and the traditional version of femininity that Milly represents for her not to get a last posthumous laugh. In her own aestheticism and idealism Milly finally exceeds the capacities of her teachers in aesthetic delights. In death she achieves the utter disinterestedness of the artist as aesthete, and in her profound impact on

Densher, she becomes a muse who rivals art's ability to stir the imagination. Indeed, it is Milly's stirring of the writer's imagination that defeats Kate. In the wake of Milly's death he finds the clarity of Kate's vision to be ultimately a delusion, protesting to her in a critique at once aesthetic and moral, "You see in everything, and you always did, . . . something that, while I'm with you at least, I always take from you as the truth itself" (389). His ultimate rebellion against the brutal modern clarity of Kate's version of the world, which aligns Kate with the popular writers of the day—clear in their ideological modernity, but deceptive in their rigid adherence to the callous marketplace—emerges in his nostalgia for the imaginative possibilities of Milly's world, symbolized by the letter she sends Densher announcing her bequest to him, which Kate ruthlessly burns:

> Then he took to himself at such hours, in other words, that he should never know what had been in Milly's letter. The intention announced in it he should but too probably know; but that would have been, but for the depths of his spirit, the least part of it. The part of it missed forever was the turn she would have given her act. That turn had possibilities that, somehow, by wondering about them, his imagination had extraordinarily filled out and refined. It had made of them a priceless pearl cast before his eyes—his pledge given not to save it—into the fathomless sea, or rather even it was like the sacrifice of something sentient and throbbing, something that, for the spiritual ear, might have been audible as a faint, far wail. This was the sound that he cherished, when alone, in the stillness of his rooms. He sought and guarded the stillness, so that it might prevail there till the inevitable sounds of life, once more, comparatively coarse and harsh, should smother and deaden it—doubtless by the same process with which they would officiously heal the ache, in his soul, that was somehow one with it. It deepened moreover the sacred hush that he couldn't complain. He had given poor Kate her freedom. (398–99)

The passage resonates with characteristic Jamesian ambiguity, since we can read the "turn" that Milly would have given her letter of bequest to Densher, and that so haunts him, as the final relic of her being, a being he had genuinely loved, or as the aesthetic impulse she embodies that still fires his own imagination ("his imagination had extraordinarily filled out and refined"). Or this "turn" and the "wail" that his imagination links with it can poignantly figure the anguish and guilt he feels at the sacrifice of his own spirit of aesthetic and creative disinterestedness and Milly's girlish idealism before Kate's sexually purchased "freedom" to corrupt and commodify all values. Most plausibly, the obliterated "turn" is a many-layered symbol of all of these things. But the general point is clear: the salvation that Milly holds out to Densher, and the language of "priceless pearl," which echoes the "pearl of great price" of Christian spiritual redemption, is nothing less than salvation through imaginative fealty to her legacy of spirit, a loyalty that necessarily involves the rejection of the commercial spirit of Kate, which still hungers for Milly's money.

Paradoxically, but appropriately, given how the novel aligns James's resistance to and subversion of a conventional courtship narrative with the resistance to commodification itself, Kate, that relentless agent of commodification who has rationalized Densher's courtship of Milly as giving her the love she craved, insists to the bitter end on reading the resonant ambiguity of Densher's refusal of Milly's bequest to him as clear proof that the story has been a conventional courtship narrative all along—that of Milly and Densher:

> "And you're afraid—it's wonderful!—to be in love with her."
>
> "I never was in love with her," said Densher.
>
> She took it, but after a little she met it. "I believe that now—for the time she lived. I believe it at least for the time you were there. But your change came—as it might well—the day you last saw her; she died for you then that you might understand her. From that hour you *did*." (402–3; emphasis in original)

Just as Kate's conventional imagination has pictured Milly as eager to experience a romantic interlude with Densher as a cosmic recompense for her mortality, here her reading remains reductive, glossing the novel as a conventional courtship narrative, albeit a failed courtship, since Densher has only finally fallen in love with Milly at her death. While this reading of a sentimental Densher as locked in a hopeless love for the dead girl is not impossible, this romance narrative is truer to Kate's conventional nature than to the narrative we see, and reductively ignores how Milly's memory, fragmented and incomplete as it is, as the burned letter suggests, has in its very incompletion become a spiritual and aesthetic icon for Densher, stimulating his imaginative powers. Through awakening Densher's imagination and his aesthetic appreciation of her selflessness, Milly posthumously defeats her rival, causing Densher to demand that Kate marry him without Milly's money, a demand he must know will be refused. So Densher's defeat of Kate's mercenary project, his insistence on not benefiting financially from his relationship with Milly, a renunciation that corresponds to James's own sense of his literary career as a single-minded refusal of popular success in search of the ideal audience, becomes—Kate's claim to the contrary notwithstanding—no sign of a failed courtship between Densher and Milly.

Rather, it marks a complete withdrawal on Densher's part from all courtship narratives and erotic or economic pursuits—the erotic and the economic having contaminated each other—and instead emblematizes how Densher transfers all his energies to an imaginative and aesthetic realm beyond the merely material. Densher's aesthetic response to Milly, signified by his refusal to benefit from her bequest, subverts traditional market-tainted courtship narratives and firmly transcends their erotic telos.

There is an implicit allegory of literary production in the way Kate's ludicity and functional use of the imagination degrades her and Densher, much as James saw most popular culture degrading true literary values, while the ethereal but ephemeral Milly embodies the ideals of disinterested use of the imagination to which Densher appreciatively and elegiacally responds. But in the novel's apotheosis of Milly and its increasingly dark reading of Kate Croy, there is also a conservative and nostalgic comment on the changing gender roles of women in fin de siècle Britain. James began his literary career when the sensation fiction furor left conservatives grumbling at the new emphasis on what Margaret Oliphant would call the "fleshly" side of feminine experience. From the seeds of that break with domestic pieties in George Eliot's work and sensation fiction would grow the more open treatments of women's discontents found in such late Victorian writers as Sarah Grand, Olive Schreiner, Henrik Ibsen, George Meredith, Thomas Hardy, and other creators of literary New Women.[35] But in *Wings of the Dove*, James's formal radicalism and sternly ironic revision of courtship narratives is put in the service of a rejection of the unsexed New Woman embodied in Kate, and of a loving nostalgia for the ethereal, nearly bodiless and naive femininity of Milly, who echoes the icons of feminine purity of the mid-Victorian era. Such a plot expresses a reading of modern femininity as coarsened and degraded by its full entry into a world of commerce, indeed, as becoming a sinister agent of the market's corrupting power. James's deployment of formal innovation to express a reactionary disdain for modern femininity anticipates and influences the similar strategies that will often characterize literary modernism. His condemnation of the literary and feminine impulses suggested by Kate Croy, with her relentless efforts to produce lucrative or at least satisfying romance narratives, is James's version of the flight from domesticity that would cause male readers to delight in the new popularity of adventure and imperial fiction in the 1880s and 1890s. James's own sensibility was far from that of the adventure writers, and indeed, he mocks the consequences of their infatuation with fantasies of heroic masculinity in the classic story "The Beast in the Jungle" (1903) where Marcher wastes his life on a sterile celibacy in blindness to the love offered him by

May Bartram simply because he sees his life as a masculine adventure and a
man "didn't cause himself to be accompanied by a lady on a tiger-hunt."[36]
But James's revisions of courtship narratives into the anticourtship narratives of texts such as *Wings of the Dove* and "The Beast in the Jungle" are re-
jections of conventional realistic courtship and domestic narratives every bit
as powerful in their different key as those of the popular adventure and fantasy tales.

If Kate and Milly embody poles of material constraint and aesthetic ideal
for Densher, the male artist, the fact that ultimately Densher loses both Kate
and Milly—both the material success desired by the one and the aesthetic
idealism embodied in the other—expresses James's profound pessimism
about an Anglo-American culture ravaged by a commercialism that he felt
subverted its highest values. Yet the mood in James's late fiction is by no
means utterly tragic and desolate; one could argue that the dramas of discrimination that mark *The Wings of the Dove* and other late James works are
covert celebrations of the fragmentation and rationalization of the literary
market—in itself a product of the market's power—into specialized realms
of high art and degraded mass culture.[37] It is hardly surprising that we see
no signs at the end of *Wings of the Dove* that Densher will return to his profession of journalism; rather, he seems in his desire to imagine Milly Theale's
last letter to be well on the way to becoming a devotee of high art and the
disinterested power of the imagination. Paradoxically, for all the underlying
pessimism about the power of the market to subvert culture's highest values,
in his late fiction James celebrates an imagination that will find refuge in the
increasing specialization of literary and creative types that the market dictates, much as James himself had done.

James's late work is admirable when it celebrates the power of the imagination and suggests the need for a more humane and less punitive attitude
toward sexuality than had characterized Victorian culture. This modernizing and tolerant sensibility is most overtly visible in *The Ambassadors* where
Strether has been commissioned by Mrs. Newsome, a wealthy industrialist
from Woolett, Massachusetts, to correct the demoralizing influence of Pari-
sian life on her son Chad and return him to bourgeois preoccupations and
moral rectitude. This narrative responds to the conventional domestic narrative of the prodigal child in which the son or daughter's moral straying becomes the occasion for familial anathematization or forgiveness. (Examples
of such narratives of the prodigal child are innumerable in nineteenth-century fiction from Dumas's *La Dame aux Camelias*, the source of Verdi's *La
Traviata*, to *David Copperfield*). Of course, this being a late James novel, *The
Ambassadors* ironically reverses the usually moral valuations of the narrative

of the prodigal child who must be redeemed from sexual dalliance when Strether finds Chad so improved by his illicit liaison with Madame de Vionnet that he upturns the moral valuations of Woolett and urges Chad to stay loyal to his lover! Similarly in *The Golden Bowl* as Maggie Verver finds that her husband, Amerigo, has been having a long-term affair with her own stepmother, we have yet another version of the plot of the woman who marries a bigamous rake, as well as the novel of adultery. But in another reversal of Victorian moralism, this adulterous betrayal is not fatal to the marriage, being contained and in a sense managed and at least partially forgiven by Maggie as the novel ends. In their firm refusal of Victorian moralism about sexual transgression, James's narratives clearly are designed to humanize and soften the punitive spirit of Anglo-American puritanism. What is poignant in each case, however, is the highly privatized and even merely psychic victory for moral compassion that James emphasizes in each case, as if he lacks all confidence that his moral stance will have a larger community to sustain it.

Ultimately, because he declines to challenge more decisively the logic of the marketplace, James's late work shows the negative power of commerce, but suggests that the refuge for human values and creativity must lie within structures the market itself creates.[38] To some extent, this means that James imagines a locus for his more refined and humanized sexual and creative values in an idealized vision of those the marketplace uplifts, the upper class. It is in this light we can understand the idealization of Milly, which is paralleled by the portrayal of Maggie Verver in *The Golden Bowl*, an idealization symptomatic of how the late fiction tends to invest itself in a redemptive fantasy of the upper class as a potential ideal reader and embodiment of humane values, almost indeed as a cocreator of the cultured and aesthetically structured realm that James's last phase maps with such deliberation. This fantasy is both poignant and disturbing. On one hand, this aspect of James's late phase suggests his dogged commitment to humane and tolerant moral values. It is highly suggestive, for instance, that in learning of her husband's adultery Maggie Verver also learns of the unexpected honesty of a Jewish jeweler, an echo of the idealistic rejection of ethnic prejudice so prominent in *Daniel Deronda*; we know that in this period James was appalled by the virulent anti-Semitism that burst into public visibility in the Dreyfus Affair. All this said, there is something self-deluding about James's desperate effort to imagine in some of his late fictions the haute bourgeoisie as the exemplary incarnation of transcendent aesthetic and civilized values. Perhaps James himself was skeptical enough about the quality of civilization possessed by the bourgeoisie of his day to treat this idealization as partly self-delusion, which is why he makes his idealized bourgeois figure a dying girl emblematic of an earlier and more idealistic bourgeois age when capitalist society seemed genuinely committed to human liberation. Looking back with nostalgia on a more heroic cultural moment in which the enthusiasm for individual freedom that Milly's aesthetic development embodies was triumphantly joined with the power that wealth grants, James expresses a wistful longing for an earlier era, tracing through the doomed girl's story the inevitable extinction of this moment of middle-class splendor, before all spiritual nobility was lost under the rising tide of commodification, and all idealism destroyed by the sickness of spiritual prostitution.

Afterword:
Modernism and the
Alienation of the Domestic

In one influential reading of the origins of literary modernism, it represents the triumph of individual style, its profusion of formal innovations reacting to the pervasive commodification of daily life while distinguishing it from the mass culture emergent in the same historical moment.[1] Valuable as this reading is, it is also essential to understand how the content of modernism, as well as its formal attributes, responds to its historical moment, and to specify the typical themes and attitudes that modernist texts tend to privilege. In exploring a genealogy of emergent modernism within Victorian literature, I have essayed this work of specification, examining one of modernism's defining themes as the problematic relation between the sexes caused by changes in gender roles, a theme often expressed through the rejection of domestic idealization as a literary mode and its replacement by the representation of the family as a matrix of individual alienation. From this perspective, the gradual emergence of alienation from the family as a central literary subject in the late Victorian period is a precondition for the emergence of high modernism, suggesting a much more intimate connection, and a greater continuity of attitudes, between modernism and its Victorian precursors than the modernists themselves would generally acknowledge.

Given the varied and conflicting impulses that contribute to the emergence of these themes, it should not surprise us that familial and sexual alienation in modernist form takes a wide variety of forms. Some modernist texts resemble fin de siècle fantasy and adventure fiction in staging an escape from, or a repudiation of, domestic space, viewed as inauthentic and confining, a rejection of domesticity which can be frankly misogynistic. In this vein Marlow, in Conrad's *Heart of Darkness* (1899), bitterly comments on women's vaunted moral idealism: "It's queer how out of touch with truth women are. They live in a world of their own, and there has never been anything like it, and never can be. It is too beautiful altogether, and if they were to set it up it would go to pieces before sunset. Some confounded fact we men have been living contentedly with ever since the day of creation would start up and knock the whole thing over."[2] This comment prepares the reader for the novella's final scene in which, under pressure from Kurtz's fiancée, Marlow tells a lie that implies that, before his death, Kurtz has remained loyal to her, the traditions of romantic love, and, ultimately the norms of European civilization, all of which the narrative has shown to be false. As the story ends, the alienation that crushes Marlow stems as much from his revulsion at women's naïveté—which embodies civilization's false ideals—as from the corruption inherent in the imperial enterprise.

If this overt misogyny is one direction modernism can take, there are versions of modernism that follow Henry James in engaging with the Victorian tradition of domestic narrative, though at times they use this tradition, as does *The Wings of the Dove*, as scaffolding with which to stage an engagement with other issues, such as dramas of developing moral and aesthetic consciousness. As we saw, *Wings* increasingly becomes a story about the moral and aesthetic discriminations made by Densher, the male writer, a process that threatens to render the courtship story in the foreground of the novel as a kind of narrative pretext. We see analogous narrative strategies in high-modernist texts such as T. S. Eliot's *The Waste Land* (1922) and James Joyce's *Ulysses* (1922). Eliot deploys many images of unhappy domestic or sexual narratives, such as the working-class Lil and her friend who tells her:

> He's been in the army four years, he wants a good time,
> And if you don't give it to him, there's others that will . . .

Lil, worn out by repeated childbearing ("She's had five already, and nearly died of young George,") seems unable to heed her insensitive friend's advice, and there are hints that the speaker has her own designs on Lil's husband; working-class domesticity is thus figured as a continuation of, rather than a respite from, a competitive and dehumanized social world. In a later section of the same poem, "The Fire Sermon," the typist's seduction by the "carbuncular" clerk is another image of sexual love reduced to routine and mechanical exploitation:

> Exploring hands encounter no defence;
> His vanity requires no response,
> And makes a welcome of indifference.
> . . . .

When lovely woman stoops to folly and
Paces around her room again, alone,
She smooths her hair with automatic hand,
And puts a record on the gramophone. (ll. 240–42, 253–56)

But, though these scenes reproduce topoi of familial and sexual alienation, they do so without Eliot's being interested in grasping the specific sources of such alienation; rather, they function merely as examples of a more general condition, embodying a pervasive alienation inherent in a modern world of degraded mass culture and spiritual desolation.

Similarly, in *Ulysses*, Joyce carefully reproduces themes of familial alienation that echo the tradition we have traced. Stephen Dedalus is determined to escape the oppressive religiosity and cultural provincialism of his origins, which are epitomized in his guilty memories of his dying mother. In the climactic moment of the "Circe" episode, her ghost stirs his guilt for refusing to pray by her deathbed and threatens him with damnation. In response, he angrily rebels against her memory with the words "*Non serviam*! [I will not serve]."[3] Like Maggie Tulliver, Dedalus feels intense alienation from his own family, which embodies cultural obstacles to his self-development. Meanwhile, Leopold Bloom's insecure masculine and cultural identity is dramatized by his well-founded fears of his wife Molly's infidelity, but he eventually finds emotional refuge in his friendship with Stephen Dedalus. In *Ulysses*, as in many narratives of the late Victorian era where transcendence seems possible through masculine solidarity, masculine bonding over communities of shared social and aesthetic values serves as a refuge from the alienated relation that men feel toward a failed domestic world. Interestingly, as in *Daniel Deronda*'s friendship between Deronda and Mordecai, in *Ulysses* a masculine bond is formed between a cultured Gentile and plebeian Jew, suggesting how such a friendship embodies a cosmopolitan humanism that transcends the specific cultural and ethnic inheritance derived from families and their confining cultural, political, and psychic structures.[4] Moreover, as in *The Wings of the Dove*, alienation from the domestic sphere provides the matrix for the aesthetic male's reaffirmation of his commitment to creative purpose.

Yet, if in works such as *Ulysses* and *The Waste Land* an alienation from domesticity figures more abstract and general issues, it is a mistake simply to dismiss the representation of alienation from domesticity in such monuments of modernism as trivial in itself.[5] For instance, in *Ulysses*, as in many other modernist texts, the transformation and modernization of gender roles is a major focus of anxiety to which the text constantly responds, even in its attempt to produce a vantage point that transcends history. It can be argued that for all its brilliant efforts to evade or resolve this topic, modernism's response to modern gender roles always possesses a provisional character, which is suggested by the tendency to place gender relations outside of history in a mythic realm. For even Molly Bloom, the archetypal female whose stream of consciousness musings lyrically conclude *Ulysses*, is a modern woman, a former professional singer, and enough a creature of the twentieth century to dismiss with scorn denunciations of feminine modernity: "that old Bishop that spoke off the altar his long preach about womans higher functions about girls now riding the bicycle and wearing peak caps and the new woman bloomers God send him sense and me more money."[6] Indeed the novel's historically overdetermined preoccupation with the modern crisis of various kinds of masculine authority (imperial, religious, literary, domestic), with Bloom's cuckolding being only the most obvious instance, suggests that *Ulysses*'s characteristically modernist mythic narrative, with its effort to transcend the nightmare of history and to create Molly as an archetypal female figure outside history, reflects Joyce's effort to contain and master his uneasy awareness that gender roles themselves are conditioned by historical change.

A writer even more palpably engaged with rewriting the Victorian tradition of domesticity and alienation is Virginia Woolf, who in *To the Lighthouse* (1927) provides an eloquent retrospective view of Victorian domesticity that emphasizes both the alienation and the creativity of the domestic sphere for women in a way that clearly derives from the Victorians themselves. In the first and longest of the novel's three sections, the central figure is a Victorian domestic icon, Mrs. Ramsay. During a family vacation in the Hebrides, we see Mrs. Ramsay, the domestic mode personified, represented from various perspectives. At her most triumphant, she is a creative artist who produces the fabric of domestic life itself and finds peace in the harmony that her feminine art of nurturance and hospitality creates:

> Just now (but this cannot last, she thought, dissociating herself from the moment while they were all talking about boots) just now she had reached security; she hovered like a hawk suspended; like a flag floated in an element of joy which filled every nerve of her body fully and sweetly, not noisily, solemnly rather, for it arose, she thought, looking at them all eating there, from husband and children and friends; all of which rising in this profound stillness (she was helping William Bankes to one very small piece more, and peered into the depths of the earthenware pot) seemed now for no special reason to stay there like a smoke, like a fume rising upwards, holding them safe together. Nothing need be said; nothing could be said. There it was, all round

them. It partook, she felt, carefully helping Mr. Bankes to a specially tender piece, of eternity; . . . Of such moments, she thought, the thing is made that endures.[7]

Though deeply aware of the continual pressure of change outside the domestic circle that she creates with such painstaking effort, Mrs. Ramsay revels in the thought that, like all artists, she is creating something "that endures."

Yet, creating a complex picture of the idealized Victorian domesticity that Mrs. Ramsay inwardly celebrates, Woolf also includes voices of characters alienated from domesticity who echo the ambivalence toward it found in the work of fin de siècle writers. Masculine impatience with domesticity is embodied in William Bankes, a friend of the Ramsays; in the scene of the dinner party in which Mrs. Ramsay exults at her triumphant domestic role, Bankes is repulsed:

> How trifling it all is, how boring it all is, he thought, compared with the other thing—work. Here he sat drumming his fingers on the table-cloth—he took a flashing bird's-eye view of his work. . . . The truth was he did not enjoy family life. It was in this sort of state that one asked oneself, What does one live for? Why, one asked oneself, does one take all these pains for the human race to go on? Is it so very desirable? Are we attractive as a species? Not so very, he thought, looking at those rather untidy boys. (89)

Mr. Bankes's fastidious bachelor disdain for family life reminds us that, even if Mrs. Ramsay's vital energy feels overpowering within the domestic sphere, from the perspective of a larger world dominated by masculine values, her world appears parochial. It is characteristic of Woolf's modernist aesthetic, with its layers of ambiguity, that while Bankes's disaffection from the familial world that nurtures him is misanthropic and unsympathetic, his basic objection to family life—that it impedes the individual's potential for sustained creative labor ("the other thing—work")—reverberates strongly in the novel as a genuine limitation of the domesticity Mrs. Ramsay embodies.

For, in a parallel to Mr. Bankes's masculine antifamilialism, Lily Briscoe represents a feminist alienation from domesticity; and for Lily, as for Mr. Bankes, a limitation of the domesticity that Mrs. Ramsay represents is its radical devaluing of individual artistic creativity, particularly the exclusion of women from such creativity. When Lily tries to capture Mrs. Ramsay's essence, she thinks:

> Arriving late at night, with a light tap on one's bedroom door, wrapped in an old fur coat . . . , [Mrs. Ramsay] would enact again whatever it might be—. . .

still always laughing, insist that she must, Minta must, they all must marry, since in the whole world whatever laurels might be tossed to her (but Mrs. Ramsay cared not a fig for her painting), or triumphs won by her (probably Mrs. Ramsay had had her share of those), and here she saddened, darkened, and came back to her chair, there could be no disputing this: an unmarried woman (she lightly took her hand for a moment), an unmarried woman has missed the best of life. (49)

Mrs. Ramsay's domestic spirit marginalizes what is central for Lily Briscoe—her painting—which emblematizes her capacity for creativity. The brusque parenthetical insistence on this marginalization suggests how axiomatic and unquestioned was the Victorian trivialization of feminine intellectual creativity.

But though the novel expresses feminist rebellion against domesticity, as a woman writer Woolf is more deeply invested than many male writers in exploring the ambivalent emotions that domesticity often generates in women. Even Mrs. Ramsay, for all the rigidity of her prescriptions for feminine behavior, is a divided character, revealing that within the domestic woman lies a kernel of alienation from the very role that she so triumphantly enacts. Amid her multitudinous social responsibilities, she finds refuge at times in simply being "herself, by herself. And that was what now she often felt the need of—to think; well, not even to think. To be silent; to be alone. All the being and the doing, expansive, glittering, vocal, evaporated; and one shrunk, with a sense of solemnity, to being oneself, a wedge-shaped core of darkness, something invisible to others" (62). The final verdict Woolf passes on Mrs. Ramsay is that she is irrevocably a figure of the past (she is abruptly killed off in the second, most impersonal, section of the novel), and the novel ends with the thoughts of Lily Briscoe, a modernist woman who by not marrying has liberated herself from Mrs. Ramsay's domestic world. Yet there lingers in the novel an elegiac nostalgia for the vanished world of Victorian domesticity, which Woolf envisions as a place of incipient feminine creativity, a powerful nostalgia that reflects her ambivalent respect for her female Victorian precursors, women who created powerful sites of domesticity, both real and fictive.[8]

These modernist examples of domestic alienation remind us that, if one source of modernism was a progressive insistence within the realist tradition on stripping away the idealizations and silences of Victorian domestic narrative, the modernist enterprise itself is paradoxically less invested in depicting reality than in elaborating countermyths that disrupt the Victorian orthodoxies and mass cultural romanticizations of erotic and sexual life. These countermyths, even in disrupting typical Victorian idealizations, also abstract, just as such idealizations did, from the concrete particularities of actual families in history. One of the characteristic components of these countermyths is their sense of the inevitability of the individual's alienation, and indeed of the writer's as well, from the domestic sphere, though by mythicizing this alienation modernist texts elide its historically determined character. I am referring here primarily to writers active in the opening decades of the twentieth century, but in some respects this modernist strategy is still with us, as the continued popularity of romantic depictions of love and courtship in mass culture gives a perpetual occasion for writers aspiring to literary prestige to distinguish themselves by producing sternly de-idealized or transgressive portrayals of love and family. The contemporary novel *Being Dead* (2000) by Jim Crace takes the unsentimentalized evocation of family life to the ultimate extreme by presenting his central characters, a married couple murdered by a transient, as decaying cadavers lying on a remote beach, a poignant image of humanity's existential plight. In a modernist marginalization of romantic love and domesticity, the couple's youthful passion for each other emerges only as fleeting memories provided elegiacally by the narrative voice. Except in such ghostly memories, the dramas of courtship and marital life are invisible, replaced by the central reality of the individual's ephemeral existence in an uncaring world.

Such a work demonstrates the endurance, though perhaps also the incipient exhaustion, of the impulse in a high cultural literary vision to reduce sentimental narratives of courtship and domesticity to a modest position. No doubt a key explanation for the persistence of thematics of alienation from domesticity and romance is that the serious writer's situation of alienation from a mass cultural marketplace, which in the late nineteenth century helped give prominence to the theme of alienation from the family, persists to this day. From the period of high modernism to our own moment, the compulsive production of narratives about alienation from, or the limits of, fulfillment in family life, like modernism's fetishism of stylistic originality, are high cultural strategies of literary specialization. As such they are forms of resistance to a commodified mass culture but also adaptations to the literary market's division into differentiated literary markets. Thus, for all the discontinuities we have traced in this study, from the perspective of the development of an increasingly market-dominated society, there is a thread of continuity between such modernist and postmodernist strategies and those of mid-Victorian domesticity. The celebration of the family toward which the narratives of a Florence Dombey or a Bob Cratchit move is a form of resistance to the marketplace and its dehumanizing domination of society, and if late Victorian and modernist texts abandon the celebration of the family, they discover a new basis for resistance to commodification in the celebration of other kinds of communities, particularly those of aesthetic value and human creativity.

Yet if the modernist de-idealization of love and family life has lost much of its avant-garde shock (leading perhaps to Crace's extreme, if macabre, plot), this may be because mass culture has become almost as open to the thematics of domestic alienation as high culture. One of the most successful examples of mass cultural fiction in our time, the Harry Potter novels, typically offer in the early chapters of each novel a comically horrific image of the family as dystopian prison. In a domestic world replete with callousness, intolerance, and materialism, the sensitive hero of the series stoically endures the incessant rejection and mistreatment meted out to him by his dysfunctional adoptive family, the Dursleys. In such a grim satire of family life, we can see that, even in children's literature, the exposure of the dark side of domesticity still feels liberating for contemporary writers and their readers.

Evidently, the ahistorical and limiting stereotypes of domestic life that often characterize Victorian literature cannot without significant modernization be a model for creativity in our own day, given how gender roles have radically changed and a greater variety of family forms than were tolerated by the Victorians have become accepted. Yet our modern myth of inevitable family alienation has limitations as surely as did the Victorian myth of domesticity triumphant. We can suggest the nature of those limits by saying that to depict the family as a creative expression of individual aspirations and yet as also part of the fabric of history remains a challenge in our own day for literature, indeed, for cultural life generally. While idealizations of the family too often ignore how family life can be complicit in larger structures of domination and oppression, it is equally reductive to isolate, in the manner of the diagnostic familial mode that the Victorians developed with such complexity and power, familial dysfunction as emblematizing or somehow explaining the majority of societal and psychic failures. Such all too common representations of the failed family, by scapegoating the family as the matrix of personal or social evil, minimize how families are created and lived within larger histories and social contexts and are profoundly influenced by the structures of the larger society. Such representations can exhibit a profound failure of the imagination, because by isolating family life and its discontents from their context, they elide the complexity and contingency of the connections between domestic troubles and the continuing realities of market forces and class inequalities that help produce them.

In contrast, in the fiction of George Eliot and, in a later generation, Virginia Woolf, we see a subtle awareness of the family both as a vital sphere in its own right but also as inescapably a product of historical change. Such writers' works might well serve as a model for nuanced portrayals of the individual's relation to the family and the family's relation to the historical forces that profoundly affect its contours and its success—or failure—in nurturing its members. So if, as Nicholas Daly suggests, fantasies of imperial adventure derived from the fin de siècle have become an enduring feature of contemporary culture, one can hope that we will eventually move beyond the impulse typical of that narrative tradition of reflexively fleeing, or trivializing, both the family and women, and of ignoring their significant place within processes of historical change.[9] Just as too much of contemporary culture marginalizes women and the family, the depictions of families that are dominant all too often lack a subtle sense of the family's place within history. In our domestic narratives, as in other kinds of stories that contemporary culture produces about itself, literature enriches itself and its readers most when it engages with the rich complexity of history's determinations, rather than attempting the fruitless task of trying to escape its power.

Notes

INTRODUCTION

1. Recent studies of the Victorian family include John Tosh, *A Man's Place: Masculinity and the Middle-Class Home in Victorian England* (New Haven: Yale University Press, 1999); A. James Hammerton, *Cruelty and Companionship: Conflict in Nineteenth-Century Married Life* (New York: Routledge, 1992); and Judith Flanders, *Inside the Victorian Home: A Portrait of Domestic Life in Victorian England* (New York: W. W. Norton, 2003). In evaluating Victorian domesticity, Hammerton and Tosh both see some evidence of an amelioration of patriarchal domination of women. See also sources cited under note 12.

2. Oscar Wilde, Preface to *The Picture of Dorian Gray* (New York: W. W. Norton, 1988), 3; Wilde's bon mot on Little Nell (the heroine of Dickens's *The Old Curiosity Shop*) is quoted in Richard Ellmann, *Oscar Wilde* (New York: Alfred A. Knopf, 1988), 469.

3. Virginia Woolf, *Women and Writing*, ed. Michele Barrett (New York: Harcourt Brace Jovanovich, 1979), 57–63.

4. Though its subject is American literature, a pioneering work arguing for the reevaluation of domestic fiction is Jane Tompkins, *Sensational Designs: The Cultural Work of American Fiction, 1790–1860* (New York: Oxford University Press, 1985).

5. D. A. Miller, *The Novel and the Police* (Berkeley: University of California Press, 1988), 219.

6. Mary Wollstonecraft, *A Vindication of the Rights of Woman* (New York: Norton, 1988), 60.

7. Tosh, *A Man's Place*, 61.

8. I discuss George Sand's influence on Eliot in chapter 3; Madame de Staël was another French writer who clearly influenced Victorian feminists.

9. Joan Perkin, *Victorian Women* (New York: New York University Press, 1993), 178–89; Christopher Hibbert, *The English: A Social History 1066–1945* (London: Grafton Books, 1988), 636–39.

10. This paragraph draws on Claire Tomalin, *The Invisible Woman: The Story of Nelly Ternan and Charles Dickens* (New York: Alfred Knopf, 1991), 84–85.

11. Dickens to Daniel Maclise, August 16, 1841, quoted in Claire Tomalin, *The Invisible Woman*, 84.

12. The literature on British literary familialism and family history is impressive and voluminous. Major contributions include Leonore Davidoff and Catherine Hall, *Family Fortunes: Men and Women of the English Middle Class, 1780–1850* (London: Hutchinson, 1987); Nancy Armstong, *Desire and Domestic Fiction: A Political History of the Novel* (New

York: Oxford University Press, 1987); Lawrence Stone, *The Family, Sex and Marriage in England, 1500–1800* (London: Weidenfeld and Nicolson, 1977).

13. For the concept of class discourse, see Fredric Jameson, *The Political Unconscious: Narrative as Socially Symbolic Act* (Ithaca: Cornell University Press, 1981), 76, 83–85.

14. Terry Eagleton, *The Rape of Clarissa: Writing, Sexuality, and Class Struggle in Samuel Richardson* (Oxford: Blackwell, 1982).

15. For the nature of familialism in this early period, see Charles Hatten, "The Politics of Marital Reform and the Rationalization of Romance in *The Doctrine and Discipline of Divorce*," *Milton Studies* 27 (1991): 95–114.

16. Max Weber, *The Protestant Ethic and the Spirit of Capitalism* (New York: Routledge, 2001).

17. John Milton, *The Riverside Milton* (New York: Houghton Mifflin, 1998), 450–51.

18. Sarah Stickney Ellis, *The Women of England: Their Social Duties and Domestic Habits*, quoted in *The Norton Anthology of English Literature*, ed. M. H. Abrams (New York: W. W. Norton, 2000), 2:1721–23.

19. For the view that Victorian domesticity is depoliticized compared to its eighteenth-century precursor, see Nancy Armstrong, *Desire and Domestic Fiction*.

20. Karl Marx, *A Contribution to the Critique of Hegel's Philosophy of Right*, quoted in *Marxism and Art*, ed. Maynard Solomon (New York: Alfred A. Knopf, 1973), 48.

21. W. H. Wills, "A Legal Fiction," *Household Words*, 21, July 1855, quoted in Catherine Peters, *The King of Inventors: A Life of Wilkie Collins* (Princeton: Princeton University Press, 1991), 128; Peters notes the likely influence of this controversy on Collins's later works.

22. Charlotte Brontë, *Jane Eyre* (New York: W. W. Norton, 2001), 93.

23. Elizabeth Barrett Browning, *Aurora Leigh*, quoted in *The Woman Question: Society and Literature in Britain and America, 1837–1883*, ed. Elizabeth K. Helsinger, Robin Lauterbach Sheets, and William Veeder, 2:146. (Chicago: Chicago University Press, 1983).

24. The phrase is Sarah Ellis's, but the ideal was a general one.

25. John Stuart Mill, *The Subjection of Woman* (1869), quoted in *The Norton Anthology of English Literature,* ed. M. H. Abrams and Stephen Greenblatt (New York: W. W. Norton, 2000), 1159.

26. Carol Dyhouse, *Feminism and the Family in England: 1880–1939* (New York: Basil Blackwell, 1989), 153–57

27. George Eliot, *Middlemarch* (New York: Penguin, 1981), 894.

28. A. James Hammerton, *Cruelty and Companionship*, 153–56.

29. This paragraph is indebted to John Tosh, *A Man's Place*, 170–94.

30. For the enthusiasm with which Kipling's work was received, see Stephen Arata, *Fictions of Loss in the Victorian Fin de Siècle* (New York: Cambridge University Press, 1996), 151–77; late Victorian gender anxieties are discussed in Elaine Showalter, *Sexual Anarchy: Gender and Culture at the Fin de Siècle* (New York: Penguin Books, 1990).

31. Carol Dyhouse, *Feminism and Family in England: 1880–1939* (New York: Basil Blackwell, 1989), 143–46.

32. For a discussion of the context of this "flight from domesticity," see Tosh, *A Man's Place.*

33. There was a corresponding reaction against Eliot herself among many late Victorian male writers, discussed in Showalter (1990), 75–79.

CHAPTER 1. DISCIPLINING THE FAMILY

1. Leonore Davidoff and Catherine Hall, *Family Fortunes: Men and Women of the English Middle-class, 1780–1850* (London: Hutchinson, 1987).

2. For an excellent discussion of how Dickens's Christmas tales promoted a reorientation of Christmas festivities in a secularized and privatized direction, see Catherine Waters, *Dickens and the Politics of the Family* (Cambridge: Cambridge University Press, 1997), 58–88.

3. N. N. Feltes, *Modes of Production of Victorian Novels* (Chicago: University of Chicago Press, 1986), 1–35.

4. Gaye Tuchman with Nina E. Fortin, *Edging Women Out: Victorian Novelists, Publishers, and Social Change* (New Haven: Yale University Press, 1989), 1–64.

5. Edgar Johnson, *Charles Dickens: His Tragedy and Triumph.* (New York: Simon and Schuster, 1952), 1:234–53; Robert L. Patten, *Charles Dickens and His Publishers* (Oxford: Clarendon, 1978), 31–44, 75–87.

6. *The Pilgrim Edition of the Letters of Charles Dickens,* ed. Madeline House and Graham Storey (Oxford: Clarendon Press, 1965). 1:165. Further citations from this edition will be cited as *Letters* followed by the volume and page numbers.

7. John Forster, *The Life of Charles Dickens* (Philadelphia: Lippincott, 1873), 1:244–45.

8. Patrick Brantlinger, "The Case Against Trade Unions in Early Victorian Fiction," *Victorian Studies* 13 (1969): 37–52; Paul Stigant and Peter Widdowson, *"Barnaby Rudge:* A Historical Novel?" *Literature and History* 2 (1975): 2–44; see also Patrick Brantlinger, *The Spirit of Reform: British Literature and Politics, 1832–1867* (Cambridge, MA: Harvard University Press, 1977), 83–96.

9. Ian Duncan, *Modern Romance and the Transformations of the Novel: The Gothic, Scott, Dickens* (Cambridge: Cambridge University Press, 1992), 220–21; Duncan's shrewd readings of Dickens's early work anticipates my argument in this chapter at numerous points.

10. Georg Lukács, *The Historical Novel,* trans. Hannah and Stanley Mitchell (London: Merlin, 1962), 19–63.

11. Walter Scott, *The Heart of Midlothian* (Oxford: Oxford University Press, 1982), 449.

12. Sandra Gilbert and Susan Gubar, *The Madwoman in the Attic: The Woman Writer and the Nineteenth-Century Literary Imagination* (New Haven: Yale University Press, 1979), 3.

13. Stephen Marcus, *From Pickwick to Dombey* (New York: Basic, 1965).

14. Charles Dickens, *Barnaby Rudge* (Harmondsworth: Penguin, 1973), 44. All later citations from the novel will be by page number in the text.

15. Scott was more generally a source of invented tradition of the British past; see Eric J. Hobsbawm and Terence Ranger, eds., *The Invention of Tradition* (New York: Cambridge University Press, 1983).

16. Richard Brodhead, "Sparing the Rod: Discipline and Fiction in Antebellum America," *Representations* 21 (1988): 67–96; Brodhead's reading of nineteenth-century American culture and mine of Victorian culture are influenced by Michel Foucault, *Discipline and Punish: The Birth of the Prison*, trans. Alan Sheridan (New York: Pantheon, 1978).

17. Charles Dickens to John Forster, June 1846, in *Letters,* 4:573.

18. For an account of Dickens's early success as part of a new mode of literary production, see N. N. Feltes, *Modes of Production of Victorian Novels* (Chicago: University of Chicago Press, 1986), 1–17, and also Richard D. Altick, *The English Common Reader: A Social History of the Mass Reading Public, 1800–1900* (Chicago: University of Chicago Press, 1957), 381–86.

19. Robert L. Patten, *Charles Dickens and His Publishers* (Oxford: Clarendon Press, 1978), 133–34, 163–71.

20. Ibid., 172.

21. Quoted in John Forster, *The Life of Charles Dickens* (Philadelphia: J. B. Lippincott, 1873), 1:207.

22. Philip Collins, ed., *Dickens: The Critical Heritage* (New York: Barnes and Noble, 1971), 212–13.

23. Thomas Carlyle, *Past and Present* (London: Chapman and Hall, 1987), 183.

24. These phrases derive from classic Victorian critiques of laissez-faire capitalism; Thomas Carlyle, *Past and Present*, 272; Friedrich Engels, *The Condition of the Working Class in England*, trans. W. O. Henderson and W. H. Chaloner (Stanford, CA: Stanford University Press, 1968), 31.

25. Critics have noted how domesticity becomes an agent of a critique of capitalism in the novel; see, for example, Helene Moglen, "Theorizing Fiction/Fictionalizing Theory: The Case of *Dombey and Son*," *Victorian Studies* 35 (1992): 159–84.

26. Charles Dickens, *A Christmas Carol*, in *The Longman Anthology of British Literature*, ed. David Damrosch et al. 3rd ed. Vol. 28, *The Victorian Age* (New York: Pearson/Longman, 2006), 26.

27. John Butt and Kathleen Tillotson, *Dickens at Work* (London: Methuen, 1957), 90–113.

28. Nina Auerbach, "Dickens and Dombey: A Daughter After All," *Dickens Studies Annual* 5 (1976): 95–114. The contrast between hard, phallic, masculine energy and fluid, emollient, feminine energy in the novel's imagery has encouraged other critics to read the work in a structuralist vein as organized around poles of "firmness and wetness" or "openness and closure": see Julian Moynahan, "Dealings with the Firm of *Dombey and Son*: Firmness v. Wetness," in *Dickens in the Twentieth Century*, ed. John Gross and Gabriel Pearson, 121–31 (London: Routledge and Kegan Paul, 1962), and Steven Connor, *Charles Dickens* (London: Basil Blackwell, 1985), 20–43.

29. Charles Dickens, *Dombey and Son*, ed. Peter Fairclough (Harmondsworth: Penguin Books, 1984), 69. Further citations from the novel will be from this edition cited in the text by page number.

30. This familial ideology is described in Steven Mintz, *A Prison of Expectations: The Family in Victorian Culture* (New York: New York University Press, 1983) and Leonore Davidoff and Catherine Hall, *Family Fortunes: Men and Women of the English Middle-class, 1780–1850* (Chicago: Chicago University Press, 1987); Davidoff and Hall stress the ideological centrality of the division between the domestic and the public sphere.

31. I draw on Catherine Gallagher, *The Industrial Reformation of English Fiction: Social Discourse and Narrative Form, 1832–1867* (Chicago: University of Chicago Press, 1985), 113–46.

32. For the prominence of class resentment in the novel, see Lewis Horne, "The Way of Resentment in *Dombey and Son*," *Modern Language Quarterly: A Journal of Literary History* 51 (1990): 44–62.

33. For the Victorian debate on female labor see Sylvia Walby, *Patriarchy at Work: Patriarchal and Capitalist Relations in Employment* (Minneapolis: University of Minnesota Press, 1986), 90–134; Jane Mark-Lawson and Anne Witz, "From 'Family Labour' to 'Family Wage'? The Case of Women's Labour in Nineteenth-Century Coalmining," *Social History* 13 (1980): 151–73, discusses how the highly publicized debate over women working in coal mining reflected changes in the process of production in that industry and the gradual obsolescence of a patriarchal organization of production. *Dombey*'s relevance to the related debates over child labor has been noted by N. N. Feltes, "To Saunter, to Hurry: Dickens, Time, and Industrial Capitalism," *Victorian Studies* 20 (1977): 245–67, especially 265.

34. Raymond Williams, introduction to *Dombey and Son*, by Charles Dickens (Harmondsworth: Penguin, 1970), 26.

35. For the relevance of these anxieties to this scene see Margaret Wiley, "Mother's Milk and *Dombey and Son*," *Dickens Quarterly* (December 1996): 217–28.

36. That Florence experiences the symbolic threat of prostitution in this scene has been argued by Joss Lutz Marsh, "Good Mrs. Brown's Connections: Sexuality and Story-Telling in *Dealings with the Firm of Dombey and Son*," *ELH* 58 (1991): 405–26.

37. On Victorian prostitution, see Frances Finnegan, *Poverty and Prostitution: A Study of Victorian Prostitutes in York* (New York: Cambridge University Press, 1979) and Judith Walkowitz, *Prostitution and Victorian Society* (New York: Cambridge University Press, 1980).

38. Michel Foucault, *Discipline and Punish: The Birth of the Prison*, trans. Alan Sheridan, (New York: Vintage Press, 1977). For "normalization" see 177–83.

39. That Dickens originally intended to unify the novel further by harping on this theme is suggested by his original plan for Walter, who was to come to naught through his dissipations.

40. That this passage alludes to prostitution has been noted: Alexander Welsh, *From Copyright to Copperfield: The Identity of Dickens* (Cambridge, MA: Harvard University Press, 1987), 90.

41. So extreme has Florence's imaginative, as much as physical, restlessness struck some critics, that they diagnose her; one argues for "unconscious feeling of hostility toward her father"; Dianne F. Sadoff, *Monsters of Affection: Dickens, Eliot, and Brontë on Fatherhood* (Baltimore: Johns Hopkins University Press, 1982), 61. Similarly, another critic has found in Edith's behavior features characteristic of Freud's "hysterical" patients; Louise Yelin, "Strategies for Survival: Florence and Edith in *Dombey and Son*," *Victorian Studies* 22 (1979): 297–319, especially 315; such critics follow the lead of the text in categorizing women into various versions of dysfunctional types, each linked by their "restlessness" or failure to maintain the proper values and boundaries within the home and separating home from society.

42. See the discussion of *Bleak House* in Miller, *The Novel and the Police*, 58–106.

43. Nancy Armstrong's argument that in the nineteenth century political impulses in fiction are increasingly displaced and contained within the domestic site, thereby depoliticizing the novel, is relevant to my argument; see Nancy Armstrong, *Desire and Domestic Fiction: A Political History of the Novel* (New York: Oxford University Press, 1987).

44. Identifying ressentiment as an important nineteenth-century ideologeme is an approach drawn from Fredric Jameson, *The Political Unconscious* (Ithaca: Cornell University Press, 1981), 88, 117, 200–205; Jameson, of course, borrows the concept from Friedrich Nietzsche.

45. Butt and Tillotson, *Dickens at Work*, 93, 103.

46. On the Victorian language of class see Geoffrey Crossick, "Classes and the Masses in Victorian England," *History Today* 37 (March 1987): 29–35.

47. See E. J. Hobsbawm, *The Age of Revolution* (New York: New American Library, 1962), 249–51, and E. Thompson, *The Making of the English Working Class* (New York: Vintage Books, 1966), 711–832; given *Dombey's* reliance on radical figurations and themes, which above all criticized the "aristocratic" political power of the wealthy whatever the origin of their wealth, and the fact that its popular success coincides with a Chartist revival, it is important to note Gareth Stedman Jones's illuminating stress on the continuity between the older tradition of political radicalism and Chartist discourse. See Gareth Stedman Jones, *Languages of Class: Studies in English Working Class History* (New York: Cambridge University Press, 1983), 90–178. Jones argues that the political language of radicalism and its Chartist descendant united the politically discontented across class lines without offering a language for articulating specifically economic grievances of workers against employers; *Dombey* (and *A Christmas Carol*), influenced by radical language, resembles such language in being primarily critical of the employer (as Jones says) "not on account of his economic role but for his political beliefs and social attitudes" (p. 145).

48. On the prominence of marital assault in the press in the early nineteenth century and in early Dickens, see Lisa Surridge, *Bleak Houses: Marital Violence in Victorian Fiction* (Athens: Ohio University Press, 2005), 15–43.

49. The novel's self-conscious emulation of Shakespeare has been demonstrated in Welsh, 87–103.

50. While the novel's polemic against Dombey resonates as a critique of capitalist inhumanity in general, the fact that he is associated with older, preindustrial modes of capitalist organization than those rapidly emerging in the novel's period shows Dickens's ambivalence toward the rise of industrial capitalists, a class that, for all its moral failings, he clearly preferred to the traditional aristocracy. For instance, Mr. Rouncewell, the iron manufacturer in *Bleak House* (1852–53), is portrayed far more positively than are aristocratic figures in that novel or in Dickens generally. Several readings of *Dombey* note the tumultous economic context for the novel and Dombey's association with archaic types of capitalism: Robert Clark, "Riddling the Family Firm: The Sexual Economy in Dombey and Son," *ELH* 51 (1984): 69–84; Jeff Nunokawa, *The Afterlife of Property: Domestic Security and the Victorian Novel* (Princeton: Princeton University Press, 1994), 40–76; Catherine Waters, *Dickens and the Politics of the Family* (Cambridge: Cambridge University Press, 1997), 38–57.

51. The Gothic's association with the subversive is suggested by the Gothic novels of such English "Jacobins" as William Godwin, Mary Wollstonecraft, and Charlotte Smith, and the notorious impropriety of Matthew Lewis's *The Monk*. (I owe my awareness of this aspect of the Gothic to Tamar Heller.)

52. See Yelin, "Strategies for Survival: Florence and Edith in *Dombey and Son*," 297–319.

53. Lisa Surridge, *Bleak Houses: Marital Violence in Victorian Fiction* (Athens: Ohio University Press, 2005), 44–71.

54. See Graham Storey and K. J. Fielding. eds., *The Letters of Charles Dickens,* 5:197n and 5:211.

55. The novel's ending has been considered problematic since French critic Hippolyte Taine's complaint in 1864 that Dombey's final reconciliation with Florence "spoils a fine novel." Hippolyte Taine, *History of English Literature* (Paris, 1863–64; trans. H. Van

Laun, 1871), quoted in Kathleen Tillotson, *Novels of the Eighteen-forties* (Oxford: Clarendon Press, 1954), 171.

56. Patrick Brantlinger, "Did Dickens Have a Philosophy of History? The Case of *Barnaby Rudge*," *Dickens Studies Annual* (2001), 30:59–74.

CHAPTER 2. *DAVID COPPERFIELD*

1. D. A. Miller, *The Novel and the Police* (Berkeley: University of California Press, 1988), 216 and 219; for a similar reading, see Gareth Cordery, "Foucault, Dickens and David Copperfield," *Victorian Literature and Culture* 26 (1998): 71–88. Though I agree with these readings in their emphasis on disciplinary thematics, I would argue that they exaggerate the novel's univocality.

2. For a reading that anticipates mine in seeing *David Copperfield* as being subversive of gender ideology, but that unpersuasively exaggerates the novel's radicalism, see Brenda Ayres, *Dissenting Women in Dickens's Novels: The Subversion of Domestic Ideology* (Westport, CT: Greenwood Press, 1998), 13–32.

3. Richard Holt Hutton, "Novels by the Authoress of John Halifax," *North British Review* 29 (1858): 466–81, quoted in Mary Lenard, *Preaching Pity: Dickens, Gaskell and Sentimentalism in Victorian Culture* (New York: Peter Lang, 1999).

4. George Henry Lewes, *Fortnightly Review,* XVII (1872), 143–51, reprinted in *Literary Criticism of George Henry Lewes,* ed. Alice R. Kaminsky (Lincoln: University of Nebraska Press, 1964).

5. The Reformation, by its attack on the Catholic doctrine of marriage as an indissoluble union, laid the basis for the liberal view of divorce, but the notionally individualist and contractual Protestant reading of marriage and its corollary of legal divorce had a limited impact in Britain due to the continued commitment of the Church of England to marriage as indissoluble. A divorce law was passed in the eighteenth century, but divorce under this statute was prohibitively expensive, leaving it available only to a miniscule portion of the population. It is this situation that Dickens attacks in *Hard Times*, where the worker Stephen Blackpool asks in anguish for "the law that helps me" obtain a divorce from his alcoholic wife; he is told that there is none for people of his social class. Charles Dickens, *Hard Times* (New York: Penguin Press, 1985), 113; for the history of British divorce, see Roderick Phillips, *Untying the Knot: A Short History of Divorce* (New York: Cambridge University Press, 1991).

6. Charles Dickens, *David Copperfield* (New York: W. W. Norton, 1990); all quotations from the novel will be cited by page number in the text.

7. In this attack on archaic legal institutions (a theme on which he would elaborate in his denunciation of Chancery in *Bleak House*), Dickens is in the tradition of nineteenth-century radicalism, which was influenced by the modernizing discourse of utilitarianism; for a persuasive argument that on such issues Dickens is closer to the utilitarians than is usually thought, see Kathleen Blake, "*Bleak House*, Political Economy, Victorian Studies," *Victorian Literature and Culture* 25 (1997): 1–22.

8. The speaker is Steerforth, but his cynical reading of the institution is supported by the novel's depiction of it; my discussion of the critique of marriage in the novel draws on Kelly Hager, "Estranging David Copperfield: Reading the Novel of Divorce," *ELH* 63 (1996): 989–1019.

9. For a reading that anticipates mine in stressing that the novel is covertly about divorce or rather its inaccessibility, see Hager, "Estranging David Copperfield."

10. Not only does Betsey Trotwood echo Mary Wollstonecraft's feminism in her indignation at Murdstone's denial of Clara's individuality, Wollstonecraft's critique of feminine education in the *Vindication of the Rights of Woman* (1792) as typically leading to excessive sensuality, lack of discipline, and incompetence echoes in the character of Dora and in the polemic that the novel directs against her miseducation. Though it is unclear whether Dickens knew Wollstonecraft's work, he clearly knew of the feminist critique of the female role (and Wollstonecraft clearly had some influence on Victorian feminism); in *Bleak House* (1852–53), the highly domestic Esther satirizes such critiques by describing the feminist discourse of Mrs. Wisk: "the idea of woman's mission lying chiefly in the narrow sphere of Home was an outrageous slander on the part of her Tyrant, Man" (Charles Dickens, *Bleak House* [Harmondsworth: Penguin, 1982], 479). Dickens's evident ambivalence about female subordination and its tension with liberal individualism is demonstrated by his sympathetic portrayal of Betsey Trotwood's feminist language to critique the masculine tyranny of Murdstone and the contrast with this antifeminist passage (and his scathing treatment of female philanthropists) in the slightly later *Bleak House*.

11. See Chris R. Vanden Bossche, "Cookery, not Rookery: Family and Class in David Copperfield," *Dickens Studies Annual* 15 (1986): 87–109.

12. Gwendolyn B. Needham, "The Undisciplined Heart of David Copperfield," repr. in *David Copperfield*, ed. Jerome H. Buckley (New York: Norton, 1990), 794–805.

13. Leonore Davidoff, "Class and Gender in Victorian England," in *Sex and Class in Women's History*, ed. Judith L. Newton, Mary Ryan and Judith R. Walkowitz, 17–71 (Boston: Routledge and Kegan Paul, 1983).

14. So pronounced is the sexualization of Steerforth and David's sycophantic hero worship of him that Oliver Buckton has argued that David is homoerotically drawn to Steerforth, only learning to suppress these feelings after Emily's seduction. The language of homoeroticism in this reading seems anachronistic, but that Dickens associates the Steerforth/David relationship with a sexualized homosociality that includes a narcissistic infatuation with masculine beauty (on both sides) is clear and confirms my sense that Dora and Steerforth represent similar temptations for David. See Oliver S. Buckton, "'The Reader Whom I Love': Homoerotic Secrets in *David Copperfield*," *ELH* 64 (1997): 189–222; for Steerforth as a decadent figure, see Vincent Newey, "Dickensian Decadents," in *Romancing Decay: Ideas of Decadence in European Culture*, ed. Michael St. John (Brookfield: Aldershot, Hants, 1999), 64–82.

15. Mary Poovey, *Uneven Developments: The Ideological Work of Gender in Mid-Victorian England* (Chicago: University of Chicago Press, 1988), 89–125.

16. J. S. Mill to Harriet Taylor, March 20, 1854, quoted in Philip Collins, ed., *Dickens: The Critical Heritage* (New York: Barnes and Noble, 1971), 297–98.

17. See Fred Kaplan, *Dickens: A Biography* (New York: Avon, 1988), 288; Dickens was disdainful of Stowe's art; see Edgar Johnson, *Charles Dickens: His Tragedy and Triumph* (New York: Simon and Schuster, 1952), 2:754.

18. John Tosh, *A Man's Place*, 170–94.

19. Lillian Nayder, *Unequal Partners: Charles Dickens, Wilkie Collins, and Victorian Authorship* (Ithaca: Cornell University Press, 2002), 101–28. In this section I am indebted to Nayder's discussion of Dickens's collaborations with Collins.

20. Dickens's original plan was to end the novel with this note of renunciation and a permanently celibate Pip. Though Pip's period of renunciation survives in the final version, Dickens was persuaded to substitute a more optimistic ending in which Pip returns to visit England and by a chance meeting is reunited with Estella.

21. For a reading of the class and gender politics of this important early detective novel, see Tamar Heller, *Dead Secrets: Wilkie Collins and the Female Gothic* (New Haven: Yale University Press, 1992), 142–63.

22. The best account of the Ternan episode is Claire Tomalin, *The Invisible Woman: The Story of Nelly Ternan and Charles Dickens* (New York: Alfred Knopf, 1991); see also Johnson, *Charles Dickens*, 2:916–26.

23. Charles Dickens to Angela Burdett-Couts, May 9, 1858, quoted in Kaplan, *Dickens: A Biography*, 388.

24. Charles Dickens to Catherine Dickens, Nov. 21, 1853, quoted in Edgar Johnson, *Charles Dickens*, 2:788–89.

25. Tomalin argues persuasively that Dickens's private sexual attitudes were less conventional and more libertine than his public image suggested. See Tomalin, *The Invisible Woman*, 84–85.

Chapter 3. The Crisis of Community

1. See, for example, Eliot's excitement at receiving a laudatory letter from Dickens in response to her fiction; Gordon S. Haight, *George Eliot: A Biography* (New York: Oxford University Press: 1968), 251–52.

2. George Eliot, *The Works of George Eliot*, ed. J. W. Cross (New York: Merrill and Baker). 21:277–78.

3. For an argument that Eliot's distrust of politics, especially working-class politics, was so strong as to make her effectively a conservative, see Evan Horowitz, "George Eliot: The Conservative," *Victorian Studies: An Interdisciplinary Journal of Social, Political, and Cultural Studies* 49, no.1 (Autumn 2006): 7–32.

4. George Eliot, *Adam Bede* (New York: J. M. Dent and Sons, 1960), 7. All subsequent quotations from the novel will be cited by page number in the text.

5. Though Walter Scott is the strongest British male predecessor for *Mill*, one critic has seen the novel as a revision of Dickens's *Dombey and Son*. There are indeed significant parallels between the two novels, such as a father's obsession with a family business and a heroine who becomes alienated from her family while being unjustly associated with sexual transgression. This parallel and likely influence supports my view that Eliot accepts much of Dickens's vision, while completely reimagining his approach to the representation of character, especially of female subjectivity; see Nancy Cervetti, "Dickens and Eliot in Dialogue: Empty Space, Angels and Maggie Tulliver," *Victorian Newsletter* 80 (1991): 18–23.

6. Margaret Anne Doody, "George Eliot and the Eighteenth-Century Novel," *Nineteenth-Century Fiction* 35 (1980): 260–91.

7. George Sand, *The Miller of Angibault*, trans. Donna Dickenson (New York: Oxford University Press, 1995), 17; subsequent quotations from this novel will be cited by page numbers in the text.

8. Mary Wollstonecraft, *A Vindication of the Rights of Woman* (New York: W. W. Norton, 1988), 45.

9. For Eliot's debt to Sand, see Patricia Thomson, *George Sand and the Victorians: Her Influence and Reputation in Nineteenth-Century England* (New York: Columbia University Press, 1977), 152–84; Paul G. Blount, *George Sand and the Victorian World* (Athens: University of Georgia Press, 1979), 5, 59–60, 93–110.

10. This significant letter, in which Eliot expresses great admiration for Sand, while admitting "I should never dream of going to [Sand's] writings as a moral code or textbook," is quoted in Haight, *Eliot*, 60.

11. Henry James, *French Poets and Novelists* (London, 1919) 182, quoted in Thomson, 164.

12. Responses to *Mill*, including a negative one from John Ruskin, were at times quite hostile, and frequently centered on the novel's alleged moral lapses in frankly representing sexual passions; see David Carroll, ed., *George Eliot: The Critical Heritage* (New York: Barnes and Noble, 1971), 145–53, 166–67.

13. George Eliot, *The Mill on the Floss* (Oxford: Oxford University Press, 1992), 490; all subsequent passages from the novel will be cited in the text by page number to this edition.

14. Susan Fraiman points out that by juxtaposing Maggie's story to Tom's bildungsroman, Eliot emphasizes how Maggie is excluded from the bildungsroman genre and from the societal concern with individual self-development; Susan Fraiman, "*The Mill on the Floss*, the Critics, and the Bildungsroman," in *"The Mill on the Floss" and "Silas Marner"* ed. Nahem Yousaf and Andrew Maunder, 31–56. (New York: Palgrave, 2002).

15. For a persuasive case that *The Moorland Cottage* influences *The Mill on the Floss*, see Ramona Lumpkin, "(Re)visions of Virtue: Elizabeth Gaskell's *Moorland Cottage* and George Eliot's *The Mill on the Floss*," *Studies in the Novel* 23, no. 4 (Winter 1991): 432–42.

16. On Eliot's debt to romanticism, see Margaret Homans, "Eliot, Wordsworth, and the Scenes of the Sisters' Instruction," in *Writing and Sexual Difference*, ed. Elizabeth Abel, 57–71 (Chicago: University of Chicago Press, 1982).

17. For a reading along these lines and a good discussion of the issue of sexuality in early Eliot, see Margaret Homans, "Dinah's Blush, Maggie's Arm: Class, Gender and Sexuality in George Eliot's Early Novels," *Victorian Studies* 36 (1993): 155–78.

18. See Susan Meyer, *Imperialism at Home: Race and Victorian Women's Fiction* (Ithaca: Cornell University Press, 1996), 126–56.

19. Margaret Oliphant, "Sensational Novels," *Blackwood's Edinburgh Magazine* 91 (May 1862): 564–80, repr. in *Varieties of Women's Sensation Fiction: 1855–1890*, gen. ed. Andrew Maunder (London: Pickering and Chatto, 2004), 1:10. In my discussion of sensation fiction, I also draw on Andrew Maunder's introduction to this series.

20. Margaret Oliphant, "Novels," *Blackwood's Edinburgh Magazine* 102 (September 1867): repr. in *Varieties of Women's Sensation Fiction* 1:171–90.

21. Oscar Wilde, *The Complete Works of Oscar Wilde* (New York: Hamlyn, 1983), 168; the association of sensation fiction and travel by train was commonplace.

22. On the relationship of one important female sensation writer, Rhoda Broughton, to Eliot, specifically *The Mill on the Floss*, and also to Charlotte Brontë, see Tamar Heller, introduction to *Cometh Up as a Flower*, in vol. 4 of *Varieties of Women's Sensation Fiction: 1855–1890*, gen. ed. Andrew Maunder (London: Pickering and Chatto, 2004). Tamar Heller has helped me understand the genre of sensation fiction and also brought Oliphant's 1867 essay on the genre to my attention.

23. Judith R. Walkowitz, *City of Dreadful Delight: Narratives of Sexual Danger in Late-Victorian London* (Chicago: University of Chicago Press, 1992), 87–89.

24. Ibid., 135–69.

CHAPTER 4. MARITAL ALIENATION

1. H. E. Harvey, "The Voice of Woman," *Westminster Review* 145 (February 1896): 193–96, in *A New Woman Reader: Fiction, Articles, Drama of the 1890s*, ed. Carolyn Christensen Nelson, 207–10 (Peterborough, Ontario: Broadview Press, 2001).

2. On the changing portrayals of the fallen woman, see Sally Mitchell, *The Fallen Angel: Chastity, Class and Women's Reading, 1835–1880* (Bowling Green, OH: Bowling Green University Press, 1981).

3. Tim Dolin, *George Eliot* (New York: Oxford University Press, 2005), 128–30.

4. Samuel Richardson, *Clarissa, or The History of a Young Lady* (Harmondsworth: Penguin, 1985), 36; emphasis in original.

5. George Eliot, *Daniel Deronda* (London: Penguin Books, 1995), 361. All later quotations from the novel will be cited by page number in the text.

6. Andrew Dowling, "'The Other Side of Silence': Matrimonial Conflict and the Divorce Court in George Eliot's Fiction," *Nineteenth-Century Literature* 50, no. 3 (December 1995): 322–36.

7. For an overview of sensationalism and an anthology of the contemporary responses, see Andrew Maunder, *Varieties of Women's Sensation Fiction: 1855–1890* (London: Pickering and Chatto), vol. 1.

8. Anne Humphreys, "Breaking Apart: The early Victorian Divorce Novel," in *Victorian Woman Writers and the Woman Question* ed. Nicola Diana Thompson, 42–59 (Cambridge: Cambridge University Press, 1999).

9. A. James Hammerton, *Cruelty and Companionship: Conflict in Nineteenth-Century Married Life* (New York: Routledge, 1992). Hammerton points out how in the wake of the Divorce Act novels of the 1860s, such as Eliot's *Middlemarch* and Trollope's *He Knew He Was Right* depict tyrannical husbands' behavior, which "offend[s] against the norms of companionate marriage by carrying their desire for mastery over their wives to extremes" (153). Hammerton argues for a general cultural effort in this period to elevate the standard of masculine behavior in marriage.

10. Lucy Bland, *Banishing the Beast: Sexuality and the Early Feminists* (New York: New Press, 1995).

11. Wilkie Collins, *The Moonstone* (New York: Oxford University Press, 1999), 454–55.

12. The likelihood that Eliot was influenced by *The Moonstone* is increased by her personal acquaintance with and approval of Collins. She and Lewes are known to have read Collins's *No Name* together. See "Collins, Wilkie," in *Oxford Reader's Companion to George Eliot*, ed. John Rignall (New York: Oxford University Press, 2000), 55. There is evidence that *Middlemarch* was influenced by another Collins novel, *The Woman in White*; see Marilyn J. Kurata, *"Italians with White Mice* Again: *Middlemarch* and *The Woman in White,"* *English Language Notes* 22, no. 4 (June 1985): 45–47. However, the use of the necklace as a motif and other plot elements in *Deronda* have been seen as derived from another sensation novel, James Payn's *Gwendoline's Harvest* (1870); Sarah M. Putzell, "The

Importance of Being Gwendolen: Contexts for George Eliot's *Daniel Deronda" Studies in the Novel* 19, no. 1: 31–45. Both novels may have influenced *Deronda*.

13. Judith Walkowitz, *City of Dreadful Delight: Narratives of Sexual Danger in Late-Victorian London* (Chicago: University of Chicago Press, 1992), 87–90.

14. For a reading that anticipates mine by emphasizing the centrality of themes of commerce to the novel, see Catherine Gallagher, "George Eliot and *Daniel Deronda*: The Prostitute and the Jewish Question," in *Sex, Politics, and Science in the Nineteenth-Century Novel: Selected Papers from the English Institute, 1983–84*, ed. Ruth Bernard Yeazell, 39–62 (Baltimore: Johns Hopkins University Press, 1986).

15. Eliza Lynn Linton, "The Girl of the Period" (1868), in *Criminals Idiots, Women, and Minors: Victorian Writing by Women on Women*, ed. Susan Hamilton, 172–76 (Orchard Park, NY: Broadview Press, 1995).

16. George Sand, *The Miller of Angibault*, trans. Donna Dickenson (New York: Oxford University Press, 1995), 18.

17. See Terence Cave's discussion of the novel's reception in the Penguin edition, Eliot (1995), xiii–xviii.

18. Susan Meyer, *Imperialism at Home: Race and Victorian Women's Fiction* (Ithaca: Cornell University Press, 1996), 157–94.

19. The idea of the Jews as a romantic and aristocratic people was not exclusively a Gentile conception, but was also promoted by Benjamin Disraeli, the famous writer and politician who was himself of Jewish origin. See Richard Dellamora, *Friendship's Bonds: Democracy and the Novel in Victorian England* (Philadelphia: University of Pennsylvania Press, 2004), 47–91; this work also usefully places *Deronda* in the context of anxieties over national decadence.

20. Letter dated June 8, 1848, in *The George Eliot Letters*, ed. Gordon S. Haight (New Haven: Yale University Press, 1954), 1:267. Further quotations from Eliot's letters will be cited in the text by as *EL* followed by volume and page number.

21. After writing this chapter, I became aware of Marlene Tromp's excellent discussion of how *Deronda* takes up themes that sensation writers had addressed: see Marlene Tromp, *The Private Rod: Marital Violence, Sensation, and the Law in Victorian Britain* (Charlottesville: University of Virginia, 2000), 199–239.

22. Terence Cave (see note 17 above) comments, for example, "That she was wholly unaware of the political and ethical problems of the displacement of the Palestinian peoples is a blindness which we may reasonably censure, but which was conditioned by the assumptions of the day . . ." (xxiii); the issue is also discussed by Meyer (1996). That Eliot shared the widespread acceptance of Britain's imperial mission and that this acceptance colored her thinking about Mordecai and Deronda's project seems clear, yet Cave and others have also noted Eliot's clear unease with the brutality and arrogance of some imperial policies.

23. Patrick Brantlinger, *Rule of Darkness British Literature and Imperialism, 1830–1914* (Ithaca: Cornell University Press, 1988), pp.34–35.

24. Amanda Anderson, *The Powers of Distance: Cosmopolitanism and the Cultivation of Detachment* (Princeton: Princeton University Press, 2001), 119–46. The complex political resonances of the Mordecai plot have been discussed by many critics; see sources mentioned in note 22.

25. Tamar Heller offered me this insight into the significance of these characters' names.

26. Quoted in Linda M. Lewis, *Germaine de Staël, George Sand, and the Victorian Woman Artist* (Columbia: University of Missouri Press, 2003), 136.

27. On Eliot's substantial debt to Sand and de Staël see Lewis, *Germaine de Staël, George Sand, and the Victorian Woman Artist*, 134–201.

28. Edmund Burke, *Reflections on the Revolution in France* (1790; New York: Penguin Press, 1968), 165.

29. Walkowitz (1992) discusses the importance of such charitable and philanthropic activities for women in the later decades of the Victorian era, for example, 52–58.

30. Jonathan Loesberg, "Aesthetics, Ethics and Unreadable Acts in George Eliot," in *Knowing the Past: Victorian Literature and Culture,* ed. Suzy Anger, 121–50 (Ithaca: Cornell University Press, 2001).

31. Matthew Arnold, "Stanzas from the Grand Chartreuse" (1855), ll. 85–86, repr. in *The Norton Anthology of English Literature*, ed. Stephen Greenblatt and M. H. Abrams (New York: W. W. Norton, 2000), 2:1493–98. This poem meditates on the sense of void left in personal values by the collapse of traditional religious faith, which was also a major concern for Eliot.

CHAPTER 5. THE SMASHED WINDOW

1. See Elaine Showalter, *Sexual Anarchy: Gender and Culture at the Fin de Siècle* (New York: Penguin, 1990); Sally Ledger "The New Woman and the Crisis of Victorianism," in *Cultural Politics at the Fin De Siècle* ed. Sally Ledger and Scott McCracken 22–44 (New York: Cambridge University Press, 1995); Stephen Arata, *Fictions of loss in the Victorian fin de siècle* (New York: Cambridge University Press, 1996).

2. Alfred Habegger, *Henry James and the "Woman Business"* (New York: Cambridge University Press, 1989).

3. The other obvious source for this story, Hawthorne's "The Prophetic Pictures," like the Browning poem, features a homicidal husband; thus James minimizes male violence against women that he finds in both of his sources; Brodhead (1986) notes James's indebtedness to the Hawthorne story.

4. Henry James, *Henry James: A Life in Letters* (New York: Viking, 1999), 91. Later quotations from this edition will be cited by *LL* followed by page number in the text.

5. Henry James, *The Bostonians* (New York: Penguin, 1984), 433.

6. Henry, James, "The Art of Fiction," in *The Art of Criticism: Henry James on the Theory and the Practice of* Fiction, ed. William Veeder and Susan M. Griffin (Chicago: University of Chicago Press, 1986), 168–69. Later quotations from this edition will be cited as *AC* followed by page number in the text.

7. Richard H. Brodhead, *The School of Hawthorne* (New York: Oxford University Press, 1986), 104–39; for the importance of Eliot to James, see Selma B. Brody, "Dorothea Brooke and Henry James's Isabel Archer," *George Eliot/George Henry Lewes Studies* (Sept. 1992): 20–21, 63–66; Anne French Dalke, "'So Much and So Little Composition': The Literary Criticism of Henry James and the Novels of George Eliot," *American Transcendental Quarterly* 58 (Dec. 1985): 63–72; Lindsey Traub, "Beyond the Americana: Henry James Reads George Eliot," in *Special Relationships: Anglo-American Affinities and Antagonisms, 1854–1936,* ed. Janet Beer and Bridget Bennett, 160–77 (Manchester: Manchester University Press, 2002); Sarah B. Daughtery, "Henry James and George Eliot: The Price

of Mastery," *Henry James Review* 10, no. 3 (Fall 1989): 153–66; George Levine, "Isabel, Gwendolen, and Dorothea," *ELH* 30, no. 3 (Sept. 1963): 244–57.

8. This phrase is from Matthew Arnold "The Function of Criticism at the Present Time" repr. in *The Norton Anthology of English Literature* (New York: Norton, 2000), 2:1514–27. James was a lifelong enthusiast for Arnold's critical project.

9. Henry James, *Letters,* ed. Leon Edel (Cambridge, MA: Harvard University Press, 1975), 2:351, emphasis in original. Further references will be given as *HJL* followed by volume and page numbers.

10. James's symbolic use of Rome echoes Eliot's use of the city in *Middlemarch*; see Q. D. Leavis, "A Note on Literary Indebtedness: Dickens, George Eliot, Henry James," *Hudson Review* 8 (1955): 423–28.

11. The source of this ending arguably is the ending of *The Scarlet Letter,* in which Hester returns to the New England community that had ostracized her; for the conservatism of Hawthorne's ending, see Sacvan Bercovitch, *The Office of the Scarlet Letter* (Baltimore: Johns Hopkins University Press, 1991), 73–154; on Hawthorne's importance for James throughout his career, see Brodhead, *The School of Hawthorne,* 104–200.

12. Henry James, *The Notebooks of Henry James,* ed. F. O. Matthiessen and Kenneth Murdock (New York: George Braziller, 1955), 192, 196.

13. On James's aversion to journalism and the cult of celebrity, see Richard Salmon, *Henry James and the Culture of Publicity* (Cambridge: Cambridge University Press, 1997).

14. For the antifeminine gender anxieties in this story, see Sandra Gilbert and Susan Gubar, *No Man's Land: The Place of the Woman Writer in the Twentieth Century, vol. 1, The War of the Words* (New Haven: Yale University Press, 1988), 134.

15. Margaret Oliphant, "The Old Saloon" *Blackwood's Edinburgh Magazine* (June 1889), 830, quoted in Solveig C. Robinson, "'At All Times Visible as Art': Henry James, Margaret Oliphant, and the Resistance to Decadence," in *Henry James Against the Aesthetic Movement,* ed. David Garrett Izzo and Daniel T. O'Hara, 97–108 (Jefferson, NC: McFarland, 2006).

16. Stephen Arata, "Realism," in *The Cambridge Companion to the Fin de Siècle,* ed. Gail Marshall, 169–87 (New York: Cambridge University Press, 2007).

17. For the authorial rebellion against mid-Victorian reticence, see Peter Keating, *The Haunted Study: A Social History of the English Novel, 1875–1915* (London: Secker and Warburg, 1989), esp. 241–84.

18. Hugh E. M. Stutfield, "Tommyrotics," repr. in *The Fin de Siècle: A Reader in Cultural History, c. 1880–1900,* ed. Sally Ledger and Roger Luckhurst, 125 (Oxford: Oxford University Press, 2000).

19. Rider Haggard, "About Fiction," *Contemporary Review* 51 (1887): 172–80, quoted in Arata (2007).

20. For discussions of James's formal innovations, see J. Hillis Miller, "Henry James and 'Focalization,' or Why James Loves Gyp," in *A Companion to Narrative Theory,* ed. and intro. James Phelan and Peter J. Rabinowitz, 124–35 (Malden, Mass: Blackwell, 2005); Peter Brooks, *Henry James Goes to Paris* (Princeton: Princeton University Press, 2007).

21. For the narrator as a stereotypical governess figure, see Priscilla L. Walton "'What then on earth was I?' Feminine Subjectivity and *The Turn of the Screw,*" repr. in Henry James, *The Turn of the Screw,* ed. Peter G. Beidler (New York: Bedford Books, 1995), 253–67.

22. For the moral ambiguity of this ending, see John Carlos Rowe, *The Other Henry James* (Durham, NC: Duke University Press, 1998), 120–54.

23. Sidney Grundy, *The New Woman* (1894), quoted in Sally Ledger, "The New Woman and Feminist Fictions," in *The Cambridge Companion to the Fin de Siècle,* ed. Gail Marshall (New York: Cambridge University Press, 2007), 153.

24. Judith R. Walkowitz comments on the symbolic centrality of the prostitute as the "quintessential female figure of the urban scene" (p. 21) and discusses the impact of narratives involving prostitution in late Victorian Britain. Judith R. Walkowitz, *City of Dreadful Delight: Narratives of Sexual Danger in Late-Victorian London* (Chicago: University of Chicago Press, 1992).

25. Ibid., 81–134.

26. On the prominence of images and narratives that demonize women in the fin de siècle, see Bram Dijkstra, *Idols of Perversity: Fantasies of Feminine Evil in Fin-de-Siècle Culture* (New York: Oxford University Press, 1986).

27. The associative link between commodification in general and prostitution is hoary indeed and found in British literature from the Renaissance. The association of writers and prostitutes, however, seems particularly characteristic of the nineteenth century and reflects the intense anxieties about commodification's effect on gender roles in that period. As early as De Quincy's *Confessions of an English Opium-Eater* (1822) one can find narratives of marginal writers identifying with prostitutes. My reading of *Daniel Deronda* in stressing how that text obsessively links women to the dangers of commodification both in their sexual aspect and as potential artists (such as Mirah) suggests that Eliot is a precursor for James's exploration of these themes.

28. The theme of individuals whose innate nobility precisely works against their success in a necessary marketing of their marks of nobility is well established in James, for instance, in the failed aristocratic models of "The Real Thing" (1892). The more general topos of the difficulty of innate nobility in marketing itself has earlier roots, for instance, Hepzibah in *The House of the Seven Gables.*

29. For a reading that anticipates mine in emphasizing how all three major characters embody imaginative projects, see Mark Conroy, "On Not Representing Milly Theale: Sacrificing for Art in *The Wings of the Dove,*" in *Henry James Against the Aesthetic Movement,* ed. David Garrett Izzo and Daniel T. O'Hara 134–56 (Jefferson, N. C.: McFarland, 2006).

30. The passage that follows also suggests a certain pride in physical health: "She looked at him now a moment as for the selfish gladness of their young immunities. It was all they had together, but they had it at least without a flaw—each had the beauty, the physical felicity, the personal virtue, love and desire of the other" (453). For the affiliation of many New Women writers with eugenicist discourses, see Iveta Jusová. *The New Woman and the Empire* (Athens: Ohio State University Press, 2005).

31. Donatella Izzo traces the lineage of the decadent woman, who is anticipated by the female aesthete, in James. As she points out, Marian Fancourt in "The Lesson of the Master," who the artistically serious writer Overt loves but who eventually abandons him to marry the cynical popular writer, is described as a female aesthete. See Donatella Izzo, "Killing Mothers: Decadent Women in James's Literary Tales" in *Henry James Against the Aesthetic Movement,* ed. David Garrett Izzo and Daniel T. O'Hara, 55–86 (Jefferson, NC: McFarland, 2006); for a reading that sees various characters in the novel as corresponding to fin de siècle visual stereotypes, see William Bysshe Stein, "*The Wings of the*

Dove: James's Eucharist of Punch," *Centennial Review* 21 (1977): 236–60; Clair Hughes notes that aesthetic dress is an influence in the novel affecting both Kate and Milly; Clair Hughes, *Henry James and the Art of Dress* (Houndmills: Palgrave, 2001), 67–89; the clearest sign that James intends his plot to have a decadent aura is his elaborate comparison of Milly and Kate's relationship to "some dim scene in a Maeterlinck play" (263). Moreover, the New Woman and the decadent woman in this period were often conflated. For a persuasive argument that James may have denigrated decadent and New Women writers because he saw them as successful rivals, see Talia Schaffer, "Some Chapter of Some Other Story: Henry James, Lucas Malet, and the Real Past of *The Sense of the Past*," *Henry James Review* 17, no. 2 (1996): 109–28.

32. Henry James, *The Awkward Age* (New York: Alfred A. Knopf, 1993), 145; for the probable allusion to *Nana*, see Terry Castle, *The Apparitional Lesbian: Female Homosexuality and Modern Culture* (New York: Columbia University Press, 1993), 159.

33. For the novel's dialogue with British aestheticism, and James's attitude toward this movement generally, I draw on Jonathan Freedman, *Professions of Taste: Henry James, British Aestheticism and Commodity Culture* (Stanford, CA: Stanford University Press, 1990).

34. For fin de siècle anxieties about Britain's cultural health and imperial role, see Patrick Brantlinger, *Rule of Darkness: British Literature and Imperialism* (Ithaca: Cornell University Press, 1988), 227–53; Sally Ledger, "The New Woman and the Crisis of Victorianism," in *Cultural politics at the Fin De Siècle*, ed. Sally Ledger and Scott McCracken 22–44 (Cambridge: Cambridge University Press, 1995); Stephen Arata, *Fictions of Loss in the Victorian Fin de Siècle* (Cambridge: Cambridge University Press, 1996).

35 For an excellent discussion of changing late Victorian gender roles, see Judith R. Walkowitz, *City of Dreadful Delight: Narratives of Sexual Danger in Late-Victorian London*.

36. Henry James, *The Great Short Novels of Henry James* (New York: Dial Press, 1944), 766; for the "flight from domesticity," see John Tosh, *A Man's Place*, 170–94.

37. The very difficulty of late Jamesian texts suggests James's willing participation in this new specialization of high literature; he theorized such specialization as inevitable in his essay on American literature "The Question of the Opportunities": "the public we somewhat loosely talk of as for literature or for anything else is really as subdivided as a chess-board, with each little square confessing only to its own *kind* of accessibility." Henry James, "American Letters," repr. in *Henry James: Literary Criticism* (New York: Library of America, 1984), 651–63.

38. For the view that James's work tends to ultimately accept market structures, see Jean-Christophe Agnew, "A House of Fiction: Domestic Interiors and the Commodity Aesthetic," in *Consuming Visions: Accumulation and Displays of Goods in America, 1880–1920*, ed. Simon J. Bronner 133–55 (New York: Norton, 1989).

Afterword

1. Fredric Jameson, *The Political Unconscious* (Ithaca: Cornell University Press 1981), 206–80; and for a development of this approach that sees the romance and adventure fiction of the turn of the century as responding in a different but parallel way to the rise of mass culture, see Nicholas Daly, *Modernism, Romance, and the Fin De Siècle* (Cambridge: Cambridge University Press, 1999).

2. Joseph Conrad, *Heart of Darkness*, repr. in *The Norton Anthology of English Literature*, ed. M. H. Abrams (New York: W. W. Norton, 2000), 2:1965.

3. James Joyce, *Ulysses* (New York: Random House, 1961), 582.

4. The bond of heterodox cosmopolitanism is explicit: "Both indurated by early domestic training and an inherited tenacity of heteredox resistance professed their disbelief in many orthodox religious, national, social and ethical doctrines." James Joyce, *Ulysses* (New York: Random House, 1961), 666.

5. Fredric Jameson comes close to this when he grumbles that a familial reading of *Ulysses* is "boring": "Has our whole experience of Mr Bloom's Dublin reduced itself to this, the quest for a 'happy ending' in which the hapless protagonist is to virilize himself and become a more successful realization of the dominant, patriarchal, authoritarian male?" See Fredric Jameson, *The Modernist Papers* (New York: Verso, 2007), 137–51.

6. James Joyce, *Ulysses* (New York: Random House, 1961), 761. Admittedly, Molly is an amalgam of modern and traditional attitudes and behaviors; her modern aspects help explain Joyce's depiction of her as stubbornly resisting masculine domination, a threat to patriarchy that the mythicization of the character attempts to contain.

7. Virginia Woolf, *To the Lighthouse* (New York: Harcourt Brace, 1981), 104–5. All subsequent quotations from this text will be by page number in the text.

8. For a more extended discussion of Woolf's ambivalent relation to domestic fiction, see Emily Blair, *Virginia Woolf and the Nineteenth-Century Domestic Novel* (Albany: State University of New York Press, 2007).

9. Nicholas Daly, *Modernism, Romance and the Fin de Siècle: Popular Fiction and British Culture, 1880–1914* (Cambridge: Cambridge University Press, 1999), 149–69.

Bibliography

Abrams, M. H., gen. ed. *The Norton Anthology of English Literature*. 7th ed. Vol. 2. New York: W. W. Norton, 2000.

Agnew, Jean-Christophe. "A House of Fiction: Domestic Interiors and the Commodity Aesthetic." In *Consuming Visions: Accumulation and Displays of Goods in America, 1880–1920*, ed. Simon J. Bronner, 133–55. New York: Norton, 1989.

Altick, Richard D. *The English Common Reader: A Social History of the Mass Reading Public, 1800–1900*. Chicago: University of Chicago Press, 1957.

Anderson, Amanda. *The Powers of Distance: Cosmopolitanism and the Cultivation of Detachment*. Princeton: Princeton University Press, 2001.

Arata, Stephen. *Fictions of Loss in the Victorian Fin de Siècle*. New York: Cambridge University Press, 1996.

———. "Realism." In *The Cambridge Companion to the Fin de Siècle*, ed. Gail Marshall, 169–87. New York: Cambridge University Press, 2007.

Armstrong, Nancy. *Desire and Domestic Fiction: A Political History of the Novel*. New York: Oxford University Press, 1987.

Arnold, Matthew. "The Function of Criticism at the Present Time." In *The Norton Anthology of English Literature*, 1514–27. New York: Norton, 2000.

Auerbach, Nina. "Dickens and Dombey: A Daughter After All." *Dickens Studies Annual* 5 (1976): 95–114.

Austen, Jane. *Pride and Prejudice*. New York: Oxford University Press, 1998.

Ayres, Brenda. *Dissenting Women in Dickens's Novels: The Subversion of Domestic Ideology*. Westport, CT: Greenwood Press, 1998.

Bercovitch, Sacvan. *The Office of the Scarlet Letter*. Baltimore: Johns Hopkins University Press, 1991.

Blair, Emily. *Virginia Woolf and the Nineteenth-Century Domestic Novel*. Albany: State University of New York Press, 2007.

Blair, Sara. *Henry James and the Writing of Race and Nation*. Cambridge: Cambridge University Press, 1996.

Blake, Kathleen. "*Bleak House*, Political Economy, Victorian Studies." *Victorian Literature and Culture* 25 (1997): 1–22.

Bland, Lucy. *Banishing the Beast: Sexuality and the Early Feminists*. New York: New Press, 1995.

Blount, Paul G. *George Sand and the Victorian World*. Athens: University of Georgia Press, 1979.

Bossche, Chris R. Vanden. "Cookery, not Rookery: Family and Class in David Copperfield." *Dickens Studies Annual* 15 (1986): 87–109.

Bourdieu, Pierre. *Distinction: A Social Critique of the Judgement of Taste*. Trans. Richard Nice. Cambridge, MA: Harvard University Press, 1984.

Brantlinger, Patrick. "The Case Against Trade Unions in Early Victorian Fiction." *Victorian Studies* 13 (1969): 37–52.

———. "Did Dickens Have a Philosophy of History? The Case of *Barnaby Rudge*." *Dickens Studies Annual* 30 (2001): 59–74.

———. *Rule of Darkness: British Literature and Imperialism, 1830–1914*. Ithaca: Cornell University Press, 1988.

———. *The Spirit of Reform: British Literature and Politics, 1832–1867*. Cambridge, MA: Harvard University Press, 1977.

Brodhead, Richard H. *Cultures of Letters: Scenes of Reading and Writing in Nineteenth-Century America*. Chicago: University of Chicago Press, 1993.

———. *The School of Hawthorne*. New York: Oxford University Press, 1986.

———. "Sparing the Rod: Discipline and Fiction in Antebellum America." *Representations* 21 (Winter 1988): 67–96.

Brody, Selma B. "Dorothea Brooke and Henry James' Isabel Archer." *George Eliot/George Henry Lewes Studies* (1992): 20–21, 63–66.

Brooks, Peter. *Henry James Goes to Paris*. Princeton: Princeton University Press, 2007.

Brontë, Charlotte. *Jane Eyre*. New York: W. W. Norton, 2001.

Buckton, Oliver S. "'The Reader Whom I Love': Homoerotic Secrets in *David Copperfield*." *ELH* 64 (1997): 189–222.

Burke, Edmund. *Reflections on the Revolution in France*. New York: Penguin Press, 1968.

Butt, John, and Kathleen Tillotson. *Dickens at Work*. London: Methuen, 1957.

Carlyle, Thomas. *Past and Present*. London: Chapman and Hall, 1897.

Castle, Terry. *The Apparitional Lesbian: Female Homosexuality and Modern Culture*. New York: Columbia University Press, 1993.

Carroll, David. *George Eliot: The Critical Heritage*. New York: Barnes and Noble, 1971.

Cave, Terence. Introduction to *Daniel Deronda*, by George Eliot. London: Penguin, 1995.

Cervetti, Nancy. "Dickens and Eliot in Dialogue: Empty Space, Angels and Maggie Tulliver." *Victorian Newsletter* 80 (1991): 18–23.

Clark, Robert. "Riddling the Family Firm: The Sexual Economy in *Dombey and Son*." *ELH* 51 (1984): 69–84.

Collins, Philip, ed. *Dickens: The Critical Heritage*. New York: Barnes and Noble, 1971.

Collins, Wilkie. *The Moonstone*. Ed. John Sutherland. Oxford: Oxford University Press, 1999.

Connor, Steven. *Charles Dickens*. London: Basil Blackwell, 1985.

Conrad, Joseph. *Heart of Darkness*. In *The Norton Anthology of English Literature*, ed. M. H. Abrams. Vol. 2. New York: W. W. Norton, 2000.

Conroy, Mark. "On Not Representing Milly Theale: Sacrificing for Art in *The Wings of the Dove*." In *Henry James Against the Aesthetic Movement*, ed. David Garrett Izzo and Daniel T. O'Hara, 134–56. Jefferson, N. C.: McFarland, 2006.

Cordery, Gareth. "Foucault, Dickens and David Copperfield." *Victorian Literature and Culture* 26 (1998): 71–88.

Corse, Sandra. "Henry James on Eliot and Sand." *South Atlantic Review* 51, no. 1 (Jan. 1986): 58–68.

Crace, Jim. *Being Dead*. New York: Farrar, Straus & Giroux, 2001.

Crosby, Christina. *The Ends of History: Victorians and "The Woman Question."* New York: Routledge, 1991.

Crossick, Geoffrey. "Classes and the Masses in Victorian England." *History Today* 37 (March 1987): 29–35.

Dalke, Anne French. "'So Much and So Little Composition': The Literary Criticism of Henry James and the Novels of George Eliot." *American Transcendental Quarterly* 58 (Dec. 1985): 63–72.

Daly, Nicholas. *Modernism, Romance, and the Fin de Siècle: Popular Fiction and British Culture, 1880–1914*. Cambridge: Cambridge University Press, 1999.

Daugherty, Sarah B. "Henry James and George Eliot: The Price of Mastery." *Henry James Review* 10, no. 3 (Fall 1989): 153–66.

David, Deirdre. *Intellectual Women and Victorian Patriarchy: Harriet Martineau, Elizabeth Barrett Browning, George Eliot*. Ithaca: Cornell University Press, 1987.

Davidoff, Leonore. "Class and Gender in Victorian England." In *Sex and Class in Women's History*, ed. Judith L. Newton, Mary P. Ryan, and Judith R. Walkowitz, 17–71. Boston: Routledge and Kegan Paul, 1983.

Davidoff, Leonore, and Catherine Hall, *Family Fortunes: Men and Women of the English Middle Class, 1780–1850*. Chicago: University of Chicago Press, 1987.

Dellamora, Richard. *Friendship's Bonds: Democracy and the Novel in Victorian England*. Philadelphia: University of Pennsylvania Press, 2004.

De Quincey, Thomas. *Confessions of an English Opium Eater*. Ed. Alethea Hayter. Harmondsworth: Penguin, 1971.

Dickens, Charles. *Barnaby Rudge*. Harmondsworth: Penguin, 1973.

———. *Bleak House*. Harmondsworth: Penguin, 1982.

———. *A Christmas Carol*. In *The Longman Anthology of British Literature*, ed. David Damrosch et al. 3rd ed. Vol. 2B, *The Victorian Age*, 1464–1513. New York: Pearson/Longman, 2006.

———. *David Copperfield*. New York: W. W. Norton, 1990.

———. *Dombey and Son*. Ed. Peter Fairclough. Harmondsworth: Penguin, 1984.

———. *Hard Times*. New York: Penguin, 1985.

———. *The Pilgrim Edition of the Letters of Charles Dickens*. Ed. Madeline House and Graham Storey. Oxford: Clarendon, 1965–.

Dijkstra, Bram. *Idols of Perversity: Fantasies of Feminine Evil in Fin-de-Siècle Culture*. New York: Oxford University Press, 1986.

Dolin, Tim. *Authors in Context: George Eliot*. Oxford: Oxford University Press, 2005.

Doody, Margaret Anne. "George Eliot and the Eighteenth-Century Novel." *Nineteenth-Century Fiction* 35 (1980): 260–91.

Douglas, Ann. *The Feminization of American Culture*. New York: Knopf, 1977.

Dowling, Andrew. "'The Other Side of Silence': Matrimonial Conflict and the Divorce Court in George Eliot's Fiction." *Nineteenth-Century Literature* 50, no. 3 (December 1995): 322–26.

Duncan, Ian. *Modern Romance and the Transformations of the Novel: The Gothic, Scott, Dickens*. Cambridge: Cambridge University Press, 1992.

Dyhouse, Carol. *Feminism and the Family in England: 1880–1939*. New York: Basil Blackwell, 1989.

Eagleton, Terry. *The Rape of Clarissa: Writing, Sexuality, and Class Struggle in Samuel Richardson*. Oxford: Blackwell, 1982.

Edel, Leon. *Henry James: 1895–1901: The Treacherous Years*. New York: J. B. Lippincott, 1969.

Eigner, Edwin M. *The Metaphysical Novel in England and America: Dickens, Bulwer, Melville, and Hawthorne*. Berkeley: University of California Press, 1978.

Eliot, George. *Adam Bede*. New York: J. M. Dent and Sons, 1960.

———. *Daniel Deronda*. Ed. Terence Cave. London: Penguin, 1995.

———. *Letters*. Vol. 5: 1869–73, ed. Gordon S. Haight. New Haven: Yale University Press, 1955.

———. *Middlemarch*. New York: Penguin, 1981.

———. *The Mill on the Floss*. Oxford: Oxford University Press, 1992.

———. *The Works of George Eliot*. Ed. J. W. Cross. Vol. 21. New York: Merrill and Baker.

Ellis, Sarah Stickney. *The Women of England*. In *The Longman Anthology of British Literature*. 3rd ed. Ed. David Damrosch et. al. Vol. 2B, *The Victorian Age*, 1632–35. New York: Longman, 2006.

Ellman, Richard. *Oscar Wilde*. New York: Alfred A. Knopf, 1988.

Engels, Friedrich. *The Condition of the Working Class in England*. Trans. W. O. Henderson and W. H. Chaloner. Stanford, CA: Stanford University Press, 1968.

Feltes, N. N. *Modes of Production of Victorian Novels*. Chicago: University of Chicago Press, 1986.

———. "To Saunter, to Hurry: Dickens, Time, and Industrial Capitalism." *Victorian Studies* 20 (1977): 245–67.

Finnegan, Frances. *Poverty and Prostitution: A Study of Victorian Prostitutes in York*. New York: Cambridge University Press, 1979.

Flanders, Judith. *Inside the Victorian Home: A Portrait of Domestic Life in Victorian England*. New York: W. W. Norton, 2003.

Forster, John. *The Life of Charles Dickens*. Vol. 1. Philadelphia: J. B. Lippincott, 1873.

Foucault, Michel. *Discipline and Punish: The Birth of the Prison*. Trans. Alan Sheridan. New York: Vintage Press, 1977.

Fraiman, Susan. "*The Mill on the Floss*, the Critics, and the Bildungsroman." In "*The Mill on the Floss*" and "*Silas Marner*," ed. Nahem Yousaf and Andrew Maunder, 31–56. New York: Palgrave, 2002.

Freedman, Jonathan. *Professions of Taste: Henry James, British Aestheticism and Commodity Culture*. Stanford, CA: Stanford University Press, 1990.

Fussell, Edwin Sill. *The French Side of Henry James*. New York: Columbia University Press, 1990.

Gallagher, Catherine. "George Eliot and *Daniel Deronda*: The Prostitute and the Jewish Question." In *Sex, Politics, and Science in the Nineteenth-Century Novel*, ed. Ruth Bernard Yeazell, 39–62. Baltimore: Johns Hopkins University Press, 1986.

———. *The Industrial Reformation of English Fiction: Social Discourse and Narrative Form, 1832–1867*. Chicago: University of Chicago Press, 1985.

Gard, Roger, ed. *Henry James: The Critical Heritage*. New York: Barnes and Noble, 1968.

Gaskell, Elizabeth. *The Moorland Cottage*. Ed. Alan Shelston. Vol. 2 of *The Works of Elizabeth Gaskell*, 1–88. London: Pickering and Chatto, 2005.

Gilbert, Sandra, and Susan Gubar. *The Madwoman in the Attic: The Woman Writer and the Nineteenth-Century Literary Imagination*. New Haven: Yale University Press, 1979.

———. *No Man's Land: The Place of the Woman Writer in the Twentieth Century*. Vol. 1, *The War of the Words*. New Haven: Yale University Press, 1988.

———. *No Man's Land: The Place of the Woman Writer in the Twentieth Century*. Vol. 2, *Sexchanges*. New Haven: Yale University Press, 1992.

Habegger, Alfred. "*The Bostonians* and Henry James Sr.'s Crusade Against Feminism and Free Love." *Women's Studies* 15 (1988): 323–42.

———. *Henry James and the "Woman Business."* New York: Cambridge University Press, 1989.

Hager, Kelly. "Estranging David Copperfield: Reading the Novel of Divorce." *ELH* 63 (1996): 989–1019.

Haight, Gordon S. *George Eliot: A Biography*. New York: Oxford University Press, 1968.

Hammerton, James A. *Cruelty and Companionship: Conflict in Nineteenth-Century Married Life*. New York: Routledge, 1992.

Harvey, H. E. "The Voice of Woman." *Westminster Review* 145 (February 1896): 193–96. Repr. in *A New Woman Reader: Fiction, Articles, Drama of the 1890s*, ed. Carolyn Christensen Nelson, 207–10. Peterborough, Ontario: Broadview Press, 2001.

Hatten, Charles. "The Politics of Marital Reform and the Rationalization of Romance in *The Doctrine and Discipline of Divorce*." *Milton Studies* 27 (1991): 95–114.

Hawthorne, Nathaniel. *The Scarlet Letter*. Intro. Nina Baym. New York: Penguin, 1986.

Heller, Tamar. *Dead Secrets: Wilkie Collins and the Female Gothic*. New Haven: Yale University Press, 1992.

———. Introduction to *Cometh Up as a Flower*, by Rhoda Broughton. In Vol. 4. *Varieties of Women's Sensation Fiction: 1855–1890*, gen. ed. Andrew Maunder, xxxiii–l. London: Pickering and Chatto, 2004.

Helsinger, Elizabeth K., Robin Lauterbach Sheets, and William Veeder, eds. *The Woman Question: Society and Literature in Britain and America, 1837–1883*. 3 vols. Chicago: Chicago University Press, 1983.

Hibbert, Christopher. *The English: A Social History, 1066–1945*. London: Grafton Books, 1988.

Hobsbawm, Eric J. *The Age of Revolution*. New York: New American Library, 1962.

Hobsbawm, Eric J., and Terence Ranger, eds. *The Invention of Tradition*. New York: Cambridge University Press, 1983.

Homans, Margaret. "Dinah's Blush, Maggie's Arm: Class, Gender and Sexuality in George Eliot's Early Novels. " *Victorian Studies* 36 (1993): 155–78.

———. "Eliot, Wordsworth, and the Scenes of the Sisters' Instruction." In *Writing and Sexual Difference*, ed. Elizabeth Abel, 57–71. Chicago: University of Chicago Press. 1982.

Horne, Lewis. "The Way of Resentment in *Dombey and Son.*" *Modern Language Quarterly* 51 (1990): 44–62.

Horowitz, Evan. "George Eliot: The Conservative." *Victorian Studies* 49, no. 1 (Autumn 2006): 7–32.

Hughes, Clair. *Henry James and the Art of Dress*. Houndmills: Palgrave, 2001.

Humphreys, Anne. "Breaking Apart: The Early Victorian Divorce Novel." In *Victorian Woman Writers and the Woman Question*, ed. Nicola Diana Thompson, 42–59. Cambridge: Cambridge University Press, 1999.

Izzo, Donatella. "Killing Mothers: Decadent Women in James's Literary Tales." In *Henry James Against the Aesthetic Movement*, eds. David Garrett Izzo and Daniel T. O'Hara, 55–86. Jefferson, NC: McFarland, 2006.

James, Henry. "The Art of Fiction." In *The Art of Criticism: Henry James on the Theory and Practice of Fiction*, 165–83. Chicago: University of Chicago Press, 1986.

———. *The Awkward Age*. New York: Alfred A. Knopf, 1993.

———. *Autobiography*. Ed. Frederick W. Dupee. New York: Criterion Books, 1956.

———. *The Complete Tales of Henry James*. 12 vols. Ed. Leon Edel. Philadelphia: Lippincott, 1964.

———. *The Great Short Novels of Henry James*. New York: Dial Press, 1944.

———. *Henry James: A Life in Letters*. Ed. Philip Horne. New York: Penguin Press, 1999.

———. *Letters*. Vol. 2, 1875–1883. Ed. Leon Edel. Cambridge, MA: Belknap Press, 1975.

———. *Literary Criticism: Essays on Literature, American Writers, English Writers*. New York: Library of America, 1984.

———. *The Notebooks of Henry James*. Ed. F. O. Matthiesen and Kenneth B. Mordoch. New York: George Braziller, 1955.

———. *The Portrait of a Lady*. New York: New American Library, 1963.

———. *The Turn of the Screw: Complete, Authoritative Text with Biological and Historical Contexts, Critical History, and Essays from Five Contemporary Critical Perspectives*. Boston: St. Martin's. 1995."

———. *The Wings of the Dove*. New York: W. W. Norton, 1978.

Jameson, Fredric. *The Modernist Papers*. New York: Verso, 2007.

———. *The Political Unconscious: Narrative as Socially Symbolic Act*. Ithaca: Cornell University Press, 1981.

Jolly, Roslyn. *Henry James: History, Narrative, Fiction*. Oxford: Clarendon Press, 1993.

Johnson, Edgar. *Charles Dickens: His Tragedy and Triumph*. 2 vols. New York: Simon and Schuster, 1952.

Jones, Gareth Stedman. *Languages of Class: Studies in English Working Class History*. New York: Cambridge University Press, 1983.

Joyce, James. *Ulysses*. New York: Random House, 1961.

Jusová, Iveta. *The New Woman and the Empire*. Athens: Ohio State University Press, 2005.

Kaplan, Fred. *Dickens: A Biography*. New York: Avon, 1988.

———. *Henry James: The Imagination of Genius*. New York: William Morrow, 1992.

Keating, Peter. *The Haunted Study: A Social History of the English Novel, 1875–1914*. London: Secker and Warburg, 1989.

King, James. *Virginia Woolf*. New York: W. W. Norton, 1995.

Kurata, Marilyn J. *"Italians with White Mice Again: Middlemarch and The Woman in White."* *English Language Notes* 22, no. 4 (June 1985): 45–47.

Leavis, Q. D. "A Note on Literary Indebtedness: Dickens, George Eliot, Henry James." *Hudson Review* 8 (1955): 423–28.

Ledger, Sally. "The New Woman and the Crisis of Victorianism." In *Cultural Politics at the Fin De Siècle*, ed. Sally Ledger and Scott McCracken, 22–44. New York: Cambridge University Press, 1995.

Lenard, Mary. *Preaching Pity: Dickens, Gaskell and Sentimentalism in Victorian Culture*. New York: Peter Lang, 1999.

Levine, George. "Isabel, Gwendolen, and Dorothea." *ELH* 30, no. 3 (Sept. 1963): 244–57.

Lewes, George Henry. "Dickens in Relation to Criticism." *Fortnightly Review*, XVII (1872), 143–51. Repr. In Literary Criticism of George Henry Lewes, 94–105. Lincoln: University of Nebraska Press, 1964.

Lewis, Linda M. *Germaine de Staël, George Sand, and the Victorian Woman Artist*. Columbia: University of Missouri Press, 2003.

Linton, Eliza Lynn. "The Girl of the Period." In *Criminals, Idiots, Women, and Minors: Victorian Writing by Women on Women*, ed. Susan Hamilton, 172–76. Peterborough, Ontario: Broadview Press, 1995.

Loesberg, Jonathan. "Aesthetics, Ethics, and Unreadable Acts in George Eliot." In *Knowing the Past: Victorian Literature and Culture*, ed. Suzy Anger, 121–50. Ithaca: Cornell University Press, 2001.

Lukács, Georg. *The Historical Novel*. Trans. Hannah and Stanley Mitchell. London: Merlin, 1962.

Lumpkin, Ramona. "(Re)visions of Virtue: Elizabeth Gaskell's *Moorland Cottage* and George Eliot's *The Mill on the Floss*." *Studies in the Novel* 23, no. 4 (Winter 1991): 432–42.

Marcus, Stephen. *From Pickwick to Dombey*. New York: Basic, 1965.

Margolis, Anne T. *Henry James and the Problem of Audience: An International Act*. Ann Arbor: UMI Research Press, 1985.

Mark-Lawson, Jane, and Anne Witz. "From 'Family Labour' to 'Family Wage'? The Case of Women's Labour in Nineteenth-Century Coalmining." *Social History* 13 (1980): 151–73.

Marsh, Joss Lutz. "Good Mrs. Brown's Connections: Sexuality and Story-Telling in *Dealings with the Firm of Dombey and Son*." *ELH* 58 (1991): 405–26.

Maunder, Andrew. General introduction to *Varieties of Women's Sensation Fiction*. Vol. 1, *Sensationalism and The Sensation Debate*, gen. Ed. Andrew Maunder, vii–xxxi. London: Pickering and Chatto, 2004.

————, gen. ed. *Varieties of Women's Sensation Fiction: 1855–1890*. 6 vols. London: Pickering and Chatto, 2004.

Mercer, Caroline. "'Consumption, Heart-Disease, or Whatever': Chlorosis, a Heroine's Illness in "*The Wings of the Dove.*" *Journey of the Mystery of Medicine* 40 (1985): 259–85.

Meyer, Susan. *Imperialism at Home: Race and Victorian Women's Fiction*. Ithaca: Cornell University Press, 1996.

Miller, D. A. *The Novel and the Police*. Berkeley: University of California Press, 1988.

Miller, J. Hillis. "Henry James and 'Focalization,' or Why James Loves Gyp." In *A Companion to Narrative Theory*, ed. James Phelan and Peter J. Rabinowitz, 124–35. Malden, MA: Blackwell, 2005.

Milton, John. *The Riverside Milton*. New York: Houghton Mifflin, 1998.

Mintz, Steven. *A Prison of Expectations: The Family in Victorian Culture*. New York: New York University Press, 1983.

Mitchell, Sally. *The Fallen Angel: Chastity, Class and Women's Reading, 1835–1880*. Bowling Green, OH: Bowling Green University Press, 1981.

Moglen, Helene. "Theorizing Fiction/Fictionalizing Theory: The Case of Dombey and Son." *Victorian Studies* 35 (1992): 159–84.

Moynahan, Julian. "Dealings with the Firm of *Dombey and Son*: Firmness v. Wetness." In *Dickens in the Twentieth Century*, ed. John Gross and Gabriel Pearson, 121–31. London: Routledge and Kegan Paul, 1962.

Nayder, Lillian. *Unequal Partners: Charles Dickens, Wilkie Collins, and Victorian Authorship*. Ithaca: Cornell University Press. 2002.

Needham, Gwendolyn B. "The Undisciplined Heart of David Copperfield." Repr. in *David Copperfield*, ed. Jerome H. Buckley, 794–805. New York: Norton, 1990.

Nelson, Carolyn Christensen, ed. *A New Woman Reader: Fiction, Articles, Drama of the 1890s*. Peterborough, Ontario: Broadview Press, 2001.

Newey, Vincent. "Dickensian Decadents." In *Romancing Decay: Ideas of Decadence in European Culture*, ed. Michael St. John, 64–82. Brookfield: Aldershot, Hants, 1999.

Nunokawa, Jeff. *The Afterlife of Property: Domestic Security and the Victorian Novel*. Princeton: Princeton University Press, 1994.

Oliphant, Margaret. "Novels." *Blackwood's Edinburgh Magazine* 102 (September 1867). Repr. in vol. 1 of *Varieties of Women's Sensation Fiction: 1855–1890*, gen. ed. Andrew Maunder, 171–90. London: Pickering and Chatto, 2004.

————. "Sensational Novels." *Blackwood's Edinburgh Magazine* 91 (May 1862): 564–80. Repr. in vol. 1 of *Varieties of Women's Sensation Fiction: 1855–1890*, gen. ed. Andrew Maunder, 8–15. London: Pickering and Chatto, 2004.

Patten, Robert L. *Charles Dickens and His Publishers*. Oxford: Clarendon Press, 1978.

Perkin, Joan. *Victorian Women*. New York: New York University Press, 1993.

Person, Leland S. *Henry James and the Suspense of Masculinity*. Philadelphia: University of Pennsylvania Press, 2003.

Peters, Catherine. *The King of Inventors: A Life of Wilkie Collins*. Princeton: Princeton University Press, 1991.

Phillips, Roderick. *Untying the Knot: A Short History of Divorce*. New York: Cambridge University Press, 1991.

Poovey, Mary. *Uneven Developments: The Ideological Work of Gender in Mid-Victorian England*. Chicago: University of Chicago Press, 1988.

Putzell, Sarah M. "The Importance of Being Gwendolen: Contexts for George Eliot's *Daniel Deronda*." *Studies in the Novel* 19, no. 1: 31–45.

Richardson, Samuel. *Clarissa, or the History of a Young Lady*. Ed. Angus Ross. Harmondsworth: Penguin, 1985.

Rignall, John, ed. *Oxford Reader's Companion to George Eliot*. Oxford: Oxford University Press, 2000.

Robinson, Solveig C. "'At All Times Visible as Art': Henry James, Margaret Oliphant, and the Resistance to Decadence." In *Henry James Against the Aesthetic Movement,* eds. David Garrett Izzo and Daniel T. O'Hara, 97–108. Jefferson, N. C.: McFarland, 2006.

Rowe, John Carlos. *The Other Henry James*. Durham, NC: Duke University Press, 1998.

Sadoff, Dianne F. *Monsters of Affection: Dickens, Eliot, and Brontë on Fatherhood*. Baltimore: Johns Hopkins University Press, 1982.

Salmon, Richard. *Henry James and the Culture of Publicity*. Cambridge: Cambridge University Press, 1997.

Sand, George. *Indiana*. Trans. Sylvia Raphael. New York: Oxford University Press, 1994.

———. *The Miller of Angibault*. Trans. Donna Dickenson. New York: Oxford University Press, 1995.

Schaffer, Talia. "Some Chapter of Some Other Story: Henry James, Lucas Malet, and the Real Past of *The Sense of the Past*." *Henry James Review* 17, no. 2 (1996): 109–28.

Scott, Walter. *The Heart of Midlothian*. New York: Oxford University Press, 1982.

Sedgwick, Eve Kosofsky. *The Epistemology of the Closet*. Berkeley: University of California Press, 1990.

Showalter, Elaine. *A Literature of Their Own: British Novelists from Brontë to Lessing*. Princeton: Princeton University Press, 1977.

———. *Sexual Anarchy: Gender and Culture at the Fin de Siècle*. New York: Penguin Books, 1990.

Solomon, Maynard. *Marxism and Art*. Ed. New York: Alfred A. Knopf, 1973.

Stein, William Bysshe. "*The Wings of the Dove*: James's Eucharist of Punch." *Centennial Review* 21 (1977): 236–60.

Stigant, Paul, and Peter Widdowson. "*Barnaby Rudge:* A Historical Novel?" *Literature and History* 2 (1975): 2–44.

Stone, Lawrence. *The Family, Sex and Marriage in England 1500–1800*. London: Weidenfeld and Nicolson, 1977.

Strychacz, Thomas. *Modernism, Mass Culture, and Professionalism*. Cambridge: Cambridge University Press, 1993.

Stutfield, Hugh E. M. "Tommyrotics." Repr. in *The Fin de Siècle: A Reader in Cultural History, c. 1880–1900,* eds. Sally Ledger and Roger Luckhurst, 120–26. Oxford: Oxford University Press, 2000.

Surridge, Lisa. *Bleak Houses: Marital Violence in Victorian Fiction*. Athens: Ohio University Press, 2005.

Thackeray, William Makepeace. *Vanity Fair: A Novel Without a Hero*. Boston: Houghton Mifflin, 1964.

Thompson, E. P. *The Making of the English Working Class*. New York: Vintage Books, 1966.

Thomson, Patricia. *George Sand and the Victorians: Her Influence and Reputation in Nineteenth-Century England*. New York: Columbia University Press, 1977.

Tillotson, Kathleen. *Novels of the Eighteen-forties*. Oxford: Clarendon Press, 1957.

Tintner, Adeline R. *The Book World of Henry James: Appropriating the Classics*. Ann Arbor: UMI Research Press, 1987.

Tomalin, Claire. *The Invisible Woman: The Story of Nelly Ternan and Charles Dickens*. New York: Alfred Knopf, 1991.

Tompkins, Jane. *Sensational Designs: The Cultural Work of American Fiction 1790–1860*. New York: Oxford University Press, 1985.

Tosh, John. *A Man's Place: Masculinity and the Middle-Class Home in Victorian England*. New Haven: Yale University Press, 1999.

Traub, Lindsey. "Beyond the Americana: Henry James Reads George Eliot." In *Special Relationships: Anglo-American Affinities and Antagonisms, 1854–1936*, ed. Janet Beer and Bridget Bennett, 160–77. Manchester, England: Manchester University Press, 2002.

Tromp, Marlene. *The Private Rod: Marital Violence, Sensation, and the Law in Victorian Britain*. Charlottesville: University of Virginia Press, 2000.

Tuchman, Gaye, with Nina E. Fortin. *Edging Women Out: Victorian Novelists, Publishers, and Social Change*. New Haven: Yale University Press, 1989.

Walby, Sylvia. *Patriarchy at Work: Patriarchal and Capitalist Relations in Employment*. Minneapolis: University of Minnesota Press, 1986.

Walkowitz, Judith R. *City of Dreadful Delight: Narratives of Sexual Danger in Late-Victorian London*. Chicago: University of Chicago Press, 1992.

———. *Prostitution and Victorian Society*. New York: Cambridge University Press, 1980.

Walton, Priscilla. "'What then on earth was I?' Feminine Subjectivity and *The Turn of the Screw*." In *The Turn of the Screw*, by Henry James. Ed. Peter G. Beidler, 253–67. New York: Bedford Books, 1995.

Waters, Catherine. *Dickens and the Politics of the Family*. Cambridge: Cambridge University Press, 1997.

Weber, Max. *The Protestant Ethic and the Spirit of Capitalism*. New York: Routledge, 2001.

Welsh, Alexander. *From Copyright to Copperfield: The Identity of Dickens*. Cambridge, MA: Harvard University Press, 1987.

Wilde, Oscar. *The Complete Works of Oscar Wilde*. New York: Hamlyn, 1983.

———. *The Picture of Dorian Gray*. New York: Oxford University Press, 1991.

Wiley, Margaret. "Mother's Milk and *Dombey and Son*." *Dickens Quarterly* (Dec. 1996): 217–28.

Williams, Raymond. *Culture and Society: 1780–1950*. New York: Columbia University Press, 1983.

———. Introduction to *Dombey and Son*, by Charles Dickens, 11–34. Harmondsworth: Penguin. 1970.

Wollstonecraft, Mary. *A Vindication of the Rights of Woman*. New York: Norton, 1988.

Woolf, Virginia. *To the Lighthouse*. New York: Harcourt Brace, 1981.

———. *Women and Writing*. Ed. Michele Barrett. New York: Harcourt Brace Jovanovich, 1979.

Yelin, Louise. "Strategies for Survival: Florence and Edith in *Dombey and Son*." *Victorian Studies* 22 (1979): 297–319.

Index

297